Lecture Notes in Computer Science 14606

The series Lecture Notes in Computer Science (LNCS), including its subseries Lecture Notes in Artificial Intelligence (LNAI) and Lecture Notes in Bioinformatics (LNBI), has established itself as a medium for the publication of new developments in computer science and information technology research, teaching, and education.

LNCS enjoys close cooperation with the computer science R & D community, the series counts many renowned academics among its volume editors and paper authors, and collaborates with prestigious societies. Its mission is to serve this international community by providing an invaluable service, mainly focused on the publication of conference and workshop proceedings and postproceedings. LNCS commenced publication in 1973.

Zuzana Kubincová · Tianyong Hao ·
Nicola Capuano · Marco Temperini · Shili Ge ·
Yuanyuan Mu · Paolo Fantozzi · Jing Yang
Editors

Emerging Technologies for Education

8th International Symposium, SETE 2023
Sydney, Australia, November 26–28, 2023
Revised Selected Papers, Part I

Springer

Editors
Zuzana Kubincová
Comenius University
Bratislava, Slovakia

Nicola Capuano
University of Salerno
Fisciano, Italy

Shili Ge
Guangdong University of Foreign Studies
Guangzhou, China

Paolo Fantozzi
LUMSA University
Rome, Italy

Tianyong Hao
South China Normal University
Guangzhou, China

Marco Temperini
Sapienza University of Rome
Rome, Italy

Yuanyuan Mu
Chaohu University
Hefei, China

Jing Yang
Zhejiang University
Hangzhou, China

ISSN 0302-9743 ISSN 1611-3349 (electronic)
Lecture Notes in Computer Science
ISBN 978-981-97-4242-4 ISBN 978-981-97-4243-1 (eBook)
https://doi.org/10.1007/978-981-97-4243-1

This Springer imprint is published by the registered company Springer Nature Singapore Pte Ltd.
The registered company address is: 152 Beach Road, #21-01/04 Gateway East, Singapore 189721, Singapore

Preface

SETE 2023 was the eighth Annual International Symposium on Emerging Technologies for Education. It was held in conjunction with ICWL 2023, under the auspices of the Hong Kong Web Society. Beside the papers presented in the SETE Main Track, this volume collects also the papers contributed by several workshops held during the conjunct events ICWL-SETE.

Fueled by ICT technologies, the e-learning environment in the education sector has become more innovative than ever before. Diversified emerging technologies containing various software and hardware components provide the underlying infrastructure to create enormous potential educational applications incorporated by proper learning strategies. Moreover, those prevalent technologies might also lead to changes of the educational environment, such as learning performance. Meanwhile, new paradigms are also emerging, with the purpose of bringing these innovations to a certain level where they are widely accepted and sustainable. Therefore, this symposium aimed to serve as a meeting point for researchers, educators, and practitioners, to discuss state-of-the-art and in-progress research, exchange ideas, and share experiences about emerging technologies for education. This symposium attempted to provide opportunities for the cross-fertilization of knowledge and ideas from researchers in diverse fields that make up this interdisciplinary research area. We hope that the findings of each work presented in this symposium, and in the attached workshops, can be used to improve the development of current and future educational environments. This year's conference was located in Sydney (Australia), where the University of Technology Sydney hosted the conjunct events, from November 26th to November 28th, 2023.

In SETE, we received 23 submissions, with one withdrawn during the review process. Each paper submission was analysed by at least three reviewers, appointed by the Program Chairs, in a single blind process. After that rigorous review process, the SETE Main Track is presenting 13 contributions, of which 8 were Full Papers, yielding an acceptance rate of 35%. These contributions covered the latest findings in various areas, such as: Artificial Intelligence in Education, Big Data Driven Education, Informal Learning in the Workplace, Data Driven Decision Making in Education, User/Student/Teacher Modeling, Learning Analytics, Modeling Complex Learning Processes with Multi-Channel Learning Data, Educational Technology and ICT for Education, Assessment in Technology Enhanced Learning, and Inclusive Education. The conjunct events also feature 3 distinguished keynote presentations and 5 workshops, which covered a wide range of topics, such as Artificial Intelligence (AI) in Education, Generative AI in Education, Support for Second Language Learning, Peer Review, Peer Assessment and Self Assessment in Education, Educational Technology and Cognitive Neuroscience for Language Learning, Digitalization in Language And Cross-Cultural Education, and Hardware and Software Systems as Enablers For Lifelong Learning.

We would like to thank the entire Organizing Committee and especially the Organization Chair Guandong Xu, for their efforts and time spent to ensure the success of the conference. We would also like to express our gratitude to the Program Committee members for their timely and helpful reviews. And, last but not least, we would like to thank all the authors for their contribution in maintaining a high-quality conference - we count on your continuing support to play a significant role in the Emerging Technologies for Education community in the future.

November 2023

Zuzana Kubincová
Tianyong Hao
Nicola Capuano
Marco Temperini
Shili Ge
Yuanyuan Mu
Paolo Fantozzi
Jing Yang

Organization

General Chair

Marco Temperini	Sapienza University of Rome, Italy

Program Committee Co-chairs

Zuzana Kubincová	Comenius University in Bratislava, Slovakia
Tianyong Hao	South China Normal University, China
Nicola Capuano	University of Basilicata, Italy

Local Organization General Chair

Guandong Xu	University of Technology Sydney, Australia

Local Organization Co-chairs

Huan Huo	University of Technology Sydney, Australia
Rafiqul Islam	Australian Institute of Higher Education, Australia

Workshop Co-chairs

Luigi Laura	International Telematic University Uninettuno, Italy
Robin Braun	University of Technology Sydney, Australia
Nana Jin	Shenzhen University, China

Publicity Co-chairs

Minjie Hu	Wellington Institute of Technology, New Zealand
Ivana Marenzi	L3S Research Center, Germany
Junjie Gavin Wu	Shenzhen Technology University, China

Proceedings Chair

Andrea Sterbini	Sapienza University of Rome, Italy

Web Chair

Kaize Shi	University of Technology Sydney, Australia

Steering Committee Representatives

Qing Li	Hong Kong Polytechnic University, China
Rynson W. H. Lau	City University of Hong Kong, China

Program Committee

Marie-Hélène Abel	Université de Technologie de Compiègne, France
Fernando Albuquerque	Costa University of Lisbon, Portugal
Jorge Luis Bacca Acosta	University of Girona, Spain
Silvia Margarita Baldiris Navarro	Fundación Universitaria Tecnológico Comfenalco, Spain
Federica Caruso	University of L'Aquila, Italy
Guanliang Chen	Monash University, Australia
Tosti H. C. Chiang	National Taiwan Normal University, Taiwan
Ruth Cobos	Universidad Autónoma de Madrid, Spain
Fisnik Dalipi	Linnaeus University, Sweden
Maya Dimitrova	Institute of Robotics, Bulgarian Academy of Sciences, Bulgaria
Jeffrey Gamble	National Chiayi University, Taiwan
Francisco José García Peñalvo	University of Salamanca, Spain
Alicia Garcia-Holgado	Universidad de Salamanca, Spain
Carina Gonzalez-González	Universidad de La Laguna, Spain
Preben Hansen	Stockholm University, Sweden
Martin Homola	Comenius University in Bratislava, Slovakia
Min Chai Hsieh	Tainan University of Technology, Taiwan
Nikolina Ilieva Nikolova	University of Sofia, Bulgaria
Tai-Chien Kao	National Dong Hwa University, Taiwan
Ján Kluka	Comenius University in Bratislava, Slovakia
Theresa Kwong	Hong Kong Baptist University, China

Luigi Laura	International Telematic University Uninettuno, Italy
Lap-Kei Lee	Hong Kong Metropolitan University, China
Yuxia Lei	Qufu Normal University, China
Carla Limongelli	Roma Tre University, Italy
Dennis Y. W. Liu	Hong Kong Polytechnic University, China
Pei-Lin Liu	National Chiayi University, Taiwan
Shiguang Liu	Tianjin University, China
Alexander Mikroyannidis	Open University, UK
Laurent Moccozet	University of Geneva, Switzerland
Ilaria Moschini	Università degli Studi di Firenze, Italy
Yuanyuan Mu	City University of Hong Kong, China
Minoru Nakayama	Tokyo Institute of Technology, Japan
Iosif Vasile Nemoianu	University POLITEHNICA of Bucharest, Romania
Patricia Paderewski	University of Granada, Spain
Natalia Padilla-Zea	Universidad Internacional de la Rioja, Spain
Luc Paquette	University of Illinois at Urbana-Champaign, USA
Ricardo Queiros	Polytechnic Institute of Porto, Portugal
Marcos Román-González	UNED, Spain
Rainer Rubira-García	King Juan Carlos University, Madrid
Filippo Sciarrone	Universitas Mercatorum, Italy
Sean Siqueira	Federal University of the State of Rio de Janeiro (UNIRIO), Brazil
Marc Spaniol	Université de Caen Normandie, France
Andrea Sterbini	Sapienza University of Rome, Italy
Shu-Yuan Tao	Takming University of Science and Technology, Taiwan
Vladimir Trajkovik	Ss Cyril and Methodius University, North Macedonia
Georgi Tuparov	New Bulgarian University, Bulgaria
Jesús Valverde-Berrocoso	Universidad de Extremadura, Spain
Pierpaolo Vittorini	University of L'Aquila, Italy
Shan Wang	University of Macau, China
Tak-Lam Wong	Douglas College, Canada
Wenxiu Xie	City University of Hong Kong, China
Wen Zhou Anhui	Philippine Normal University, Philippines
Yingyi Zhuang	Chinese University of Hong Kong, Shenzhen, China

Additional Reviewers

Aldino, Ahmad Ari
Leung, Alven C. Y.

Workshops Organizing Committees

CNLL: 1st International Workshop on Cognitive Neuroscience of Language Learning

Jing Yang	Zhejiang University, China
Zhisheng Edward Wen	Hong Kong Shue Yan University, China
Helen Zhao	University of Melbourne, Australia

DLCCE: 2nd International Workshop on Digitalization in Language and Cross-Cultural Education

Yuanyuan Mu	Chaohu University, China
Yinggen Ke	Chaohu University, China
Rongqi Yu	Chaohu University, China

ETLL: 6th International Workshop on Educational Technology for Language Learning

Shili Ge	Guangdong University of Foreign Studies, China
Martin Weisser	Guangdong University of Foreign Studies, China
Menglian Liu	Guangdong University of Foreign Studies, China
Christina Alexandri	University of Athens, Greece
Rou Song	Guangdong University of Foreign Studies, China

HASSELL: 2nd Workshop on Hardware and Software Systems as Enablers for Lifelong Learning

Paolo Fantozzi	LUMSA University, Italy
Valerio Rughetti	Uninettuno University, Italy
Giacomo Valente	University of L'Aquila, Italy
Eleonora Veglianti	Lille Catholic University, France

PRASAE: 9th International Workshop on Peer Review, Peer Assessment, and Self Assessment in Education

Zuzana Kubincová	Comenius University in Bratislava, Slovakia
Martin Homola	Comenius University in Bratislava, Slovakia

Contents – Part I

Contents – Part II

Workshop ETLL

Workshop HASSELL

Workshop PRASAE

SETE Main Track

Perceptions of High School Mathematics Students in the Use of Technologies for Educational Purposes

Hassan Hossein-Mohand[1], Hossein Hossein-Mohand[2](✉), Nabil Mohamed-Chemlali[1], and Sara Osuna-Acedo[1]

[1] National University of Education at Distance – UNED, Madrid, Spain
hassan@melilla.uned.es, nmohamed63@alumno.uned.es, sosuna@edu.uned.es

[2] University of Granada, Granada, Spain
hossein.h.m@ugr.es

Abstract. The availability of technological resources at homes does not correlate with the educational use of RICT by secondary school Mathematics students. The use of technological resources, their use in the classroom and the educational level are some of the factors that could influence students' perceptions of RICT (Relationship, Information and Communication Technologies). This study evaluates the perceptions of Secondary Mathematics students towards the use of RICT for educational purposes, analyzing their relationship with the use of technological resources, their participation in the classroom activities and their educational level. A total of 2018 secondary school students were tested in this ex post facto cross-sectional study with a validated 6-item questionnaire extracted from the general instrument. Bayesian analysis suggests the existence of a predominantly positive perception in secondary school students' perception of the use of technologies. This perception decreases as the level of education increases. Furthermore, a significant positive correlation is observed between the perception that RICT can improve their grades and the use of technological resources in their studies.

Keywords: Mathematical Education · Educational Technologies · Academic Performance

1 Introduction

The progressive evolution of Relationship, Information and Communication Technologies (RICT), term coined in 2016 by Marta-Lazo and Gabelas-Barroso, has introduced a wide range of possibilities to improve the teaching-learning process in different areas of knowledge, including Mathematics [1, 2]. In this context, digital technologies are understood as educational scenarios for relationships and collaboration, rather than mere instruments or tools [3]. Far from this instrumentalist conception of digital technologies, to understand secondary school students' perceptions on the use of RICT for educational purposes becomes a key factor in optimizing academic performance and promoting

Z. Kubincová et al. (Eds.): SETE 2023, LNCS 14606, pp. 3–15, 2024.
https://doi.org/10.1007/978-981-97-4243-1_1

meaningful and motivating learning [4, 5]. Access to technological resources at homes [1, 6] and schools [7] is a key factor in the use of RICT for educational purposes [8, 9]. Recent studies show that the availability of technology at schools is positively associated with the students' academic performance [10], compared to a negative association with technological resources at homes [11]. However, there are remaining challenges in terms of connectivity and access to devices in some areas, which can lead to social differences and limit equal learning opportunities [12, 13].

The concept of "digital natives", was developed by Marc Prensky in 2001, later replaced by the author himself by the concept of "digital savants" in 2009, is used to describe those who have grown up in an climate surrounded by digital technology since birth or at an early age [14, 15]. These individuals exhibit an inherent familiarity with electronic devices and a natural ability to use RICT [16]. However, the level of digital literacy of these individuals is insufficient for their full use in education [15, 17], which can have a negative impact on the learning of mathematics with educational tools [18, 19]. Therefore, it is necessary to promote training actions to improve this competence in the educational climate and encourage the appropriate use of RICT as a tool to facilitate learning [20].

Nowadays, the use of RICT in mathematics teaching is a generalized practice in many educational centers [10]. Various applications and customized software are used for problem solving, conceptual visualization of mathematical ideas and assessment in learning [21–23]. In addition, online learning platforms and digital resources offer a wide range of materials and activities to improve the students' experience [24]. Despite progress and technological advances, challenges persist in the effective integration of RICT [25, 26] in mathematics education [11] such as the choice of appropriate methodologies and pedagogical models, digital teacher training, appropriate selection of technological resources [27, 28] and overcoming social and eco-nomic barriers by vulnerable learners. All of these are influential factors to take into account [25].

Despite the reservations about incorporating RICT, it is mandatory to implement changes, as lecture classes show low effectiveness [29]. Therefore, the secondary school educator must implement new methodological strategies [30] and have efficient feedback tools to evaluate students' mathematical understanding [31].

This study proposes to assess tics students' perceptions of the use of RICT for educational purposes, analyzing their relationship with the use of technological resources, their participation in the classroom work and their educational level. By understanding these associations and perceptions, it is expected to contribute to the continuous improvement of the teaching-learning process and the enhancement of the potential of RICT as a tool for improving secondary school students' mathematical learning.

1.1 Objectives

The objectives of this work are as follows:

General Objective. To evaluate the perceptions of secondary school mathematics students regarding the use of Relationship, Information and Communication Technologies (RICT) for educational purposes.

The specific objectives are:

Specific Objective 1. To analyse secondary school students' perceptions of the use of RICT for educational purposes in the teaching of Mathematics.

Specific Objective 2. To examine/analyze the possible relationship between students' perceptions of the use of RICT for educational purposes and the use of technological resources, their use in class work and their educational level.

This study aims to obtain an initial approximation of how secondary school students understand and use RICT in education, which will allow the identification of areas for improvement and opportunities to optimize the teaching-learning process in Mathematics, and finally, to favour a more rewarding and equitable academic development for all students.

2 Materials and Methods

The current cross-sectional research employs a non-experimental, ex post facto method utilizing a sealed survey as the means of data gathering. Mathematics grades serve as a predictive indicator of students' academic achievement in Mathematics [32, 33].

2.1 Participants

The research participants consisted of students of Mathematics in the A.C. of Melilla. To form the study population, certain criteria were applied, including being below 18 years of age, residing in the City, and attending secondary and high school during the 2018/2019 academic year. With these conditions, the total population amounted to 5,875 individuals, with females accounting for 50.84% of the total. The sample selection method used was a non-probabilistic convenience sampling.

Initially, there were 2,039 students in the sample, but after an initial analysis, 21 incomplete questionnaires were identified and subsequently removed from the study. The final number of participants in the study was 2,018 students (53.40% females) from every school and educational level in the C.A. of Melilla. The sample was categorized based on educational levels, including 1° secondary school (417), 2° secondary school (473), 3° secondary school (394), 4° secondary school (417), 1° Baccalaureate (233), and 2° Baccalaureate (84).

2.2 Instrument

The current research is a component of a comprehensive investigation that concentrates on secondary and high school students in theton of Melilla. To conduct this study, a survey comprising 135 closed-ended items of 6 dimensions and 31 indicators was utilized, following the method proposed by Rosenbluth et al., (2016) [34].

This study presents fractional findings concerning 6 items within the "B. Learning Mathematics" and "E. RICT and Mathematics learning" dimensions of the total questionnaire. Its aim was to explore potential connections between RICT students' perceptions. A different Likert scale of 4 is used. For items TGM, TTM, TMN and ATC

(1, none; 2, a little; 3, enough; and 4, a lot). The Likert-scale for RTC is (1, No; 2, Yes), for NEC is (1, 1° Secondary; 2, 2° Secondary; 3, 3° Secondary; 4, 4° Secondary; 5, 1° High School; and 6, 2° High School).

Table 1 shows the variables evaluated, their indicators and the relationship with them, and the dimensions.

Table 1. Relationships among dimensions, indicators, and items

Dimension	Indicators	Code	Items
A. General data	A.1Student´s data	NEC	What level of education are you studying?
B. Learning of Mathematics	B.1 Affinity	TGM	Do you like Mathematics?
E. RICT and Mathematics learning	E.1 At Home	RTC	Do you use the technological resources that you have at home to study Mathematics?
	E.3 Perception	TTM	Do you think you work on Mathematics more and better using RICT?
		TMN	Do you think RICT makes you improve your marks in Mathematics?
	E.4 Tasks	ATC	Does your teacher propose homework, exercises, tasks or projects to do by using RICT in the classroom?

2.3 Instrument Validation

A team of four researchers in Mathematics education, three secondary school principals, and four heads of Mathematics departments validated the questionnaire´s content. With more than fifteen years of academic experience, the team evaluated both the writing level and the appropriateness of the items used. Additionally, twenty students were administered with a pilot test to identify potential areas for improvement.

Subsequently, the internal data matrix was studied to confirm that, in its composition, there is coherence in the conjunction of the heterogeneous items, using the Kaiser–Guttman criterion and the Tucker–Lewis index. Initially, the instrument was structured around 6 dimensions, but the algorithm determined that the optimal number of axes is three. For validation, generalized low-rank models (GLRM) and principal component analysis (PCA) were employed. To validate the instrument, a dual exploratory factor analysis was conducted.

The first analysis aimed to test the dimensions based on the initial statement. The second employed varimax rotation to identify potentially removable variables. The findings of the initial exploratory factor analysis are Mean item complexity = 1.2. Testing the hypothesis shows that 5 factors are sufficient. The null model had 15 degrees of freedom and an objective function of 0.15, with a chi-square value of 302.63. Tucker-Lewis index of factoring reliability = 1.052. Considering both the initial dimensions of the instrument and the fact that the Tucker-Lewis index of factoring reliability exceeded 0.9, a choice of 5 axes must be executed to optimize the instrument. This was also confirmed by the lower Bayesian information criterion (BIC) when taking 5 dimensions instead of the initial 6. The second exploratory factor analysis, using varimax rotation, calculated uniqueness and analyzed the residual matrix. The proportion of variability, designated as communality, was appraised by subtracting uniqueness from 1. A suitable factor model exhibits low uniqueness and high communality values. The validation of the instrument met these findings, conducing to the removal of 7 variables. The results indicated that variables with values close to 0 were well represented in all cases.

2.4 Data Set Key Variables

In this study, Naive Bayes is employed to conduct our analyses. The focus is on conducting a examination in a academic level-differentiated analysis the potential connections between the students perceptions on RICT and specific academic variables detailed below. Initially, the dataset comprised 2018 observations and 137 variables. However, for the purpose of this study, only the following variables and indicators in Table 1 are taken into consideration.

2.5 Data Collect Process

The process of collecting data was intricate due to its execution during school hours; although this was deemed essential to ensure data reliability. This required the active participation of school management, the RICT coordinator, and the mathematics and technology departments of each institution to distribute the questionnaires with minimal disruption to school operations. Adequate classroom and technological resources were also arranged. Google Forms was utilized to guarantee data collection reliability, and a specific procedure was adopted to minimize coder transcription errors [35]. The questionnaires were distributed in a computer classroom during school hours to mitigate bias, and they were distributed to all secondary and high schools in the A.C. of Melilla. Throughout the data collection process, a Mathematics teacher was designated to each school to address questions related to the questionnaire, and another teacher from the technology department was assigned to handle technical concerns. After completing the online questionnaire, each student returned to its respective classroom to return to its studies.

Because participants are under 18 years-old, the questionnaire was evaluated by the local educational authorities, and approved for distribution within the High School during school hours. Furthermore, all voluntary participants were provided with comprehensive information regarding the research's purpose. In addition, this study adheres to the ethical principles highlighted in the Declaration of Helsinki and follows the code of ethics for educational research established by the AERA (American Educational Research Association).

3 Results and Discussion

The following is a Bayesian analysis as a first approach to the study of secondary school Mathematics students' perceptions of RICT for educational purposes. This analysis shows the percentages corresponding to the independent variable TMN, which has been previously defined, with the conditional values of the other variables related to it. The results of this analysis are detailed in Tables 2, 3 and 4.

Table 2. Naive Bayes for TMN A-priori probabilities.

None	A little	Enough	A lot
0,223639	0,3025993	0,3094654	0,1642962

Table 2 shows that the students' perception of the impact of Relationship, Information and Communication Technologies (RICT) on their Mathematics grades is predominantly positive. 77.64% of students say that RICT have a positive influence on their academic performance in this area. This number is formed by those who selected the categories "A little" (30.26%), "Enough" (30.95%), and "A lot" (16.43%). However, 22.36% have a negative perception towards the role of RICT in improving their grades. These students selected the option " None", which suggests that they do not see or do not trust the potential of RICT to improve their academic performance in Mathematics.

These results have suggested the existence of a mixed opinion among students about the impact of RICT on their academic results in Mathematics [36]. While a significant part of the participants in the questionnaire has a positive view of the use of RICT in the learning of this subject, other smaller groups have a more neutral or negative opinion on the subject. In this sense, Gorjon et al., (2023) report that the excessive use of RICT in the classroom has a negative impact on students' perceptions [37].

Table 3. Naive Bayes. Conditional probabilities TTM/TMN

TTM/TMN	None	A little	Enough	A lot
None	0,76096491	0,15350877	0,05701754	0,02850877
A little	0,06320908	0,66450567	0,25121556	0,02106969
Enough	0,01584786	0,19651347	0,70206022	0,08557845
A lot	0,0119403	0,05970149	0,24179104	0,68656716

Regarding the TTM scores conditioned by the TMN values, Table 3 shows that as the belief that RICT improves marks in Mathematics (TMN) increases, so does the perception that with RICT students work more and better in the subject (TTM). This is clearly shown in the significant percentages, where within the group "None" in TMN, a remarkable 76.10% also believe "None" in STM, indicating a strong correlation between the two views. Furthermore, the analysis shows that in the extreme TMN groups, "None" and "A lot", the relationship with TTM is more defined. In the "A lot" group in TMN, a significant 68.66% also believe "A lot" in TTM, demonstrating that those who have a high belief in the positive impact of RICT on their grades also have a strong perception that RICT contributes to a better academic performance in Mathematics. In the "None" group in TMN, a large 76.10% believe "None" in TMT, indicating that those who do not believe that RICT influences their grades also have a negative perception of its usefulness in improving their work in the subject.

This relationship suggests that the perceived usefulness of RICT is related to the expectation of improved grades [38, 39]. Furthermore, it indicates that stronger beliefs about the impact of RICT on marks are linked to more definite perceptions of its utility. It also maintains that the belief in the positive impact of RICT on grades can have an effect on students' motivation [40, 41] and approach to RICT use [42].

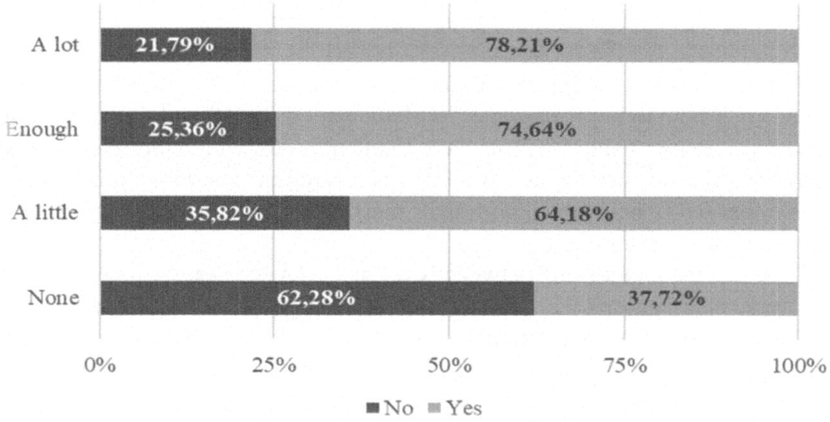

Fig. 1. A Naive Bayes. Conditional probabilities RTC/TMN.

From the RTC/TMN relationship, Fig. 1 shows an association between the perception of the usefulness of RICT in improving grades in Mathematics (TMN) and the use of technological resources at homes to study Mathematics (RTC). As the belief that RICT helps to improve grades in Mathematics (TMN) increases, the percentage of those who do use technological resources to study the subject also tends to increase, and vice versa. In other words, among those who scored "None" in TMN, a considerable majority (62.28%) do not use technological resources to study Mathematics. In contrast, among those who scored "A lor" in TMN, a significant majority (78.21%) do use technological resources to study Mathematics. Furthermore, it can be observed from Fig. 1 that the relationship between TMN and RTC seems to be more accentuated in the extremes of TMN (i.e., "None" and "A lot"), while in the middle groups (i.e. "A little" and "Enough"), the relationship between the two variables is less pronounced.

Students with a stronger belief that RICT can improve their grades in Mathematics are also more likely to use technological resources in their studies [6]. On the other hand, those students with a weaker belief in the impact of RICT on their grades tend to use fewer technological resources to study [38]. These findings are relevant for education, as they highlight the importance of encouraging a positive perception of RICT use in science learning [43, 44]. Teachers can create awareness of how the appropriate use of RICT can improve academic performance [45] and motivate their students to use technological resources in their studies [46].

Table 4. Naive Bayes. Conditional probabilities ATC/TMN

ATC/TMN	None	A little	Enough	A lot
None	0,64473684	0,19078947	0,08114035	0,08333333
A little	0,47811994	0,32090762	0,1280389	0,07293355
Enough	0,45007924	0,26624406	0,17591125	0,10776545
A lot	0,40298507	0,21492537	0,1761194	0,20597015

Regarding the role of a teacher, Table 4 shows a positive correlation between the belief that RICT help to improve grades in Mathematics (TMN) and the perception that teachers send activities using RICT in class. In other words, within the "None" group in TMN, 64.47% also answer "None" in ATC, which suggests that those students who do not believe that RICT helps them with their marks, also feel that their teachers do not send them activities using RICT in class.

In this sense, the relationship between NMT and CTA seems to be more pronounced in the extreme NMT groups (i.e., "None" and "A lot"), while in the middle groups (i.e., "A little" and "Enough"), the relationship between the two variables is less significant.

This suggests that students who believe in the potential of RICT to improve their grades also feel that teachers use RICT more frequently in their teaching [45, 47, 48]. If students perceive that teachers use RICT frequently to administer activities, this could influence their own beliefs about the impact of RICT on their grades [36, 49]. These findings could represent a challenge for teachers who would like to promote the use of RICT in the classroom [50], as students who do not believe in its usefulness may not be motivated to adopt it in their studies [40].

Figure 2 shows the conditional relationship between educational level and student perception. This analysis suggests that educational level may influence students' perceptions of the impact of RICT on their Mathematics grades. Students in the lower levels of education (1° and 2° ESO) are likely to have a higher belief that RICT can improve their Mathematics grades, while this belief tends to gradually decrease as they advance through the levels of education.

These results can be explained by several factors, such as familiarity with RICT [39], previous experience in using RICT for educational purposes [36], and expectations about how RICT can benefit their learning. In other words, other authors argue that younger students may be more familiar and exposed to RICT from an early age as "digital natives" [14], which could lead to a more positive perception of its impact on academic performance [51].

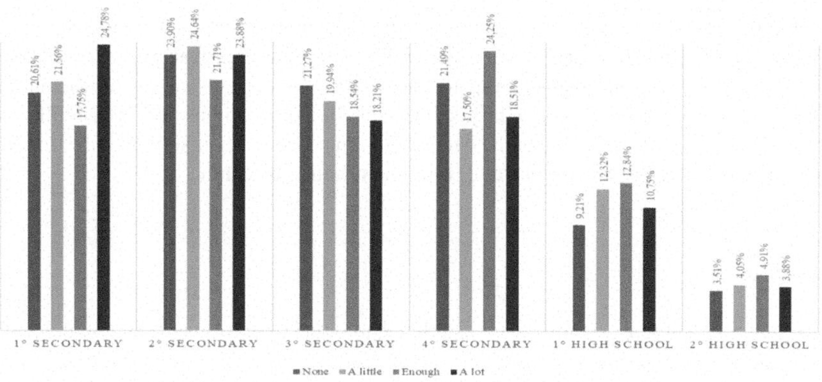

Fig. 2. A Naive Bayes. Conditional probabilities NEC/TMN.

4 Conclusion

The main conclusions of this study are presented according to the proposed objectives. Regarding the objective of analyzing secondary school students´ perceptions of the use of RICT for educational purposes in Mathematics teaching, the results obtained suggest that more than 70% of the students show a positive predisposition that RICT can improve their grades in Mathematics.

Regarding objective 2, our results point to a significant correlation between educational level and students' perception of the impact of RICT on their Mathematics grades. Another factor that has a significant influence is their educational use in the classroom. In this aspect, teachers, and the education system in general should adapt the teaching approach and encourage the use of RICT according to the characteristics and expectations of the students at each educational level. It is also concluded that those Mathematics students who strongly believe in the potential of RICT to improve their grades may be more motivated to use technological resources in their studies.

These findings should be considered with certain limitations in mind. First, the study design does not allow for establishing causal relationships between the variables. Secondly, the Bayesian analysis is presented only as a first descriptive approximation without using an inferential analysis. Finally, the geographical limitation should be noted, as the study focused on students from the Autonomous City of Melilla, which means that the generalization of the results to other regions or educational contexts is limited. Future lines of research could address this analysis by conducting a longitudinal study to assess the evolution of secondary school students' perceptions of the educational use of RICT. Diversification of the sample is also recommended. Extending the sample to other geographical regions or types of schools could provide a more complete picture of students' perceptions in different educational contexts. It is also interesting to include mixed methods combining quantitative approaches with qualitative methods, such as interviews, to provide a better understanding of students' perceptions and the reasons behind their beliefs.

Acknowledgments. We would like to express our gratitude to the Provincial Directorate in Melilla of the Ministry of Education and Vocational Training for the approval given to conduct this study in all schools. We are also grateful to the directors and heads of the Mathematics and Technology departments of the secondary schools of the Autonomous City of Melilla, whose valuable collaboration was essential in the data collection process. Their support and commitment have been fundamental for the successful development of this research.

References

1. INE. Encuesta sobre equipamiento y uso de tecnologías de información y comunicación en los hogares. INE (2019)
2. Colomo-Magana, E., Soto-Varela, R., Ruiz-Palmero, J., Gómez-García, M.: University students' perception of the usefulness of the flipped classroom methodology. Education Sciences **10** (2020). https://doi.org/10.3390/educsci10100275
3. Marta-Lazo, C., Gabelas-Barroso, J.A.: Diálogos posdigitales: Las TRIC como medios para la transformación social; Editorial Gedisa (2023)
4. Abidin, Z., Mathrani, A., Hunter, R.: Gender-related differences in the use of technology in mathematics classrooms: student participation, learning strategies and attitudes. Int. J. Inf. Learn. Technol. **35**, 266–284 (2018). https://doi.org/10.1108/ijilt-11-2017-0109
5. Areepattamannil, S., Santos, I.M.: Adolescent students' perceived information and communication technology (ICT) competence and autonomy: examining links to dispositions toward science in 42 countries. Comput. Hum. Behav. **98**, 50–58 (2019). https://doi.org/10.1016/j.chb.2019.04.005
6. Skvarc, D.R., Talbot, M., Harries, T., Wilson, C.J., Joshua, N., Byrne, L.K.: Home information and communication technology use and student academic performance: encouraging results for uncertain times. Front. Psychol. **12** (2021). https://doi.org/10.3389/fpsyg.2021.638319
7. INE. Estadística de la Sociedad de la Información y la Comunicación en los centros educativos no universitarios. Curso 2018–2019 (2020)
8. Weber, M., Becker, B.: Browsing the web for school: social inequality in adolescents' school-related use of the internet. Sage Open **9** (2019). https://doi.org/10.1177/2158244019859955
9. Kim, S.: ICT and the UN's sustainable development goal for education: using ICT to boost the math performance of immigrant youths in the US. Sustainability **10**, 4584 (2018). https://doi.org/10.3390/su10124584
10. Chaves-Barboza, E., Manuel Trujillo-Torres, J., Antonio Lopez-Nunez, J., Sola-Martinez, T.: Actions and achievements of self-regulated learning in personal environments. Research on students participating in the graduate program in preschool education at the university of granada. J. New Approaches Educ. Res. **6**, 135–143 (2017). https://doi.org/10.7821/naer.2017.7.236
11. Wakefield, J., Frawley, J.K.: How does students' general academic achievement moderate the implications of social networking on specific levels of learning performance? Comput. Educ. **144**, 103694 (2020). https://doi.org/10.1016/j.compedu.2019.103694
12. Levine, L.: Broadband adoption in urban and suburban California: information-based outreach programs ineffective at closing the digital divide. J. Inf. Commun. Ethics Soc. **18**, 431459 (2020). https://doi.org/10.1108/jices-04-2020-0041
13. Ballesta Pagán, F.J., Lozano Martínez, J., Cerezo Máiquez, M.C.: Internet use by secondary school students: a digital divide in sustainable societies? Sustainability **10**, 3703 (2018)
14. Prensky, M., Gonzalez Calatayud, V.: Entrevista a Marc Prensky. RiiTE Revista Interuniversitaria de Investigación en Tecnología Educativa, 12–21 (2018). https://doi.org/10.6018/riite/2018/354791

15. Prensky, M.H.: Sapiens digital: From digital immigrants and digital natives to digital wisdom. Innovate J. Online Educ. **5** (2009)
16. Wang, H.Y., Sigerson, L., Cheng, C.: Digital nativity and information technology addiction: age cohort versus individual difference approaches. Comput. Hum. Behav. **90**, 1–9 (2019). https://doi.org/10.1016/j.chb.2018.08.031
17. Botuzova, Y.V.: Experience of using ICT tools for teaching mathematical analysis to future teachers of mathematics. Inf. Technol. Learn. Tools **75**, 153–169 (2020)
18. Eger, L., Klement, M., Tomczyk, L., Pisonova, M., Petrova, G.: Different user groups of university students and their ITC competence: evidence from three countries in Central Europe. J. Balt. Sci. Educ. **17**, 851–866 (2018)
19. Frolova, E.V., Rogach, O.V., Ryabova, T.M.: Digitalization of education in modern scientific discourse: new trends and risks analysis. Eur. J. Contemp. Educ. **9**, 313–336 (2020). https://doi.org/10.13187/ejced.2020.2.313
20. López Núñez, J.A., Campos Soto, M.N., Aznar Díaz, I., Rodríguez Jiménez, C.: Digital competence of the teaching staff to attend to students with learning difficulties. A theoretical review. Revista Electronica Interuniversitaria De Formacion Del Profesorado **23**, 143–154 (2020). https://doi.org/10.6018/reifop.418171
21. Roanes-Lozano, E., Galán-García, J.L., Solano-Macías, C.: Some reflections about the success and impact of the computer algebra system DERIVE with a 10-year time perspective. Math. Comput. Sci. **13**, 417–431 (2019). https://doi.org/10.1007/s11786-019-00404-9
22. Melfi, G., Schwarz, T., Stiefelhagen, R.: An inclusive and accessible LaTeX editor. In: Miesenberger, K., Kouroupetroglou, G. (eds.) ICCHP 2018. LNCS, vol. 10896, pp. 579–582. Springer, Cham (2018). https://doi.org/10.1007/978-3-319-94277-3_90
23. Scharpf, P., Mackerracher, I., Schubotz, M., Beel, J., Breitinger, C., Gipp, B., Assoc Comp, M.: AnnoMathTeX - a formula identifier annotation recommender system for STEM documents. In: Recsys 2019: 13th ACM Conference on Recommender Systems, pp. 532–533 (2019). https://doi.org/10.1145/3298689.3347042
24. Olofsson, A.D., Lindberg, O.J., Fransson, G.: Students' voices about information and communication technology in upper secondary schools. Int. J. Inf. Learn. Technol. **35**, 82–92 (2018). https://doi.org/10.1108/ijilt-09-2017-0088
25. Gonzales, A.L., Calarco, J.M., Lynch, T.: Technology problems and student achievement gaps: a validation and extension of the technology maintenance construct. Commun. Res. **47**, 750–770 (2020). https://doi.org/10.1177/0093650218796366
26. Sánchez-Prieto, J.C., Huang, F., Olmos-Migueláñez, S., García-Penalvo, F., Teo, T.: Exploring the unknown: the effect of resistance to change and attachment on mobile adoption among secondary pre-service teachers. Br. J. Educ. Technol. **50**, 2433–2449 (2019). https://doi.org/10.1111/bjet.12822
27. Chen, I.-H., Gamble, J.H., Lee, Z.-H., Fu, Q.-L.: Formative assessment with interactive whiteboards: a one-year longitudinal study of primary students' mathematical performance. Comput. Educ. **150**, 103833 (2020). https://doi.org/10.1016/j.compedu.2020.103833
28. Mercader, C.: Explanatory model of barriers to integration of digital technologies in higher education institutions. Educ. Inf. Technol. **25**, 51335147 (2020). https://doi.org/10.1007/s10639-020-10222-3
29. Vergara, D., Paredes-Velasco, M., Chivite, C., Fernández-Arias, P.: The challenge of increasing the effectiveness of learning by using active methodologies. Sustainability **12**, 8702 (2020). https://doi.org/10.3390/su12208702
30. Mora, H., Signes-Pont, M.T., Fuster-Guillo, A., Pertegal-Felices, M.L.: A collaborative working model for enhancing the learning process of science & engineering students. Comput. Hum. Behav. **103**, 140–150 (2020). https://doi.org/10.1016/j.chb.2019.09.008

31. Sánchez-Matamoros, G., Fernández, C., Llinares, S.: Relationships among prospective secondary mathematics teachers' skills of attending, interpreting and responding to students' understanding. Educ. Stud. Math. **100**, 83–99 (2019). https://doi.org/10.1007/s10649-018-9855-y
32. Córdoba, L., García, V., Luengo, L., Vizuete, M., Feu, S.: How academic career and habits related to the school environment influence on academic performance in the physical education subject. Retos. Nuevas tendencias en Educación Física, Deporte y Recreación **21**, 9–13 (2012)
33. Barca, A., Peralbo, M., Porto, A., Marcos, J., Brenlla, J.: Metas académicas del alumnado de Educación Secundaria Obligatoria (ESO) y Bachillerato con alto y bajo rendimiento escolar. Revista de educación **354**, 341–368 (2011)
34. Rosenbluth, A., Cruzat-Mandich, C., Ugarte, M.L.: Methodology to validate a competencies assessment tool for psychology students. Universitas Psychologica **15**, 303–314 (2016)
35. Cohen, L., Manion, L.: Research Methods in Education. Chatham (1990)
36. Hossein-Mohand, H., Gómez-García, M., Trujillo-Torres, J.-M., Hossein-Mohand, H., Boumadan-Hamed, M.: Uses and resources of technologies by mathematics students prior to COVID-19. Sustainability **13**, 1630 (2021). https://doi.org/10.3390/su13041630
37. Gorjon, L., Oses, A.: The negative impact of information and communication technologies overuse on student performance: evidence from OECD countries. J. Educ. Comput. Res. **61**, 723–765 (2023). https://doi.org/10.1177/07356331221133408
38. Coyne, B., McCoy, S.: Forbidden fruit? Student views on the use of tablet PCs in education. Technol. Pedagogy Educ. (2020). https://doi.org/10.1080/1475939x.2020.1754897
39. Valverde-Berrocoso, J., Acevedo-Borrega, J., Cerezo-Pizarro, M.: Educational technology and student performance: a systematic review. Front. Educ. **7**, 916502 (2022). https://doi.org/10.3389/feduc.2022.916502
40. Hossein-Mohand, H.: Influence of motivation on the perception of mathematics by secondary school students. Front. Psychol. **13**, 16 (2023). https://doi.org/10.3389/fpsyg.2022.1111600
41. Jiménez Villalpando, A., et al.: Student motivation towards mathematics at blended learning and place-based classroom high schools motivación hacia las matemáticas de estudiantes de bachillerato de modalidad mixta y presencial. Revista Educación **44**, 96–109 (2020). https://doi.org/10.15517/revedu.v44i1.35282
42. Prasojo, L.D., Mukminin, A., Habibi, A., Hendra, R., Iqroni, D.: Building quality education through integrating ICT in schools: teachers' attitudes, perception, and barriers. Qual. Access Success **20**, 45–50 (2019)
43. Simo, V.L., Lagaron, D.C., Rodríguez, C.S.: STEM education for and with a digital era: the role of digital tools for the performance of scientific, engineering and mathematic practices. Red-Revista De Educacion a Distancia **20**, 31–34 (2020). https://doi.org/10.6018/red.410011
44. Lavicza, Z., et al.: Integrating STEM-related technologies into mathematics education at a large scale. Int. J. Technol. Math. Educ. **27**, 3–11 (2020). https://doi.org/10.1564/tme_v27.1.01
45. Polymeropoulou, V., Lazaridou, A.: Quality teaching: finding the factors that foster student performance in junior high school classrooms. Educ. Sci. **12**, 20 (2022). https://doi.org/10.3390/educsci12050327
46. Smith, J., et al.: Linking high school students' achievement goal orientations with their competence beliefs and their perception of teachers' emotional support during the COVID-19 pandemic. Front. Educ. **7**, 7 (2022). https://doi.org/10.3389/feduc.2022.762766
47. Strelan, P., Osborn, A., Palmer, E.: Student satisfaction with courses and instructors in a flipped classroom: a meta-analysis. J. Comput. Assist. Learn. **36**, 295–314 (2020). https://doi.org/10.1111/jcal.12421

48. Hossein-Mohand, H., Trujillo-Torres, J.-M., Gómez-García, M., Hossein-Mohand, H., Campos-Soto, A.: Analysis of the use and integration of the flipped learning model, project-based learning, and gamification methodologies by secondary school mathematics teachers. Sustainability **13**, 2606 (2021). https://doi.org/10.3390/su13052606
49. Trujillo-Torres, J.-M., Hossein-Mohand, H., Gómez-García, M., Hossein-Mohand, H., Hinojo-Lucena, F.-J.: Estimating the academic performance of secondary education mathematics students: a gain lift predictive model. Mathematics **8**, 2101 (2020). https://doi.org/10.3390/math8122101
50. Gómez-García, M., Hossein-Mohand, H., Trujillo-Torres, J.M., Hossein-Mohand, H.: The training and use of ICT in teaching perceptions of Melilla's (Spain) mathematics teachers. Mathematics **8**, 1641 (2020). https://doi.org/10.3390/math8101641
51. Partovi, T., Razavi, M.R.: The effect of game-based learning on academic achievement motivation of elementary school students. Learn. Motiv. **68**, 101592 (2019). https://doi.org/10.1016/j.lmot.2019.101592

Social Innovation on Educational AI Developments. A Case Study on Social Participation on Designing AI Generative Models for Diversity

Roberto Feltrero(✉) and Sara Osuna-Acedo

UNED - National Distance Education University, Madrid, Spain
rfeltrero@edu.uned.es

Abstract. Social engagement processes are critical to technology development if we want to ensure inclusivity, equity, and responsiveness to diverse populations. Generative AI tools require new models of technology development due to the complexity of their structure, from the creation of large datasets to the adjustment of biases to ensuring fairness of their results. The use of community-based research approaches to involve diverse groups and citizen sensitivities in the research and development process seems a good strategy to guarantee the ethical design and use of these knowledge-generating technologies.

A particular case it is presented regarding the potential of AI generative tools to simplify legal, administrative, or educational texts by providing new translation tools. This is a multidisciplinary project that requires consideration of ethical and legal consequences and that can be addressed by a social engagement development model. Requires civil and democratic engagement in two areas: 1) democratically selecting the type of texts and translations needed, and 2) involving citizens, experts, and non-experts to produce and validate real examples of legal texts with cognitive adaptations. These adaptations will feed the AI algorithms used to learn how to translate the texts. The social value of this model extends beyond the design of a text simplification tool. The model aims to establish participation and validation criteria to prevent legal, social, and equity biases in the design of generative AI tools for social purposes, improving the design of validation and explainability processes guided by human experts.

Keyword: AI for Social Development · Responsible AI · Cognitive Accessibility · Easy-to-read

1 Introduction

To ensure accessibility and inclusion, any computational design must have tools for the accessibility of its functions and to guarantee a certain control and social fairness to its outcomes. If we are dealing, as in the case of AI, with tools that are generative of information and knowledge, the accuracy of those results must also be guaranteed through the elimination of biases and the explainability of their results [1, 2].

Z. Kubincová et al. (Eds.): SETE 2023, LNCS 14606, pp. 16–26, 2024.
https://doi.org/10.1007/978-981-97-4243-1_2

The popular text generation development *ChatGPT* has shown us that it is possible to make a universal machine for all kinds of content and topics [3]. But it has also shown us that in order to use the possibilities of a machine with as many functions as this one, a rather complicated interface is needed. Not only do we have countless options to choose from when ordering one type of text or another, but there are also different procedures to learn in order to really get the most out of it [4]. If we want to use such a machine to facilitate the interaction of people with cognitive difficulties with their environment, we cannot do it with a tool that is difficult to use and understand. Moreover, the proprietary nature of this technology prevents access to information on its operation, reducing the explainability of its results and, therefore, making it hard to implement validation systems. Other examples of more specialized AI developments on easy-to-read texts are inaccessible, simply because they are only commercially available (see https://readeasy.ai/). There should be free technological alternatives promoted by public institutions in addressing such sensitive social problems for equality and equity.

It is not easy to influence the design of large technology companies to ensure these requirements of accessibility and fairness in their AI models. Fortunately, there is a whole ecosystem of open Large Language Models (LLM) allowing their modification and adjustment, both in the design of their interaction interfaces and in the fine-tuning of their datasets and model behavior in response to user prompts [5]. The community works on the basis of already trained models that, although not having the power of the best known ones, have been made available for free use by the community. This opens up the possibility of the adaptation of the various LLM for educational uses [6, 7]. In addition, there is the emergence of low-power models that can be trained on cheap web servers and, moreover, can run locally on consumer equipment (the ones we all have at home), the option of democratizing the design and adaptation of generative AI is open to all kinds of initiatives and proposals [8, 9].

Taking all this in mind, a fruitful social innovation project could be to design a truly accessible AI machine for translation and generation of easy-to-read texts managed and financed by public institutions. Such system can help people with cognitive difficulties to read complicate educational or legal documentation. At the same time, this machine could incorporate an easy to use and perfectly customizable interface for all. Being a public driven development, it will involve a further layer of supervision, and that is the control of the training data used on the AI system. This will improve explainability and validation of such AI system.

This research will particularly explore how to design a social participation system for the development of the necessary criteria and civil participation for the development of such AI generative model. Models of responsible AI that must take into account the requirements of people with special needs regarding their cognitive abilities to understand complex administrative, educational and legal texts. This means defining and understanding the: a) the who? (stakeholders involved), b) the why? (social, legal and ethical reasons) and c) the how? (criteria, regulations, etc.)

Responsible research and innovation (RRI) framework will be adapted for AI tools to ensure that everyone will be able to share in the benefits of innovation [10, 11], and to produces democratic innovations, that is to say, everyone must have the possibility to participate in the decisions of the innovation process [12]. A democratic and inclusive model of participation and social innovation includes people with disabilities and people at risk of discrimination.

The design process should prioritize equity alongside the social function of the tools being developed. Instead of becoming an obstacle to RRI, this principle can become an asset if we involve citizens in the design process itself [13, 14]. This is especially important in the development of AI and machine learning tools, which require large amounts of data to learn. The more people involved in selecting, elaborating, or validating the data and algorithms used in these tools, the better the outcome will be [15].

In order to achieve democratic innovation, it is important to have a diverse range of voices and criteria involved in the design process. However, when it comes to people with cognitive disabilities, there are specific considerations that must be taken into account in order to ensure responsible innovation. These considerations will be explored in detail in the paper.

1.1 Stay of the Art: Cognitive Diversity and Easy-to-Read Solutions

People with intellectual disabilities have limitations in their cognitive abilities, mainly in information processing: attention, perception, memory, problem solving, comprehension and analogies [16]. This does not mean that they can not cope with certain tasks. It only means that they have different cognitive abilities to do so. It is important to provide them with a communicational environment that is tailored to their needs in order to facilitate their ability to complete tasks. This is particularly important in technological environments, where many individuals face similar challenges [17]. Approximately 30% of the global population experiences difficulty in understanding certain types of information [18]. This percentage is increasing rapidly due to the prevalence of advanced technologies that mediate public and private interactions without human assistance. Even individuals without cognitive disabilities may struggle with these technologies due to differences in education, age, and social or educational background. As a result, cognitive accessibility aids are necessary to ensure that everyone can understand the environment and information around them in a way that is easy and accessible, regardless of their capabilities, culture, language, or background.

Individuals with hard intellectual disabilities face specific challenges in their interactions with the environment. These challenges primarily stem from difficulties in understanding information due to memory, concentration, or analytical problems. In particular, they struggle with comprehending written information, especially if it includes acronyms or excessive technical language that requires prior knowledge. Additionally, they may have difficulties in navigating unfamiliar situations or dealing with unexpected events, which can be further exacerbated by their struggles in communicating with unfamiliar individuals. These difficulties are often linked to their heightened sensitivity to stress. As a result, individuals with hard intellectual disabilities may exhibit slower comprehension of instructions and decision-making processes [19].

The challenges faced by individuals with intellectual disabilities are influenced by both their own abilities and the barriers or obstacles present in their surroundings. By creating a more accessible and accommodating environment, individuals with intellectual disabilities can experience fewer difficulties and better navigate the world around them [20]. There are tools and approaches that can help alleviate these difficulties and facilitate understanding. Cognitive accessibility is related to the design of environments, spaces, services, products, processes, and texts that are easy to understand and use. This approach benefits not only individuals with cognitive disabilities, but also anyone who may experience cognitive difficulties. An environment that meets the conditions of cognitive accessibility allows all individuals to access and understand their surroundings, and to receive appropriate personal attention from services trained in attention to functional diversity. This type of environment is essential for enabling individuals to fully express their abilities and participate in community life on equal terms. However, when spaces, public services, or products do not offer easily understandable information, individuals with intellectual disabilities may encounter serious difficulties in accessing, using, and enjoying them. This includes educational centers and education itself. In contrast to physical disabilities, which can be addressed through physical modifications to the environment, cognitive disabilities require a more adaptable approach. The cognitive environment is highly changeable, with new texts, signals, and informational messages constantly emerging. While it is not feasible to create a cognitive environment permanently adapted to everyone's needs, AI technologies offer tools to accompany individuals with cognitive disabilities in their daily activities and to translate texts, messages, signals, and conversations in real time. AI has the potential to remove accessibility barriers, such as computer vision to help the blind perceive the visual world and speech recognition and translation technologies for the hearing impaired. However, there is still a long way to go in terms of the usability, utility, and effectiveness of such assistive technology tools [21].

Considering the needs of users with disabilities can help technologists identify high-impact challenges that can advance the state of AI for all users. However, cognitive impairment presents unique challenges that require novel designs to address ethical considerations such as inclusivity, bias, privacy, error, expectation setting, simulated data, and social acceptability. Providing individuals with intellectual disabilities the appropriate supports to understand information in a language they can comprehend will allow them to participate and use spaces, services, and products with greater autonomy. It is also important to establish training processes for individuals with disabilities on how to use and care for AI technologies, how to select appropriate datasets or algorithms to generate easy-to-understand documents, and how to use these tools in accordance with the rights of individuals with disabilities. Legal texts are an interesting case in this regard, as they require AI to accomplish functions that no other technology or social process can achieve. By addressing these challenges, we can ensure that AI is developed in a just and fair manner that benefits all users.

Regarding legal texts and new frameworks of personal autonomy, persons with disabilities have legal capacity on an equal footing with others, and with respect to them it is appropriate to adopt whatever measures are necessary to provide them with the support they may need in the exercise of that legal capacity, measures that must be guided by the principles of necessity and proportionality.

This is deduced from the International Convention on the Rights of Persons with Disabilities, made in New York on December 13, 2006, which Spain, for instance, has ratified and whose adaptation to our legal system is the origin of the legislative amendments contained in Law 8/2021, of June 2. The previous system was based on the substitution in decision-making for individuals with disabilities, but the new system is based on respect for the will and preferences of the disabled person. Only in situations where support cannot be provided in any other way will representation in decision-making be provided. The new regulation is applicable to any person who needs this type of protection, regardless of whether their disability situation has obtained administrative recognition. The regulation also attends to personal aspects, such as decisions related to the vicissitudes of ordinary life.

People with disabilities have particular difficulty in reading court rulings. The new configuration of disability in the legal system states that they can be autonomous on court. But the adaptation and integration of people with disabilities is a pending task of Spanish Justice. In this sense, at present there is no general mechanism that allows the assistance and full participation of any person present in the courtroom, regardless of their physical or cognitive condition. This kind of regulation demands very dynamic tools since each pronouncement is different. Also, each interaction on court may differ in so many ways. Therefore creating easy-reading texts needs to be done every time and at the best possible speed, but always producing texts that, despite simplicity, are written according to legal principles. We need cognitive criteria, but also legal criteria to evaluate texts.

1.2 The Relevance of Validation in AI Tools for Easy-Reading

Up to now, AI tools with natural language processing (NLP) systems to produce generative adapted texts seems to be a good choice for the tasks of easy-reading to translate texts cognitively adapted so that people with intellectual disabilities, but also other groups such as the elderly, or those who do not know the language of the host country, can easily understand it.. But in the case of social and legal texts, is not enough to implement a series of guidelines that makes more easy the lexicon, semantics and even the organization and structure of the text. The validation of such a NLP tool for easy-reading requires attendance of a lists of guidelines from different institutions and points of view. And this validation tasks are very difficult and involve public participation at different levels. The methodology to decide how to implement that kind of public engagement on the very design of datasets, models and interfaces of AI easy-reading tools, is both a social and a technical problem that will be addressed on this research.

2 Methodology

The Responsible Research and Innovation (RRI) framework aims to promote socially responsible, inclusive, and sustainable innovation. Participatory design is a useful tool for achieving these objectives, as it involves the active involvement of end users in all steps of the design process. This ensures that all aspects of the design, including biases and ethical and social implications, are validated by stakeholders. To apply this participatory model to the creation of an AI system that translates legal, administrative, and educational texts into easy-to-read formats, it is necessary to identify the stakeholders involved. In this case, stakeholders participate in the main task of feeding a machine learning system with appropriate sample text, samples of pictographic languages, creative algorithms, and bias avoidance algorithms. This process can be broken down into four steps: 1) creation of text samples to feed the machine learning systems; 2) disability experts to validate the cognitive adaptability of easy-to-read texts; 3) ethics and social values experts to validate bias-free datasets and algorithms; 4) legal experts to validate the legal accuracy of the texts produced.

This model incorporates social participation, including validation, in all four steps, and also involves the technological appropriation of AI systems to enhance and automate the participatory design process. To implement this model within the RRI framework, it is essential to provide justification for the ethical, legal, and cognitive considerations that underlie the validation steps in each of these four processes.

2.1 Cognitive Accessibility Experts and End Users

Civil participation is essential for translating legal and administrative texts into easy-to-read formats. While some legal texts have already been translated into easy-to-read formats, a robust dataset requires hundreds of such texts. Governments can collaborate with social and civil associations that work on behalf of individuals with intellectual or developmental disabilities and their families to create local and national areas specialized in Cognitive Accessibility.

These areas should be composed of a group of experts in the adaptation of texts, documents, or information to easy reading. Typically, these experts are individuals with intellectual disabilities who are the end users of these texts. Adapting legislative texts to easy-reading is a complex process that involves expressing legal concepts in simpler language and providing examples to clarify technical terms. The structure and layout of the document must also be reorganized, with adjustments such as enlarging the font or line spacing. In addition to linguistic adaptations, paratextual elements such as pictographic symbols or color-coding must be used to enhance comprehension. These graphical elements complement the written text and are based on both NLP and graphic generators.

End users with intellectual disabilities have a crucial role in validating the adapted texts. They review the texts and provide feedback on their comprehensibility, suggesting improvements and proposing solutions to enhance accessibility. They will be involved on the reviewing of the adapted texts to determining whether it is comprehensible in terms of terminology, organization, and use of paratextual elements.

2.2 Experts and Public Participation to Avoid Social Biases

Inclusivity of AI systems is related to their effectiveness for diverse user populations. There are many discussions regarding a lack of, age, gender and racial diversity in training data for AI systems, and how these biases can be exacerbated in the case of people with disabilities [22]. AI designs that use fairness approaches to avoid biases related to gender There are many studies on how we should design AI solutions for people with disabilities avoiding biases [23]. Fairness may be a good methodology to do so [24, 25] since is a main principle to be respected. But maybe it is not enough for cognitive disabilities because of is multiple variations and individual differences [23]. A more comprehensive approach based on differences instead of equality can be used to design individual interfaces suitable for each case. Only individual users or very limited and specialized groups of users with cognitive disabilities can understand how a set of data or particular outcomes of an AI translation machine. Civil participation is needed to work together with engineers to refine the fairness of datasets and outcomes and to provide insights on how to integrate them into the interfaces for interaction with those texts.

2.3 Validation of Legal Translations: Steps to Improve Legal Accuracy

When creating easy-to-read translations from a legal perspective, it is important to engage experts to validate the translations. Their expertise can help ensure that the translations adhere to legal principles and maintain the intended meaning of the original text. These experts specialize in the amendments to regulations made at national Civil Codes that must be followed. For instance, the title XI of book one of the Spanish Civil Code is rewritten and renamed "On support measures for persons with disabilities for the exercise of their legal capacity", in which voluntary measures -those that can be adopted by the person affected by the disability himself/herself- are strengthened, as a consequence of the principle that informs the reform.

The main support measure of judicial origin for persons with disabilities becomes the guardianship. It is intended to provide support in the exercise of legal capacity, along the lines of excluding, as far as possible, actions of a representative nature, and only in cases where necessary, and only exceptionally, representative functions may be attributed to the guardian.

In this case, expertise and public engagement is driven by some detailed principles that allow the selection of legal texts and legal procedures where easy-reading and, eventually, an AI translation aid, are needed. Those principles are: a) informing principles on the support measures for persons of legal age or emancipated minors who need them for the proper exercise of their legal capacity will be intended to allow the full development of their personality and their legal development under conditions of equality, and only in the absence or insufficiency of the will of the person in question, may have a legal or judicial origin; b) support measures of a voluntary nature are those established by the person with disability, in which he/she designates who should provide him/her with support and to what extent, which may be accompanied by the necessary safeguards to ensure respect for the will, wishes and preferences of the person. The legal status of the person -in this case with capacity limitations- has many derivatives and affects a multiplicity of situations that require multiple regulation.

The task of feeding datasets and learning algorithms for easy-reading translations of legal and administrative texts is a huge one that requires the involvement of a group of legal experts, specialists in the amendments to regulations made at national Civil Codes. This task must be done for each regulatory framework in every country. Engagement of experts to validate translations from a legal point of view is often overlooked when discussing easy-reading and must be included on public projects like the proposed here.

2.4 AI Solutions to Integrate Participation and Validation

To address the need for a practical and policy-oriented definition of AI, as well as criteria for evaluating AI technologies based on cognitive diversity, it is important to break down AI systems into their constituent parts. This will enable users and experts in different fields to understand how to modify the outcomes of these systems. Additionally, technology should provide easy ways to implement policy encounters between civil society groups, allowing for multiple points of intervention in AI reflection and repair work. Some proposals go beyond simple reflection tools and involve a policy of community participation and activism [26].

In order to design AI tools for cognitive disabilities that respect fairness, legal requirements, and avoid biases, it is necessary to implement practical mechanisms within AI itself. This involves the application of defined principles of civil participation on four levels of combined expert criteria, creating a collective cognition that is aided by AI systems. The collaboration between people and artificial text translation systems in social uses of easy-reading translation systems presents a wide range of cases that need to be trained on the model. Automating this training process could be a potential solution. Some experiments suggest that the cognitive capabilities of human experts can be "cloned" and trained as collective intelligence on models of generative adversarial networks [27]. The discriminator component of these models can be duplicated to replicate the four groups of expert criteria outlined in our participation model. It can also be trained to include both human and artificial discriminators working together. This allows for civil participation to collaborate with its own cognitive artificial clones, speeding up the process of neural network training and improving accuracy with human intervention. From a technical standpoint, civil participation in this model can be seen as a design solution that involves learning machines specifically designed to evaluate various principles, legal frameworks, and social biases on generative and translation machines. This approach allows for a more comprehensive assessment of AI systems.

3 Conclusion

The text discusses the importance of Artificial Intelligence (AI) for social development, taking into account a social participation system to design such technological resources in order to improve civic and democratic participation in the process of developing such innovations for all. It has been presented a particular case of a participatory model for designing equal access to legal or administrative procedures, which requires cognitive adaptability due to the complexity of legal or administrative language. The use of AI for that purpose can make educational and administrative processes more accessible for people with cognitive disabilities, older people, or citizens at risk of educational or social discrimination.

Social innovation for individuals with diverse cognitive skills involves a validation process that includes various stakeholders. This process is driven by social, legal, and ethical reasons. In order to ensure that social innovation is inclusive and accessible, criteria and regulations must be established. The question about who is involved in the validation process for social innovation for individuals with diverse cognitive skills has been answered: stakeholders may include individuals with cognitive disabilities, their families and caregivers, disability advocates, policymakers, researchers, and technology developers. The four main dimensions of citizen engagement tasks include: a) experts for writing easy-to-read texts and examples to feed learning AI systems, b) cognitive experts to validate the examples and create analogies with graphical information, c) legal experts to validate and adjust biases and fairness of the system, and d) disability users and experts to validate final results and create interfaces and simple procedures to use NLP machines.

The reasons why this validation process is important for social, legal, and ethical reasons has been deployed addressing the potential biases and ethical concerns that may arise in the development and implementation of social innovation on AI generative tools. By involving citizens in these social innovation procedures, trust in the use of AI tools can be improved by increasing transparency, efficiency, accountability, and legitimacy of the designed tools. This approach allows people to participate in the development of ethical standards for the use, validation and explainability of these technologies, and also for the data used on the training processes.

The ways on how can the validation process for social innovation for individuals with diverse cognitive skills be facilitated has been answered through the establishment of criteria and regulations that ensure inclusivity and accessibility. Implementing these innovations requires policies and policy recommendations to apply and disseminate AI social tools. One approach to achieving this is through citizen engagement in the design and use of AI tools for public services. This engagement can be facilitated through a participatory system that involves experts from various fields. Additionally, it is beneficial to improve educational tools for lifelong learning using AI models and educate individuals about AI models. Integrating outreach, education, and social participation in innovative educational processes can help make educational and assistive technologies developed with AI accessible to all, promoting responsible and social innovation.

Acknowledgements. This publication has been supported by the Cátedra Paulo Freire de Educomunicación, financed by MESCYT (Dominican Republic) and UNED (Spain). This text also participates in the activities derived from the PID I+D+i project PID2021-127124OB-I00 (financed by MCIN/ AEI/10.13039/501100011033/ and by "FEDER Una manera de hacer Europa").

References

1. Masters, K.: Ethical use of artificial intelligence in health professions education: AMEE guide no. 158. Med. Teach. **45**, 574–584 (2023). https://doi.org/10.1080/0142159X.2023.2186203
2. Mhlanga, D.: Open AI in education, the responsible and ethical use of ChatGPT towards lifelong learning (2023). https://doi.org/10.2139/ssrn.4354422, https://papers.ssrn.com/abstract=4354422
3. Mhlanga, D.: ChatGPT in education: exploring opportunities for emerging economies to improve education with ChatGPT (2023). https://papers.ssrn.com/abstract=4355758
4. Gozalo-Brizuela, R., Garrido-Merchan, E.C.: ChatGPT is not all you need. A state of the art review of large generative AI models (2023). https://doi.org/10.48550/arXiv.2301.04655, http://arxiv.org/abs/2301.04655

5. Bozkurt, A., Xiao, J., Lambert, S., Pazurek, A., et al.: Speculative futures on ChatGPT and generative artificial intelligence (AI): a collective reflection from the educational landscape (2023). https://doi.org/10.5281/ZENODO.7636568
6. Aydin, C.C., Tirkes, G.: Open source learning management systems in e-learning and Moodle. https://doi.org/10.1109/EDUCON.2010.5492522
7. Tian, J., Chen, H., Xu, G., Yan, M., et al.: ChatPLUG: open-domain generative dialogue system with internet-augmented instruction tuning for digital human (2023). https://doi.org/10.48550/ARXIV.2304.07849
8. Gerhard-Young, G., Anantha, R., Chappidi, S., Hoffmeister, B.: Low-resource adaptation of open-domain generative chatbots. In: Proceedings of the Second DialDoc Workshop on Document-grounded Dialogue and Conversational Question Answering, pp. 23–30. Association for Computational Linguistics, Dublin (2022). https://doi.org/10.18653/v1/2022.dialdoc-1.3
9. Schmidt, B., Duderstadt, B, Anand, Y., Nussbaum, Z.: Gpt4all: training an assistant-style chatbot with large scale data distillation from gpt-3.5-turbo (2023). http://static.nomic.ai.s3.amazonaws.com/gpt4all/2023_GPT4All_Technical_Report.pdf
10. Conover, W.: Review of responsible innovation: managing the responsible emergence of science and innovation in society. J. Chem. Educ. **91**, 1513–1514 (2014)
11. Sherborne, T., Young, G., Okada, A.: Innovative teaching of responsible research and innovation in science education. eLearning Papers **8** (2015)
12. von Hippel, E.: Democratizing Innovation. MIT Press, Cambridge (2005)
13. Robinson, D.K., Simone, A., Mazzonetto, M.: RRI legacies: co-creation for responsible, equitable and fair innovation in Horizon Europe. J. Responsible Innov. **8**, 209–216 (2021)
14. Stahl, B.C., Wright, D.: Ethics and privacy in AI and big data: Implementing responsible research and innovation. IEEE Secur. Priv.Secur. Priv. **16**, 26–33 (2018)
15. Birhane, A., et al.: Power to the people? Opportunities and challenges for participatory AI. In: Equity and Access in Algorithms, Mechanisms, and Optimization, pp. 1–8 (2022)
16. Googin, G., Newell, C.: Digital Disability. Rowan & Littlefield, United Kingdom (2003)
17. Kolatch, E.: Designing for users with cognitive disabilities (2000). http://www.otal.umd.edu/UUGuide/erica/
18. G3ict: The accessibility imperative. Implications of the convention on the rights of persons with disabilities for information and communication technologies. http://g3ict.org/resource_center/g3ict_book_-_the_accessibility_imperative
19. Navas, P., Verdugo, M., Gómez, L.: Diagnóstico y clasificación en discapacidad intelectual. Psychosoc. Interv.. Interv. **17**, 143–152 (2008)
20. Cuesta, J.L., de la Fuente, R., Ortega, T.: Discapacidad intelectual: una interpretación en el marco del modelo social de la discapacidad. Controversias y Concurrencias Latinoamericanas **10**, 85–106 (2019)
21. Smith, P., Smith, L.: Artificial intelligence and disability: too much promise, yet too little substance? AI Ethics. **1**, 81–86 (2021). https://doi.org/10.1007/s43681-020-00004-5
22. Morris, M.R.: AI and accessibility: a discussion of ethical considerations. Commun. ACM (2020)
23. Whittaker, M., et al.: Disability, Bias, and AI. AI Now Institute (2019)
24. Guo, A., Kamar, E., Vaughan, J.W., Wallach, H., Morris, M.R.: Toward fairness in AI for people with disabilities SBG@a research roadmap. SIGACCESS Access. Comput. **2**, 1 (2020). https://doi.org/10.1145/3386296.3386298

25. White, J.J.G.: Fairness of AI for people with disabilities: problem analysis and interdisciplinary collaboration. SIGACCESS Access. Comput. **3**, 1 (2020). https://doi.org/10.1145/3386296.3386299
26. Krafft, P.M., et al.: An action-oriented AI policy toolkit for technology audits by community advocates and activists. In: Proceedings of the 2021 ACM Conference on Fairness, Accountability, and Transparency, pp. 772–781. Association for Computing Machinery, New York (2021). https://doi.org/10.1145/3442188.3445938
27. Terziyan, V., Gavriushenko, M., Girka, A., Gontarenko, A., Kaikova, O.: Cloning and training collective intelligence with generative adversarial networks. IET Collab Intel Manufact. **3**, 64–74 (2021). https://doi.org/10.1049/cim2.12008

Empowering Collaboration Through Immersive Technologies: Fostering Intercultural Competencies

Nicia Guillén-Yparrea[1](✉), Felipe Hernández-Rodríguez[1], and María Soledad Ramírez-Montoya[2]

[1] School of Engineering and Sciences, Tecnologico de Monterrey, Monterrey, Mexico
nicia.gy@tec.mx
[2] Institute for the Future of Education, Tecnologico de Monterrey, Monterrey, Mexico

Abstract. Intercultural collaboration promotes diversity as a strength and builds more effective, creative, and understanding teams in a globalized world. This study explores and evaluates university students' perceptions of their intercultural competencies and acceptance of emerging technology tools, specifically Metaverse, for virtual collaboration with people from other cultures. This research employs qualitative research methodology, specifically a case study design. The sample consisted of 55 interdisciplinary undergraduate students, and data were collected through surveys and focus group discussions. The analysis focused on three main components: intercultural collaboration, international experience, and metaverse. The results highlighted that (a) most students know how to deal respectfully with different intercultural perspectives, (b) students do not always feel motivated to interact with other students from different cultural backgrounds, but they are aware that they can learn a lot from each other, (c) students who have had an international experience are more willing to involve people from different backgrounds in collaborative assignments, and (d) students think that it would be interesting and enriching to collaborate with students from other countries in the Metaverse. This study aims to be of value to academic and research communities, and to those interested in education, internationalization, and educational innovation.

Keywords: Intercultural competencies · Metaverse · Internationalization · Collaborative learning · Educational innovation · Higher education

1 Introduction

Educational technology is essential in enhancing and updating learning through digital tools, platforms, and resources. It allows for customizable, responsive, and efficient education that caters to diverse student needs in the digital age. Intelligent learner modeling and group modeling are concepts in educational technology that focus on using data and technology to understand and support the learning process of individual learners and groups of learners. These concepts are often used in personalized learning environments and online education platforms. Immersive technologies aim to involve users deeply in

Z. Kubincová et al. (Eds.): SETE 2023, LNCS 14606, pp. 27–36, 2024.
https://doi.org/10.1007/978-981-97-4243-1_3

digital encounters, making them feel fully engaged within virtual or digital surroundings; these technologies establish a feeling of being present and actively involved in a simulated realm, often engaging multiple senses like vision, hearing, and occasionally touch. Their primary goal is to create a more authentic and captivating user experience. For example: virtual environments have gained significant attention due to the opportunities they offer in distance education, enabling interaction between students and teachers solely through the internet [1]. The Metaverse is currently very popular because of the unique experience that it offers. It is a combination of virtually enhanced reality and physical-persisted virtual space, which includes items mapped from or augmented from the real world and the virtual creations [2]. In the need to adapt to virtual education and the search for the best tools to provide students that can fully develop their competencies, immersive technologies give the hope of this possibility.

On the other hand, internationalization in higher education is essential for students, institutions, and societies. It fosters intercultural understanding and a global perspective and enhances education through diverse methods and standards. Intercultural competencies involve having the right and relevant knowledge about specific cultures, maintaining open attitudes that facilitate establishing and maintaining relationships with people from different cultural backgrounds, and having the necessary skills to benefit from the exchange of knowledge and attitudes during interactions [3]. Interaction with diverse peers fosters adaptability and intercultural competence, while promoting global citizenship to address universal challenges. This approach inspires robust professional collaboration around shared goals, building partnerships that facilitate knowledge transfer, multilingual environments that enhance language skills, and ultimately, an internationalized education that cultivates well-informed, innovative, and responsible global citizens. To date, significant collaborations have been made at the international level [4], as evidenced by the progress of the Sustainable Development Goals towards the 2030 Agenda [5], but there is still a long way to go in higher education to create awareness of shared responsibility and the need to form a perspective of global citizenship that encourages voluntary contribution with the initiative to work for common goals.

In this context, the central goal of this study is to explore and assess university students' insights into their intercultural competencies and possible acceptance of immersive technology tools, specifically Metaverse, for virtual collaboration with people from other cultures. This includes examining the differences between those who have had international experiences or exchanges and those who have not, their opinions about a previous study of virtual collaboration using Metaverse, and their perceptions of the potential of using Metaverse to simulate international experiences that help them develop intercultural competencies to improve their collaborative skills.

2 Methodology

After conducting exploratory research on the implementation of playful activities to enhance interdisciplinary collaboration and observing a very good level of acceptance [6], in which it is worth mentioning that this Metaverse activity showed a natural collaboration among the participants, where each member contributed their knowledge and skills to solve the exercise, it was decided to use the same sample for this study to explore students' perceptions and the possibility of using this type of immersive technology to develop transversal skills, specifically intercultural competencies.

The sample consisted of 55 interdisciplinary students, of whom 40% (n = 22) were female and 60% (n = 33) were male. All participants were undergraduate students enrolled in the 8th (55%), 9th (9%), and 10th (36%) semesters of a university located in northern Mexico. The selection represented a variety of fields, including Industrial and Systems Engineering (36%, n = 20), Bachelor in Strategy and Business Transformation (29%, n = 16), Civil Engineering (9%, n = 5), and Information Technology Engineering (5%, n = 3), which accounted for 80% of the sample. The remaining 20% were from various other disciplines. Of the sample group, 71% (n = 39) of the students had international academic exposure, while 29% (n = 16) had no international academic experience.

The implementation of this experimental study and the ethical implications involving individuals in this study was regulated and approved by the Tecnologico de Monterrey, and the technical support of the Writing Lab of the Institute for the Future of Education.

Because of their ability to explore human opinions, attitudes, and perspectives, qualitative studies have gained significant traction in various disciplines, with a notable emphasis on the social sciences and education [7]. This investigation employs qualitative research methodology, specifically a case study design. Data was collected through surveys and focus group discussion, aimed to explore how students cooperate with each other on the Metaverse, their attitudes towards intercultural collaboration, and their views on academic collaboration with students from foreign countries via the Metaverse. A comprehensive literature review was carried out which included a thorough investigation of tools used in previous studies, and an analysis was performed on the collected data using a questionnaire conducted to assess intercultural competencies perception among university students. The online survey received responses from all the 55 students from the sample. A Likert scale was used for the questionnaire, with the following response options: 1-Strongly disagree, 2-Disagree, 3-Agree, and 4-Strongly agree. The Cronbach's Alpha coefficient was designed to assess the reliability and internal consistency of multi-item research instruments. Therefore, calculating and communicating this coefficient, particularly when using Likert-type scales, is essential. This coefficient's range is between 0.00 and 1.0, with a value of 0.00 indicating a lack of consistency and 1.0 indicating perfect consistency. Normally, a value between 0.70 to 0.90 is deemed acceptable [8].

Focus groups are an established mechanism for data collection across qualitative, mixed method, and quantitative methodologies [9]. This technique allows researchers to gather in-depth and rich qualitative data, because the participants are encouraged to openly discuss their thoughts, feelings, and experiences, which can provide insights into their attitudes, opinions, and perceptions. The focus group study can also facilitate a deeper exploration of complex or nuanced topics by allowing participants to build on each other's ideas and contribute to a more comprehensive understanding. From the whole sample, three 9th semester students were carefully selected for the focus group discussion:

- Student 1 (S1): Who has had an international academic experience, studying in Ireland for a year to learn English after high school and before enrolling in the university.

- Student 2 (S2): Who has had an informal international experience by attending a summer camp in France and another in Italy during high school.
- Student 3 (S3): With no international experience.

Questions were designed to deepen the results obtained from the survey and their perceptions of the previous Metaverse experience, aligning three key elements: (a) intercultural collaboration, (b) the relevance of international experiences for the development of transversal competencies, and (c) the use of immersive technology, specifically Metaverse, for intercultural interactions. The session was conducted in a Gessell room (Fig. 1), a special room for focus group discussions, moderated by a professor from the same institution, and lasted 55 min.

Fig. 1. Focus group scenario.

3 Results

Based on the results from the questionnaire, Table 1 shows the distribution of responses to the questions, according to the Likert scale applied as a rubric to the 55 students. Acceptance predominates in all the items mentioned above, with 49% of responses in rating 5-Strongly agreed. To ensure that the reliability of the survey is preserved, the calculation of the Cronbach's Alpha coefficient statistic was carried out to evaluate the internal consistency of the measurement scale, resulting in an acceptable value of consistency with $\alpha = 0.76$.

The research team surveyed participants about their attitudes toward collaborating with individuals from different cultures. As shown in Fig. 2, students with international experience were slightly less likely to agree strongly (50%, $n = 8$) or agree (44%, $n = 7$) than students without such experience, of which 59% ($n = 23$) strongly agreed and 36% ($n = 14$) agreed. Only approximately 5% of the overall sample disagreed with the statement.

Figure 3 depicts the perspective of students concerning the importance of being tolerant towards diverse opinions from people from other cultures. Out of all participants, 75% ($n = 12$) fully concurred while 25% ($n = 4$) concurred. For students with international experience, 54% ($n = 21$) completely agreed while 46% ($n = 18$) agreed.

Table 1. Distribution of Likert scale responses.

	With international experience		Without international experience	
Variable	f	%	f	%
Strongly agree	49	61%	94	49%
Agree	28	35%	86	45%
Disagree	3	4%	12	6%
Strongly disagree	0	0%	1	1%

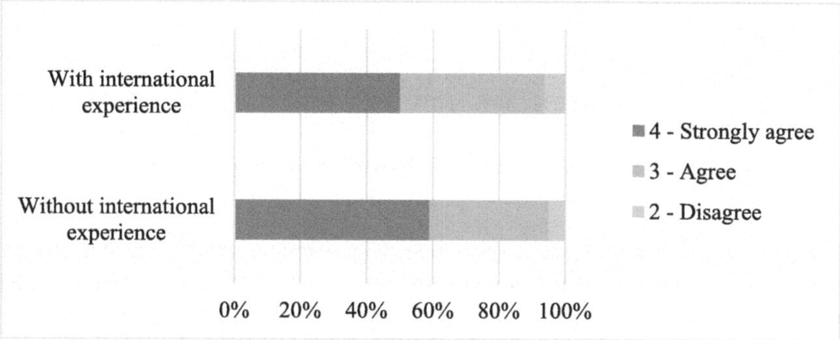

Fig. 2. Collaborating with people from different cultures is enjoyable.

The outcomes of this question give us insight to the significance of having firsthand experience of working with different cultures for a more profound comprehension of interaction.

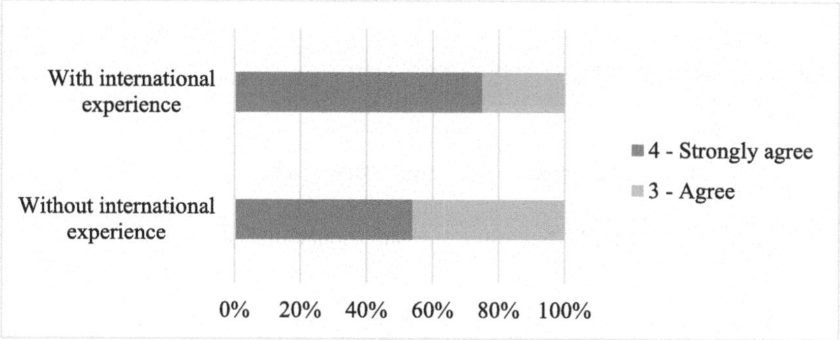

Fig. 3. Demonstrating respect towards differing opinions.

Figure 4 illustrates the degree of interest among the students to discuss current issues, indicating the levels of agreement from strongly agree to strongly disagree. The distribution of these responses is as follows: for the group with international experience, 56% (n = 9) strongly agreed, 44% (n = 6) agreed, and 6% (n = 1) disagreed, while for the group without international experience, 36% (n = 14) strongly agreed, 46% (n = 18) agreed, 15% (n = 6) disagreed, and 3% (n = 1) strongly disagreed.

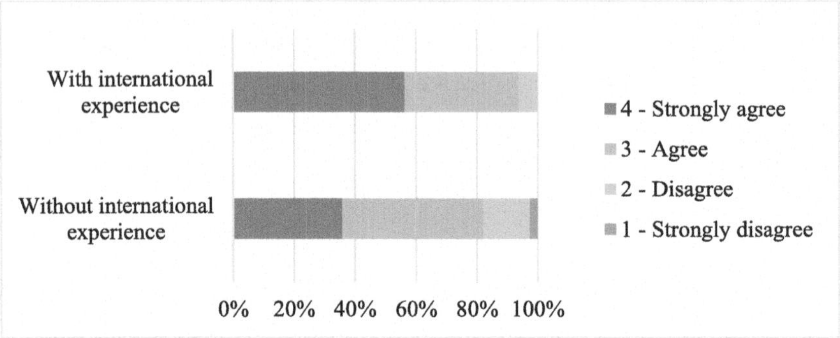

Fig. 4. Talking with individuals from diverse cultures about current topics.

In the group with international experience, 13 participants totally agreed (81%) and three agreed (19%) that they were interested in learning about cultures different from their own and found it enriching. In contrast, in the group without international experience, 21 participants (54%) totally agreed, 17 participants (44%) agreed, and one participant (3%) disagreed (Fig. 5).

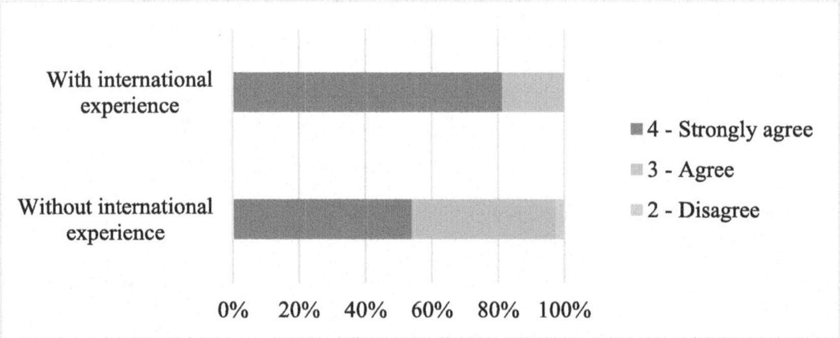

Fig. 5. Interest in learning about cultures.

Figure 6 displays the students' views on the inclusion of individuals from other cultures in joint activities, with 44% (n = 7), 50% (n = 8), and 6% (n = 1) of those with international background responding strongly agree, agree, and disagree respectively. On the other hand, 38% (n = 15), 54% (n = 21), and 8% (n = 3) of participants without professional experience showed similar strong agreement, agreement, and disagreement levels.

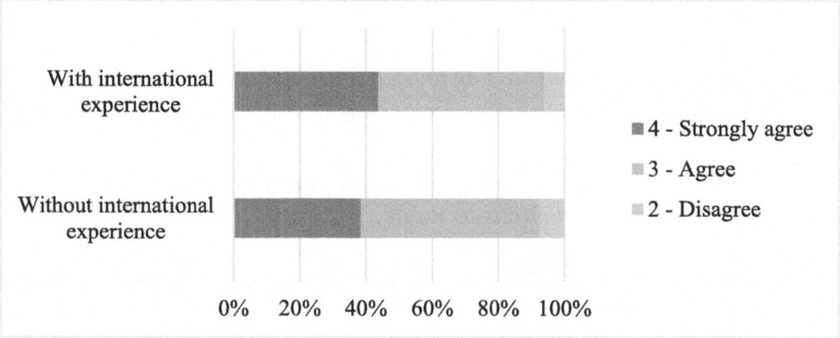

Fig. 6. Incorporating people from varied backgrounds in collaborative assignments.

As results from the focus group discussion, it can be highlighted (a) the students showing a genuine interest in knowing from other cultures, (b) the difficulty of adapting at first when interacting with students from other countries, (c) the good improvement they perceived after having these international experiences when collaborating with others, (d) their comments about the good experience they have using the Metaverse for collaboration by the first time, and (e) the enthusiasm shown about the proposal of intercultural collaboration activities and interactions through the Metaverse. Here is a transcript of some of their reflections during the discussion:

- About if they enjoy interacting with people from different cultures:

  S3: *"I really like to get close to students when they are foreigners, from other states of Mexico, because I like the food and I like to ask them about that and their customs, social issues."*

  S1: *"The fact in terms of culture, food, environment, customs of the different states are very different within Mexico itself, but after doing some work you can make friends with other people."*

- About how to carry out the intercultural collaboration and show respect:

  S2: *"New ways of thinking academically from our society or from other societies that are found elsewhere, you learn a lot."*

  S1: *"I find it attractive, but if we agree on what language we speak and how to navigate correctly in the metaverse, you can see people's gestures and walking in spaces, you feel closer to others."*

- About what motivate them to communicate with people from diverse cultures and how it will be doing it through the Metaverse:

  S2: *"The incentive to seek relationships with other people from other cultures would be from the part of something that interests you."*

  S3: *"To collaborate in, for example, the Metaverse, I would find it interesting, yes... to have contact with them, to see how we could understand each other..."*.

- About the interest in learning about cultures:

  S3: *"It would be a tool not only to talk to each other, but also to interact and learn about their cultures and that helps personally, it motivated me to do different things!"*

  S2: *"It's interesting to interact with other cultures because you have no idea how they respond to the same situations as we do."*

- About Metaverse to interact and how to incorporate people from diverse cultural backgrounds in collaborative tasks:

  S3: *"The facilities provided by, for example, Zoom, are more beneficial than just WhatsApp messages, but as for the benefit of being in the Metaverse, it fosters greater communication, greater interaction... With my classmates, for example, I could not see them physically, but I could see a complete avatar, and I liked that a lot because you interact differently."*

  S1: *"I had a class with a group of Germans who were on exchange, and when it was our turn to choose a team, our team and I decided to include them because we thought that maybe they knew more about the subject because they were German... It was very interesting to work with them, it was different, because my classmates and I had to speak in English and then with engineering concepts that they did not use in English in their country if not in German, it was a challenge, but we learned a lot..."*

4 Discussion and Conclusions

When interacting with people from different cultures, whether in-person or through immersive technologies, it is crucial to communicate effectively and treat other learners' diverse perspectives with respect. Figure 3 shows that the students know how to deal respectfully with the different perspectives that can emerge in intercultural collaboration, and as students commented in the focus group discussion, it is essential for this to happen that they can fully interact with their partners, not only verbally, but also facial and body expressions are relevant and very important. The detrimental effects of verbal and non-verbal language, as well as cultural barriers, enjoy a robust global consensus due to their profound impact on our personal and professional spheres [10]. The opportunity to interact with people from different cultures in different contexts and to gain a range of experiences can enable students to develop a heightened sensitivity and improve their communication skills. The Metaverse provides both the platform and the tools to facilitate such interactions, even in the realm of distance learning.

Promoting intercultural competence involves not only improving academic skills, but also fostering a global perspective on contemporary issues. Although this interaction occurs naturally with people who share similar interests in proximal contexts, it can be extended to a wider range through the use of immersive collaborative technologies. Students do not always feel motivated to interact with other students from different cultural backgrounds, but they are aware that they can learn a lot from each other (Figs. 4, 5).

As in the results from the focus group session, they need an incentive, perhaps something of their own interest, to seek out and build these relationships, but also curiosity about other people's culture can make them start the conversation. Motivation is a critical factor to consider for the success of any collaboration [11], because individuals make commitments out of desire, not just obligation. Motivation is the impetus that drives individuals and teams to actively engage, contribute, and persevere in collaborative efforts. It fosters a shared sense of purpose, commitment, and enthusiasm that is critical to maintaining momentum, overcoming challenges, and achieving collective goals. Having stimuli and all kinds of tools, from their avatars, texting, the use of emoticons, the possibility of translated comments, and spaces to explore like in the Metaverse, helps to make the interaction attractive to the students, leading them to exchange opinions and ideas with their partners.

Involving everyone in an intercultural collaborative activity promotes diversity as a strength and builds more effective, creative, and understanding teams in a globalized world. Students who have had an international experience are more willing to incorporate people from varied backgrounds in collaborative assignments than the students with no international experience (Fig. 6). Exposure to different cultural environments and interaction with people from diverse cultural backgrounds can lead students to appreciate contrast in perspectives and feel more secure in communication. As in the focus group, students commented that working with peers from other countries was a unique and challenging experience, but ultimately proved to be an invaluable learning opportunity. Diversity of thought and approach is naturally seen as beneficial to the innovation process, which by its very nature thrives on creative tension and changing perspectives [12]. Different cultural perspectives can lead to unique and innovative solutions to complex problems through the diversity of approaches and ideas brought to the table; a range of cultural viewpoints ensures a more comprehensive examination of issues and enables the team to approach challenges from different angles.

This research underscores the invaluable benefits that the Metaverse can provide in facilitating diverse group academic activities. Its importance extends beyond distance learning, as it also provides a complementary benefit within traditional classrooms. The potential of the platform lies in bringing together students from different institutions and countries, thereby enriching fundamental cross-cutting skills such as collaboration, communication, and intercultural competencies.

Acknowledgement. The authors acknowledge the technical and financial support of Writing Lab, Institute for the Future of Education, Tecnologico de Monterrey, Mexico, in the production of this work.

References

1. Turan, Z., Karabey, S.C.: The use of immersive technologies in distance education: a systematic review. Educ. Inf. Technol. (Dordr.) **28**, 1604116064 (2023). https://doi.org/10.1007/s10639-023-11849-8
2. Agustini, K., Putrama, I.M., Wahyuni, D.S., Mertayasa, I.N.E.: Applying gamification technique and virtual reality for prehistoric learning toward the metaverse. Int. J. Inf. Educ. Technol. **13**, 247–256 (2023). https://doi.org/10.18178/ijiet.2023.13.2.1802

3. Leeds-Hurwitz, W.: Competencias interculturales: marco conceptual y operative (2017)
4. United Nations: Goal 17: Revitalize the global partnership for sustainable development (2015). https://www.un.org/sustainabledevelopment/globalpartnerships/
5. UN General Assembly: Transforming our world: the 2030 agenda for sustainable development (2015)
6. Guillén-Yparrea, N., Hernández-Rodríguez, F.: Reinforcement of collaborative work in the metaverse through playful activities. In: Proceedings of the 2023 IEEE/ACIS 21st International Conference on Software Engineering Research, Management and Applications (SERA), pp. 307–312. IEEE (2023)
7. Akyildiz, S.T., Ahmed, K.H.: An overview of qualitative research and focus group discussion. Int. J. Acad. Res. Educ. 7, 1–15 (2021). https://doi.org/10.17985/ijare.866762
8. Adeniran, A.O., Olaniyi, A.A.: Application of likert scale type and Cronbach's alpha analysis (2019)
9. Pearson, D., Vossler, A.: Methodological issues in focus group research
10. Abu-Arqoub, I.A., Alserhan, F.A.: Non-verbal barriers to effective intercultural communication (2019)
11. Bista, K., Glass, C.: Journal of International Students: 10th Anniversary Series, 4th edn. OJED/STAR (2020)
12. Jones, G., Chirino Chace, B., Wright, J.: Impact of diversity on innovation. Int. J. Innov. Sci. **12**, 323–343 (2020)

Investigating the Adoption of Machine Translation in Foreign Language Learning: The Instructors' Perspective

Giada Pantana[1,2](✉) and Ilaria Torre[2]

[1] COASIT, Melbourne, Australia
[2] University of Genoa, Genoa, Italy
giada.pantana@edu.unige.it, ilaria.torre@unige.it

Abstract. Advances in machine translation brought by the use of artificial neural networks and large language models are giving impetus to research and studies on its possible use for educational purposes. In this paper we contribute to the investigation about how this technology can be used to support language learning, particularly, taking into account the instructors' perspective. Building upon the state of the art in this field, we first conducted an experimental evaluation of machine translation quality and then a survey with language teachers and assistants on their perception of machine translation quality, their opinion about machine translation, and its use in educational activities, with the aim to investigate at what extent this emerging technology can support language learning and possibly be integrated into didactic practices.

Keywords: Technology-Enhanced Learning · Neural Machine Translation · Foreign Language Learning

1 Introduction

Starting from 2016 when Google introduced artificial neural networks in Google Translate, Neural Machine Translation (NMT) has gained significant popularity and rapidly outperformed traditional Statistical Machine Translation (SMT) methods [1,3]. Advances in Machine Translation (MT) brought by the use of neural networks, specifically of deep learning, and large language models, have increased its use and gave rise to research and studies on its possible adoption to support language learning. Machine translation is seen to be most helpful in Foreign Language Learning (FLL) when used for writing tasks, translating single words or short sentences, and for intermediate students (i.e., students who can critically select the most appropriate option using their linguistic knowledge) [13].

Many articles in current literature focus on students' perspective in the use of MT for FLL [2,14], which is understandable, since the student is the final user and learner. Conversely, instructors' perspective is rarely taken into account,

Z. Kubincová et al. (Eds.): SETE 2023, LNCS 14606, pp. 37–52, 2024.
https://doi.org/10.1007/978-981-97-4243-1_4

while it would allow a wider comprehension of the possibilities for MT to be used in FLL support, and even for incorporating this technology into instructional design. The few available studies report divergent opinions among teachers [7, 8,18]. While some of the teachers envisage great potentials, others are sceptical mostly due to the perceived low quality of MT [13,17].

These findings and the limited number of studies that take teachers' perspective into account call for further investigations about the actual quality of MT compared to the perceived one and a deeper analysis of foreign language instructors' perspective and uses of MT in the classroom. This is what we investigated. Specifically, the study addresses the following Research Questions (RQs):

1. What is the performance of machine translation in terms of translation quality for the selected language pair on the given corpus?
2. Are there any discrepancies between the MT quality perceived by the instructors and the quality assessed in the evaluation?
3. Is machine translation useful to be used in foreign language learning and how, according to the instructors?
4. To what extent the findings from the MT quality evaluation can be useful to highlight unexplored uses of MT for foreign language learning?

The study we conducted to address the RQs includes an experimental comparison on the quality of three specific MT engines, i.e., Google Translate, DeepL, Systran Translate, and a survey with language teachers and language assistants in secondary and primary schools in Melbourne, Australia. The study uses English-Italian as language pair for the two evaluations and their joint analysis of results. The goal and contribution of the paper is to shed light on possible unexplored uses of MT for educational purposes in FLL and possible discrepancies between the actual MT quality and the instructors' perception, reflecting on MT adoption in the language classrooms. The idea behind the joint design of the two studies is that a high quality of MT outputs can help unfold new possible uses and contributions for this technology in FLL classrooms, especially using it according to some language proficiency aspects like writing, speaking, vocabulary expansion, pronunciation, spelling, and both written and oral comprehension.

2 Related Works and Background

One specific challenge of Computer Assisted Language Learning (CALL) is to investigate whether MT is capable of helping in FLL in addition to mere translation. MT in CALL has become even more popular since 2016, when a major shift was made from Statistical models into Neural models. Neural Machine Translation (NMT) models can capture complex linguistic patterns and handle dependencies more effectively [10]. The improvements in MT increased also thanks to the use of Large Language Models (LLMs). Thanks to these improvements, MT is more frequently adopted as a learning tool in schools and universities [3]. The common conclusion in literature is that the use of MT tools is beneficial for FLL

[9,13], but the level and areas of its benefits are still under survey. Instead, the opinions on its use in FLL diverge in opposite directions among instructors.

As reported by Lee in [13], "although an increasing number of studies have reported its pedagogical benefits, studies have also revealed that language teachers are still sceptical about using MT for various reasons. Most of all, they have limited trust in MT quality and the effectiveness of using MT in foreign language learning". Similar results can be found in Stapleton [17], which assesses that teachers are very sceptical about using MT in the classrooms since the tools still make a large number of errors. Also, dishonesty is a recurrent theme in current literature. For this reason, instructors are worried about the students' dependence from these tools, while students do not feel like they are cheating [18]. The research conducted by Zhu [18] also shows that the teachers' negative view is most commonly due to a low level of knowledge of these tools on their part. "Instructors without understanding said technology tools cannot truly leverage the advantages of these tools and help students to achieve their further proficiency in language learning" [18]. Similarly, Delorme [3] states that the didactic potential of these tools remains widely unexploited. Likewise, Jolley and Maimone [7] observe that MT will become unavoidable in the language learning process, and instructors and students alike would benefit from training regarding how to best use MT tools to support language teaching and learning. In this respect, the study by Zhu [18] emphasizes the need of "rethink[ing] and adapt[ing] didactic methods and tools when faced with recent technological developments".

However, currently, very few works analyse the specific support that MT can provide in order to incorporate these tools in didactic methods. In our survey, we consider this point and focus our analysis particularly on exploring possible uses of MT to support learning aspects such as writing, listening, vocabulary, accuracy and fluency, starting our investigation from the manual evaluation of MT quality, with a focus on these aspects. In literature, MT quality assessment has been performed using both automatic and manual methods. One of the most comprehensive studies using automatic methods is conducted by Intento Inc. [6], an enterprise MT hub that annually releases the "State of Machine Translation" by comparing the translation quality of the commercial versions of several MT and GenAI (Generative Artificial Intelligence) engines. In the study conducted in April 2023 [6] they compared 37 MT engines (including different GenAI models) on 22 language pairs and 9 domains, and found an average increase of quality compared to the past year, according to COMET, BERT, and BLEU scores, with accuracy scores over 0.90 for all the three metrics for the best performing MT tool. Translations to English are on average the best performing, with less differences among the engines, while higher differences exist when English is the source, depending on the engine, the domain, and the language pair.

Human evaluation has been performed in smaller evaluation tasks [16] and has shown overall that NMT models have better sensitivity to sentence structure, word order, and grammar, resulting in translations that preserve the meaning and intent of the source text more accurately, compared to SMT. The study by Rivera [16] concludes that automatic evaluation by itself is not enough to determine which system worked better and that human evaluations play an essential role to determine MT quality. In this paper we will focus on human evaluation using the MQM framework that will be described in the next section. The aim is to obtain a more accurate evaluation and to take into account specific features of MT quality, in particular vocabulary, accuracy and fluency, which we aim to investigate for the purpose of using MT for language learning support.

3 Method

To address the RQs we conducted two distinct studies, one on the evaluation of MT quality and the other on MT use for teaching, and we analysed the results jointly. Since past studies show overall good MT quality from Source Languages to English and higher variability of quality from English to Target Languages, as seen in Sect. 2, we limited our study to the evaluation of MT quality from English to a Target Language, Italian, and therefore, coherently, the survey is performed with Italian instructors in Melbourne schools.

3.1 MT Quality Evaluation

MT Engines. For the purposes of this research we used three MT engines in their free, not pre-trained version, and without glossaries. Google was chosen because it is very popular and used by a wide amount of researches [16]. DeepL was chosen because it is considered as one of the best MT engines and is widely used [6]. Instead, Systran Translate was chosen because in 1995 it was the first-ever provider to offer public MT services. These systems were all used to automatically translate the corpus from English to Italian.

Corpus. The corpus used for this MT quality evaluation regards the language combination English-Italian in the economic and financial domain. It is composed of 1722 segments, divided in 52 source texts, with an average of 604 words per text. Every source text has a corresponding human translation and three machine translations, one for each tool (Google Translate, DeepL, Systran Translate). The corpus is designed to ensure balance across the range of genres (articles in newspapers, blog posts, web guides, and institutional texts). The corpus is diachronic (the period selected ranges from 2008 to 2022), and the texts refer mostly to the informative type, according to Reiss's functional approach [15].

Participants. The human evaluation of the machine-translated texts from English to Italian was performed by Italian graduates in Foreign Languages, 29 in total, of which 28 are enrolled in the Master's degree course in Specialised Translation and Interpreting at the University of Genoa, Italy, and 1 already graduated in the same Master's degree.

Evaluation Metrics. The metrics used for the evaluation are based on the Multidimensional Quality Metrics (MQM) Framework, which is commonly used in the current literature to identify quality issues in translation by marking the error types and the severity of these errors in the evaluated translations. This method is open, standardised, and widely adopted for human evaluation of translations [4,11]. According to its developers, MQM is reliable for the focus it has on objectivity, for the fact that it is simple to explain and to understand for the evaluators, and because it is easy and fast to work with [11]. The framework includes a core set of metrics and additional optional metrics that can be selected based on the specific objectives of the evaluation.

For this study, we selected three metrics for Quality Dimensions (Accuracy, Fluency, Terminology) and also the "Other" Dimension. Definitions of these dimensions are available in the MQM website [11]. Each Quality Dimension is associated to one or more Issue Types. For Accuracy, the Issue Types are the following: Mistranslation, Addition, Omission, and Untranslated. For Fluency the Issue Types are: Grammar and Syntax (examples: function words, word order, word form), Grammatical Register, Inconsistency (examples: abbreviations, links), Spelling (example: capitalisation), Typography (examples: punctuation, white space). According to MQM, translation errors are to be classified on a scale of severity (0, 1, 10, 100), which corresponds respectively to none, minor, major, or severe error.

Procedure. (1) Before performing the evaluation task, participants attended a series of lessons on how MT tools work other than on post-editing, which was also taught in previous courses attended by the students. Moreover, before starting the task, the MQM framework was thoroughly explained in preliminary in-class and remote meetings where participants had the chance to ask questions and make a trial. (2) Participants were provided with 2 texts translated by the three MT engines, anonymised, and in different orders to avoid biases. (3) Participants were given two weeks to complete the evaluation task, which consisted in: a) post-editing the machine translations and timing the process, b) performing the manual evaluation by selecting the category to which errors belonged to, and scoring them according to the severity error scale of the MQM framework. (4) Participants ended the task by submitting the evaluation file.

3.2 Survey Study with Instructors

The second study we performed is a survey study with instructors about their perception of MT quality and their use of MT in language learning.

Participants. The participants of the current study were Italian language teachers and Italian language assistants in secondary and primary schools in Melbourne, Australia. The participants were recruited through an email message sent to all the instructors, inviting them to take part in the survey. The invitation was accepted by N = 26 instructors, of which 16 assistants (61.5%) and 10 teachers (38.5%), in an age range between 22 and 62 years old (AVG = 54.6).

The schools involved are a total of 18, of which 15 being secondary schools and 3 being primary schools. One participant works in two schools. The number of participants per school varied between 1 and 3 per each school. The distribution is the following: primary school (3); year 7 (19); year 8 (18); year 9 (15); year 10 (10); year 11 (9); year 12 (11).

Instrument. The survey questionnaire used in this study is composed of closed- and open-ended questions intended to provide value and depth to the analysis, taking advantage of the fact that the subjects were not too numerous. It is organised in five sections and includes 11 Likert questions on a 7-points scale, 7 multiple-choice questions, 5 checkbox questions with an "other" option to provide more information, and 5 open-ended questions, other than 4 more text questions for demographic information. The sections that compose the survey are detailed below. The complete questionnaire is available online[1].

- *Demographics*: questions in this section regard type of school (primary or secondary), profession (teacher or assistant), languages taught (Italian is mandatory to be part of the participants), years of service, school years actually teaching.
- *Personal Use of MT*: to understand the level of knowledge and personal use of MT, frequency of use, types of usage, and the knowledge of the MT engines.
- *Opinion on MT Quality:* to identify possible discrepancies between the instructors' believes and the findings from the MT quality evaluation and from the literature. This section deals also with specific translation aspects like accuracy, fluency, and vocabulary that we aim to investigate specifically for the purpose of language learning support.
- *Use of MT in Class:* to investigate whether the instructors incorporate MT use in language learning, which are the common uses and to which classes they encourage it for, whether they are aware of the advantages and disadvantages of MT tools, and whether they have explained them to their students.
- *Opinion on the Use of MT in Language Learning:* to analyse the opinion the instructors have on using this tool for FLL. More specifically, whether they think MT is a valid tool for FLL and which are the aspects it can foster. The open-ended questions in this part deal with the factors that influence instructors' decision to use or not to use MT in class, their opinion on advantages and disadvantages, whether there are any aspects they would like to know more of, and feedbacks for new practices.

For all the sections except for *Demographics*, the study of Jolley and Maimone [8] was taken as a source, adapting the questions to a wider spectrum of MT tools and to multiple aspects of the translation quality described above. A comparison of Jolley and Maimone results and this survey's results will be provided in Sect. 5.

[1] https://forms.gle/1VP3wrEc5sWhhrWX9.

4 Results

In this section, the results of the MT quality analysis and the instructors' survey will be reported in their own dedicated subsections.

4.1 MT Quality Results

We report a summary of the main results obtained from the human evaluation of the translation quality performed by the three MT engines considered, described in Sect. 3.1. We remind that the types of errors taken into account by the evaluators are based on the set of MQM metrics selected for this study.

As regards the total *number of errors*, we can observe that the MT engine with fewer errors is DeepL (1039), followed by Systran (1474), and then Google (1516). Since not all errors have the same weight, as it depends on *error severity*, the weighted average was counted. DeepL has the lowest error weighted average (173.41), Google has the highest number (n.) of errors, yet it has not the highest weighted average (244.04), Systran has a total n. of errors lower than Google, but they are marked as more severe, thus the weighted average is higher (275.57).

This data is confirmed if we count all the times that the n. of errors is minimum for each translation system. We find that DeepL scored 41 times as the MT tool with the fewest errors in the whole corpus, which is 78.84% of the corpus. Systran reports a total of 7 times (13.46%) and Google only 4 (7.69%).

If we look at the *error categories*, Fig. 1 shows the data according to each MT tool: Google has the major n. of errors in the categories Grammar/Syntax, Register and Spelling; DeepL has the highest n. of errors in Untranslated/DNT and Other; Systran has the highest n. of errors in Mistranslation, Addition/Omission, Inconsistency and Terminology. On the other hand, we now consider in which categories they have the least number of errors. Google has the lowest n. of

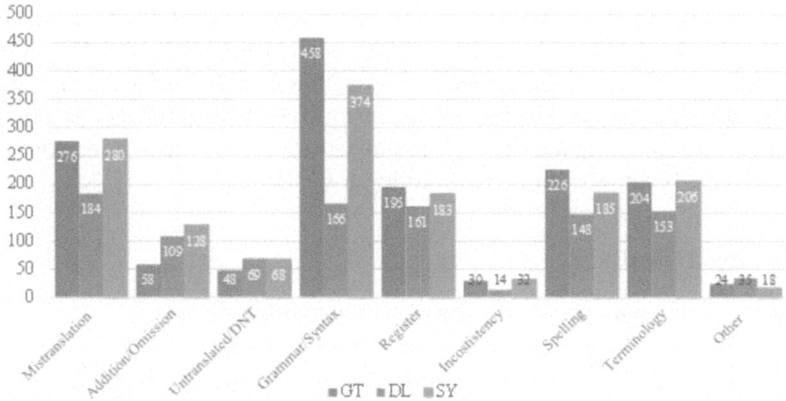

Fig. 1. MQ quality: errors analysis using MQM-based human evaluation for GT (Google Translate), DL (DeepL), SY (Systran Translate).

errors in Addition/Omission and in Untranslated/DNT; DeepL has the lowest n. of errors in Mistranslation, Grammar/Syntax, Register, Inconsistency, Spelling and Terminology; lastly, Systran is better in Other.

To summarise, DeepL is the translation tool that makes less errors (overall) in five different categories, while both Google and Systran have the maximum n. of errors in 11 categories and of different severities. If we look at the *quality dimensions* for MQM, Google is reported to have problems in Fluency (909 errors vs 774 Systran and 489 DeepL), and Systran has difficulty in dealing with Accuracy (476 errors vs 382 Google and 362 DeepL). The worst MT for Terminology issues is Systran (206 errors), but Google is not so far (204 errors), while DeepL has apparently less problems with that (153 errors). Regarding texts, DeepL's superiority in our study is confirmed, since 4 of the translated texts contain 0 errors; Systran comes next with 3 texts with 1 error each; at the end comes Google with only 1 text translated with only 1 error. These findings are coherent with the results on *average time required for post-editing*, which can be seen as an indirect measure of translation quality. DeepL resulted as the translation tool with the lowest average time required for post-editing (23 min 23 s), followed by Systran (26 min 53 s) and then by Google (32 min 14 s).

Additional Analysis. To investigate if the results might have any *correlation* with the features of the corpus, we used Pearson r correlation. The first parameter we took into account is the text readability, calculated using the Fog Index and Flesch-Kincaid Index [19,20]. We wanted to understand if a lower degree in readability impacts on the translation quality result. The hypothesis is that a higher reading difficulty might result in lower translation quality scores, (i.e., higher n. of errors). The second parameter we considered is the length of the texts. We found that indeed translation quality is correlated with the text readability. Specifically, results of the Pearson's correlation indicated that there is a significant moderate positive correlation between reading difficulty and translation errors, with an average correlation for the three MT tools of 0.324 using the Fog Index and 0.337 using the Flesch-Kincaid Index at $p < 0.05$. Conversely, the text length resulted to have a weak negative correlation with translation errors, which however is non significant ($p > 0.05$). This is coherent with the working mechanism of the Neural Machine Translation which exploits the context and thus lengthy texts are generally not penalized, yet they may have some weak positive effects. Results data are available on GitHub[2].

4.2 Survey Results

In this section we analyse the results of the instructors' survey.

Personal Use of MT. The answers to the questionnaire show that 73.1% of the participants use or have used MT before, while 26.9% claims not to use it (or have never used it). 80.7% also claims to use MT infrequently (answers 1–2–3

[2] https://github.com/teldh/MT.

of the Likert scale, with 1 being "never"). Their personal use, if infrequent, is still varied. The most selected option is to understand texts (10); to write (8); to communicate orally (3); to translate or to look for alternative translations (3); for pronunciation and spelling (2 each); for proofreading and confirming understanding (1 each); 4 people claim they do not use it at all. For the question on which is the MT tool that the participants use the most, there was a bit of confusion, because the reported answers included tools that are not MT tools, such as Reverso Context and Word Reference. For this reason, these questions, for a total of 6 votes, were left out of the reported results. We found that the most popular MT engine among the participants is DeepL (7); Google (7); Reverso Tranlsate (3) and 4 votes for none. Interestingly, the majority of the participants claimed that they know how to use MT: 61.5% of them (16 people) voted for options 5–6–7 of the Likert scale, with 7 being "strongly agree" to the assumption "I know how to use MT".

Opinion on MT Quality. The first question investigated here is the instructors' opinion on the current MT quality. This answer is balanced with 9 people assessing it as "very positive" (options 5–6 of the Likert scale), 10 people finding it negative (options 1–2–3) and 7 people assuming it is neutral. Then we investigated some specific aspects of translation, which are respectively fluency, accuracy and vocabulary. 65.3% doesn't agree that MT produces fluent outputs, and 53.8% thinks that MT does not produce accurate outputs. For the appropriateness of vocabulary of MT, 50% is neutral in their answers. The last question is the instructors' opinion on which MT tool is the best performing. The same situation as above occurred, where participants indicated Reverso Context and Word Reference as MT tools: their answers are again left out of these results. DeepL is the best performing tool for this analysis, receiving 11 votes; Google received 7 votes; just two votes for "I do not know".

Use of MT in Class. A neat majority (92.3%) of instructors does not incorporate MT in class and an even higher number (96.1%) does not encourage it to be used by their students, with 34.6% of them strongly disagreeing and another 42.3% disagreeing to encourage it. For the few ones who encourage MT use in class, we look at 5 people encouraging it in year 12, which are the VCE classes (Victorian Certificate of Education) and just 2 people encouraging it in year 10, 11, and 7. Some feedbacks report that the instructors instead encourage the use of dictionaries, and for primary school an instructor stated "I don't encourage [MT] in primary school because I believe the students don't have the tools to use it appropriately and efficiently yet. I would use it with older students who have more developed language skills and more awareness about the language structure and the MT itself".

For what concerns the activities for which MT is used, the majority use it for vocabulary lookup (12), pronunciation (4), reading activities (3), translation and writing (2 each), 10 votes for "none". The instructors were asked whether they encouraged a specific MT tool to students and the majority of them (80.8%) answered "no". Of the few "yes" answers, the most common ones used DeepL most frequently (3) because it is believed to perform better than Google, or because it is believed to have more options for vocabulary. The rest (2) voted for Google Translate. Other votes for this question were not classified, but a common trait is that the instructors explicitly specified they would not use Google Translate.

A final point was asking the instructors about the advantages and disadvantages of MT and whether they think they have a good understanding of it: 65.3% agrees on knowing MT engines, 15.4% is neutral, and another 19.2% disagrees. While, interestingly enough, if we look at whether they have explained the pros and cons of these tools to their students, the percentages drop quite consistently. Just 46.1% agrees to having explained them; 19.2% is neutral and 34.6% of the instructors disagrees.

Opinion on the Use of MT in Language Learning. The first question is aimed at attesting at what extent the instructors agree on MT being a valid tool for language learning. 50% of the instructors disagrees, while 23.1% remains neutral, and just 26.9% agrees on that.

We then asked which are the aspects for which MT can be useful in FLL, and a huge number of votes was for vocabulary lookup and extension (21), 8 for syntax, 5 for fluency, 4 for grammar, 3 for accuracy, 2 votes each for pronunciation and spelling, 2 votes for "none", 1 vote for word order.

In this section, 4 open-ended questions were also asked to the instructors. We will briefly report the questions and the most frequent and common answers, due to space constraints. For the question: "What factors influence your decision to use or not to use machine translation tools in your language teaching?", the answers diverge into positive (40%) and negative views (60%). The negative ones point out the translation is too literal and not accurate. Many students seem to use MT because they are just lazy, and they use it improperly (translate whole paragraphs or sentences) for the instructors. For this reason, instructors are worried that these tools do not entice students' use of grammar and syntax learned in class, rather their pupils would have a fossilisation of incorrect language forms. The teachers and assistants suggest instead to use the dictionaries (online ones, too), and make errors, since they can spot the students using the tools exactly from this, i.e. error making. On the other hand, teachers support that MT tools are so quick and easy to access and notice a certain keenness in the students to use them. Some (10%) encourage vocabulary lookups or free writing tasks to extend their vocabulary; while some other think they are also useful to help poor-performing students. Some of them trust their students in using the tools for translation or to check their translations, since they think the digital instruments have improved and are accurate (if enough context is provided); other prefer to use them along with other methods (like dictionaries).

About the question on the main advantages and disadvantages of MT in the language learning process, we have similar results for the question reported above on pros and cons on MT, so we briefly report them. Some unprecedentedly-reported advantages of using this method in class are for example that students can look for words in context to have a better understanding of a text piece. For the negative sides, the instructors noticed that the students who tend to rely on these methods cannot remember new words or know how to properly structure a sentence on their own; another remark is that these instruments should be used by advanced students, since a good language knowledge is required to understand when the machine fails, and for this reason they are easy to misuse. Some (15%) would like the MT to be able to explain some syntax and word order to be a useful tool. A final opinion by the instructors is that these machines convince students that they are more capable than they actually are.

Another question asked to instructors was whether there is something they would like to know that could incite them to introduce these tools in class. Some (30%) of the participants candidly admitted to be in need of an introduction or they showed little knowledge of MT functioning in their answers. Some others (30%) are curious for new techniques or activities to integrate in their classrooms. Others (40%), would like to know more about their accuracy in translation and about the proven advantages of using these tools in FLL.

A final question was intended to ask the instructors on some feedbacks or additional ideas they had on MT. It was reported that the use of these systems should be regulated. Some positive insights come from a few instructors that would like to have a classroom-use mode with limits to the translator or with grammar explanations, for example; or, they see it as "the way of the future for student numbers forever declining". The survey results are available on GitHub[3].

5 Discussion and Limitations

A discussion regarding the results of the two studies we conducted and a comparisons with Jolley and Maimone's research [8] are reported in this section. The joint interpretation of the results provides useful insights to address the four Research Questions of this study.

RQ1. The experimental evaluation of MT quality was intended to address the first RQ. Results from many different calculations in the human evaluation for the given corpus in the English-Italian language combination show that DeepL resulted the best performing engine, followed by Google and at a wider distance by Systran. As a further contribution to the literature, the results of the human evaluation through the MQM metrics provide specific feedback about MT quality in terms of accuracy, fluency, and terminology, showing a lack of accuracy and fluency from Google and Systran especially. Whereas, DeepL reveals to have the most satisfying results both in terms of number of errors and of severity of errors. This is a relevant outcome in our opinion, since the goal of this research was to understand not only where machine translation is most lacking compared to the human translation, but also to understand what specifically it succeeds in, in order to be used to support FLL.

[3] https://github.com/teldh/MT.

RQ2. The second RQ was aimed at investigating whether any discrepancies exist between the MT quality perceived by the instructors and the quality levels resulted from the evaluation. Comparing the results from the two studies we can assess that:

- The evaluation of MT based on the MQM framework shows that the results are quite clear about its high quality, whereas, the answers of instructors about MT quality are divided evenly between a positive and a negative perception.
- There is a clear misunderstanding among the instructors of what MT actually is. We noticed a certain confusion when the survey asked specifically to name which is the most used MT tool by the participants, and they named also tools which offer translation features but are not MT engines, e.g., Word Reference and Reverso Context (which are a dictionary, the former, and an application using large multilingual corpora that enable users to look for translations in context, the latter).
- The results about the best-performing MT engine for the instructors actually match with the research on quality, crowning DeepL as the best-performing one. Google comes as second in both the evaluations. Systran comes third, but is not mentioned by the instructors.
- For Fluency, 65.3% of the participants assessed that MT does not produce fluent outputs, and this aspect is quite in line with the quality assessment, since Fluency has the highest number of total errors compared to Accuracy and Terminology for all the three translation tools.
- For Accuracy, the instructors agreed for the 53.8% that MT does not produce accurate outputs. This percentage is lower than the one for Fluency, and the trend is similar in the quality evaluation: Accuracy has a lower number of total errors for all the three MT tools. This means that machine translation is better at Accuracy rather than Fluency for both of the analyses.
- For Terminology, 50% of the instructors are neutral about MT providing appropriate vocabulary. The quality assessment reports an even smaller amount of total errors in this category than the other two aspects, thus the analysis suggests that MT is more reliable for specific terminology and vocabulary rather than Accuracy and Fluency. Moreover, it suggests that half of the instructors underestimate the good quality of Terminology in MT.

We can conclude that, overall, instructors have a conforming opinion for quality of MT with respect to the actual results of the quality evaluation of MT, e.g. DeepL is the best-performing tool, and that the results on Accuracy, Fluency and Terminology are consistent in both analyses, however there are several misunderstandings, lack of knowledge of these tools, and underestimation of terminology quality for machine translation.

RQ3. The third research question was aimed at investigating at what extent MT can be useful to support FLL according to the instructors. Results concerning the "Use of MT in Class" and "Opinion on the Use of MT in FLL" evidently suggest that MT is not incorporated and encouraged enough in the FLL class. Jolley and Maimone's research [8] has instead a wider evidence of MT use in the classroom, reporting more than 80% using it for personal or teaching purposes combined. Among those who encourage MT in this study, most of the instructors use it with more experienced students (year 12). We have also seen a certain consistency in encouraging DeepL among the instructors, because it is believed to have better performances than Google. This data is confirmed by the quality evaluation results. Unfortunately, we have seen that the instructors do not explain advantages and disadvantages of MT too often to their students, and this is somewhat because they are not confident in what they know about MT. For what concerns the opinion of the instructors about using MT in the language learning process, only 26.9% agreed on it being a valid tool. This data is confirmed by Jolley and Maimone's study [8], finding that just 30.77% of instructors agreed (none strongly agreed) that the use of free online MT tools has a positive impact on the language learning process.

RQ4. The goal of this RQ was to highlight the potentials of incorporating MT into teaching practices from the analysis of MT quality. We think both the studies we conducted can provide insights in this respect. The former is specifically useful to highlight that, at least for the conditions of this research, DeepL should be considered as the most reliable engine in fluency, accuracy and vocabulary. In addition, the error analysis, which dealt with assigning the types of errors and severity, seems to suggest that instructors should take these Quality Dimensions into account when designing activities that use ML. They should make students more aware about possible issues, always considering to be trained first, so that they could explain how the tools work, clarifying its advantages and disadvantages. This is in line with Jolley and Maimone [8], suggesting the need of a framework that addresses the pedagogical implications of the MT tool usage. In particular, we found that, even if the comparison of MT quality shows good performances, instructors are still reluctant to adopt these methods to teach a foreign language, partially contrasting past results in the literature. Another conclusion to be drawn is that instructors' previous knowledge and personal use impact on their opinions, but there is also evidence of teachers and assistants who know these tools well, who are still doubtful of using them freely in their classrooms. There are concerns about how these tools should be used, because it is understood that the students' language proficiency level is crucial for the correct and efficient use of these tools; and also that the instructors are unsure of how to exploit these tools at their maximum potential, because this would require more knowledge [5]. There are also instructors who highly regard these instruments as a way to make students interested in languages, in the same way we would say CALL does [12].

We conclude analysing the MT uses for FLL from the survey, supported by the results from the quality evaluation. First of all, results suggest the value of using MT in student activities for improving the appropriateness of vocabulary in the sentence context. This result comes from the survey and is confirmed by the quality evaluation, since the categories of terminology and vocabulary are the ones with the lowest number of errors in all the three MT engines analysed. It is worth noting that, differently from the services that use multilingual corpora, NMT is not limited to, although wide, finished corpora, but can generate new sentences to be used in the activities. Writing tasks and written comprehensions are widely used by the instructors. They are frequently used with other support methods such as online dictionaries or corpora. Other common activities are to listen to pronunciation and look for the spelling of words, or directly to verify a student's translation using MT as a proofread method.

Findings from these two studies make a contribution in providing results about MT quality and showing misconceptions that may hinder the introduction of MT in the learning process, however caution is required in drawing conclusions and generalizations, due to the specific features and limits of this study. We refer in particular to the restricted sample of texts, the number of instructors involved, and the focus on a single language pair. However, in this respect, it is worth noting that while the focus on a single language pair is a limitation, on the other hand, the same focus on English-Italian in both the studies allowed a coherent and consistent analysis helping to strengthen the results already achieved in the literature, and advancing them with further evidences like it does with the results reported by Jolley and Maimone [8]. This comparison is done by underlining that the scope, goals and methods of this research and Jolley and Maimone's have points in common (the use of the survey, the theme investigated, the instructors as subjects of the survey), but also differences (they considered students in the survey, they structured the survey differently, etc.). Further works can widen the number of languages and teachers taken into account, involve students in the survey, analyse results diachronically.

6 Conclusion

The objective of this research was twofold. The first was to study the state-of-the-art machine translation quality and contribute with more specific analysis concerning in particular the evaluation of terminology and vocabulary, accuracy, and fluency. This first objective was functional to the second one that meant to investigate how these MT tools can be used in Foreign Language Learning. More specifically, we analysed which are the practices of MT in the classroom and the instructors' perspective of using these instruments for L2 teaching. We found that, generally speaking, the MT quality assessment and the MT quality perceived by the instructors do not overlap, but there is agreement on the best-performing tool (DeepL), and on the perception of three specific parameters (Accuracy, Fluency, Terminology). We also found that even if some teachers and assistants know the advantages and disadvantages of these tools, they are not frequently used in language learning due to a lack of preparation and knowledge about them. We also reported the main usages the instructors already do in the class and at which year level they are thought to be used more appropriately, underlining also which are the instructors' needs to make MT more wide-spread and reliable in the classroom.

References

1. Aiken, M.: An updated evaluation of google translate accuracy. Stud. Linguist. Lit. **3**, 253 (2019). https://doi.org/10.22158/sll.v3n3p253
2. Briggs, N.: Neural machine translation tools in the language learning classroom: students' use, perceptions, and analyses. JALT CALL J. (2018)
3. Delorme Benites, A., Lehr, C.: Neural machine translation and language teaching - possible implications for the CEFR. Bull. Suisse de Linguistique Appliquee **114**, 47–66 (2022)
4. Freitag, M., Foster, G., Grangier, D., Ratnakar, V., Tan, Q.: Experts, errors, and context: a large-scale study of human evaluation for machine translation. Trans. Assoc. Comput. Linguist. **9**, 1460–1474 (2021)
5. Hellmich, E., Vinall, K.: FL instructor beliefs about machine translation. ecological insights to guide research and practice. Int. J. Comput.-Assist. Lang. Learn. Teach. **11**, 1–18 (2021)
6. The state of machine translation 2023. An independent multi-domain evaluation of MT engines (2023). https://inten.to/machine-translation-report-2023/
7. Jolley, J.R., Maimone, L.: Thirty years of machine translation in language teaching and learning: a review of the literature. L2 J. **14**(1) (2022)
8. Jolley, J.R., Maimone, L.: Free online machine translation: use and perceptions by Spanish students and instructors. In: Central States Conference on the Teaching of Foreign Languages, p. 181–200 (2015)
9. Klimova, B., Pikhart, M., Benites, A.D., Lehr, C., Sanchez-Stockhammer, C.: Neural machine translation in foreign language teaching and learning: a systematic review. Educ. Inf. Technol. **28**(1), 663–682 (2023). https://doi.org/10.1007/s10639-022-11194-2
10. Koehn, P.: Neural machine translation. CoRR **abs/1709.07809** (2017). http://arxiv.org/abs/1709.07809
11. MQM Council: Multidimensional quality metrics (MQM), (2016). https://themqm.org/
12. European Commission, Directorate-General for Education, Youth, Sport and Culture, Szonyi, E., Siarova, H., Le Pichon-Vorstman, E.: The future of language education in Europe – Case studies of innovative practices – Executive summary, Publications Office (2020). https://data.europa.eu/doi/10.2766/81169
13. Lee, S.M.: The effectiveness of machine translation in foreign language education: a systematic review and meta-analysis. Comput. Assist. Lang. Learn. **36**(1–2), 103–125 (2023)
14. Murtisari, E.T., Widiningrum, R., Branata, J., Susanto, R.D.: Google translate in language learning: Indonesian EFL students' attitudes. J. Asia TEFL **16**(3), 978–986 (2019)
15. Reiss, K.: Text types, translation types and translation assessment. In: Readings in Translation Theory, p. 19771989 (1989)
16. Rivera-Trigueros, I.: Machine translation systems and quality assessment: a systematic review. Lang. Resourc. Eval. **56**(2), 593–619 (2022). https://doi.org/10.1007/s10579-021-09537-5
17. Stapleton, P., Becky Leung, K.K.: Assessing the accuracy and teachers' impressions of google translate: a study of primary l2 writers in Hong Kong. English for Specific Purposes **56**, 18–34 (2019)
18. Zhu, X.: Machine translation in foreign language learning classroom-learners: indiscriminate use or instructors discriminate stance. English Linguist. Res. **9**(4), 1–5 (2020)

19. Mostafa, Z., Pooneh, H.: Readability of texts: state of the art. Theor. Pract. Lang. Stud. **2** (2012). https://doi.org/10.4304/tpls.2.1.43-53
20. William, D.: The Principles of Readability. CA **92627949**, 631–3309 (2004)

On the Dynamic Generation of Items Within an Assessment Test Using Genetic Algorithms

Popescu Doru Anastasiu[1(✉)] and Bold Nicolae[2]

[1] Department of Mathematics and Computer Science, Pitești University Center, National University of Science and Technology POLITEHNICA Bucharest, Bucharest, Romania
dopopan@gmail.com

[2] Faculty of Management and Rural Development, University of Agronomic Sciences and Veterinary Medicine Bucharest, Slatina Branch, Bucharest, Romania

Abstract. The generation of assessment test is a vast area within the educational assessment design process. In this matter, the type of the question is one of the most important parameters of this process, due to its impact on the development of the assessment implementation phase. This paper presents a development of a model of an assessment test generation using genetic algorithms with an additional type of item which is dynamically generated. The item has a form of a parametric structure, e.g. the quadratic function for a given set of parameters. The purpose of this paper is to present the schema of the additional part of the model and its integration within the assessment model developed and described in previous papers.

Keywords: genetic algorithm · assessment · item

1 Introduction

Designing a learning test involves creating an assessment tool that measures the level of understanding and retention of information by pupils or students. A well-designed test must be fair, valid and provide relevant information about the knowledge and skills acquired by the participants. Also, the generation of the assessment test must be made in an optimized manner, the automatic generation being one of the most facile method of optimizing educational assessment.

In this matter, this paper presents the development of a model which has been described in previous research papers of the authors using specific types of questions. This improvement of the model is related to the generation of assessment tests formed of questions that are automatically generated based on a parametric structure of the question. In this manner, using a template of a question and generating parameters that characterize the question can lead to various questions that have different outcomes. For example, a test can be

Z. Kubincová et al. (Eds.): SETE 2023, LNCS 14606, pp. 53–67, 2024.
https://doi.org/10.1007/978-981-97-4243-1_5

generated using only a question related to solving a particular case of a quadratic function, the generated questions having different parameters for the three values of the quadratic function.

In this matter, the main research issues/questions that the approach relates are determined by the dynamic generation of questions for an educational assessment test related to STEAM (Science, Technology, Engineering, Art and Mathematics) starting from a specific parametric template of a question for which several values are generated. The values for these parameters are generated using a genetic algorithm, allowing the assessor to generate a harder or easier question depending on the closeness of the incorrect values to the correct value.

In order to accomplish this purpose of the paper, several sections were developed. Section 2 shows a short review of the area of educational assessment in this direction. The Model description presents in a detailed manner the development of the entire model related to the generation of tests [4,19] using genetic algorithms [2,5] and the final sections present several outcomes of the model presentation.

2 Literature Review

One of the most important aspects of the educational assessment process is a good design of the assessment tools, which will lead to better results for the assessee, which will permit the inclusion of assessment content in real-life situations [16]. A good design [23] is related to the assessment objectives and must be made in respect to several characteristics such as validity, reliability, equity, question types, item analysis and contextual factors [17] or requirements.

Validity refers to the extent to which a test accurately measures what it is intended to measure [1]. The literature discusses various types of validity, such as content validity (whether the test adequately covers the studied content), construct validity (whether the test measures the specific concept or ability), and criterion validity (whether the test results accurately predict subjects' subsequent performance). The validity aspect plays an important role in the assessment and its inclusion within the design of the assessment has a great impact on the assessment results [6].

Reliability refers to the consistency of measurements [3]. A reliable test will produce similar results when administered repeatedly to the same population.

The item analysis aspects of the assessment [12] have a more accentuated statistical character [18] and this analysis is used especially for the validation of the development of a good design of the assessment, as well as other aspects [8,10], such as the influence of the degree of difficulty on the assessment results.

The type of the questions has also a great impact on the results of the assessment. The most usual types of questions used in assessment are multiple-choice, short and essay questions. The literature presents more and more studies related to the automatic generation of the questions based on a corpus of text [13] and also the automatic checking of answers [20] using NLP (Natural Language Processing) tools, as well as the statistical and psihometric aspects of the question type. Regarding the specific type of multiple-choice tests [11], their widespread usage in the assessment process [24], as well as their presence within the studies in the literature shows the easiness of usage within the assessment process. Every aspect of this type of question has been researched and a special part is given to the distractor development [22]. The distractors [9] are the wrong choices of the question, which can lead to a more difficult or to an easier question for the user.

3 Model Description

3.1 General Considerations

A more developed model, described in [14,15], presents the generation of the item sequences based on several requirements. The main components of the model are the questions, named items after the generation process, the test, referred as the item sequence, the requirements and the generation mechanism. In the model, the nature of the item was a secondary approach for the research, the implementation using predominantly static multiple-choice items. This paper shows the development of the generation mechanism by including dynamically-generated items that can also have multiple choices that must also be related to the generated items.

3.2 Components

Items. This paper aims to introduce novel types of questions which are generated dynamically. These types of questions are primarily related to the Science, Technology, Engineering, Arts and Mathematics (STEAM) field, but the generation methodology includes items that are generated based on several parameters.

For this specific purpose, an item $q(id; st; sdd; cdd; V; P; T; c)$ is an object formed of the next components:

- the identification number of the item id, which has the role of being the unique identifier of the item in the implementation phase;
- the statement st, which is formed of a phrase or a set of phrases that describes the initial data and the requests of the item, which must be solved, as well as the mathematical/numerical expression;
- the set of keywords kw, which consists in the list of keywords that describe the best the topic of the item;
- the statistical degree of difficulty sdd, $sdd \in [0, 1]$; the degree of difficulty is calculated as the ratio between the number of incorrect answers at a specific item and the total number of answers;
- the degree of difficulty based on choices cdd, $cdd \in [0, 1]$, which is calculated as described in Eq. 4;
- the number of correct choices c the item will have in its final form;

- choices set V (wherever necessary), which can be formed of a list of correct and incorrect values for the given expression in the statement st:

$$V = \{(V_i), i = 1, nv\} \tag{1}$$

where nv is the number of choices from the item;
- parameters tuple P, which contains the tuple of the numerical parameters needed in order to generate the item with the same statement, but various numerical values:

$$P = (p_i | i = 1, np) \tag{2}$$

where np is the number of parameters needed within the expression. The number of parameters is defined by the expression, whether it requires a fixed cardinal or a variable one;
- the type of parametric expression T, which consists in the definition of the category of the expression, e.g. general mathematical expression, logarithmic function. The type of the parametric expression will be expressed as a set of categories, which will be introduced by the administrator. This paper will take as an example the quadratic equation type.

The structure of each item provides the opportunity to generate series of items that have the same template, in form of a parametric expression, e.g. a mathematical function or an expression that must be calculated.

The choices set is determined dynamically, by following two processes, which will be denoted by:

- $I - Solving$, which consists in the determination of the correct choice by solving the expression given in the statement;
- $I - Distractor$, which consists in the generation of distractors [7] or the wrong choices of the item.

The degree of difficulty can be weighted [7] for a specific type of question by determining the "closeness" of the wrong answers, also known in the literature as distractors [21], to the correct one. This closeness degree acts as a measure of the proficiency of the student based on how easily an answer can be differentiated from another when several values are close.

$$sid_j = |\frac{V_j - V_a}{V_a}| \tag{3}$$

This degree of difficulty can be expressed as an average of the similarity indexes between the correct answer and the wrong answers. In order to determine a value for this degree, the next value will be taken into consideration:

$$cdd_q = \frac{\sum_{j=1}^{nv} sid_j}{nv - c} \tag{4}$$

where sid is the similarity index, nv is the number of choices, V_j is the value of the jth wrong choice and V_a is the value of the correct answer. Related to this expression, the a higher value of the *cdd* shows an easier question, while a lower value of the *cdd* shows a more difficult item.

In the case of the items that have several correct answers, the degree of difficulty will be established as a matter of relationship with either the correct answers. As a result, the value of the similarity index of a wrong choice in case of an item with more than one correct answer will be determined as a minimum of the values determined for the similarity index with all the correct answers:

$$sid_j = min(\frac{V_j - V_{a_i}}{V_{a_i}}) \tag{5}$$

where V_{a_i} is the i_{th} correct choice, $i = 1, V$.

Depending on the desired degree of difficulty of the item, the distractors will be generated with the same numeric correct answer type (integer, float, complex etc.) as the correct choice (choices), thus ensuring that these will take part in the same category of the correct choice in order to create a more difficult question.

Answers. An item answer $a(id; V)$ is an object formed of the next components:

- the identification number of the item *id*, which has the role of being the unique identifier of the item in the implementation phase;
- the correct values of the expression for the item q_{id}; when $|V| = 1$, the question has a single correct answer.

Regarding the number of correct choices that the assessor desire to show, the single requirement that an item must comply with is that the number of desired choices must be lower or equal to the number of correct values of the item ($c_q \leq |V|$).

Sequence of Items. A sequence of items *SI* is the model formulation of a set of questions of, more informally, known as an assessment test. Formally, a test is a set of items, as follows:

$$SI = \{q_i | i = 1, nsi\} \tag{6}$$

where:

- q_i is the ith item within the sequence, as described in Subsect. 3.2;
- nsi is the number of items within the test, usually given by the user.

In order to differentiate a sequence of items that has a structure based on a variation of parameters from other types of generated items described in previous research papers, we will denote it by *PSI* (Parametric Sequence of Items).

The sequences of items are generated based on attributing several parameters to a given type of item T. As a result, a sequence of item will contain variations of the same item. In order to formulate a model for the described case, any *PSI* is a tuple $(id; q; nsi; nT; T; dt; dd)$ characterized by the next aspects:

- the identification particle *id*, which uniquely identifies the generated test;
- the number of items nsi within the sequence;
- the set of items q that form the sequence;
- the timestamp of the generation of the sequence *dt*, which contains the date and time the sequence was generated;
- the number of types of the items nT;
- the type of the sequence T, formally considered as a set of types of items q_T. This leads to the consideration of two main forms of a sequence, based on the type of items:
  - simple form (PSI_{SF} - Parametric Simple Form), where $nT = 1$ and the set T has a single value. In other words, the simple form is a sequence of items obtained as a variation of a single type of item by changing the parameter values. This paper shows a case of generating simple sequences of quadratic function type.
  - mixed form (PSI_{MF} - Parametric Mixed Form), where $nT > 1$ and the set T is a set of types q_T, with each type being represented by a number of items nTs. In this matter, nTs is formally described as:

$$nTs = \{nTs_i | i = 1, nT\} \tag{7}$$

    with the property that

$$\sum_{i=1}^{nT} nTs_i = nT \tag{8}$$

    This form treats the case of a sequence with several types of items. Based on these considerations, the simple form is basically a particular case of the mixed form, where $nT = 1$ and $|T| = 1$;
- the degree of difficulty *dd*, *dd* $\in [0, 1]$, which consists in the average of the values of the degrees of difficulty (*cdd*) for each item within the PSI:

$$dd = \frac{\sum_{i=1}^{nsi} cdd}{nsi} \tag{9}$$

Furthermore, a sequence of items can be formed of items that can have the structure described in Subsect. 3.2, but also a structure that has been described in previous research papers of the authors [15]. Basically, a sequence of items can have items that are generated based on a variation of parameters and also items that are selected from a database or generated based on a corpus of text. In this matter, we will consider a hybrid form of a sequence of items (SI_{HF}), which will be described and implemented in future research works.

3.3 Requirements

In order to comply with the formal structure of the assessment process, the model comprises two main roles:

- the Assessor (Ar), which is the role which has the main privilege of generating items and sequences of items, usually a teacher;

- the Assessee (Ae), which must solve the generated sequences of items, usually a student.

The items and the sequences of items will be generated based on requirements given by the Ar. In this matter, the requirements are related to the phase of the generation, either item generation ($q - G$) or sequence of items generation ($PSI - G$). For the $q - G$ generation, the main requirements are related to:

- $R_q(1)$: the type of the item T_q;
- $R_q(2)$: the degree of the difficulty of the item cdd_q.

For the $PSI - G$ generation, the main requirements are related to:

- $R_{PSI}(1)$: the categories of the items of the sequence T_{PSI};
- $R_{PSI}(2)$: the degree of the difficulty of the item dd_{PSI}.

The purpose of the $q - G$ generation is related to the generation of items that have a given type and their degree of difficulty is close to a degree given by the Ar. Similarly, the purpose of the $PSI - G$ generation is related to the generation of items which are related to the same category and their degree of difficulty is close to a degree given by the Ar. In this matter, for both the generation processes, the authors provide a similar modality of generation: the items are filtered and several clusters related to the categories are created (for the PSI_G generation) and the closeness of the degree of difficulty of the item or the sequence to the one desired by the Ar is computed.

3.4 Generations of the Items and Sequences of Items

The components of the model described below will be used to form items and sequences of items. The generation process will take into consideration the requirements described in Subsect. 3.3 and will be made using evolutionary algorithms, specifically genetic algorithms. The phases and steps of the algorithms are presented in the next subsections.

The Parametric Item Generation ($q - G$) In order to implement the generation of an item, we will formulate the model related to the generation of an item using genetic algorithms. In this matter, we will use the next components of an algorithm:

- the gene g_q, which codifies a wrong choice within the item;
- the chromosome Ch_q, which codifies the set of wrong choices of the item;
- the fitness function f_q, which is built based on the calculation of the degree of difficulty given by the Ar (DD_q) and is calculated as the absolute difference between the DD_q and the cdd_q. The lower the value of the function f_q, the fitter will be the chromosome;
- the initial population NP, which will be formed of the initial population of the genetic algorithm;
- the number of generation NG, which determines the number of generation of the genetic algorithm;

- the operations of the genetic algorithm:
  - the selection (GS) operation, which consist in the calculation of the fitness function for each chromosome, the sort of the chromosomes and the selection of the best chromosomes;
  - the mutation (MS) operation, which consist in the mutation of the chromosome Ch_q, meaning the replacement of a gene g_q within the chromosome with a randomly-generated gene;
  - the mutation rate r_m, which determine the frequency of the mutation operation;
  - the crossover (CS) operation, consisting in the replacement of parts of chromosomes with correspondent parts of other chromosomes;
  - the crossover rate r_c, which determine the frequency of the crossover operation.

The steps of the genetic algorithm for $q - G$ are:

Step 1: The item type T_q and the parameters tuple P are read.
Step 2: The correct answers are computed using the specific methodology of calculation. The result is the answer a and the correct choices V_a are established.
Step 3: The genetic algorithm is applied, as follows:
(a) the generation of the initial population of wrong choices is made;
(b) the mutation operation is applied;
(c) the crossover operation is applied;
(d) the resulted chromosomes are selected;
(e) after NG generations, the best chromosome is selected.
Step 4: The resulted choices from the genetic algorithm are input and stored in the database.

The substeps from (b) to (d) in Step 3 are repeated for a number of NG times. The algorithm in pseudocode is presented in Algorithm 1.

The Generation of the Sequence of Items (*PSI* − *G*). The generation of the sequence of items is similar to the one presented in Subsect. 3.4. In this matter, the components of the genetic algorithm are similar, but they codify slightly different values, as follows:

- the gene g_{PSI} codifies the item within the sequence;
- the chromosome Ch_{PSI} codifies the sequence of items;
- the fitness function f_{PSI}, which is built based on the calculation of the degree of difficulty given by the Ar (DD_{PSI}) and is calculated as the absolute difference between the DD_{PSI} and the cdd_{PSI}. The lower the value of the function f_{PSI}, the fitter will be the chromosome.

The rest of the genetic algorithm components remain unchanged. As for the steps of the genetic algorithm for $q - PSI$, they are:

Algorithm 1: $q - G$ algorithm

```
Data: T_q, P = (P_j | j = 1, np)
Result: V_q
                                        ▷ The input data is read
T_q ← type;
for i ← 0 to np do
  | p_i ← P_i
end
nv ← |V| − c;
                                        ▷ The correct answers are generated
V_a ←
                                        ▷ The initial population is generated
for i ← 0 to NP do
  | Ch_i ← null
  | for j ← 0 to (nv do
  |   | g_{q_j} ← random
  | end
end
                                        ▷ The genetic algorithm starts
k ← 0;
while k ≤ NG do
  |                                     ▷ The mutation operation is applied
  | mc ← random(1,NP);
  | pmc ← random(1,nv);
  | if r_m < random(0,1) then
  |   | Ch_{mc_{pmc}} ← random(1,nv);
  | end
  |                                     ▷ The crossover operation is applied
  | cc1 ← random(1,NP);
  | cc2 ← random(1,NP);
  | pcc ← random(1,nv);
  | if r_c < random(0,1) then
  |   | for i ← 0 to pcc do
  |   |   | Ch_{cc2_i} ← Ch_{cc1_i}
  |   | end
  |   | for i ← pcc to nv do
  |   |   | Ch_{cc1_i} ← Ch_{cc2_i}
  |   | end
  | end
  |              ▷ The selection operation is applied - fitness calculation
  | f ← 0;
  | for i ← 0 to NP do
  |   | for j ← 0 to nv do
  |   |   | f ← f + cdd_{Ch_{i_j}};
  |   | end
  |   | f_{Ch_i} ← |DD_q − (f/nv)|;
  |   |                                 ▷ The selection operation is applied - sort
  |   | if f_{Ch_i} < min then
  |   |   | min ← f_{Ch_i};
  |   |   | sort;
  |   | end
  | end
end
                                        ▷ The first chromosome is selected
V_q ← Ch_1;
```

Step 1: The item types T_{PSI}, the set of categories T_{PSI}, the number of each items desired for each category nT_{PSI} and the number of items within the sequence nsi are read.
Step 2: The clusters related to the set of categories T_{PSI} are built. For each category in the set, a distinct cluster is formed.
Step 3: The genetic algorithm is applied, as follows:
(a) the generation of the initial population of items is made;
(b) the mutation operation is applied;
(c) the crossover operation is applied;
(d) the resulted chromosomes are selected;
(e) after NG generations, the best chromosome is selected.
Step 3: The resulted choices from the genetic algorithm are input and stored in the database.

Besides the formation of clusters, the algorithm in pseudocode remains the same as the algorithm presented in Algorithm 1.

Item Usage. In order to create a dynamic environment, the items and sequences that are generated using the presented processes are stored in a database (denoted in the model by BD, which has the following structure (Fig. 1):

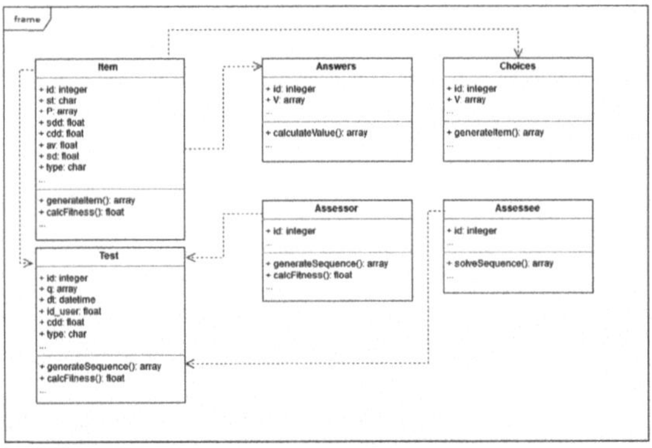

Fig. 1. The schema of the environment deployed for the item re-usage

- *Item* is a table that contains the fields related to an item that were described previously, as well as the statistical fields, e.g. the statistical degree of difficulty, average, standard deviation;
- *Choices* is a table that contains the wrong choices related to an item;
- *Answer* is a table that contains the fields related to the correct answers of an item;

- *Test* is a table that contains the fields related to a sequence of items that were described previously, as well as the ones related to the generation of the sequence of items (e.g., timestamp, author) or statistical data related to the sequence of items;
- *Assessors* is a table that contains the fields related to the users that generate items or sequences of items;
- *Assesses* is a table that contains the fields related to the users that solve sequences of items.

The storage of the items and sequences of items is established in the form of re-usage, as shown in Fig. 2, which can lead to the formation of sequences of items using items generated before or which can permit the re-usage of the sequences for several times.

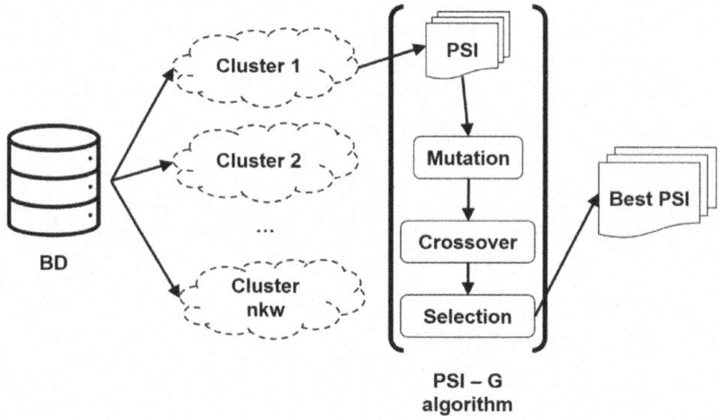

Fig. 2. The re-usage of the items

Also, the storage allows the determination of statistic-based data used in the item analysis, a useful tool for the determination of a good design of an item or of a test.

The final aspects of the model take into consideration the hybrid usage of the generated items and the items stored in the database *DB* which have the same topic, as shown in Fig. 3.

4 Discussions and Results

The genetic algorithm presented in section Algorithm 1 is an algorithm used for the generation of distractors for a specific parametric item. In this matter, we have implemented a genetic algorithm that follows the structure presented in Model description for a specific function, the quadratic function. In this matter, we have obtained specific data for the parameters of the genetic algorithm. For the quadratic function $x^2 + 4x + 4$, a number of 5 choices for each item, the question would have the next form:

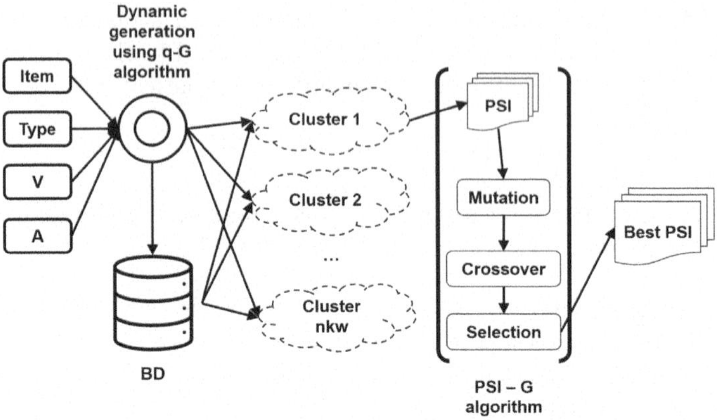

Fig. 3. The general schematic view of the model

Find the correct solutions for the given equation:
$x^2 + 4x + 4$:
a) -3 b) -4 c) -2 d) 2 e) -1

Obviously, the correct values are -2 and 2. The values for the degree of difficulty given by Ar (DD), the obtained fitness value for the example and the obtained distractors are shown in Table 1. The values were obtained for $NP = 100$, $NG = 50$ and $rm = 0.5$.

Table 1. Values of generated distractors for a given example

No	DD	dd	Distractors
1	0.0	0.67	−3 −4 −1
2	0.1	0.56	1 −3 0
3	0.2	0.46	−1 −3 −4
4	0.3	0.36	−3 0 −1
5	0.4	0.26	−4 −3 −1
6	0.5	0.16	−4 −1 −3
7	0.6	0.06	−3 −1 −4
8	0.7	0.03	−1 −4 −3
9	0.8	0.03	−1 0 −4
10	0.9	0.06	−3 0 −4
11	1.0	0.00	−1 1 −4

The obtained values show that the degree of difficulty of the item decreases once the desired degree of difficulty increases, thus the item is considered to be more difficult.

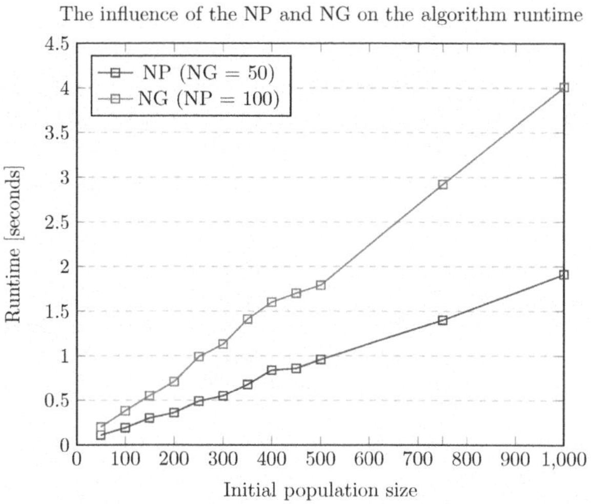

The impact of the number of generations and the initial population size is a large one once the values increase. In this matter, the values of the runtime obtained for the initial population size of 1000 chromosomes is situated almost at 2 s, while for 1000 generations, the runtime goes to almost 4 s. On the other hand, the bigger runtime leads to finer results, the fitness function decreasing for the same value of DD ($DD = 0.5$), meaning that the results are finer for the same degree of difficulty.

The evaluation of the validity of the generated results will be made using two evaluation criteria:

- the statistical criteria, which will use Item Analysis (IA) tools to determine the validity of the generated items and generated sequences;
- the human assessor criteria, which will give a comparison base for a given item template and generated distractors.

5 Conclusions

Distractors in multiple-choice questions are incorrect, plausible, and attractive choices or options that are included alongside the correct answer. The role of the distractors is to effectively test participants' understanding and critical thinking, helping to differentiate between those who have the appropriate knowledge and those who might guess or fumble in their answer choice. For this matter, the $q-G$ generation process takes into account the differentiation of weaker distractors to stronger ones based on the closeness of the choices to the correct answer. Also, the genetic algorithm for the generation of sequences of items can help in creating tests from single items based on a parametric approach. Also, the re-usage of the items helps at determining the validity of the design of the test and a better understanding of the assessees learning process.

Limitations of the paper approach are related to the manual selection of the item template (quadratic, logarithmic etc.), as well as the brute form of the item generation related to distractors, which can have finer results. Future work will consist in the inclusion of the implementation of the $q-G$ algorithm in the larger assessment model and to extend the types of the numeric functions used in the assessment, as well as the evaluation procedures described above.

References

1. Aloisi, C.: The future of standardised assessment: validity and trust in algorithms for assessment and scoring. Eur. J. Educ. **58**(1), 98–110 (2023)
2. Balcau, C.: Combinatorica si teoria grafurilor. Editura Universitatii din Pitesti (2007)
3. Black, P., Wiliam, D.: The reliability of assessments. In: Assessment and Learning, pp. 149–167 (2006)
4. Constantin, D., State, L.: An improved algorithm for estimating the ICA model concerning the convergence rate. In: Perales, F.J., Fisher, R.B. (eds.) AMDO 2008. LNCS, vol. 5098, pp. 400–408. Springer, Heidelberg (2008). https://doi.org/10.1007/978-3-540-70517-8_39
5. Constantin, D., State, L.: Successive approximations-based algorithm for independent component analysis. In: 2008 The Third International Conference on Digital Telecommunications (ICDT 2008), pp. 82–87 (2008). https://doi.org/10.1109/ICDT.2008.15
6. Divjak, B., Svetec, B., Horvat, D., Kadoić, N.: Assessment validity and learning analytics as prerequisites for ensuring student-centred learning design. Br. J. Edu. Technol. **54**(1), 313–334 (2023)
7. D'Sa, J., Al-Harbi, M., Visbal-Dionaldo, M.: The relationship between item difficulty and non-functioning distractors of multiple choice questions. Int. J. Nurs. Educ. **10** (2018). https://doi.org/10.5958/0974-9357.2018.00065.X
8. Ferketich, S.: Focus on psychometrics. aspects of item analysis. Res. Nurs. Health **14**(2), 165–168 (1991)
9. Gierl, M.J., Bulut, O., Guo, Q., Zhang, X.: Developing, analyzing, and using distractors for multiple-choice tests in education: a comprehensive review. Rev. Educ. Res. **87**(6), 1082–1116 (2017)
10. Gierl, M.J., Lai, H., Pugh, D., Touchie, C., Boulais, A.P., De Champlain, A.: Evaluating the psychometric characteristics of generated multiple-choice test items. Appl. Measur. Educ. **29**(3), 196–210 (2016)
11. Haladyna, T.M.: Developing and Validating Multiple-Choice Test Items. Routledge, London (2004)
12. Moses, T.: A review of developments and applications in item analysis. In: Advancing Human Assessment: The Methodological, Psychological and Policy Contributions of ETS, pp. 19–46 (2017)
13. Nwafor, C.A., Onyenwe, I.E.: An automated multiple-choice question generation using natural language processing techniques. arXiv preprint arXiv:2103.14757 (2021)
14. Popescu, D.A., Cristea, D., Bold, N.: On an integrated assessment for the students within an academic consortium. In: Frasson, C., Mylonas, P., Troussas, C. (eds.) ITS 2023. LNCS, vol. 13891, pp. 518–529. Springer, Cham (2023). https://doi.org/10.1007/978-3-031-32883-1_46

15. Popescu, D.A., Domsa, O., Bold, N.: The determination of the learning performance based on assessment item analysis. In: Ustalov, D., Savage, S., van Berkel, N., Liu, Y., Smirnova, A. (eds.) Proceedings of the 4th Crowd Science Workshop on Collaboration of Humans and Learning Algorithms for Data Labeling co-located with ACM International WSDM Conference (WSDM 2023), Singapore, 3 March 2023. CEUR Workshop Proceedings, vol. 3357, pp. 59–76. CEUR-WS.org (2023). https://ceur-ws.org/Vol-3357/paper3.pdf
16. Popîrlan, C.I., Tudor, I.V., Dinu, C.C., Stoian, G., Popîrlan, C., Dănciulescu, D.: Hybrid model for unemployment impact on social life. Mathematics **9**(18) (2021). https://doi.org/10.3390/math9182278, https://www.mdpi.com/2227-7390/9/18/2278
17. Popîrlan, C.I., Tudor, I.V., Dinu, C.C., Stoian, G., Popîrlan, C., Dănciulescu, D.: Influence of certain social aspects on most likely internet usage scenarios. Sustainability **14**(12), 1–20 (2022). https://ideas.repec.org/a/gam/jsusta/v14y2022i12p7129-d835759.html
18. Quaigrain, K., Arhin, A.K.: Using reliability and item analysis to evaluate a teacher-developed test in educational measurement and evaluation. Cogent Educ. **4**(1), 1301013 (2017)
19. Radovici-Marculescu, P., Balcau, C.: O aplicatie a metodei funcţiilor generatoare în combinatorica, pp. 437–444 (2005)
20. Saikia, M., Chakraborty, S., Barman, S., Chettri, S.K.: Aptitude question paper generator and answer verification system. In: Kalita, J., Balas, V.E., Borah, S., Pradhan, R. (eds.) IC3 2018. AISC, vol. 740, pp. 129–136. Springer, Singapore (2019). https://doi.org/10.1007/978-981-13-1280-9_12
21. Shin, J., Guo, Q., Gierl, M.J.: Multiple-choice item distractor development using topic modeling approaches. Front. Psychol. **10** (2019). https://doi.org/10.3389/fpsyg.2019.00825, https://www.frontiersin.org/articles/10.3389/fpsyg.2019.00825
22. Tarrant, M., Ware, J., Mohammed, A.M.: An assessment of functioning and non-functioning distractors in multiple-choice questions: a descriptive analysis. BMC Med. Educ. **9**(1), 1–8 (2009)
23. Wiggins, G., McTighe, J.: Understanding by Design. Gale Reference, Association for Supervision and Curriculum Development (2005). https://books.google.ro/books?id=hL9nBwAAQBAJ
24. Xu, X., Kauer, S., Tupy, S.: Multiple-choice questions: tips for optimizing assessment in-seat and online. Scholarsh. Teach. Learn. Psychol. **2**(2), 147 (2016)

Engagement at a Distance: Online Instructor Behaviors to Encourage Student Success

Shawn Berglund(✉) and Sabine Graf

Athabasca University, Athabasca, Canada
sberglund1540@gmail.com, sabineg@athabascau.ca

Abstract. In-person education has had its fair share of research and best practices developed, however, understanding the educational needs of students enrolled in online courses, specifically needs that are fulfilled by their instructor, requires further research. Knowing what instructor activities and behaviors support student success can have a confound impact on how instructors teach in the future to improved learning experiences of students. This paper aims at identifying instructor behaviors that impact student success in online courses and that can be supported by data available from online learning platforms. Following the literature, this paper identifies six specific online behaviors of instructors that are expected to increase student satisfaction when completing online courses, which has been related to student overall success. These behaviors include supporting students with their own time management, providing personalized and timely feedback, soliciting feedback from students, being present and actively utilizing the online learning system, encouraging peer to peer interactions, and ensuring students have access to technical support when required. This paper further breaks down these behaviors into specific auditable online activities that can then be further analyzed for their effectiveness in supporting students' success. Such analysis can be extremely valuable in providing evidence-based research to support specific instructor online behaviors that encourage student success.

Keywords: Teaching Analytics · Online Educator Behavior · Online Instructor Behavior · Student Success

1 Introduction

Online education is becoming more popular due to promises of more flexible learning opportunities and decreased overall costs for students in the hopes to bridge the socioeconomic gap seen between wealthy and more vulnerable populations due to geographic constraints [1]. Universities, such as open universities, have been offering distance and online education for decades [2], providing an opportunity for researchers to compare quality of learning and student success between the two modalities. This has helped to identify issues around the stresses of online learning among groups of students and professors alike [3]. The aim for this paper is to improve our understanding on what, if any, impact instructors have on student success through their actions online and to identify specific behaviors that instructors can use to increase student success.

Z. Kubincová et al. (Eds.): SETE 2023, LNCS 14606, pp. 68–78, 2024.
https://doi.org/10.1007/978-981-97-4243-1_6

Building off previous research that indicates that immediacy behaviors by instructors have an impact on student learning and satisfaction (e.g., [4, 5]), this paper suggests specific instructor behaviors and activities that can be validated using the data collected within online learning platforms. These results can then be expanded on by analyzing the behavioral patterns of educators to validate specific and measurable actions educators can do online to increase student success, and reduce student drop out or failure rates.

The following section outlines the current literature that explores related works and theoretical frameworks to identify relevant instructor behaviors that support student success. Section 3 discusses the approach on how literature was examined. In Sect. 4, online instructor behaviors as well as actionable behavior patterns in online learning platforms are introduced that, according to literature, can lead to student success. Section 5 concludes the paper and highlights the benefits and contributions of this work.

2 Review of Related Literature

Research on student online behavior and how it relates to their success is abundant in the literature, however, a focus on instructor behaviors and activities has not had as much attention. Generalized research can be found on topics such as instructor presence [6], instructor immediacy [4, 5], quality of instruction [7, 8], fostering an interactive community for students and instructors [9], and their positive impact on student persistence and satisfaction, all supporting students to be successful. However, there is a need to evaluate instructor behavior more thoroughly and explore the relationship between instructor presence and immediacy, and their impact on student learning.

The Community of Inquiry model is a widely accepted learning model that can be used to identify the different aspects that impact a student's learning experience, including instructor actions. As described by Garrison et al., Community of Inquiry as a learning experience can be conceptualized as containing three overlapping parts: cognitive presence, social presence, and teacher presence [6]. Each of these constructs describes aspects of the learning journey that impact a learner's ability to conceptualize and understand the intended teachings. As a well-documented framework [6], this paper uses the Community of Inquiry model's use of cognitive, social and teacher presence as a basis for identifying instructor behaviors to support students.

Student success and persistence to complete online courses are impacted by a variety of variables. For example, Hart found that student's persistence in online learning were most influenced by how close the student is from graduating, the flexibility of the program and their own time management skills, commitment, current program grade, quality of instructor communication, satisfaction with faculty, self-motivation, social connections with peers, and both emotional and technical support [10].

Research has shown that student satisfaction and student success are influenced by each other [9]. As student satisfaction is impacted by the quality of instruction [7, 8], observable activities such as forum posts, messaging, and general activities in the online course by students can increase student success [7, 10]. Instructor immediacy, or response to messages and course assignment feedback in a timely manner, has also shown to increase student satisfaction [10, 11], along with instructors encouraging student to student interactions [9].

3 Methodology

The search for papers on online instructor behaviors that support student success was carried out between June 2022 and September 2022 using Google Scholar. In this search, we focused on both new promising research as well as strong evidence-based papers. In the first phase of the literature search, literature was identified using combinations of the following keywords: online, post-secondary, university, behavior, patterns, educator, success, failure, dropout, student, attrition, satisfaction, learning module, and performance indicators. The following three inclusion criteria were used: publications need to (1) be published in 2010 or later, (2) have at least 5 citations, and (3) be published as either refereed journal articles, conference papers or book chapters. In addition, any publications that did not report on or discuss online instructor behaviors that contribute to student success were discarded. At the end of this phase, 9 high-quality publications were identified.

In the second phase, recurring themes were identified from the 9 publications. Furthermore, the literature references used within those 9 publications were further explored for additional information regarding the themes. From this step, 6 more relevant publications were identified.

In the third phase, information from the 15 publications was used to identify concrete instructor behaviors from the themes and related instructor activities that support those behaviors. Given that one of the aims of this research is to identify instructor activities that are observable in an online learning platform, those activities were further refined after evaluating available data in a commonly used learning platform (i.e., Moodle) to ensure that the activities could be reported on to validate their impact on student success.

4 Online Instructor Behaviors Supporting Student Success

Given the findings from the literature search and available data from commonly used online learning platforms (e.g., Moodle), this paper proposes the following instructor behaviors and auditable instructor activities to increase student success in online learning.

4.1 Behavior 1: Managing Time and Commitments

For students struggling to manage their time and commitments, instructors can initiate conversations to provide resources or additional support. This can be done by increasing their teacher presence in the online learning platform and supporting their cognitive presence to help students set time aside in their day to absorb the course material. Ahmad et al. identified the importance that good time management and learning tactics has on students' success [12]. In their study, they evaluated the time students spent on preparation, looking ahead, revisiting previous lessons, and catching up in their coursework. They found that students who employed a balanced approach to these activities were more successful than students who did not [12]. As such, helping students to set time aside and develop a balanced approach to studying can lead to more success for students.

Activity 1 – Time Commitment Messaging and Late Assignments. Both Hart and Bao recognize the importance of students to manage their personal time effectively and how that relates to student persistence in completing online courses [10, 11]. This activity postulates that time commitment issues for students can be identified by instructors when assignments are turned in late, or not at all. Using online messaging directed to students by recommending they focus on their time management skills, or providing tools for students to better focus their time for studying should increase their persistence and success in online courses [10]. The following behavior pattern outlines how instructors can support students struggling to submit their assignments on time:

Supportive Behavior Pattern. When marking student assignments and finding that either an assignment is missing or submitted after the due date, the instructor should reach out to the student through the messaging tool in the online learning platform suggesting that the student should focus on submitting their assignments on time. These messages can be either in the form of a direct message to the student or through the feedback functionality of the assignment itself. The messaging should focus on building the students' time management skills by recommending tools or techniques they can utilize for future courses or assignments.

Activity 2 – Time Commitment Messaging and Low Grades. Harrell and Bower found that student Grade Point Average (GPA) is a predictor in student persistence [13]. As identified in Activity 1, time management also impacts student persistence. This activity suggests that this association can be manipulated by instructor behaviors to purposefully reach out and communicate with students that are struggling with their grades with tools and strategies to complete their course work in a timely manner through developing their time management skills.

Supportive Behavior Pattern. Once an assignment is graded, if that grade is below an acceptable level, instructors should message the student through the assignment feedback functionality, or through direct messaging to support that student with time management tools or strategies to improve future assignment grades. The messaging should focus on building the students' time management skills by recommending tools or techniques they can utilize for future courses or assignments.

Activity 3 – Time Commitment Messaging and Low Participation. A strong link has been found between student participation in online activities in a class and overall success [14]. This participation can be either reviewing course content, reading forums posts, or creating their own discussions in the online learning platform. In Morris et al.'s research, students that participated in online classes and spent less than 6.84 h reviewing discussion pages, less than 8.74 h reviewing course content, less than .39 h in creating posts, or less than .29 h responding to posts were not successful [14]. This can be used as a basis for future student interaction expectations. However, course specific features should be considered when determining a threshold for instructors to act on when students fall behind on participation.

Supportive Behavior Pattern. Instructors should routinely evaluate student interactions with the online learning platform throughout the course through reporting capabilities to ensure that they are accessing the course material, reviewing forum posts, and participating in online discussions. The instructors should follow up with any students who are falling behind on participation, as identified above, by messaging the students directly about the importance of participating in the online courses with references to managing their time more effectively.

4.2 Behavior 2: Personalized and Timely Feedback

This behavior focusses on instructors providing personalized and timely communication to students when marking assignments, corresponding in forums, or messaging. A timely feedback loop with direct instructions from instructors on how to improve their work or solidify concepts is expected to increase student satisfaction, and in relation, support student success [15]. Ensuring that communication is constructive and specific to students' learning needs has also supported student success [16].

Activity 4 – Personalized Feedback on Assignments. Hart recognizes that quality, non-ambiguous feedback from instructors contribute to student persistence [10]. As students with very high grades do not generally need additional feedback, this activity focusses on students with mid-range to lower grades and ensuring that instructors are providing quality interactions to increase their success and persistence in the course.

Supportive Behavior Pattern. When an instructor grades an assignment that is of mid-range to low quality, the instructor should provide constructive feedback through the assignment feedback functionality. To determine that the feedback from the instructor is of high quality, this activity does assume that the comments would not be similar from student to student, and instead have a high degree of disparity between assignments and students.

To check the quality of the feedback, a linguistic model is proposed to analyze individual instructor feedback throughout a course. Each feedback response is compared against other already given responses to identify how unique it is. The model is based on a simple word-by-word analysis.

In the following paragraphs, two examples are provided to demonstrate the model and how it distinguishes between generic feedback and personalized feedback. In the first example, Responses A and B are both generic feedback:

Response A: Great work, David! However, there are a few problems in your assignment. Have a great Spring Break!
Response B: <u>Great work,</u> Shawn! But <u>there are a few problems</u>. I hope you <u>have a great Spring Break!</u>

Underlined words in Response A and B visually represent duplicate words between the two responses. For each new response (i.e., Response B), a similarity score is calculated by determining the percentage of same words used. In this example, Response B has 17 words, 12 of which are not unique, giving it a score of 12/17 = 71%. The second example shows personalized feedback in Responses C and D:

Response C: Well-crafted essay, Shelly! I appreciate the detail in Section A and the way you compared cloud and cloudlets. Your references section is not in proper APA, please watch this in future assignments!
Response D: <u>Your essay</u> contains novel ideas on how VR may be more widely accepted in business settings. <u>I</u> would have liked to see more recent <u>references</u> on <u>the</u> risks of long-term use to make <u>your</u> arguments stronger <u>in Section</u> B as <u>the</u> ones <u>you</u> used were from over 10 years ago.

In this example, Response D has 50 words, with only 10 found in respond C, leading to a score of 20%. In a real-life setting where there are multiple students and multiple assignments in a class, this model compares every new feedback response against the existing feedback responses in the class, flagging high percentage responses as being unsupportive of this behavior.

Activity 5 – Timely Feedback on Assignments. To support students managing their time commitments, it has been shown that instructors need to provide timely feedback when marking assignments [7, 17]. Specifically, Bunn indicates that by not providing timely feedback to students, their persistence is affected, increasing students risk of dropping out of the course [17]. Fortunately, many institutions post their service standards for instructors to provide feedback for students.

Supportive Behavior Pattern. When a student submits an assignment, the instructor should mark and provide feedback on that assignment in a timely manner (e.g., within the approved institution's policy guidelines). This can be evaluated by comparing the assignment submission date to the date the instructor graded their assignment.

Activity 6 – Personalized Messaging. Ivankova and Stick highlighted the necessity of building a rapport and community with students online, both through student-to-student interactions and instructor-to-student communication [18]. When instructors communicate with their students on a personal level, student retention has also been shown to rise [7].

Supportive Behavior Pattern. This activity requires that instructors use both the messaging functionality and forums posts in the online learning platform to communicate with their students. While the messages need to be informative, it is important to ensure they are not generic to help build a connection with the students. Since this activity compares instructor responses for uniqueness, the linguistic model proposed for Activity 4 (Personalized Feedback for Assignments) can also be used for this activity.

Activity 7 – Timely Messaging. This activity focusses on the messages that are sent directly to the instructor through the messaging functionality of the online learning platform. The intent of this activity is to ensure that instructors are responding to messages sent to them in a timely manner, supporting the need for increasing instructor immediacy behavior to decrease the potential for misunderstandings that can occur in distance learning [5]. Building on Moore's transactional distance theory that increased communication between instructor and student can help bridge the communication gap that is found in online learning, this activity surmises that responding to student messages will reduce misunderstandings and increase student success in a course. Similar to Activity 5, service standards published by the educational institution (e.g., 2 business days) can be used to set a threshold for timely responses.

Supportive Behavior Pattern. When an instructor receives a message from a student through the messaging system in the online learning platform, the instructor should respond in a timely manner (e.g., within 2 business days or within their organizations service standards).

Activity 8 – Monitoring Forums. Throughout the course, instructors should continually monitor student forum posts for any queries or struggles, and respond to them with advice, additional resources, or to guide peer discussions to resolve the issues. these actions align with the instructor presence requirements of the Community of Inquiry model and previously mentioned Moore's transactional distance by keeping communication flowing in a course between students and the instructor, supporting student persistence and increasing their likelihood of success in the course [6].

Supportive Behavior Pattern. The instructor should monitor forum posts through the online learning platform for queries looking for support and responding to them with direction, resources, or links to help resolve any issues students may be having.

4.3 Behavior 3: Soliciting Feedback from Students

Bocchi et al. found that student's success was linked to continuous feedback and interactions with instructors and peers [16]. This behavior looks to see if instructors can help increase student satisfaction by soliciting feedback throughout the course, encouraging engagement, and potentially increasing student success as part of the social and teacher presence aspects of the Community of Inquiry model. This feedback loop can support instructors to identify whether students are struggling with technology, the teaching strategy, or their own time management. In addition, results of the feedback can also help inform future course content or design changes [16].

Activity 9 – Soliciting Feedback During the Course. While online learning platforms can formally survey students throughout the course, such surveys have often low response rates and the anonymity of surveys makes it very difficult for instructors to provide direct feedback, causing a disconnect for students and reduces participation [19]. This activity instead proposes to use the forum functionality in the online learning platform for instructors to solicit feedback on the course content, instructor presence, and checking to see if their students' educational needs are being met. in addition, the instructor should respond to student feedback, addressing what actions will be taken as a result of their posts [19].

Supportive Behavior Pattern. The instructor should submit a forum post to their class, soliciting feedback on the course. This post should be an open-ended request for feedback from students on their online experience with the course. Once posts are made, instructors should respond in a timely manner.

4.4 Behavior 4: Active Use of the Online Learning Platform

Through consistent utilization of the online learning platform, instructors can capitalize on learning opportunities with students. An instructor's continuous use of the system has a positive association with student usage and engagement through instructor presence [5]. Apart from the previous messaging and feedback activities, online instructor presence can also be recognized by students through regular usage of the online learning platform, including the use of announcements and forum posts throughout the course.

Activity 10 – Instructor Use of Announcements. Through the research conducted by Williams, a significant portion of students indicated that email and the use of announcements in the online learning platform were their preferred mode of communication from their instructor [20]. Many online learning tools have an announcements feature that allows instructors to post a forum-type announcement in the system that students will see as they log into their course. For online learning platforms that do not utilize this feature, similar pinned forum posts can also act as a course announcement.

Supportive Behavior Pattern. Instructors should use the announcement feature, or a pinned forum post to highlight important deadlines or information throughout the course. As an example, in a project management course, an instructor who posts a news article about a recent failed major Information Technology project for discussion, may solicit input from students related to current learnings.

4.5 Behavior 5: Peer to Peer Support

To help build a sense of community or camaraderie, that in turn supports retaining students in online courses, instructors should encourage students to connect and converse with other students using the online learning platform [6]. The act of engaging in online discussions using the forums do not just build those relationships, it also helps increase student understandings of the course content when coupled with teaching presence as identified through the Community of Inquiry model [21].

Activity 11 – Encouraging Peer to Peer Support. To encourage this behavior in students, instructors should set expectations at the beginning of the course by explaining the benefits of peer-to-peer support and the expectation that students communicate and discuss with each other about the course topics.

Supportive Behavior Pattern. At the beginning of the course, the instructor should post an announcement or forum post encouraging students to talk and discuss with each other, similar to "As this is an online course, it is expected that you will participate by posting and replying to other students' posts, similar to class discussions in a face-to-face classroom setting. As this course is provided asynchronously, you are encouraged to post questions, discuss issues with your peers, and support your peers." While course design may already encourage participation through participation marks, instructor behavior that explicitly asks for constructive discussions among students will encourage the use of peer support in the course.

4.6 Behavior 6: Ensure Students Have Timely Access to Technical Support

Bunn identified in his research that students found the lack of technical support when an issue arises to be more of a barrier than the technical issues themselves [17]. Bunn adds that this lack of support culminates in a feeling of isolation, reducing student satisfaction and raises the risk of student attrition in completing online courses [17]. Instructors can help reduce this feeling of isolation by proactively providing contact information and resources to students in their courses before they run into technical problems. This behavior is further supported by Rotar, who identified that technical support for students need to be provided at key times in a learning cycle, including during orientation, and proactively reaching out to students with support prior to them requiring it. [22] This activity supports both the teacher presence and social presence needs from the Community of Inquiry model, reducing isolation, and increasing engagement by removing technical barriers.

Activity 12 – Provide Technical Support Resources. This activity focusses on supporting students at the beginning of the course and throughout the course to ensure that technical issues do not hinder their ability to be successful. Proactively, instructors need to ensure students know how to obtain technical support, either by online resources, or a student helpdesk [17, 22].

Supportive Behavior Pattern. At the beginning of the course, either through announcement functionality or forum posts, the instructor should post available resources for students that may run into technical issues. This post needs to contain a technical support path for students to follow, such as the phone number for a help desk, support documentation, or external links to support resources.

4.7 Evaluating the Effectiveness of the Instructor Behaviors

The proposed behavior patterns have been derived from literature and intentionally designed to be easily monitored and evaluated using readily available data routinely logged in online learning platforms. Most of these behavior patterns can be validated for their effectiveness by using a control and experiment group, whereas the instructor either exhibits the behavior identified in the activities or does not, and comparing student success in both groups by evaluating student grades throughout the course. Activity 9 (Soliciting Feedback During the Course) needs to be evaluated over multiple courses as student feedback may influence instructor behavior and course design over time, with the expectation that overall student success or grades would increase after each iteration.

5 Conclusion

This paper contributes to improving our understanding in the area of teaching analytics by identifying six behaviors and 12 specific activities that instructors can do to help increase their student's success in online courses. By analyzing existing research pertaining to instructor behaviors that influence student success in online courses and using a Community of Inquiry approach, specific online behaviors supporting the cognitive, teacher, and social presence of the educational experience were identified. These behaviors consist of supporting students to manage their time and commitments appropriately, providing personalized and timely feedback, soliciting feedback throughout the course, actively engaging in the use of the online learning platform, encouraging peer to peer support, and offering technical support as required. Each behavior identified has been designed to be easily monitored and evaluated using data captured by most online learning platforms. Online instructors can adopt these online behaviors within their courses and expect to see an increase in student participation, student satisfaction, and overall success.

While this paper identifies specific activities that can be validated using online learning platforms, the research is based on available literature. Future work includes further practical applications of these activities in a live online learning platform and evaluating the efficacy of the identified activities. In addition, expanding this research to more interactive tools, such as video, instant messaging apps [23], or research into virtual reality classrooms could provide additional opportunities to increase social, cognitive and teacher presence in online learning platforms and contribute to the understanding of what online behaviors instructors can do to support their students.

Acknowledgments. The authors acknowledge the support of the National Science and Engineering Research Council of Canada (NSERC) [RGPIN-2020–05837].

References

1. Protopsaltis, S., Baum, S.: Does online education live up to its promise? A look at the evidence and implications for federal policy. Cent. Educ. Policy Eval, 1–50 (2019)
2. Bozkurt, A.: From distance education to open and distance learning. In: Handbook of Research on Learning in the Age of Transhumanism, pp. 252–273. IHI Global (2019)
3. Kabir, M., Seward, B., Dhuey, E.: Higher Education in Canada During COVID-19. FutureSkills Research Lab (2021)
4. Arbaugh, J.B.: How instructor immediacy behaviors affect student satisfaction and learning in web-based courses. Bus. Commun. Q. **64**(4), 42–54 (2001)
5. Baker, C.: The impact of instructor immediacy and presence for online student affective learning, cognition, and motivation. J. Educators Online **7**(1) (2010)
6. Garrison, D.R., Anderson, T., Archer, W.: The first decade of the community of inquiry framework: a retrospective. Internet High. Educ. **13**(1–2), 5–9 (2010)
7. Després-Bedward, A., Avery, T.L., Phirangee, K.: Student perspectives on the role of the instructor in face-to-face and online learning. Int. J. Inf. Educ. Technol. **8**(10), 706–712 (2018)
8. Kim, D., Lee, Y., Leite, W.L., Huggins-Manley, A.C.: Exploring student and teacher usage patterns associated with student attrition in an open educational resource-supported online learning platform. Comput. Educ. **156**, 103961 (2020)
9. Garrison, D., Cleveland-Innes, M., Fung, T.: Student role adjustment in online communities of inquiry: model and instrument validation. J. Asynchronous Learn. Netw. **8**, 61–74 (2004)
10. Hart, C.: Factors associated with student persistence in an online program of study: a review of the literature. J. Interact. Online Learn. **11**(1) (2012)
11. Bao, W.: COVID-19 and online teaching in higher education: a case study of Peking University. Hum. Behav. Emerg. Technol. **2**(2), 113–115 (2020)
12. Ahmad Uzir, N.A., Gašević, D., Matcha, W., Jovanović, J., Pardo, A.: Analytics of time management strategies in a flipped classroom. J. Comput. Assist. Learn. **36**(1), 70–88 (2020)
13. Harrell, I.L., Bower, B.L.: Student characteristics that predict persistence in community college online courses. Am. J. Distance Educ. **25**(3), 178–191 (2011)
14. Morris, L.V., Finnegan, C., Wu, S.: Tracking student behavior, persistence, and achievement in online courses. Internet High. Educ. **8**(3), 221–231 (2005)
15. Ojokheta, K.O.: A path-analytic study of some correlates predicting persistence and student's success in distance education in Nigeria. Turk. Online J. Distance Educ. **11**(1), 181–192 (2011)
16. Bocchi, J., Eastman, J.K., Swift, C.O.: Retaining the online learner: profile of students in an online MBA program and implications for teaching them. J. Educ. Bus. **79**(4), 245–253 (2004)
17. Bunn, J.: Student persistence in a LIS distance education program. Aust. Acad. Res. Libr. **35**(3), 253–270 (2004)
18. Ivankova, N.V., Stick, S.L.: Collegiality and community-building as a means for sustaining student persistence in the computer-mediated asynchronous learning environment. Online J. Distance Learn. Adm. **8**(3) (2005)

19. Keane, E., Labhrainn, I.M.: Obtaining student feedback on teaching & course quality. https://www.universityofgalway.ie/media/celt/files/coursedesign/ReviewofTeachingEvaluationMethods.pdf. Accessed 20 Apr 2023
20. Williams, K.: Student perceptions of instructor communication and instructor presence online [Doctoral dissertation]. The University of Alabama, Tuscaloosa (2022)
21. Garrison, D.R.: Online community of inquiry review: Social, cognitive, and teaching presence issues. J. Asynchronous Learn. Netw. **11**(1), 61–72 (2007)
22. Rotar, O.: Online student support: a framework for embedding support interventions into the online learning cycle. Res. Pract. Technol. Enhanc. Learn. **17**(1), 1–23 (2022)
23. Li, N.: How technology promotes educational change: studies of virtual learning environment in higher education [Doctoral dissertation, Liverpool University]. University of Liverpool (2022). https://livrepository.liverpool.ac.uk/3158265/1/201317890_Jul2022.pdf

EduPort: An Intelligent Learning System Based on Deep Learning - A Preliminary Evaluation

Alessandro Cuneo[1], Stefano D'Urso[1], Filippo Sciarrone[1], and Marco Temperini[2(✉)]

[1] Faculty of Economics, Universitas Mercatorum, Rome, Italy
{alessandro.cuneo,stefano.durso}@studenti.unimercatorum.it, filippo.sciarrone@unimercatorum.it

[2] Sapienza University of Rome, Rome, Italy
marte@diag.uniroma1.it

Abstract. The recent developments in Deep Learning Generative methods provided significant new and developing assets in Technology Enhanced Learning, with the production of conversational agents able to sustain a dialogue with the learner, and answer direct questions about the topic to learn. The possibility to help students at any time, about the topic of a study course, is important at any level of education, and it is almost crucial when it comes to students in Massive Open Online Courses, where the possibility to have direct interaction with the teacher, could be extremely limited. In this paper we present *Eduport*, a system designed to answer questions posted by learners in natural language. The system is based on a multi-tiered virtual interaction, ranging from using FAQs to generating responses grounded in the course material. One of its main feature is the use of OpenAI API, specifically utilizing the GPT 3.5-turbo model, for more refined assistance on the question at hand. This paper delineates the Eduport system and shares preliminary findings, encouraging outcomes in two primary dimensions: 1) the significant adherence of Eduport's responses to the established learning materials, and 2) the proficient harnessing of the OpenAI GPT 3.5-turbo model, to yield answers closely aligned with the course's didactic content.

Keywords: Intelligent Chatbots · MOOCs · ChatGPT

1 Introduction

One most intriguing characteristic of young generations is in the "need for speed". It is apparent in several fields of their life, where what is needed is expected (i) to be available right when its need is showing, and (ii) to be consumed as soon as possible. One of such fields is Education, where, on the other hand, the above demands are quite difficult to be satisfied in full: learning activities need patience and time much more than, say, *TikTok* videos, in order to

Z. Kubincová et al. (Eds.): SETE 2023, LNCS 14606, pp. 79–93, 2024.
https://doi.org/10.1007/978-981-97-4243-1_7

produce effective and long-lasting results. However, the research area of Technology Enhanced Learning (TEL) is working for decades about making it possible to study in effective ways, supported by various aspects of technology and in particular by a combination of Pedagogy and Information and Communication Technology [10,11]. Important tools in TEL, are those that support answering to learner's questions while the teacher, especially due to a huge numbers of enrolled people, could be not available. Several approaches are known, in TEL, such as those based on Learning Analytics [21,25], on students collaboration [2,19,22,24,29], and on peer learning and assessment [7,12,28,30,32] The recent development of Generative methods of Deep Learning have provided a significant boost, with the production of *Conversational Agents* or *Chatbots*, able to sustain a dialogue with the learner, or at least able to answer a direct question about the topic to learn [23,31]. To date, ChatGPT, by OpenAI[1], is, among the best performing intelligent chatbot available on the internet. It is able to converse and give meaningful answers across many knowledge domains, having been trained on very large databases, of which, for instance, Wikipedia covers only 3% [9,15,16,26]. Also, in recent years, chatbots are being developed so that they can help students with special needs (such as, for instance, presenting dyslexia or autism) [1,8,17,20].

The possibility to help students at any time, about the topic of a study course, is important at any level of education, and it is almost crucial when it comes to students in Massive, Open Online Courses (MOOCs), where the possibility to have direct interaction with the teacher, could be extremely limited [13,14,25].

In this paper we present a web-based system, called *EduPort*[2] able to receive and answer questions prompted by the learner in natural language. In Eduport we assume the learner is enrolled in a given course, where a set of learning materials is selected and made available by the teacher. Then the learner can submit questions to the system, related to the course topics, and they can receive an answer according to the following levels of virtual interaction: 1) The answer is selected from the list of Frequently Asked Questions (FAQ); in this case the best match with the question is selected, if available; 2) if the answer is not available, or if the learner asked for more, the EduPort's Chatbot generates an answer, based on the learning material associated to the course; 3) if the answer is unavailable or if the learner searches for further information, EduPort formulates an inquiry to be processed through the OpenAI's APIs, leveraging the capabilities of the turbo 3.5 models. This inquiry is then transmitted to the learner to facilitate a deeper understanding and exploration of the topic at hand. There is in fact an appendix-service: if the learner is not satisfied by the system's answer, and does not intend to try with differently worded questions, Eduport would initiate the process of creation of a new element in the FAQ dataset, by an inquiry to the teacher. EduPort's chatbot leverages a robust, multi-tiered architecture grounded in both the BART Transformer model [4,6] and the GPT-3.5 turbo engine to facilitate a nuanced approach to automated responses. As we

[1] openAI.com.
[2] Available at https://app.alessandrocuneo.it/.

further this discourse, we are in the midst of a comprehensive experimentation to rigorously evaluate the system's performance and effectiveness.

In this paper, we describe the Eduport system and provide the reader with an experimentation of its use. The experiment is based on a simulation of the system's use, based on a set of questions we selected, and three sets of related answers, generated by Eduport (under the second level of service), and through two different ways of using ChatGPT (third level). The experiment investigates two hypotheses formulated during the inception and nascent stages of Eduport, and it is based on the following Research Questions (RQs).

RQ1. *How close are the answers provided by Eduport and by ChatGPT to the learning material corpus?*
The corpus is the learning material that the teacher decided to provide for the students, and inform the course on. The conjecture to validate, here, is in that Eduport would produce answers closer to the corpus, than ChatGPT. In our interpretation the answers' closeness to corpus would let the students concentrate mainly on the course content (so implementing solely the teacher's learning strategy, while answers from ChatGPT might let a student have further stimuli, and deal with concepts that are not fully treated in the course. This might be an advantage for the curious student, or a disadvantage (see next point).

RQ2. *Is it possible to constraint ChatGPT, so to produce answers closer to the course corpus, than it would be if the chatbot were not constrained? And, would that be doable without proceeding through fine tuning, which would be cumbersome for the teacher to perform?*
Basically, here we are looking at the possibility to have ChatGPT answers being sufficiently close to the course corpus, so to preserve the chance for the student to have further stimuli, and yet avoid letting the learner, say, wander too much around, maybe collecting information and suggestions that would make the learning process harder, rather than smoother.

The above RQs are related to the usefulness, for the student, 1) to get answers deeply rooted into the course's learning material (from the Eduport Chatbot), and 2) to get answers based on an ampler source of data, which might help the learner connect concepts of the course with other, external, concepts. They are discussed in Sect. 4. Before of that, Sect. 2 illustrates some related works, while Sect. 3 describes the architecture of Eduport, and some implementation issues. Section 5 provides, then, some observations that will inform future work.

2 Related Work

Chatbot-based learning systems are applications that use artificial intelligence to provide an interactive learning experience through virtual conversations. These educational chatbots provide students with a personalized and accessible learning environment where they can ask questions, receive explanations, and access relevant educational resources. Moreover, in recent years, thanks also to the pandemic from COVID-19, MOOCs have grown a lot, both as the number of affiliated students and the number of courses offered on the Web. In this section we try to compare our system with other similar proposals in the literature.

In [3], is proposed a chatbot architecture acting as teaching assistance to answer queries faced by learners in MOOCs. The chatbot is trained on the course material using ALBERT, a lite BERT model, to develop its knowledge base. The chatbot tries to answer a large number of student's queries, thus reducing the workload of the instructor(s) to answer all the queries. Our system is a pipe-based system that uses ChatGPT as the last step in the answer generation and enriches its knowledge base with the new questions posted by students. This approach allows for a more articulated and complete response. Moreover, our system has been designed having the zone of proximal development, as the pedagogical baseline.

The system *AI4Architect* is proposed in [18]. In this paper the authors present an intelligent support system, to assist students to create and develop their projects in the Design domain. The system is configured as a Web application and is based on the use, in a pipe configuration, of ChatGPT and DALL-E[3] The authors investigate, through a controlled experiment, if the use of the system impacts the project creation process in any way. In fact, those students who use the system, show more creative design than the control group. This system, as a support to the student, does not present a chain of possibilities but provides a one-shot answer, also equipped with graphic suggestions. The EduPort system is a multi-domain system and therefore potentially suitable for providing answers to the student on any knowledge domain, provided an effort to adapt the system to the teaching material entered by the teacher.

In [5], the authors present *LineBot*, a Question Answering System in educational domain. The system is based on Word Embedding, Latent Dirichlet Allocation and Text Summarization method. It retrieves data from different knowledge bases and provides proper answers to the student. Through this learning platform, students can search for similar sentences in three knowledge bases respectively. After entering the sentence, similar sentences will be provided, and through the selection of sentences, the system responses the position of the video and the article chapter and page number of the article. When students get this information, it can help students understand the content more quickly and solve problems quickly. Our system, differently, has a different architecture, based both on a level of services answer, i.e., four different steps, and in particular, we use the ChatGPT model, further trained on the knowledge domain of the course, to build a generative answer.

In [14], a MOOC recommender system for facebook Messenger called *MOOCBuddy* is proposed. This system is a recommender system based on a user's social media profile and interests. The authors mentioned that the recommender system had scope for improvement with respect to having a larger category of user characteristics. Differently, our system does not profiles users, but, as it is used, it builds answers taking into account old questions.

---

[3] Available at: https://design-edu.bubbleapps.io/.

3 The Eduport System

This section describes the architecture and the functional modules of the system. EduPort, is a web-based educational platform, aiming at improving students' learning process in MOOCs, where teachers cannot manage students individually. The overall design includes two sets of features offered, one for the teacher and one for the student.

Teachers are given the opportunity to enter FAQs for each course. Through a simple web-form, a teacher can enter into EduPort a question together with its answer, building in this way a question-answer knowledge base. The second feature provided for teachers includes the possibility, for each course, to upload their own learning material (text files, PDFs), which will be used to automatically feed the machine learning engine that generates the answers to the questions asked by students.

Students have the possibility to be helped by a chatbot, in order to speed up and improve their learning process. In fact, students' queries, based on a managed system with multiple levels of service, tries to provide them with an answer that is relevant and appropriate to the knowledge domain related to that course in which they are learning. The question is posted in natural language and is assumed to be related to the knowledge domain of the course. The following three different levels of service are available:

- In the first level, a Question/Answer (QA) search is carried out, using a pattern matching technique, exploiting the QA knowledge base provided by the teacher by the FAQ off-line module. This level is the one that provides answers that are fully consistent with the content of the course.
- To make up for the limitation of the first level, a second level of service was integrated. It takes full advantage of the potential of AI. In fact, after analyzing the question, the system will search in a very broad context, generating an answer to be prompted to the student. The system will use the transformer-based *BART* bidirectional learning model for Natural Language Processing (NLP). It is responsible for analyzing the question provided in input by the student, generating a valid answer, using the database (handouts) provided by the teacher. This methods, aims to be able to provide the student with a reliable answer within the knowledge domain of the course;
- In order to make the educational experience stimulating and exploratory, a third level of service was integrated. It leverages the capabilities of the OpenAI's GPT-3.5 turbo engine through a suitable API: the system transmits the student's query to this engine, obtaining detailed answers to facilitate enriched interaction with the student.

3.1 The Architecture

The system architecture of the student layer is illustrated in Fig. 1, and consists of the following functional blocks:

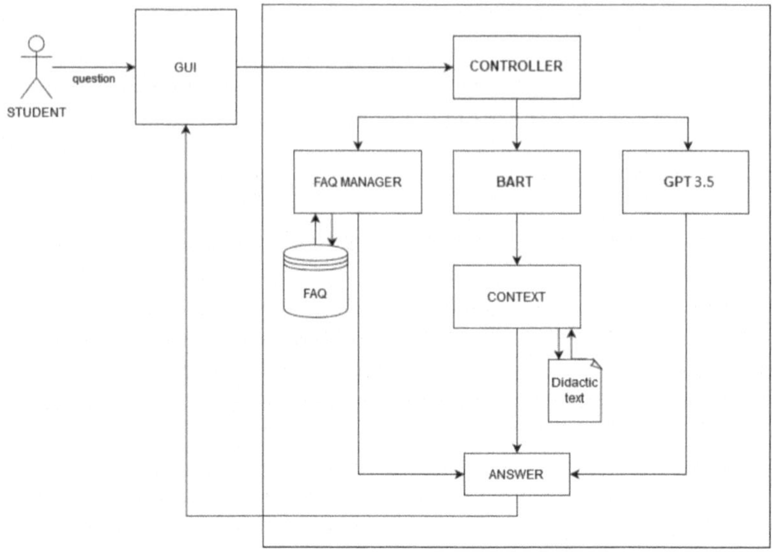

Fig. 1. The system architecture of the student layer, consisting of several functional modules.

- *The student*: this is the main actor using the system. It can be any student in a MOOC who needs support during her learning process;
- The *Graphical User Interface (GUI) module*: it is used by the system to interact with students. Each student can directly enter the question and wait for the chatbot's response. A suitable theme was used for the GUI, chosen so that to ensure the best visualization for users and ensure the best adaptability to any computing device;
- The *Controller*: this is the module that connects what is submitted through the GUI to the modules that process and generate the response;
- The *BART* module: it implements a standard transformer model architecture using both encoder and decoder blocks and uses a bidirectional encoder. The choice of the BART model turns out to be the best performing model because of some of its features that are a good fit for the goals set by the project: BART has been trained on large amounts of text data and has been shown to achieve high quality results on many natural language processing tasks;
- The *FAQ MANAGER* module. This is the module responsible for storing and managing the FAQ knowledge base, the repository of predefined QAs entered by the teacher, with the possibility to be extended by users;
- The *CONTEXT* module. This module manages the context, that is the dataset containing all the subject-related data entered by the teacher and subsequently enriched by the QA process. This dataset could be a large text containing a lecture or a generic learning material in text format. Given a student's question, the BART engine processes both the context and the question, producing an answer for the student. Subsequently, the learner will

evaluate its correctness and validity, providing feedback to improve her performance;

- *GPT3.5*. This module provides the student with the answer to their question using the GPT-3.5 turbo model, which is queried using the RESTful API capabilities provided by OpenAI;
- The *ANSWER* module. The task of this module is to transmit the system-generated answer to the GUI, which will be displayed into the user'student's screen, asking for her satisfaction, for a valuable feedback.

3.2 The Implementation

The system was developed as a web application, based on Linux Ubuntu 22.04, PHP 8.0 and MariaDB 11.0. The registration form is shown in Fig. 2, the student can register into the system and enroll to a particular course.

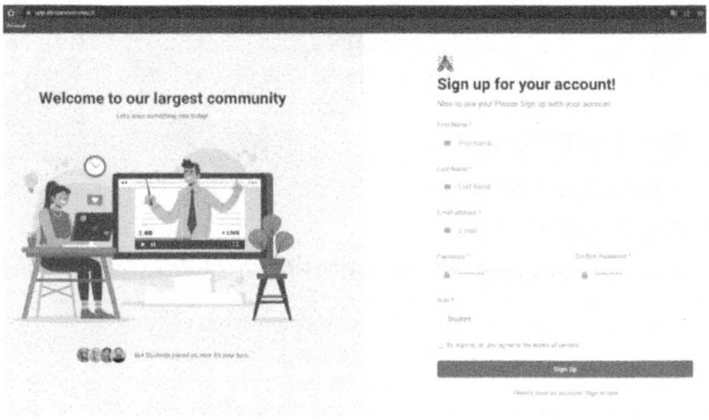

Fig. 2. The registration form.

The portal consists of three main modules that communicate and exchange data through the use of HTTPS requests, as shown in Fig. 3:

- The *Front-end*: developed with the PHP Laravel framework and a Bootstrap graphic theme, it provides users with the visibility of all the features provided by the web platform, according to their permissions and roles;
- The *Back-end*: this is Laravel's MVC pattern implementation of the layers functionalities. For example, for those which have the role of implementing the chatBot logic, it searches for questions among the FAQs, sends requests to the Machine Learning module, queries ChatGPT and makes available to the front-end module what it has processed. It is also responsible for managing and storing the internal data in the MariaDB database and providing full access to all expected functionality;

- The *Machine Learning* module: this is the engine that performs the answer generation through the BART deep learning engine. It is based on the question provided by the student and uses the documentation already stored by the teacher. Developed entirely in Python, it uses *Haystack*[4] to perform embedding of the learning material and queries with the BART model. To run the machine learning engine, the system uses the *Colab* deep learning platform, accessible directly by the browser[5]. It provides excellent computing power also through the use of CPU, GPU and TPU, which allow to greatly improve performance in terms of speed. It supports many machine learning libraries that can be easily loaded and used for deep learning projects.

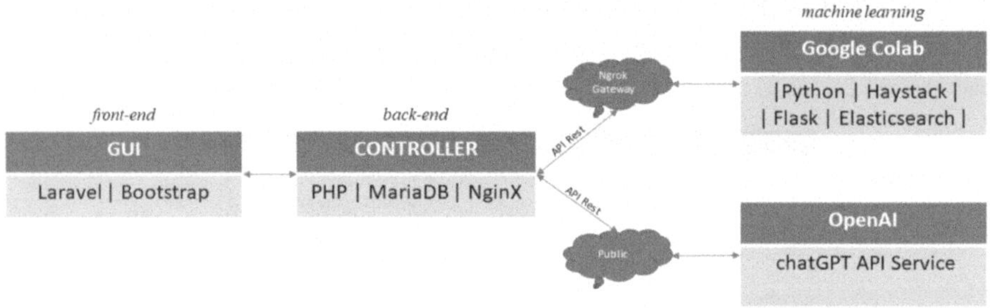

Fig. 3. The implementation architecture.

4 First Evaluation

In this Section we explore the use of Eduport, and of two of its levels of service, namely those related to the generation of an answer by 1) the system, using the learning material added into the system by the teacher, and 2) by GPT 3.5.

About RQ1, we would expect that the Eduport generative subsystem would produce answers better close to the course corpus, than the applications of ChatGPT (constrained and unconstrained).

About RQ2, we have to notice that GPT 3.5 constraining can be performed basically in two ways:

- Through traditional fine tuning [27]: in our case that is further training the GPT pre-trained model over the course corpus.
- By a "constraining preamble" that could be placed before of each question to GPT 3.5.

As a matter of facts, the second approach seems to be easier and more controllable by the teacher.

[4] https://haystack.deepset.ai/.
[5] https://colab.research.google.com/.

4.1 Method

The experiment was prepared based on the following elements:

1. A course was defined in Eduport, where the corpus is made of 53 pdf/text documents ($\{source_i, i \in [1, ..., 53]\}$), of about 1000 pages overall. The documents were taken mostly from Wikipedia, and from two books from the *Project Gutenberg.* (Copyright on the books had expired already).
2. The general topic of the course is *The French Revolution, and Napoleon.*
3. A list of 11 questions was produced.
4. GPT 3.5 was used in two flavors: *GPT_free*, and *GPT_constrained.* By interrogating *GPT_free*, we would get an answer by the plain, unconstrained, version of the chatbot. By interrogating *GPT_constrained*, we would get an answer by the chatbot, where the question was preceded automatically by a preamble, explaining the chatbot that it is answering to help a student with respect to the topics of the course.

Then we collected the answers coming from 1) Eduport generative engine, 2) *GPT_free*, and 3) *GPT_constrained.*

We obtained 11 answers from each one of the above mentioned service level, described by the three following sets:

- $\text{ANS}_{Eduport} = \{ans_i^{edu}, i \in [1, ..., 11]\}$,
- $\text{ANS}_{GPT-free} = \{ans_i^{free}, i \in [1, ..., 11]\}$,
- $\text{ANS}_{GPT-constrained} = \{ans_i^{constr}, i \in [1, ..., 11]\}$,

For each answer, ans_j^*, we computed the distances between the answer and each one of the documents in the corpus: $\{d_{j,k}^*, k \in [1, ..., 53]\}$ where $d_{j,k}^*$ is the distance between the document $source_k$ and the answer ans_j^*, and $*$ is one of *Eduport, GPT-free, GPT-constrained.*

We used the *doc2vec* deep learning model in order to compute all the distances. First, each question was embedded in a dense vector; then each didactic material, in txt and pdf format, were embedded in a dense vector as well. Subsequently, all the distances were computed using the cosine similarity distance.

The distance, here is to be interpreted as *closeness* of the answer to the document. So, eventually we had a sequence of 53 closeness values for each one of the (33) answers. This data gives the distance of each answer from each document in the course corpus.

In determining the approach to assess the mean closeness of an answer relative to the corpus of learning materials, we devised a strategy to not just observe the results, yet also discern potential trends. Our analytical process involved examining a representative subset of documents from the corpus, as well as the entire set, to foster a comprehensive understanding of the answer's alignment with the course materials. We selected three distinct tiers for this evaluation:

- 20% (11 documents): This initial step facilitates a preliminary analysis, offering insights based on a focused subset of documents. It serves as a starting point to gauge the early indications of the answer's closeness to the educational content.

- 41% (22 documents): Expanding the scope to include a wider portion of the corpus allows for a balanced analysis, providing a middle ground to evaluate the answer's adherence to a broader yet still controlled set of learning materials.
- 100% (53 documents): This comprehensive approach encompasses the entire corpus, offering a holistic view of the answer's alignment with the full breadth of course materials. It ensures a rigorous evaluation, pinpointing the exact degree of closeness the answer shares with the complete set of learning materials.

We hypothesized that this graduated approach would reveal if a discernible trend emerges in the analysis, helping to ascertain not only the immediate alignment but also the broader trends that could guide future optimizations and strategies.

So, we then computed the average and the standard deviation of the closeness of each answer ans^*_j to the corpus, $\{d^*_{j,k}, k \in [1, ..., 53]\}$: In particular, this computation was done, as devised, in three different ways:

avg closeness by 11 For each answer ans^*_j in ANS_* the average closeness is computed by averaging on the greatest 11 elements of the set $\{d^*_{j,k}, k \in [1, ..., 53]\}$;

avg closeness by 22 Same as above, but using the greatest 22 distances in $\{d^*_{j,k}, k \in [1, ..., 53]\}$ to compute the average.;

avg closeness by 53 For each answer ans^*_j in ANS_* the average closeness is computed by averaging on all the elements of the set $\{d^*_{j,k}, k \in [1, ..., 53]\}$.

Finally we grouped our answers in order of service level, so to compute the average value of the distances of the service answers from the corpus, and be eventually able to draw some conclusions about our RQs.

The reason for adopting average closeness as our primary metric is to emphasize the proximity of the generated answer to the entire corpus, rather than solely assessing correctness. We believe this approach aligns with our specific research objectives.

Our aim is not to determine the correctness of the answer in isolation but to understand how closely the answer aligns with the content of the entire corpus. This perspective offers a broader assessment of the quality of the generated response, which is especially relevant in scenarios where multiple plausible answers may exist within the corpus. By evaluating the distance between the generated answer and all documents in the corpus, we gain insights into how well the answer relates to the knowledge contained within the corpus as a whole. This approach allows us to identify answers that may be contextually relevant even if they are not the "correct" answer according to a specific criterion.

We acknowledge that measuring distance to all documents in the corpus may seem too exhaustive, but it is intentional and designed to provide a holistic view of how well the generated response aligns with the knowledge within the corpus. This approach serves our research goals, which are more focused on the informativeness and contextual relevance of the answers rather than their correctness in isolation.

4.2 Results

Figures 4, 5, and 6 show the results of the computations.

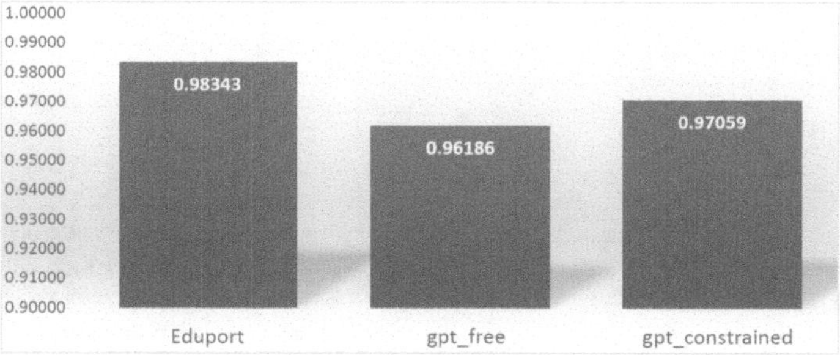

Fig. 4. Average performance of Eduport, gpt_free, and gpt_constr when the means are computed out of the 11 greatest distances of each answer from the corpus (the total number of distances is 53).

The values of average of the closeness appear to be all quite high, and not extremely different, probably as an effect of the ways of computation of the distances. Moreover, the standard deviation was in the range $SD = [0.10, 0.20]$, with lowest values for *avg closeness by 11*. These values confirm the goodness of the average as valid representation of the distributions.

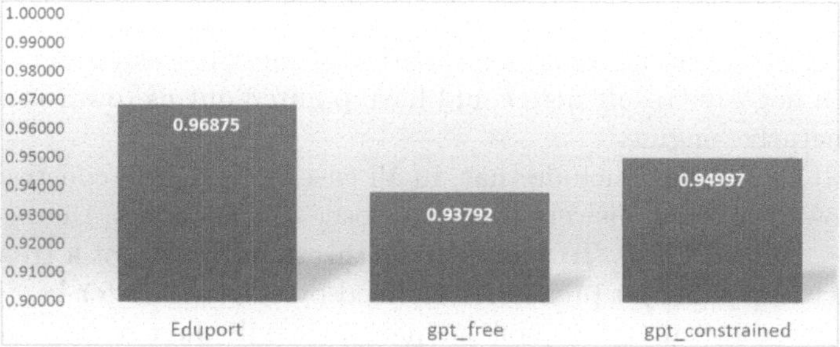

Fig. 5. Average performance of Eduport, gpt_free, and gpt_constr when the means are computed out of the 22 greatest distances of each answer from the corpus (the total number of distances is 53).

Figure 6 provides figures quite lower than the other two, as it was expectable: an answer might probably refer to a subset of the corpus, and be closer to a subset of the documents forming the corpus; so averaging on all documents has a "diluting" effect, reported by the picture. However we can appreciate two preliminary observations: two trends appear to be established, with

a) EduPort providing the answers closest to the corpus, and
b) Cgpt_constrained generating answers closer to the corpus than Cgpt_free.

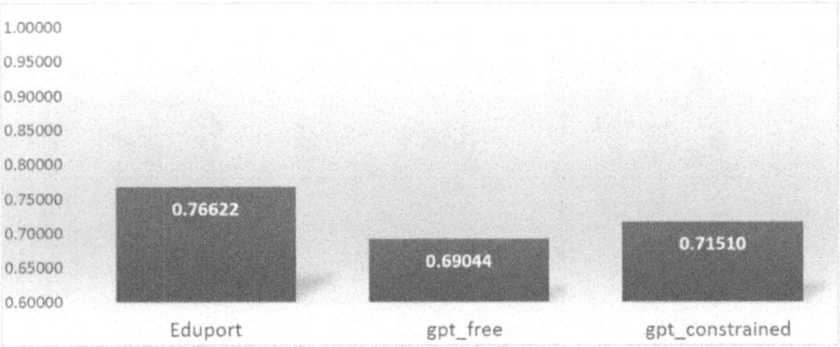

Fig. 6. Average performance of Eduport, gpt_free, and gpt_constr when the means are computed out of all the distances (53) of each answer from the corpus (the total number of distances is 53).

4.3 Discussion

Coming back to our Research Questions, basically they both appear to be supported (although with less enthusiasm than was in the authors expectation, when they devised this limited investigation).

About RQ1, basically Fig. 4, Fig. 5, and Fig. 6, do confirm that the answers generated by Eduport are more centered on the learning content of the course. This result is not overwhelming: as a matter of facts it was expectable; on the other hand a negative result here could have pointed out us towards bugs in the internal generative engine.

About RQ2, we can conclude that, in all cases, our lightly constrained usage of GPT allowed to have answers that are closer to the corpus, than those given by an unconstrained GPT. To some extent this is indicative of a trend, and we might expect that different preambles, defined by the teacher for her/his course, and placed automatically on top of the questions, will allow to have answer that are progressively more or less distant from the course corpus, according to the teacher's preference.

5 Conclusion

This paper has presented an investigation into the Eduport web-based system, which is designed to assist inquisitive learners by providing answers through a three-layered service approach. Our approach includes the use of FAQs, the generation of answers from provided course materials, and the provision of direct interaction with GPT 3.5 when needed for more extensive research.

Our primary emphasis has been on validating the Eduport's internal generative engine's ability to reflect the depth and nuances of course materials as instructed by the teacher. We are committed to maintaining strict alignment with the teacher-provided course content as it forms the foundation of our development philosophy.

However, in light of the rapidly evolving educational landscape, we acknowledge the importance of adapting and improving our architecture. As educational technologies and methodologies continue to advance, we aim to enhance our system by integrating tools and orchestrators that offer even greater benefits to learners. We recognize the intrinsic value of nurturing learners' curiosity and encouraging them to explore intellectual pathways that may extend beyond the confines of the course materials. This navigational freedom can lead to innovative insights and perspectives, enriching the learning experience. Our design philosophy is to strike a balance between guiding learners along the core content provided by the teacher and allowing a margin for exploratory learning. This margin ensures that learners can seek diverse answers while remaining within a protective radius that upholds the educational integrity and focus of the course.

We draw inspiration from Lev Vygotsky's Zone of Proximal Development and see an opportunity to modernize this concept within a deep-learning-based educational environment, with some necessary adjustments. This might involve a method to constrain GPT 3.5, resulting in answers that align closely with the course contents, offering guided and fruitful exploration. By integrating tools and orchestrators that facilitate such guided exploration, we aim to support learners in their quest for alternative answers while enhancing their overall learning experience. These alternative answers will complement the course content and align with the teacher's intended learning outcomes. As we continue to adapt and improve our architecture in this ever-changing educational landscape, our goal remains to empower learners while maintaining a strong connection to the core educational content.

References

1. Abd-alrazaq, A.A., Alajlani, M., Alalwan, A.A., Bewick, B.M., Gardner, P., Househ, M.: An overview of the features of chatbots in mental health: a scoping review. Int. J. Med. Inform. **132**, 103978 (2019)
2. Alfonseca, E., Carro, R.M., Martín, E., Ortigosa, A., Paredes, P.: The impact of learning styles on student grouping for collaborative learning: a case study. User modeling and user-adapted interaction. Special Issue: User Model. Support Groups Communities Collab. **16**(3–4), 377–401 (2006). http://www.springerlink.com/content/k203641n28n86m17
3. Amarnani, S., Bhagat, N., Ekade, H., Gupta, A., Sahu, S.: A complete chatbot based architecture for answering user's course-related queries in MOOC platforms. In: 2021 International Conference on Computing, Communication and Green Engineering (CCGE), pp. 1–7 (2021). https://doi.org/10.1109/CCGE50943.2021.9776437
4. Bloom, B.: Taxonomy of Educational Objectives. David McKay Comp. Inc., Philadelphia (1964)

5. Chen, L.E., Cheng, S.Y., Heh, J.S.: Chatbot: a question answering system for student. In: 2021 International Conference on Advanced Learning Technologies (ICALT), pp. 345–346 (2021). https://doi.org/10.1109/ICALT52272.2021.00110
6. De Bruyn, M., Lotfi, E., Buhmann, J., Daelemans, W.: Bart for knowledge grounded conversations. In: Converse@ KDD, vol. 2666 (2020)
7. Dmoshinskaia, N., Gijlers, H.: Giving feedback to peers in an online inquiry-learning environment. In: Noroozi, O., De Wever, B. (eds.) The Power of Peer Learning: Fostering Students' Learning Processes and Outcomes, pp. 289–304. Springer, Cham (2023). https://doi.org/10.1007/978-3-031-29411-2_13
8. Dosovitsky, G., Pineda, B., Jacobson, N., Chang, C., Bunge, E.: Artificial intelligence chatbot for depression: descriptive study of usage. JMIR Format. Res. **4**(11), 1–13 (2020)
9. Du, H., et al.: Chat with chatgpt on intelligent vehicles: an IEEE TIV perspective. IEEE Trans. Intell. Veh. 1–7 (2023). https://doi.org/10.1109/TIV.2023.3253281
10. Duval, E., Sharples, M., Sutherland, R.: Technology Enhanced Learning. Springer, Cham (2017). https://doi.org/10.1007/978-3-319-02600-8
11. Fiume, A.F., Sciarrone, F., Temperini, M.: A new metric to help teachers unveil meaningful learning in concept maps. In: Temperini, M., et al. (eds.) MIS4TEL 2022. LNNS, vol. 580, pp. 65–74. Springer, Cham (2023). https://doi.org/10.1007/978-3-031-20617-7_9
12. Hadzhikoleva, S., Hadzhikolev, E., Kasakliev, N.: Using peer assessment to enhance higher order thinking skills. TEM J. **8**(1), 242–247 (2019)
13. Han, S., Lee, M.K.: FAQ chatbot and inclusive learning in massive open online courses. Comput. Educ. **179**, 104395 (2022). https://doi.org/10.1016/j.compedu.2021.104395
14. Holotescu, C.: Moocbuddy: a chatbot for personalized learning with MOOCs. In: Romanian Conference on Human-Computer Interaction (2016)
15. Limongelli, C., Gasparetti, F., Sciarrone, F.: WIKI course builder: a system for retrieving and sequencing didactic materials from Wikipedia. In: 2015 International Conference on Information Technology Based Higher Education and Training (ITHET), pp. 1–6. IEEE (2015)
16. Limongelli, C., Lombardi, M., Marani, A., Sciarrone, F.: A teacher model to speed up the process of building courses. In: Kurosu, M. (ed.) HCI 2013. LNCS, vol. 8005, pp. 434–443. Springer, Heidelberg (2013). https://doi.org/10.1007/978-3-642-39262-7_50
17. Limongelli, C., Marani, A., Sciarrone, F., Temperini, M.: Measuring the similarity of concept maps according to pedagogical criteria. IEEE Access **10**, 27655–27669 (2022)
18. Abrusci, L., Dabaghi, K., D'Urso, S., Sciarrone, F.: Ai4architect: an intelligent help system to support students in the design domain. In: Milrad, M., et al. (eds.) MIS4TEL 2023. LNNS, vol. 764, pp. 65–72. Springer, Cham (2023). https://doi.org/10.1007/978-3-031-41226-4_7
19. Magnisalis, I., Demetriadis, S., Karakostas, A.: Adaptive and intelligent systems for collaborative learning support: a review of the field. IEEE Trans. Learn. Technol. **4**(1), 5–20 (2011)
20. Mateos-Sanchez, M., Melo, A.C., Blanco, L.S., García, A.M.F.: Chatbot, as educational and inclusive tool for people with intellectual disabilities. Sustainability **14**(3) (2022)
21. Misiejuk, K., Wasson, B.: Learning analytics for peer assessment: a scoping review. In: Noroozi, O., De Wever, B. (eds.) The Power of Peer Learning: Fostering

Students' Learning Processes and Outcomes, pp. 25–46. Springer, Cham (2023). https://doi.org/10.1007/978-3-031-29411-2_2
22. Morita, J., Ohmoto, Y., Hayashi, Y.: Integrating knowledge in collaborative concept mapping: cases in an online class setting. In: Cristea, A.I., Troussas, C. (eds.) ITS 2021. LNCS, vol. 12677, pp. 99–106. Springer, Cham (2021). https://doi.org/10.1007/978-3-030-80421-3_12
23. Peyton, K., Unnikrishnan, S.: A comparison of chatbot platforms with the state-of-the-art sentence BERT for answering online student FAQs. Results Eng. **17**, 100856 (2023)
24. Sciarrone, F.: Machine learning and learning analytics: integrating data with learning. In: 2018 17th International Conference on Information Technology Based Higher Education and Training (ITHET), pp. 1–5 (2018). https://doi.org/10.1109/ITHET.2018.8424780
25. Sciarrone, F., Temperini, M.: K-openanswer: a simulation environment to analyze the dynamics of massive open online courses in smart cities. Soft. Comput. **24**(15), 11121–11134 (2020)
26. Shoufan, A.: Exploring students' perceptions of chatgpt: thematic analysis and follow-up survey. IEEE Access **11**, 38805–38818 (2023). https://doi.org/10.1109/ACCESS.2023.3268224
27. Simonyan, K., Zisserman, A.: Very deep convolutional networks for large-scale image recognition (2015)
28. Sterbini, A., Temperini, M.: Learning from peers: motivating students through reputation systems. In: Proceedings of International Symposium on Applications and the Internet. SAINT 2008 (2008)
29. Sterbini, A., Temperini, M.: Collaborative projects and self evaluation within a social reputation-based exercise-sharing system. In: Proceedings of IEEE/WIC/ACM International Joint Conference on Web Intelligence and Intelligent Agent Technology, pp. 243–246 (2009)
30. Sterbini, A., Temperini, M.: Supporting assessment of open answers in a didactic setting. In: Proceedings of 12th IEEE International Conference on Advanced Learning Technologies. ICALT 2012 (2012)
31. Sáiz-Manzanares, M.C., Marticorena-Sánchez, R., Martín-Antón, L.J., González Díez, I., Almeida, L.: Perceived satisfaction of university students with the use of chatbots as a tool for self-regulated learning. Heliyon **9**(1), e12843 (2023)
32. Zhan, Y., et al.: Effects of online peer assessment on higher-order thinking: a meta-analysis. Br. J. Educ. Technol. Open Access **54**(4), 817–835 (2023)

Examining the Technological Pedagogical Content Knowledge (TPACK) of Biology Educators: A Case Study on Pre-service and In-service Teachers in Preparation for Applying STEM Education

Chen Fei(✉) and Alex Wing Cheung Tse

The University of Hong Kong, Hong Kong SAR, China
u3597957@connect.hku.hk, awctse@hku.hk

Abstract. Despite the growing popularity of STEM education as an emerging concept in various educational fields, limited research exists on in-service and pre-service educators in STEM-related disciplines, especially biology. By using the STEM-TPACK framework, the first phase of this research project adopted a quantitative approach and found the differences in readiness of in-service and pre-service biology teachers to implement STEM education as reflected in their views of Technological Pedagogical Content Knowledge (TPACK). As the second phase of this research project [1], this study used a qualitative approach that went deeper, aiming to examine the differences, strengths, and weaknesses of biology educators in implementing STEM education in Guangdong Province, the most populous province of China. Interviews were conducted to collect insights from 12 participants. The results revealed that pre-service teachers demonstrated enthusiasm and willingness to learn educational technologies, as well as a strong grasp of pedagogical knowledge. However, their lack of teaching experience and limited familiarity with biology and STEM content posed challenges when implementing STEM education. In-service teachers, on the other hand, exhibited stronger expertise in biology and STEM-related subjects, along with well-developed teaching skills and confidence. However, they were less inclined to embrace emerging technologies and may have fixed thinking patterns. Suggestions from in-service teachers to pre-service teachers varied, focusing on meeting student needs, learning from experienced teachers, and developing technological skills. These findings aligned with previous studies and highlighted the need for continuous professional development to enhance technical expertise and effectively integrate technology into teaching practices for both pre-service and in-service educators. However, it is important to acknowledge the limitations of this case study and future research should consider exploring the implementation of STEM education across various disciplines in mainland China.

Keywords: STEM education · Technological Pedagogical Content Knowledge (TPACK) · Mainland China · Biology teachers

Z. Kubincová et al. (Eds.): SETE 2023, LNCS 14606, pp. 94–110, 2024.
https://doi.org/10.1007/978-981-97-4243-1_8

1 Introduction

In recent years, the Technological Pedagogical Content Knowledge (TPACK) framework has emerged as a valuable theoretical framework for understanding and enhancing teachers' proficiency in integrating technology effectively into their teaching practices. While TPACK has been widely studied in various subjects, there is a need to explore its application specifically within the domain of biology education. This study aims to examine the readiness of biology educators in implementing STEM education, using the revised TPACK framework. STEM education has gained significant attention in recent years due to its potential to develop students' 21st-century skills, foster innovation, and promote interdisciplinary learning. However, the successful integration of STEM education requires educators to possess a deep understanding of the interplay between technology, pedagogy, and content knowledge, as emphasized by the TPACK framework.

By conducting the case study, this study investigated the technological pedagogical content knowledge of biology educators in the context of preparing for the integration of STEM education. Specifically, this study addressed a topic that lacked research but was important: the readiness of STEM educators, including pre-service teachers and in-service teachers [2]. The STEM-TPACK framework, which is a TPACK model specific to STEM education, was adopted in this research to examine the related information of the pre-service and in-service biology teachers and guided the design of the interview form used in the teachers' interviews [3, 4]. The following research questions guided this study:

1 What are the differences in TPACK in implementing STEM education between the pre-service and in-service biology teachers?
2 What are the strengths and weaknesses of pre-service and in-service biology teachers in implementing STEM education?
3 What can be suggested to the pre-service biology teacher in implementing STEM education?

2 Literature Review

2.1 STEM Education

Contemporary education places significant importance on science, technology, engineering, and mathematics (STEM). Policymakers, educators, and various stakeholders are no longer content with teaching individual disciplines but are actively exploring interdisciplinary integration. This integration is commonly referred to as STEM [5], which has become a popular trend in the field of education. STEM education places great emphasis on 21st-century learning [6], which highlights the integration of diverse disciplines, effective communication, collaboration, self-directed learning, problem-solving skills, and critical thinking [7, 8].

In the context of this study situated in mainland China, it is important to discuss STEM education within this specific context. In mainland China, there exists a relatively official and concise definition of STEM education. The 2017 edition of the Science Curriculum Standard for Compulsory Education in Primary Schools [9] provides a localized definition of STEM education in Chinese: "STEM refers to a curriculum organization approach guided by project-based learning and problem-solving. It seamlessly integrates science, technology, engineering, and mathematics, to foster students' innovative abilities."

2.2 Pre-service and In-service Biology Teacher in Mainland China

In mainland China, biology is often considered a subsidiary subject and is frequently neglected by teachers, students, and parents. This poses challenges for biology teachers in adapting to the new curriculum reform, which emphasizes student-centered and inquiry-based learning [10]. Furthermore, factors such as the lack of resources, inadequate teacher training, and the pressure of exam-oriented education have exacerbated these challenges. Additionally, the prevailing teaching approach remains predominantly teacher-centered, making it difficult to ignite students' interest and motivation for self-directed learning. Moreover, students may face difficulties in acquiring effective learning methods while studying under the strong authority of teachers in the classroom [11]. Therefore, it is necessary to implement measures that enhance the ability of contemporary biology teachers in various ways. Reforms in the biology curriculum and the development of new teaching approaches can help revitalize biology education in mainland China. In this context, incorporating STEM education into the biology curriculum emerges as a promising strategy to achieve this goal.

2.3 Theoretical Framework of STEM-TPACK

The TPACK framework was initially developed to identify the essential components of teacher expertise necessary for the successful integration of technology in the classroom [12]. As illustrated in Fig. 1, the seven-dimensional framework revolves around the convergence of three foundational areas: 1) Content Knowledge (CK), 2) Technological Knowledge (TK), and 3) Pedagogical Knowledge (PK) [13]. The framework also encompasses 1) Technological Content Knowledge (TCK), 2) Technological Pedagogical Knowledge (TPK), 3) Pedagogical Content Knowledge (PCK), and 4) Technological Pedagogical Content Knowledge (TPACK) as the remaining four dimensions. Importantly, the TPACK framework exhibits flexibility, allowing for adaptations to suit diverse research topics [14]. In the current study, the TPACK framework was specifically revised to STEM-TPACK, aligning it more closely with the research theme [3].

The STEM-TPACK framework represents a theoretical model that combines the principles of STEM with TPACK, guiding the effective implementation of STEM education. Both STEM and TPACK emphasize the role of technology and recognize the significance of 21st-century skills [5, 15]. Building upon the TPACK framework, researchers such as Chai, Rahmawati, and Jong expanded its scope to encompass STEM disciplines, thereby synthesizing a more comprehensive theoretical framework [3]. They concluded that pre-service teachers could benefit from interdisciplinary STEM communities within a social context by employing the TPACK framework. Essentially, the STEM-TPACK framework offers a holistic and integrated approach to STEM education that considers the complex relationships between content, pedagogy, technology, and the contextual factors influencing teaching and learning. Figure 1 illustrates the revised theoretical framework, which is practical for this study and applicable in STEM and biology, making it suitable for the topic of this research.

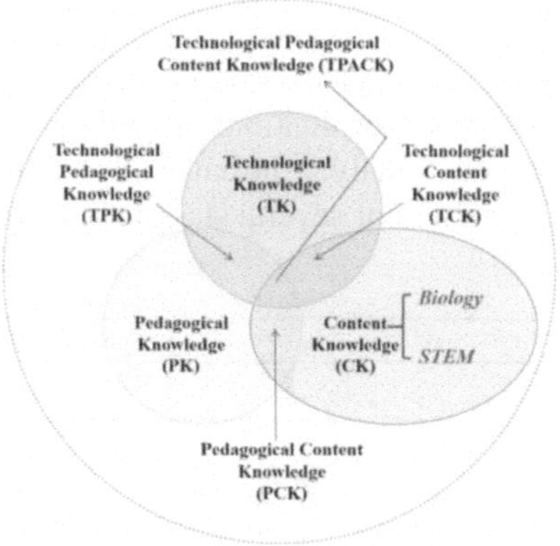

Fig. 1. The theoretical framework (revised from the graph from http://tpack.org/).

3 Methodology

3.1 Research Design

The first phase of this research project has been completed, which involved the use of a t-test to examine the STEM-TPACK of pre-service and in-service biology teachers. The results indicated that in-service teachers outperformed pre-service teachers in dimensions such as CK, PK, PCK, TPACK, and total scores [1]. Moreover, in-service teachers demonstrated higher levels of expertise due to their teaching experience, while pre-service teachers showed higher potential for integrating emerging technologies in future teaching practices despite their limited experience. However, further analysis of these two groups of teachers was necessary. After collecting and analyzing the quantitative data collected from 70 teachers, this study, as the second phase of this research project, selected 12 teachers from the 70 participants in the first phase and conducted interviews to have a more comprehensive investigation. The sample size of 70 teachers in the first phase allowed for the collection of sufficient quantitative data for more comprehensive analysis, providing a broader perspective on the research topic. In this study, the smaller sample included the three highest and three lowest-scoring pre-service and in-service teachers, ensuring better representation and enabling a more detailed understanding of their experiences and perspectives.

This study adopted a case study approach to comprehensively analyze teachers' views on TPACK in implementing STEM education. The participants consisted of pre-service and in-service biology teachers from Guangdong Province, the most populous province of China. After obtaining informed consent from the teachers, an interview was designed to gather detailed information about their views on TPACK in STEM education. The sample size included 12 teachers, comprising 6 pre-service and 6 in-service teachers. The interview form was revised from Chai's original version of the STEM-TPACK framework, which contained seven dimensions: TK, CK, PK, TCK, TPK, PCK, and TPACK (Read Sect. 2.3 for the full form of these abbreviations) [3]. The revised interview form contained 10 questions (e.g. How do you use a variety of teaching strategies to improve students' learning outcomes?) to investigate both pre-service and in-service teachers' self-evaluations according to these seven dimensions. Thematic analysis was employed to analyze the data collected from the online interviews. The entire research design consisted of several stages as shown in Fig. 2.

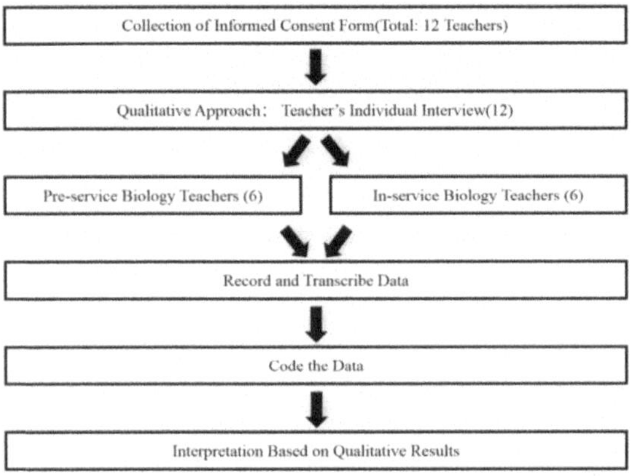

Fig. 2. The entire design of research methods.

3.2 Data Collection

Data for this study were collected through online interviews. Six pre-service teachers were recruited from various universities in Guangdong Province, including teacher trainees and normal biology students. Similarly, six in-service biology teachers were invited from different schools in Guangdong Province. After the interviews were completed, the data were transcribed and coded. Recorded data that did not meet the targeted quality requirements or irrelevant content, were excluded from the analysis.

3.3 Data Analysis

Qualitative data analysis was conducted after collecting adequate data. Thematic analysis was employed to compare their views on TPACK in implementing STEM education among pre-service and in-service biology teachers across seven dimensions and overall performance. The results were interpreted to gain insights into the differences, strengths, and weaknesses of both pre-service and in-service biology teachers. Additionally, these findings contributed to addressing the research questions and resolving the relevant issues.

3.4 Ethical Measures

Upon the design of the two-phase research project, an ethical review application form was submitted to and approved by the Office of Research at the University. Before they participated in this research project, both pre-service and in-service biology teachers were provided with consent forms that clearly outlined the objectives and significance of the study. Throughout the research process, participants were informed of their right to withdraw from the interviews at any stage. It is worth noting that all data and participants' information were treated with strict anonymity and confidentiality during the analysis.

4 Results and Findings

As stated before, the participants included six pre-service biology teachers and six in-service biology teachers. For coding and analysis, each participant was assigned a unique identifier, with "PT1" representing the first pre-service teacher and "IT1" representing the first in-service teacher then so and so. This coding approach of participants allowed for a systematic and organized analysis of the interview data, which was closely aligned with the research questions and objectives.

The interviews conducted in this study revealed several key themes that explained the phenomenon rarely covered in past research. Participants PT1, PT3, PT6, and IT4 stated that they did not incorporate STEM into their biology teaching practice. This was attributed to a variety of factors including insufficient class hours and learning resources, personal perceptions of the difficulty in implementing STEM, and lack of relevant knowledge and training. Specifically, over half of the participants expressed positive attitudes towards STEM and had experience incorporating STEM into their biology courses. However, most participants chose to integrate only specific disciplines such as mathematics, English, or chemistry. Notably, all participants were more familiar with science and mathematics compared to technology and engineering in the context of STEM education. This trend reflected the lack of emphasis on STEM education in mainland China and the traditional approach of teaching every discipline in isolation. The more detailed results and findings are presented below according to these three themes: TPACK differences (including technological knowledge, content knowledge, and pedagogical knowledge), strengths and weaknesses, and in-service teachers' suggestions.

4.1 TPACK Differences in Implementing STEM Education Between the Pre-service and In-service Biology Teachers

Technological Knowledge

In the context of technology and its impact on curriculum, all participants involved expressed that integrating technology into biology education is beneficial for improving students' learning outcomes. However, none of the participants had experimented with various technologies that are commonly used in STEM education and evaluated their effects on biology instruction. Table 1 shows the technological knowledge of pre-service and in-service teachers.

Table 1. The technological knowledge of pre-service and in-service teachers.

Dimension	Theme	Codes	Pre-service teachers	In-service teachers
Technological Knowledge	The use of different technologies	PowerPoint; 3D printing; AR; VR; Hi-Teach Interactive Whiteboard; Virtual Simulation Technology; Multimedia Equipment	Virtual Simulation Technology; AR; VR	Hi-Teach Interactive Whiteboard
			Hi-Teach Interactive Whiteboard; Multimedia Equipment	Hi-Teach Interactive Whiteboard; PowerPoint
			Hi-Teach Interactive Whiteboard; Multimedia Equipment; 3D printing	Hi-Teach Interactive Whiteboard; Video Editing
			Technologies within the field of biology; 3D printing; Python	PowerPoint; Video Editing
			PowerPoint; Video Editing	Flash Animation
			PowerPoint; Video Editing	PowerPoint

Notably, the "Hi-Teach Interactive Whiteboard" was mentioned by participants PT2, PT3, and IT1 as the most frequently used technology in their teaching. This innovative tool enabled teachers to seamlessly integrate multimedia content and interactive resources into their lessons, enhancing student engagement and effectiveness. One participant, PT1, expressed expectations for the development of Virtual Simulation Technology to provide students with a more intuitive understanding of biological structures from scientists' perspectives. Additionally, 3D printing was commonly mentioned as a valuable technology for presenting complex biological models. Although participants PT3 and PT4 acknowledged the benefits of 3D printing, they did not possess the necessary skills to use it effectively. Apart from technologies irrelevant to the biology discipline, participant PT4 referred to some technologies within the field of biology, including Polymerase Chain Reaction sequencing, instruments such as spectrophotometers, and instruments for detecting nitrites and reducing sugars. While these technologies can certainly be helpful for ontology teaching, integrating interdisciplinary technological engineering is necessary to enhance students' problem-solving abilities. Furthermore, participant PT4 explored the use of Python in course design, which improved the effectiveness of the presentation process beyond the limitations of PowerPoint.

Regarding the integration of technology into the curriculum, pre-service biology teachers generally demonstrated a more innovative mindset and proposed ideas for future implementation. Conversely, in-service teachers tended to opt for common teaching technologies such as PowerPoint, Video Editing, and Flash Animation, which were more feasible in the authentic classroom environment.

Content Knowledge

The six pre-service biology teachers generally showed very low confidence in STEM and moderate to low confidence in their biology expertise. The six in-service biology instructors, on the other hand, displayed both expectations and modesty toward STEM and showed high confidence in their grasp of the biology content. Table 2 shows the content knowledge of pre-service and in-service teachers.

The apparent lack of creative thinking, poor practical skills, and gaps in teaching experience may be responsible for the pre-service biology teachers' lack of confidence. As participant PT1 stated, "I can deal with the textbook and meet the basic requirements of the teaching content, but it's difficult to teach the knowledge integrated and expand students' interest." Participant IT3 stated, "I am confident in biology because I have

Table 2. The content knowledge of pre-service and in-service teachers.

Dimension	Themes	Codes (Levels)	Pre-service teachers	In-service teachers
Content Knowledge	Confidence in biology	High; Medium; Low	Medium "It is difficult for me to make biology lessons logical and rigorous."	High (case unfound)
			Low "I don't have comprehensive knowledge of biology."	High (case unfound)
			Low "My biology knowledge is poor."	High (case unfound)
			High (case unfound)	High (case unfound)
			Medium (case unfound)	High (case unfound)
			Medium (case unfound)	High (case unfound)

(*continued*)

Table 2. (*continued*)

Dimension	Themes	Codes (Levels)	Pre-service teachers	In-service teachers
	Confidence in STEM	High; Medium; Low	Low "I don't have any knowledge about STEM."	Medium "I have no experience with STEM, but I know what is STEM education."
			Low "STEM education is time-consuming."	Low "I don't have any knowledge about STEM."
			Medium "STEM will attract students."	Medium "I have no experience with STEM, but I know what is STEM education."
			Low "I don't have relevant knowledge of STEM."	Low "STEM knowledge is unfamiliar to me."
			Low "STEM is unfamiliar to me."	Medium "I have no experience with STEM, but I know what is STEM education."
			Low "STEM is unfamiliar to me."	Medium "I have no experience with STEM, but I know what is STEM education."

taught high school seniors, and I feel that I have organized the learning process quite well."

The interview data revealed that in-service teachers exhibited greater confidence in their biology content knowledge and held a more optimistic outlook toward the integration of STEM education in the future. They recognized the potential for students' development and were committed to seeking out additional knowledge to construct a comprehensive framework of biology knowledge for their students. In contrast, pre-service teachers tended to confine themselves to textbook knowledge, focusing on conducting biology lessons that centered around the textbook.

Pedagogical Knowledge

In the context of pedagogy, each participant expressed their preferred teaching strategy especially useful in implementing STEM education and provided a reasonable explanation. Table 3 shows the pedagogical knowledge of pre-service and in-service teachers.

Table 3. The pedagogical knowledge of pre-service and in-service teachers.

Dimension	Theme	Codes	Pre-service teachers	In-service teachers
Pedagogical Knowledge	The use of different teaching strategies	Contextual Learning; Combining Theory with Practice; Problem-based Learning; Project-based Learning; Create Mind Maps; Collaborative Inquiry	Contextual Learning	Contextual Learning
			Combining Theory with Practice	Problem-based Learning
			Contextual Learning	Collaborative Inquiry
			Create Mind Maps	Project-based Learning
			Combining Theory with Practice	Problem-based Learning
			Problem-based Learning	Project-based Learning

Participants PT1 and IT1 mentioned contextual learning, which emphasized the authenticity of the content and its relationship with daily life to increase students' interest in the lesson and improve their understanding of the course material. This approach highlighted that what students learn should ultimately serve a purpose in the real world. Contextual learning and STEM education hold similar learning outcomes, which aim to cultivate students' problem-solving abilities, emphasize the importance of practice and application, and cultivate students' innovative thinking [6]. Participants PT2 and PT5 stressed the significance of combining theory with practice in biology education and developing students' hands-on abilities. As participant PT5 stated, "If a student has conducted an experiment at school, they will have a deeper understanding of some of the experimental knowledge." This underscored the importance of providing students with opportunities to apply theoretical concepts in practical settings to reinforce their understanding and enhance their skills. Moreover, participant PT4 guided students to create mind maps of each unit, while participants PT6 and IT5 chose the problem-oriented strategy. The use of this approach can stimulate students' critical thinking skills and increase their engagement in the subject, fostering a more focused classroom environment. Furthermore, participant IT3 suggested collaborative group inquiry to promote students' collaboration, while participant IT6 preferred project-based learning. The latter approach enabled students to engage in a coherent and independent exploration of knowledge through pre-class curriculum design.

Both in-service and pre-service teachers had some experience when it came to their pedagogical knowledge. Impressively, in-service biology teachers can suggest more pedagogy conducive to implementing STEM education like collaborative inquiry, project-based learning, and problem-based learning.

4.2 Strengths and Weaknesses

The strengths and weaknesses of implementing STEM in the future were also discussed with interviewees, two types of interviewees showed similar opinions. Table 4 shows the strengths and weaknesses of biology teachers using STEM education.

Table 4. Teachers' statements of strengths and weaknesses in implementing STEM education.

Dimension	Themes	Codes	Examples (Pre-service teachers)	Examples (In-service teachers)
Self-evaluation of implementing STEM education	Strengths	Knowledge; Support; Understanding; Passion; Innovation	"I can organize STEM teaching activities."	"I am familiar with biology."
			"I support STEM."	"I am more passionate."
			"I have some knowledge about STEM."	"I integrated chemistry and math with biology."
			"I have a great passion for learning."	"My learning ability is relatively high."
			"I would like to try something new."	"I embrace various disciplines."
			"I embrace different technologies."	"I have interdisciplinary experience."

(*continued*)

Table 4. (*continued*)

Dimension	Themes	Codes	Examples (Pre-service teachers)	Examples (In-service teachers)
	Weaknesses	Insufficient knowledge; No experience; Lack of support; Time-consuming; Superficial	"Insufficient knowledge."	"No STEM experience."
			"No STEM experience."	"Lack of support."
			"Lack of technical skills."	"No STEM experience."
			"Insufficient knowledge."	"Hard to apply STEM"
			"Interdisciplinary teaching is challenging."	"Learning technologies is time-consuming."
			"I don't have much time."	"My understanding of STEM is superficial."

Firstly, these teachers expressed a desire to learn more about STEM and integrate STEM education into their biology courses in the future. However, there were still several challenges that need to be addressed, including teachers' insufficient knowledge, conflicts with the existing education system requirements in mainland China (see the example below), inadequate technical resources, time constraints, and potential negative impacts on students' original biology scores. As participant PT2 stated, "The advantage is that I am more in favor of STEM education, so I am willing to explore it and try to integrate it into my classroom. The disadvantage is a more realistic problem. STEM may not be in line with the requirements of the school, such as the requirements of class hours and grades, which may hinder me." This emphasized how crucial it is to take into account teachers' competencies and willingness to incorporate STEM, as well as the challenges of doing so in an actual teaching and learning setting.

4.3 In-service Teachers' Suggestions

The suggestions given to pre-service biology teachers by in-service biology teachers focused on different aspects, including meeting students' needs, learning from veteran teachers, and developing more emerging technological skills. Table 5 shows in-service biology teachers' suggestions for implementing STEM education.

Table 5. In-service biology teachers' suggestions for implementing STEM education.

Theme	Codes	Examples
Suggestions for implementing STEM education	Content Knowledge; Understand Students; Educational Technology; Teaching Strategies; Learn from Others; Patient; Creative; Innovative	1) Enhance the content knowledge of biology 2) Observe and understand students 3) Design the teaching content from the student's point of view
		1) Learn more about educational technology 2) Master some technologies that can enhance personal competitiveness
		1) Observe more exemplary open classes 2) Master comprehensive teaching strategies
		1) Create a solid knowledge base of biology 2) Learn more from people in different fields 3) Strive to build a more comprehensive knowledge system for students
		1) Be patient 2) Be creative and have your own thoughts 3) Maintain the state of lifelong learning
		1) Have innovative ideas 2) Pay more attention to students' backgrounds

5 Discussion

This study conducted interviews with 12 biology educators to examine their differences, strengths, and weaknesses in implementing STEM education in Guangdong Province. Additionally, suggestions were collected from in-service biology teachers to benefit pre-service biology teachers.

5.1 Interpretations of Research Findings

Overall, pre-service biology teachers expressed a greater willingness to learn and utilize different emerging technologies in their course design. They were also well aware of the areas in their teaching that needed improvement and possessed comprehensive pedagogical knowledge that could be applied in the future. This group of teachers demonstrated innovation, creativity, and energy in teaching and learning. However, due to their lack of teaching experience, some of their ideas may not be suitable or feasible in an authentic learning environment, which can result in lower-than-expected teaching effectiveness. Furthermore, pre-service teachers may not be as familiar with biology and STEM content at the middle or high school level, posing challenges for them when it comes to implementing STEM in biology courses during their lessons.

When it comes to understanding biology and STEM subjects, in-service biology instructors were better prepared than pre-service teachers. They possessed more experience in organizing diverse learning activities to enhance students' learning outcomes. This group of teachers demonstrated confidence, strong teaching skills, individualized teaching styles, and the ability to achieve notable teaching results. However, precisely because of their confidence in teaching, they were more prone to be less proactive in exploring emerging teaching technologies. Consequently, they may encounter difficulties when implementing STEM education and applying different technologies. Furthermore, in-service biology teachers provided a variety of suggestions to pre-service biology teachers, each with different focuses and priorities. Some emphasized the importance of meeting students' needs, while others recommended learning from experienced teachers. Additionally, some suggested the development of technological skills as a means of enhancing future teaching and learning design.

5.2 Comparison with the Results and Findings in Other Studies

The mentioned findings are consistent with previous studies. Dong [16] identified educational technology and information and communication technologies (ICT) integration as key components of teacher preparation courses. The results of this study aligned with the finding that in-service teachers outperformed pre-service teachers in terms of technology expertise. However, the report acknowledged that younger teachers had the opportunity to develop higher levels of technical expertise if they received appropriate teacher preparation courses. According to Dong's research and the findings of this study, pre-service teachers possess certain advantages for the future. While in-service teachers may lean towards a more traditional approach and be reluctant to change, pre-service teachers tend to be more creative and open to integrating technology into the classroom. Therefore, both pre-service and in-service educators require continuous professional development to enhance their technical expertise and effectively implement technology in their teaching practice.

The findings about TK, TCK, and TPK from Cakir's [17] study also supported the results mentioned above. Both pre-service and in-service teachers in Cakir's study expressed support for the use of educational technology in the data analysis. Pre-service teachers scored higher on their attitudes towards technologies and their perceived usefulness of these tools compared to in-service teachers. In addition, in-service teachers reported using these technologies less frequently than their pre-service counterparts. The distinctions between pre-service and in-service teachers were made clear by these findings. Teachers who were in the classroom had more experience with educational technology, and as a result, they had a better grasp of their viability and effectiveness.

However, pre-service teachers learned more about emerging educational technologies at the university, so they had more confidence in these technologies without authentic teaching practices [18].

5.3 Limitations and Suggestions

Although this study answered the research questions, the limitations should not be ignored. A potential limitation of this case study is its lack of applicability due to the non-representative nature of the individual case. In addition, due to the limited time, the strengths and weaknesses between pre-service and in-service biology teachers were not comprehensively discovered, which needs further analysis to develop relevant teachers' preparation and development training. To further validate the findings, future studies should consider larger sample sizes and more rigorous sampling methods. Additionally, promoting research on the implementation of STEM education in specific disciplines across mainland China beyond biology would be a valuable area of inquiry. Furthermore, future studies should explore ways to combine the innovation of pre-service teachers and the rich experience of in-service teachers to better prepare pre-service teachers and promote in-service teachers.

6 Conclusion

This study was the second phase of the research project about pre-service and in-service biology teachers' STEM-TPACK backgrounds in Guangdong Province, which collected quantitative data from 70 biology teachers in the first phase and qualitative data from 12 biology teachers in the second phase. The data collection procedures adhered to ethical standards and this research was conducted ethically and responsibly. The findings from this study contributed to addressing the gap in the first phase of the research project. The overall research addressed the gap in the study of STEM implementation in specific disciplines and regions and revealed significant differences in seven dimensions between pre-service and in-service biology teachers [1].

Analysis of the qualitative data indicates that in-service teachers exhibited more confidence than pre-service teachers during interviews due to their extensive experience in teaching. In contrast, pre-service teachers had a lack of content and pedagogy knowledge and expressed low confidence in teaching biology and implementing STEM education in the future. These results aligned with expectations, as in-service teachers had more opportunities to consolidate their biology content knowledge, practice teaching skills, compare different pedagogical strategies, and plan for integrating STEM education into the biology course.

On the other hand, pre-service teachers exhibited more innovation in implementing educational technologies, but the reasons for this phenomenon were complex and multifaceted. It may be due to pre-service teachers' exposure to innovative teaching methods and emerging technologies during their training at the university. In contrast, in-service teachers' rich experience in authentic teaching and learning environments may reveal the problem in implementing some technologies and hinder their efforts to discover new educational technologies, or they may have tried various technologies but found them impractical or inefficient in the realistic biology course, particularly when integrating STEM education.

When it comes to the suggestions for pre-service biology teachers, in-service teachers indicated the importance of biology content knowledge, pedagogical knowledge, focusing on students' background and needs, and learning more educational technologies to supplement the teaching, which was obtained from their daily teaching experience and common shortages of contemporary teachers.

Although this study answered the research questions, the limitations should not be ignored. The sample size of 12 participants, selected through random sampling from the previous 70 participants in the first phase of the research, may have introduced errors and biases in the results. In addition, the strengths and weaknesses between pre-service and in-service biology teachers need further analysis to develop relevant teachers' preparation and development training. Furthermore, exploring the implementation of STEM education in specific disciplines across mainland China, beyond the scope of biology, holds great potential and value for future research endeavors.

References

1. Chen, F., Tse, A.W.C.: A survey of pre-service and in-service biology teachers' technological pedagogical content knowledge (TPACK) in implementing STEM education. In: Proceedings of the 15th International Conference on Education Technology and Computers (ICETC 2023). University of Barcelona (2023)
2. Wu, B., Hu, Y., Wang, M.: Scaffolding design thinking in online STEM preservice teacher training. Br. J. Edu. Technol. **50**(5), 2271–2287 (2019)
3. Chai, C.S., Rahmawati, Y., Jong, M.S.Y.: Indonesian science, mathematics, and engineering preservice teachers' experiences in STEM-TPACK design-based learning. Sustainability **12**(21), 9050 (2020)
4. Horzum, M.B.: An investigation of the technological pedagogical content knowledge of pre-service teachers. Technol. Pedagog. Educ. **22**(3), 303–317 (2013)
5. Lucietto, A., Russell, L., Schott, E. : STEM educators, how diverse disciplines teach. J. STEM Educ. **19**(3) (2018)
6. Rifandi, R., Rahmi, Y.L.: STEM education to fulfil the 21st century demand: a literature review. J. Phys. Conf. Ser. **1317**(1), 012208 (2019)
7. Cavlazoglu, B., Stuessy, C.: Changes in science teachers' conceptions and connections of STEM concepts and earthquake engineering. J. Educ. Res. **110**(3), 239–254 (2017)
8. Ring, E.A., Dare, E.A., Crotty, E.A., Roehrig, G.H.: The evolution of teacher conceptions of STEM education throughout an intensive professional development experience. J. Sci. Teacher Educ. **28**(5), 444–467 (2017)
9. Li, M., Chen, H., Wang, H.: Statistical comparative analysis of key words in science curriculum standard for compulsory education primary school. Training Primary Secondary Sch. Teachers **07**, 59–62 (2020)
10. Wei, S.: A preliminary study on the present situation and optimization strategy of biology teaching in junior middle school under the new curriculum reform. Learn. Wkly **29**, 78–80 (2022)
11. Wu, Q.: Re-examining the "Chinese learner": a case study of mainland Chinese students' learning experiences at British Universities. High. Educ. **70**, 753–766 (2015)
12. Mishra, P.: Considering contextual knowledge: the TPACK diagram gets an upgrade. J. Digit. Learn. Teacher Educ. **35**(2), 76–78 (2019)

13. Koehler, M., Mishra, P.: What is technological pedagogical content knowledge (TPACK)? Contemp. Issues Technol. Teacher Educ. **9**(1), 60–70 (2009)
14. Zhang, W., Tang, J.: Teachers' TPACK development: a review of literature. Open J. Soc. Sci. **9**(7), 367–380 (2021)
15. Chai, C.S., Hwee Ling Koh, J., Teo, Y.H.: Enhancing and modeling teachers' design beliefs and efficacy of technological pedagogical content knowledge for 21st century quality learning. J. Educ. Comput. Res. **57**(2), 360–384 (2019)
16. Dong, Y., Chai, C.S., Sang, G.Y., Koh, J.H.L., Tsai, C.C.: Exploring the profiles and interplays of pre-service and in-service teachers' technological pedagogical content knowledge (TPACK) in China. J. Educ. Technol. Soc. **18**(1), 158–169 (2015)
17. Cakir, R., Yukselturk, E., Ercan, T.O.P.: Pre-service and in-service teachers' perceptions about using Web 2.0 in education. Participatory Educ. Res. **2**(2), 70–83 (2015)
18. Bull, G., et al.: Connecting informal and formal learning experiences in the age of participatory media. Contemp. Issues Technol. Teacher Educ. **8**(2), 100–107 (2008)

Online Performance Prediction Combined Prior Knowledge and Deep Learning Models

Zhao Xie[1], Meixiu Lu[1](✉), and Xing Pan[2](✉)

[1] School of Information Science and Technology/School of Cyber Security, Guangdong University of Foreign Studies, Guangzhou, China
xiez022@163.com, meixiulu@mail.gdufs.edu.cn

[2] Center for Contemporary Education Technology, Guangdong University of Foreign Studies, Guangzhou, China
xingpan@mail.gdufs.edu.cn

Abstract. With the rapid development of information technology, an increasing number of student learning activities are taking place in online environments. Analyzing online learning behavior data can further improve teaching and assessment methods, enhance learning outcomes, and promote independent learning. However, it is a challenge for teachers to evaluate learning status and academic performance of each student through online learning systems. This study aimed to explore an efficient method for assessing student academic performance. A performance prediction method combined prior knowledge and deep learning models was proposed. Before putting learning behavior data into deep learning models, a weight matrix for learning behaviors was reconstructed. And the learning behavior features derived from this weight matrix along with the raw learning behavior data were imported into a custom Dense layer network. Additionally, an attention mechanism was incorporated into the model to improve model prediction accuracy. Experimental results showed that this method could effectively predict academic performance, identify high-risk students who may need assistance and improve the quality of online teaching.

Keywords: Online Performance Prediction · Deep Learning · Neural Networks · Prior Knowledge

1 Introduction

Student performance prediction is the practice of forecasting a student's future academic performance based on factors such as course information, historical data, and other relevant variables. In recent years, it has gradually become a hot research topic in the area of educational data mining. In the post-pandemic era, an increasing number of student learning activities are conducted online, making it challenging for educators to track individual student's progress and provide immediate feedback, thereby compromising the quality of online education. Therefore, researches on online performance prediction and the development of effective predictive models are crucial for educators to identify students at risk and offer timely assistance, harnessing the potential advantages of online education.

Z. Kubincová et al. (Eds.): SETE 2023, LNCS 14606, pp. 111–120, 2024.
https://doi.org/10.1007/978-981-97-4243-1_9

In recent years, numerous scholars have conducted related researches in this field. Early research predominantly employed machine learning methods, utilizing student historical grades and learning behavior data to construct predictive models for future performance. For instance, Zhang et al. focused on "Educational Cloud Computing" course offered by Huazhong Normal University's Haster teaching platform and adopted an optimized logistic regression algorithm to predict student performance [1]. Zhou et al. collected campus network access records with over 10,000 students and adopted a naïve Bayes classifier to construct a predictive model for students' offline performance [2]. Figueroa-Canas et al. analyzed students' network logs to understand learning behaviors and outcomes, employing a binary decision tree to predict student performance [3]. These findings revealed significant correlations between factors like learning time, frequency, content, and interaction patterns in network logs and student performance [4]. As artificial intelligence, big data, and related technologies have rapidly advanced. Deep neural networks and big data methods have also been applied to performance prediction. Leveraging extensive datasets contain personal information, learning behavior data and social network data.

Currently, existing machine learning and deep learning methods often rely on data, which can lead to unsatisfactory results [5]. Particularly limited data is available for predicting learning outcomes. Traditional machine learning methods are relatively simple and highly interpretable but require manual feature selection and extraction, along with domain expertise. In contrast, deep learning methods offer excellent predictive performance and enhance understanding through data visualization but lack interpretability in the decision-making process, especially for complex models.

To address these challenges, this paper proposed an online performance prediction method that integrated prior knowledge with deep learning models. Leveraging previous research findings, we reconstructed a weight matrix for learning behavior features, emphasizing the importance of certain learning behaviors. Before building the LSTM network, we added a Dense layer network, enabling the input of student time-series learning behavior data and the reconstructed weight matrix into LSTM model, thereby enhancing prediction accuracy.

2 Related Work

Student learning behavior data exhibits significant time-series characteristics, and deep neural networks have the capability to capture complex nonlinear relationships between features, boasting strong expressive and fitting abilities. Many scholars have delved into this area of research with promising outcomes. For instance, Karimi H and colleagues proposed a deep learning model for predicting online learning behavior performance based on click-through rates and demographic data to forecast students' performance in courses [6]. Subsequently, they constructed a knowledge graph encompassing relationships between students, courses, teachers, and subjects within online systems, and trained and predicted on this graph using a graph neural network (R-GCN) to predict student performance [7]. Corrigan and others gathered interaction data from virtual learning environments and the number of times students accessed the Moodle platform as inputs for their predictive model, employing a Long Short-Term Memory network (LSTM) to predict student learning performance, with results showing favorable performance [8]. Gardner and colleagues approached student dropout prediction from two perspectives: forum data and learning platform click data [9]. W. Feng et al. leveraged attention mechanisms to learn activity features and introduced a context-aware feature interaction network model to predict grades [10]. Q. Hu and collaborators represented relationships between students and courses as graphs, enhanced the relationships between students and courses using attention mechanisms, and proposed an attention-based graph convolutional neural network method for predicting academic performance [11].

Prior knowledge typically refers to the knowledge that has been acquired about data, models, or tasks before the learning task at hand. This prior knowledge can be obtained from domain experts or conclusions drawn from previous related research. Existing research has shown that combining neural networks with prior knowledge can yield favorable results. For example, Jin X introduced a technique based on distillation and route constraint optimization to extract prior knowledge from complex models and transfer it to smaller models to enhance their performance [12]. Ganin Y proposed a domain-adversarial training approach, incorporating a domain classifier into the network to divide input features into different domains, thereby improving the network's generalization to diverse data domains [13]. Heo and collaborators introduced a knowledge distillation method to transfer knowledge from a complex network to a simpler network, resulting in improved performance for the simpler network [14].

The aforementioned research on performance prediction has mainly utilized machine learning or neural network methods, with limited studies focusing on the integration of prior knowledge into deep learning models. In this paper, we reconstruct a weight matrix for learning behavior, input learning behavior data along with the learning behavior features derived from this weight matrix into a Dense layer network, and subsequently process the data through the Dense layer before feeding it into a deep learning model. Additionally, an attention mechanism has been incorporated into the model.

3 Dataset

3.1 Data Description

This study utilized relevant data from the Open University Learning Analytics Dataset (OULAD), specifically focusing on the FFF course [15]. The dataset comprises information from 22 Open University courses offered in 2013 and 2014, along with data from 32,593 students. The dataset includes student personal information, exam results, and interaction data between students and the Virtual Learning Environment (VLE) online learning platform. The student information includes geographic location and level of education. Student information related to various learning interactions is stored in the VLE, such as access to resources. The exam results includes student assessment scores, ranging from 0 to 100, with scores below 40 indicating a fail. It summarized 20 categories of learning behaviors from the dataset (Appendix).

This experiment specifically utilized the data from students who participated in the FFF course(Mathematics), which includes information such as course name, subject area, semester, the number of students, course duration in weeks, and the status of passed or not. This analysis focused exclusively on those students with learning records.

The academic performance was categorized into four classes: Excellent, Pass, Fail, and Withdraw. Previous research carried by Karimi et al. found that predicting four categories had a low accuracy rate, and the distribution of results among different categories was imbalanced [7]. Hence, this experiment employed binary classification, wherein Excellent and Pass were categorized as Pass, and Fail and Withdraw were categorized as Fail (Table 1).

Table 1. The description of the dataset

Name	Domin	Period	Student	Weeks	Outcomes (pass/fail)
FFF	STEM	2013B	1,510	35	51.78%/48.22%
FFF	STEM	2013J	2,098	39	52.19%/47.81%
FFF	STEM	2014B	1,363	35	47.98%/52.02%
FFF	STEM	2014J	2,121	39	52.66%/47.34%

3.2 Data Preparation

Before conducting the experiment, data preprocessing was carried out. Firstly, student information was read, missing and incomplete data were filtered out, and the data was consolidated. Next, a dictionary was created to map student learning behaviors to indices, extracting all the student learning behavior data. Subsequently, the data was split into a training set and a test set. To represent click features, the weekly clicks made by students were calculated, such as forum clicks and resource access times. Then, label was applied to encode the target variable, where 'fail' was encoded as 0 and 'success' as 1. Lastly, it was transformed into a one-dimensional array and fitted before scaling the data, followed by data scaling using logarithmic transformation.

4 Proposed Model

Existing research indicated that student activities on forums and click rates showed a significant impact on performance prediction [7, 16, 17]. Based on these prior knowledge, the pre-LSTM model was introduced and designed to extract important online behavioral features, such as forum click counts, wiki click counts, etc. Then a weight matrix for these features was reconstructed. Subsequently, the weights of these features were increased and fed into the neural network layers. Firstly, the weight matrix was constructed as follows:

$$w = f(x) \quad (1)$$

In this process, where 'x' represents the input data and 'f' denotes the mapping function used to create and modify the weight matrix 'W'.

Initiate a feature matrix was created with all values set to 1. The weight values 'wh' and 'wf' for two features, namely "homepage" and "forumng" were adjusted to fall within the range of 'wh' ∈ (1.0–2.0) and 'wf' ∈ (1.0–2.0), while the other features remained at 1.

Following this, an improved multi-layer Recurrent Neural Network (LSTM) model was constructed for predicting academic performance. Before building the LSTM model, a Dense layer was added, which took the student learning data and the weight matrix as inputs. The Dense layer calculated based on the input student learning data and the weight matrix. For each element of the input vector 'X,' it was multiplied with the corresponding column of the weight matrix 'w' and then the results were summed up, followed by adding a bias vector 'b' Nonlinear transformation was applied to the results through the activation function 'g()' yielding an output vector 'A' which served as the output of this layer. The calculation process was as follows:

$$\left(Z = X * w^\wedge T + b\right) \tag{2}$$

$$A = g(Z) \tag{3}$$

Next, the length of the time series for all students was set to 'T' ∈ (0, 20) weeks. For each 't' ∈ [1, T], the learning data was inputted into an LSTM unit. The main focus here was the computation of output and storage units. The formula 4 was adopted to calculate the output gate vector. And the formula (5) was for storage unit computation, ultimately resulting in a single LSTM output vector (6).

$$o_t = \sigma(W_o x_t + U_o y_{t-1} + b_o) \tag{4}$$

$$c_t = f_t \circ c_{t-1} + i_t \circ \mathcal{G}(W_c x_t + U_c h_{t-1} + b_c) \tag{5}$$

$$y_t = o_t \circ \mathcal{G}(c_t) \tag{6}$$

where 'i_t' was the input gate vector, 'f_t' was the forget gate vector, 'O_t' was the output gate vector, 'y_t' was the LSTM output cell vector, 'c_t' was the storage unit vector, 'W,' 'U,' 'b' were parameters of the LSTM network, 'σ' was the sigmoid function, 'G()' was the activation function. Additionally, the model utilized binary cross-entropy as the loss function, the sigmoid function as the activation function, and employs the Adam optimizer for model optimization.

Attention mechanisms dynamically allocated weights to different parts or features of the input data based on their importance. Here, a self-attention mechanism was introduced to focus the model on critical time behavior features. Where 'M' represented a Multi-Layer Perceptron (MLP), and 'A_t' was the attention score vector output from the attention component. The formula was as follows:

$$o_t = \sigma(W_o x_t + U_o y_{t-1} + b_o) \tag{7}$$

$$E(t) = M(h_t) \tag{8}$$

$$A_t = \frac{\exp(E_t)}{\sum_{t=1}^{T} \exp(E_t)} \tag{9}$$

Finally, the pre-LSTM model was depicted in Fig. 1.

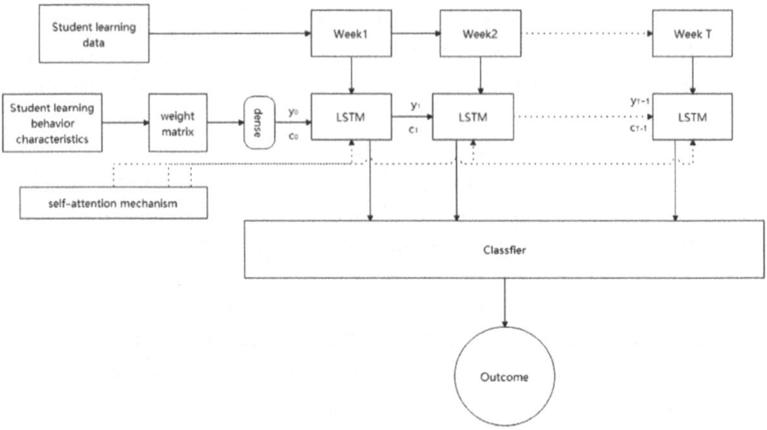

Fig. 1. The student performance prediction model.

5 Experiment and Result Analysis

5.1 Experimental Settings

This study conducted comparative experiments to validate the effectiveness of the proposed model. Specifically, three commonly used deep learning models, namely CNN [18], LSTM [19], and GRU [20], were evaluated. In the experiment, the proposed model was configured with 300 hidden layer neurons, a learning rate of 0.01, a total of 100 iterations, and a batch size of 100 samples (students). The evaluation metrics included accuracy and precision.

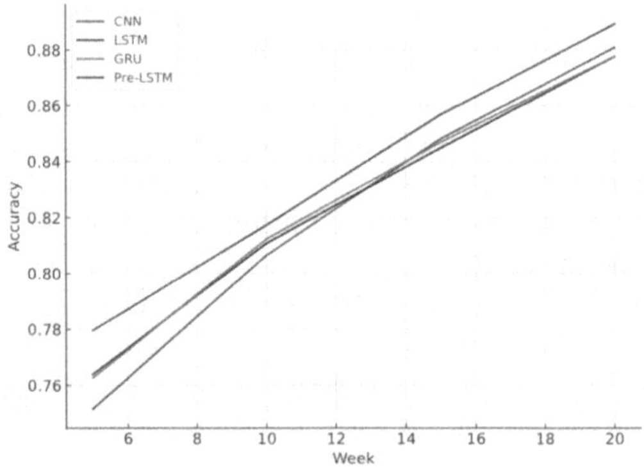

Fig. 2. The accuracy of different model

5.2 Result Analysis

The comparison of different models in Fig. 2 and Fig. 3 showed that the binary classification results for the FFF course. The results respectively illustrated the different

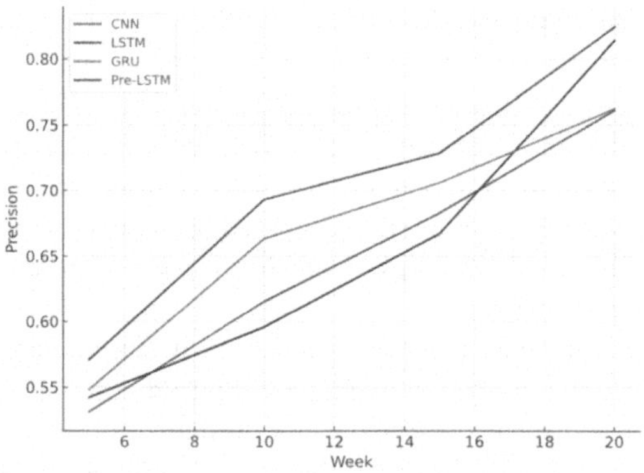

Fig. 3. The precision of different model

models based on varying click data for 5 weeks, 10 weeks, 15 weeks, and 20 weeks (Fig. 2 & Fig. 3). The improvement in precision showed that pre-LSTM's ability to extract time features from click behavior indeed affected the model's predictive accuracy (Fig. 3). Furthermore, incorporating prior knowledge, adjusting feature weights, and introducing the attention mechanism lead to significant improvements in various performance metrics for performance prediction model. This study also confirmed that student engagement in forum discussions significantly impacts their result to pass final academic examination during online learning [16].

Throughout the duration of the course, the more click data we incorporated, the better our method's predictions became. Additionally, compared to CNN, LSTM, and GRU, the pre-LSTM model showed higher improvements. Moreover, it demonstrated a very high accuracy in predicting grade outcomes by the 20th week of the course. This can provide valuable information for educational administrators to take timely intervention measures to assist students with risky learning behaviors.

5.3 Discussion

According to previous research, the vast majority of researchers trained their models using data from an entire semester to improve prediction accuracy. Course configurations are not uniform, and the learning requirements for students vary across different courses, with even greater variations across different disciplines. For instance, in the study conducted by Karimi H [7], when a model trained on data from one course was used to predict results for another course, there was a significant drop in prediction accuracy.

This study aimed to predict students' final academic test results as quickly as possible, specifically by the mid-semester, using limited data. This allows us to promptly provide feedback to educators, which has practical significance. This approach is built upon the foundations of prior research, adding prior knowledge, such as constructing a weight matrix and adjusting the feature weights that have a greater impact on students' final grade results, can indeed effectively enhance prediction accuracy.

6 Conclusion and Future Work

A method for online performance prediction that combined prior knowledge with deep learning models was proposed, focusing on the most significant learning behaviors during the process of online learning. Experimental results demonstrated the effectiveness of the proposed method, which significantly enhanced prediction accuracy. In comparison to other approaches, this method focused on the impact of process-oriented learning behavior data on final test results.

Education evolves with the changing times, and it can be challenging to adapt to changes in course instruction based solely on past experiences. Future work will consider how different types of courses correspond to the influence of learning behaviors on the final prediction results, aiming to improve the model's time efficiency and accuracy. In addition, the integration of our research findings into a module of engineering projects that can be incorporated into online education systems in the future. This will have a positive impact on online education.

Acknowledgments. This study was funded by the MOE Project [Foreign Language Proficiency Assessment System in the New Era, China #2] under Grant [number 22JJD740019]; the Ministry of Education of Humanities and Social Science Project under Grant [number 20YJCZH124].

Disclosure of Interests. The authors have no competing interests to declare that are relevant to the content of this article,*corresponding author.

Appendix

Learning Behavior Categories

Index	Learning Behavior Category	Illustration
0	resource	Total number of clicks on PDF resources
1	url	Total clicks on the links to audio/video
2	homepage	Total clicks on course homepage
3	subpage	Total clicks to access other websites during the course
4	glossary	Total clicks on vocabulary related to the course
5	forumng	Total clicks on the discussion forum
6	oucollaborate	Total clicks of online video discussions
7	dataplus	Total clicks on additional resources, such as videos, websites, etc
8	quiz	Total on the course quiz
9	ouelluminate	Total clicks in online tutorial sessions

(continued)

(*continued*)

Index	Learning Behavior Category	Illustration
10	htmlactivity	Total clicks on HTML interaction
11	dualpane	Total clicks on website related information and activities
12	sharedsubpage	Total clicks to access shared pages
13	questionnaire	Total clicks on the questionnaires related to the course
4	page	Total clicks on the information related to the course
15	externalquiz	Total clicks for additional quizzes
16	ouwiki	Total clicks accessing Wiki
17	repeatactivity	Total clicks on the course contents from previous weeks
18	folder	Total clicks on course related files
19	oucontent	Total clicks on the contents of the assignment

References

1. Zhang, W., Huang, X., Wang, S., Shu, J., Liu, H., Chen, H.: Student performance prediction via online learning behavior analytics. In Proceedings of the 2017 International Symposium on Educational Technology (ISET), Hong Kong, China, pp. 153–157 (2017). https://doi.org/10.1109/ISET.2017.43, https://ieeexplore.ieee.org/document/8005410
2. Zhou, Q., Zheng, Y., Mou, C.: Predicting students' performance of an offline course from their online behaviors. In: Proceedings of the 2015 Fifth International Conference on Digital Information and Communication Technology and Its Applications (DICTAP),Beirut, Lebanon, 29 April–1 May 2015, pp. 70–73 (2015). https://doi.org/10.1109/DICTAP.2015.7113173, https://ieeexplore.ieee.org/document/7113173
3. Figueroa-Canas, J., Sancho-Vinuesa, T.: Early prediction of dropout and final exam performance in an online statistics course. IEEE Rev. Iberoam. Tecnol. Aprendiz. **15**, 86–94 (2020). https://doi.org/10.1109/RITA.2020.2987727, https://ieeexplore.ieee.org/abstract/document/9064814
4. Wu, B., Qu, S., Ni, Y., Zhou, Y., Wang, P., Li, Q.: Predicting student performance using weblogs. In: Proceedings of the 14th International Conference on Computer Science and Education, ICCSE 2019, Toronto, ON, Canada, 19–21 August 2019, pp. 616–621 (2019). https://ieeexplore.ieee.org/document/8845440
5. Von Rueden, L., Mayer, S., Beckh, K., et al.: Informed machine learning–a taxonomy and survey of integrating prior knowledge into learning systems. IEEE Trans. Knowl. Data Eng. **35**(1), 614–633 (2021). https://doi.org/10.1109/TKDE.2021.3079836, https://arxiv.org/pdf/1903.12394.pdf
6. Karimi, H., Huang, J., Derr, T.: A deep model for predicting online course performance. Assoc. Adv. Artif. Intell. (2020). https://tylersnetwork.github.io/papers/aaai-ai4edu2020-predicting_online_course_performance.pdf
7. Karimi, H., Derr, T., Huang, J., et al.: Online academic course performance prediction using relational graph convolutional neural network. Int. Educ. Data Min. Soc. (2020). https://files.eric.ed.gov/fulltext/ED608007.pdf

8. Corrigan, O., Smeaton, A.F.: A course agnostic approach to predicting student success from vle log data using recurrent neural networks. In: Lecture Notes in Computer Science, vol. 10474, pp. 545–548. Springer, Cham (2017). https://doi.org/10.1007/978-3-319-66610-5_59
9. Gardner, J., Brooks, C.: Dropout model evaluation in MOOCs. In: Proceedings of the AAAI Conference on Artificial Intelligence, vol. 32, p. 1, April 2018. https://doi.org/10.1609/aaai.v32i1.11392
10. Feng, W., Tang, J., Liu, T.X.: Understanding dropouts in MOOCs. Assoc. Adv. Artif. Intell. (2019). https://doi.org/10.1609/aaai.v33i01.3301517
11. Hu, Q., Rangwala, H.: Academic performance estimation with attention-based graph convolutional networks. In: Proceedings of The 12th International Conference on Educational Data Mining (EDM 2019), vol. 168, pp. 69–78. ERIC (2019). https://doi.org/10.48550/arXiv.2001.00632
12. Jin, X., Peng, B., Wu, Y., et al.: Knowledge distillation via route constrained optimization. In: Proceedings of the IEEE/CVF International Conference on Computer Vision, pp. 1345–1354 (2019). https://doi.org/10.48550/arXiv.1904.09149
13. Ganin, Y., Ustinova, E., Ajakan, H., et al.: Domain-adversarial training of neural networks. J. Mach. Learn. Res. **17**(1), 2096–2030 (2016). https://doi.org/10.48550/arXiv.1505.07818
14. Heo, B., Lee, M., Yun, S., Choi, J.Y.: Knowledge transfer via distillation of activation boundaries formed by hidden neurons. Proc. AAAI Conf. Artif. Intell. **33**(01), 3779–3787 (2019). https://doi.org/10.1609/aaai.v33i01.33013779
15. Kuzilek, J., Hlosta, M., Zdrahal, Z.: Open University Learning Analytics dataset. Sci. Data **4**, 170171 (2017). https://analyse.kmi.open.ac.uk/open_dataset
16. He, C., Ma, P., Zhou, L., Wu, J.: Is participating in mooc forums important for students? a data-driven study from the perspective of the supernetwork. J. Data Inf. Sci. **3**(2), 62–77 (2018). https://doi.org/10.2478/jdis-2018-0009
17. Paszke, A., et al.: Pytorch: an imperative style, high-performance deep learning library. In: Advances in Neural Information Processing Systems, pp. 8024–8035 (2019). https://doi.org/10.48550/arXiv.1912.01703
18. Lecun, Y., Bottou, L., Bengio, Y., Haffner, P.: Gradient-based learning applied to document recognition. Proc. IEEE **86**(11), 2278–2324 (1998). https://doi.org/10.1109/5.726791. https://ieeexplore.ieee.org/document/726791
19. Hochreiter, S., Schmidhuber, J.: Long short-term memory. Neural Comput. **9**(8), 1735–1780 (1997). https://doi.org/10.1162/neco.1997.9.8.1735
20. Cho, K., Van Merriënboer, B., Gulcehre, C., et al.: Learning phrase representations using RNN encoder-decoder for statistical machine translation. arXiv preprint rXiv:1406.1078 (2014). https://arxiv.org/pdf/1406.1078.pdf

On the Impact of Augmented Reality for Rehabilitation Treatment: Early Results from a Study with Children

Maria Paola Colatei[1], Eleonora De Piano[2], and Pierpaolo Vittorini[1(✉)]

[1] University of L'Aquila, P.le S. Tommasi, 67100 L'Aquila, Italy
{mariapaola.colatei,pierpaolo.vittorini}@univaq.it

[2] Associazione Italiana Terapisti della Neuro e Psicomotricità dell'Età Evolutiva, Rome, Italy

Abstract. Virtual, augmented or mixed reality (VAMR) has recently gained attention in rehabilitation, given the possibilities technology offers to integrate traditional approaches. In this context, the paper reports on a study involving two children groups for five months. The first group (group A) followed an integrated intervention (traditional plus augmented reality). The second group (group B) underwent only the traditional approach. The results show larger improvements for group A in almost all investigated areas, suggesting a possible benefit of VAMR-supported interventions. On the other hand, the limited size and heterogeneity of the sample represent a clear limitation of this study. Nevertheless, we consider these early results as further evidence of the possible positive impact of technologies – in this case, VAMR – in rehabilitation in the developmental age.

Keywords: Augmented Reality · Rehabilitation treatments · Developmental age

1 Introduction

Rehabilitation in the developmental age is a complex process that promotes psychophysical well-being and integrates the best quality of relational and emotional life, as desirable by the minor and his family. While rehabilitation in adults deals with the problem of restoring functions that one assumes to be intact before the injury, in the developmental stage, the pathologies are grafted onto the more general process of development and learning. Therefore, given that there is no previous "normal" condition in the child that can be taken as a point of reference, the rehabilitation process in the developmental age must focus on the child in his physical, mental, emotional, communicative and relational aspects, and involves the family and the socio-educational environmental context. In all rehabilitation processes in the developmental age, the child is required to learn and strengthen his/her skills related to different aspects that depend on the specific disability.

Z. Kubincová et al. (Eds.): SETE 2023, LNCS 14606, pp. 121–129, 2024.
https://doi.org/10.1007/978-981-97-4243-1_10

The application of virtual, augmented or mixed reality (VAMR) has been explored in recent years in terms of the possible benefits in different fields, like education [15], in teaching rehabilitation practices (e.g., [4]), physical therapy [5], after stroke [6] or in paediatrics [8]. In the specific context of children's rehabilitation, the research is even more recent and usually includes gamification (e.g., [12,20,21]).

In this latter context, the paper reports on a small study involving children who used a commercial system during a five-month rehabilitation period. The rehabilitation process supported by VAMR included the execution of tasks supported by serious games of different categories, each aiming at stimulating the different developmental areas affected by the disability.

In particular, the paper describes the main system functionalities (Sect. 2), then delves into the study and its results, discussed in terms of all the limits related to the sample size and heterogeneity (Sect. 3). The paper then ends with short conclusions (Sect. 4).

2 Background

The use of technology to support rehabilitation in children has a long tradition. It includes devices (e.g., [7]), adaptive technologies (e.g., [1,3]), virtual/augmented reality (e.g., [8]) usually supported by gamification (e.g., [20]), to make the rehabilitation process more engaging for patients in the developmental age.

In this latter context, the authors used a commercial system[1] to support the rehabilitation of a small cohort of children. Through the system, a child/patient is immersed in a "sensory room" where he/she can operate and interact with different scenarios, more or less realistic. The different scenarios are projected on a wall and the floor, offering stimuli to the patient with whom to interact. The system is based on a marker-less motion acquisition and analysis: a patient can move freely, using the needed aids (e.g., wheelchair, walker), without additional equipment (e.g., glasses, gloves). Moreover, the system offers a gamified approach to exercises, the therapies can be customised to each patient, and sensory feedback is provided during exercises (i.e., acoustic and visual) to stimulate the patient further and help him improve his skills. Figure 1 shows a sample session with the system.

The software that controls the system has a web-based interface and can manage a database of patients and personalised therapies made up of sequences of exercises. The available exercises are offered as games and belong to different categories:

Motion. Exercises finalised to improve the coordination of all body segments, like (i) walking on a bridge without touching the lateral ropes, (ii) "cleaning" a window to discover a hidden pet, (iii) moving clouds to find a hidden game

[1] The name and brand of the system are not reported in the paper, as well as any proprietary hardware/software, to avoid any conflict of interest or unwanted advertising.

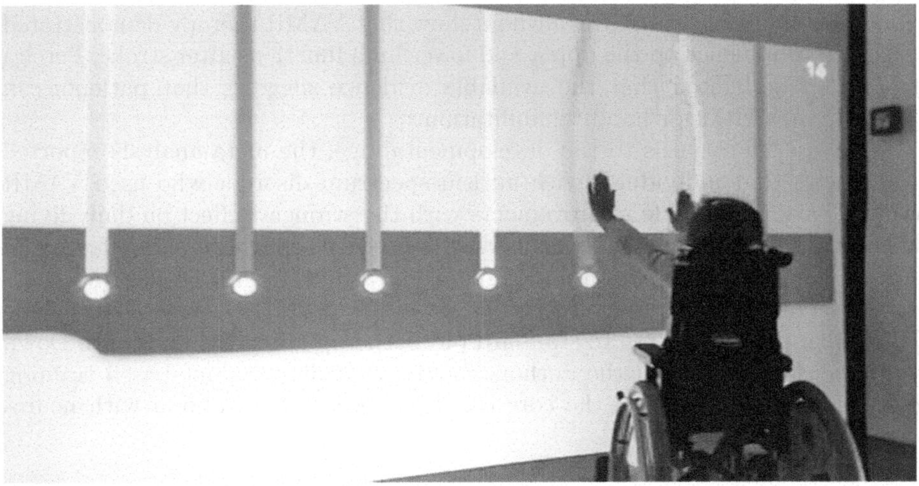

Fig. 1. A sample session with the system

(e.g., amusement park carousel, colourful balloons), and (iv) paint freely on the wall;

Grasping. Exercises finalised to simulate the gripping and repositioning of an object, like (i) find the black sheep and move them into a fence, (ii) find the dirty clothes in the wardrobes, grab and put them in the washing machine, (iii) pick the apples from the tree and store them in a basket, (iv) find among the shelves the items indicated on a list, grab and place them in the shopping cart;

Games. Exercises finalised to keep the attention and interest high, like (i) throwing a black disk into the opponent's goal using a virtual joystick, (ii) breaking a wall using a coloured ball;

Sprites. Exercises that require movements aimed at reaching and touching a series of objects to train cognitive, spatial and orientation skills, like (i) reordering the letters of the alphabet, (ii) touching the coloured rectangles to discover the related fruit, (iii) touching the numbers in the correct sequence (the number becomes red in case of a mistake, green otherwise);

Follow me. Exercises to follow moving objects to train the visuospatial skills, orientation and spatial cognition, like (i) following a dog or a panda, (ii) walking on footprints that appear on the sand (the footprint becomes red in case of mistake, green otherwise);

Hunt. Exercises in which the patient must reach various elements that appear randomly to stimulate eye-eye coordination, motor skills and attention levels, like (i) reaching coloured balloons and popping them, (ii) tapping the mole.

In terms of effectiveness, the results available in the scientific literature show general agreement regarding the positive effect of VAMR systems in rehabilitation.

For instance, in [10,14], the authors show that VAMR therapy demonstrated a significant influence on the upper and lower limb functions after stroke; Pereira et al. [13] highlighted that the available evidence suggests that patients can benefit from VARM for hand rehabilitation.

With specific regards to the developmental age, the meta-analysis reported in [9] shows that individuals with autism spectrum disorder who used VAMR training have remarkable improvements with the strongest effect on daily living skills; in [17], the results show that VAMR-based interventions are effective in improving sustained attention and vigilance measures, even if no improvements were observed in impulsivity responses; Stander et al. [19] suggest to include VAMR therapy in addition to standard physiotherapy in individuals with Down syndrome; finally, in [16], the authors showed that digital game-based training could significantly enhance the core cognitive abilities of children with neurodevelopmental disorders.

3 The Study

3.1 Materials and Methods

The sample consists of 8 subjects. The children are all males, born between 2015 and 2017 (average age 6.2[2]). The pathologies involving the examined patients were intellect disability, genetic syndrome, autism spectrum disorder and motor coordination disorder. The subjects were selected and divided into two homogeneous groups (group A and group B). Therefore, both groups were equal for the number of components (4 children each), age, pathology and number of prescribed therapy sessions (2 sessions per week). Children belonging to group B performed classical neuro-psychomotor therapy biweekly. The classic treatment includes sitting or standing games/exercises involving only one part of the body or several parts simultaneously to be done with the therapist's support. Children belonging to group A replaced one session with a different one using the system (group A).

Group A was made up of R.F. aged 7 (intellect disability); P.D. aged 4.11 (genetic syndrome – Sotos syndrome); B.F. aged 6.2 (autism spectrum disorder); G.D. aged 6 (motor coordination disorder). Group B was made up of G.M. aged 7.8 (intellect disability); A.R. of 5.11 years (genetic syndrome – Down syndrome); G.B. aged 6.2 (autism spectrum disorder); G.S. aged 6 (motor coordination disorder).

The study lasted 5 months, from October 2022 to February 2023. It included the patients' evaluation and the treatment, which lasted 4 months (15 weeks). All patients in group A received 15 therapies with VAMR support.

The VAMR session lasted 45 min and was organised by selecting a subset of the available exercise for each category. Specifically, the proposed exercises were:

- 6 of the motion category (clean animals, clean window, discover the landscape, find the coloured balloon, find the red balloon, amusement park);

[2] All ages are at the beginning of the study.

- 6 of the grasping category (bring the black sheep in the fence, cooking, laundry, pick the apples, pick the oranges, supermarket);
- 1 of the games category (break the wall);
- 7 of the sprites category (alphabet and count to – only for the already educated patients, the colour of fruits, moon, guitar, memory for kids, trumpets);
- 2 of the follow me category (escape the dog, follow footprints in the sand);
- 2 of the hunt category (balloons and tap the mole).

The questionnaires used to evaluate the patients are the APCM-2 (Abilitá Prassiche e della Coordinazione Motoria – Praxic and Motor Coordination Skills) [18] and the VMI test [2]. The APCM-2 investigates the following areas: (A_{01}) balance and coordination, (A_{02}) oculomotion, (A_{03}) observe, memorise and execute actions sequentially, (A_{04}) dynamic coordination, (A_{05}) motor/graphic skills, (A_{06}) manual skills, (A_{07}) symbolic gestures, (A_{08}) praxic skills, (A_{09}) hands/fingers movements, (A_{10}) orofacial movements. As for the VMI, in this paper, we report only the standardised VMI values for vision and motion abilities. All values of both tests are numerical: the higher the value, the better the performance in the corresponding ability.

A developmental neuro and psychomotricity therapist performed the therapies and tests. Such a health professional collaborates with the other disciplines in the paediatric area. He/she carries out interventions for rehabilitating child neuropsychiatric disorders in neuro-psychomotricity, neuropsychology and developmental psychopathology.

3.2 Results

Table 1 summarises the results of the APCM-2 test. In the rows, it reports the results for each patient, for all areas at the beginning of the study (pre), at the end of the study (post) and the observed difference (diff). We also report on the average value for each group to easily discuss the results. Note that missing values indicate that the specific part of the test was not executed (e.g., because the child was too young for the task). In contrast, zeros indicate that it was executed with a result equal to zero.

Table 2 instead focuses on the VMI test. It reports the results for each patient, for the visual and motion abilities, at the beginning of the study (pre), at the end of the study (post) and the difference (diff). Like Table 1, we also report on the average difference for each group.

A note is worth about negative differences that seem to indicate a regression. Negative differences may take place because of at least the following reasons:

- The performance remained stable, but – given that four months passed from the first test – the same execution, normalised for the actual age, corresponds to a value that appears as a regression when it should be considered the lack of the expected progress;
- The protocol to be followed by the children has changed – once again because of the difference of four months between test and re-test – and therefore, the gap is emphasised.

Table 1. Summary of the results regarding the APCM-2 test: for each patient, for all the areas, the test result at the beginning of the study (pre), at the end (post) and the corresponding difference (diff). For each group and area, the average difference is also reported.

		A_{01}			A_{02}			A_{03}			A_{04}			A_{05}		
Subject	Group	Pre	Post	Diff	Pre	Post	Diff	Pre	Post	Diff	Pre	Post	Diff	Pre	Post	Diff
1 RF	A	43.8	81.3	37.5	56.1	71.4	15.3	35.7	42.9	7.2	87.5	100.0	12.5	50.0	50.0	0.0
2 PD	A	45.8	83.3	37.5	70.0	90.0	20.0	37.5	76.7	39.2	40.0	50.0	10.0	45.5	92.9	47.4
3 BF	A	18.8	25.0	6.2	57.5	64.3	6.8	0.0	14.3	14.3	75.0	75.0	0.0	0.0	25.0	25.0
4 GD	A	10.0	12.5	2.5	30.0	50.0	20.0	9.4	21.4	12.0	60.0	75.0	15.0	0.0	0.0	0.0
	Avg.	29.		*20.9*			*15.5*			*18.2*			*9.4*			*18.1*
5 MG	B	68.8	81.3	12.5	85.7	85.7	0.0	57.1	71.4	14.3	100.0	100.0	0.0	100.0	100.0	0.0
6 AR	B	15.0	12.5	-2.5	60.0	57.1	-2.9	0.0	0.0	0.0	10.0	50.0	40.0	0.0	0.0	0.0
7 GB	B	25.0	37.5	12.5	28.6	28.6	0.0	28.6	28.6	0.0	100.0	100.0	0.0	0.0	25.0	25.0
8 GS	B	50.0	0.0	-50.0	40.0	35.7	-4.3	9.4	9.4	0.0	80.0	75.0	-5.0	61.1	75.0	13.9
	Avg.			*-6.9*			*-1.8*			*3.6*			*8.8*			*9.7*

(a) APCM-2 (first five areas)

		A_{06}			A_{07}			A_{08}			A_{09}			A_{10}		
Subject	Group	Pre	Post	Diff	Pre	Post	Diff	Pre	Post	Diff	Pre	Post	Diff	Pre	Post	Diff
1 RF	A	62.5	81.3	18.8	57.1	71.4	14.3	90.0	90.0	0.0	40.9	77.3	36.4	91.7	91.7	0.0
2 PD	A	44.4	66.7	22.3	87.5	95.8	8.3	55.0	81.3	26.3						
3 BF	A	50.0	56.3	6.3	64.3	85.7	21.4	50.0	80.0	30.0	18.2	31.8	13.6	83.3	83.3	0.0
4 GD	A	41.7	56.3	14.6	75.0	64.3	-10.7	7.1	10.0	2.9		27.3			50.0	
	Avg.			*15.5*			*8.4*			*14.8*			*25*			*0.0*
5 MG	B	81.3	81.3	0.0	71.4	85.7	14.3	90.0	90.0	0.0	45.5	63.6	18.1	58.3	75.0	16.7
6 AR	B	58.3	18.8	-39.5	87.5	64.3	-23.2	7.1	10.0	2.9		9.1			75.0	
7 GB	B	31.3	50.0	18.7	50.0	78.6	28.6	50.0	70.0	20.0	40.9	86.4	45.5	83.3	91.7	8.4
8 GS	B	100.0	43.8	-56.2	41.7	57.1	15.4	92.9	60.0	-32.9		9.1			75.0	
	Avg.			*-19.3*			*8.8*			*-2.5*			*31.8*			*12.6*

(b) APCM-2 (last five areas)

3.3 Discussion

The results show that group A (i.e., the subjects that integrated the treatment with virtual reality) has achieved – on average – better performance modifications in almost all areas if compared with group B (see Table 1, "Diff" columns).

By focusing on the children of group A, the subject with the intellectual disability greatly improved his performance, particularly in the area of balance and coordination, as well as hand and finger movements; the subject with a genetic syndrome improved his performance homogeneously in all areas of interest; the child with autism spectrum disorder changed his performance except for the area of dynamic coordination; finally, the subject with motor coordination disorder slightly improved his performance in all areas, except for the graph motor skills and symbolic gestures.

On the other hand, the VMI returns contradictory results (see Table 2, "Diff" columns): group A shows greater improvements for vision, whereas group B has larger improvements regarding motion. A possible explanation for this difference is twofold. First, the motion part investigated in the VMI is only related to motor-graphic skills and – even in the APCM-2 – this area does not show large improvements. Second, the two tests have slightly different executions: the APCM-2 requires a child to make a controlled scribble from right to left, then left

Table 2. Summary of the results regarding the VMI test: for each patient, for the vision and motion abilities, the standardised VMI at the beginning of the study (pre), at the end (post) and the corresponding difference (diff). For each group and ability, the average difference is also reported.

		Vision			Motion		
Subject	Group	Pre	Post	Diff	Pre	Post	Diff
1 RF	A	80	70	-10	102	100	-2
2 PD	A	93	99	6	107	114	7
3 BF	A				60	61	1
4 GD	A	51	85	34	53	61	8
	Avg.			*10*			*3.5*
5 MG	B	75	80	5	91	99	8
6 AR	B				57	60	3
7 GB	B	116	111	-5	53	72	19
8 GS	B	73	85	12	113	107	-6
	Avg.			*4*			*6*

to right; the VMI instead requires a child to draw a shape following a pre-defined path.

From a qualitative point of view, the attitude of all patients in group A changed during the 15 therapies. All patients in the first session approached the instrument as if it were a touch screen technology, whereas, at the end of the treatment, they could interact only through movement (avoiding touching the wall). They were also all capable of self-correction, self-managing and limiting requests for help to the operator. A general reduction was noted regarding motor agitation, especially for the exercises belonging to the "games" and "hunt" categories (see Sect. 2), particularly for the patient with motor coordination disorder. There was also a reduction in verbal and motor stereotypies by the patient with autism spectrum disorder: initially, they appeared very frequently (when he succeeded in the task, when he had difficulties, at the end and the beginning of each exercise); finally, at the end of the treatment, the stereotypies appeared only between the exercises.

However, due to the different pathologies, the sample is small and not homogeneous. Although the two groups included the same number of children with the same type of disability, these two factors represent clear limitations of the study. Moreover, it is also possible that the apparent improvement of the VAMR session in Group A may just be a Hawthorne effect [11].

4 Conclusions

The paper summarised the results of a study regarding the use of a VAMR during rehabilitation in developmental age. The study shows better improvements in children who substituted one traditional session with a VARM-supported one than children who followed the traditional approach. Moreover, qualitative observations confirmed the improvements.

On the other hand, the small number of subjects and the different pathologies of the patients represent clear biases that limit the generalisability of the findings.

Anyway, this study represents further evidence of the possible positive impact of augmented reality in rehabilitation.

The following steps in this research – given these encouraging results – include the extension of the sample and the development of protocols tailored to the specific disabilities, to be revised cyclically in the light of the measured efficacy.

Acknowledgements. The authors thank Dr. Donatella Olivia and the "LARS" rehabilitation centre for their work and support during the VAMR therapy.

References

1. Alrifai, M., Gennari, R., Vittorini, P.: Adapting with evidence: the adaptive model and the stimulation plan of TERENCE. In: International Workshop on Evidence-Based Technology Enhanced Learning. AISC, vol. 152, pp. 75–82 (2012). https://doi.org/10.1007/978-3-642-28801-2_9
2. Bernstein, J.H.: Developmental test of visual motor integration. In: The Corsini Encyclopedia of Psychology, p. 1 (2010). https://doi.org/10.1002/9780470479216.CORPSY0268
3. Di Giacomo, D., et al.: The silent reading supported by adaptive learning technology: influence in the children outcomes. Comput. Hum. Behav. **55** (2016). https://doi.org/10.1016/j.chb.2014.09.053
4. Erdoğan, K., Ceylan, R., Albayrak Gezer, I.: The use of augmented reality in the teaching and training of basic exercises involved in the non-surgical treatment of neck pain. Virtual Real. **27**(1), 481–492 (2023). https://doi.org/10.1007/S10055-022-00739-Y
5. Gil, M.J.V., Gonzalez-Medina, G., Lucena-Anton, D., Perez-Cabezas, V., Del Carmen Ruiz-Molinero, M., Martín-Valero, R.: Augmented reality in physical therapy: systematic review and meta-analysis. JMIR Serious Games **9**(4) (2021), https://doi.org/10.2196/30985
6. Gorman, C., Gustafsson, L.: The use of augmented reality for rehabilitation after stroke: a narrative review. Disability and rehabilitation. Assist. Technol. **17**(4), 1–9 (2022). https://doi.org/10.1080/17483107.2020.1791264
7. Health Quality Ontario: Bilateral cochlear implantation: a health technology assessment. Ontario Health Technol. Assess. Ser. **18**(6), 1–139 (2018). https://pubmed.ncbi.nlm.nih.gov/30443278/
8. Kacmaz, K.S., Kaçmaz, C.: Bibliometric analysis of research in pediatrics related to virtual and augmented reality: a systematic review. Curr. Pediatric Rev. **19** (2023). https://doi.org/10.2174/1573396319666230214103103
9. Karami, B., Koushki, R., Arabgol, F., Rahmani, M., Vahabie, A.H.: Effectiveness of virtual/augmented reality-based therapeutic interventions on individuals with autism spectrum disorder: a comprehensive meta-analysis. Front. Psychiatry **12** (2021). https://doi.org/10.3389/FPSYT.2021.665326
10. Leong, S.C., Tang, Y.M., Toh, F.M., Fong, K.N.: Examining the effectiveness of virtual, augmented, and mixed reality (VAMR) therapy for upper limb recovery and activities of daily living in stroke patients: a systematic review and meta-analysis. J. NeuroEngineering Rehabil. **19**(1) (2022). https://doi.org/10.1186/S12984-022-01071-X

11. McCambridge, J., Witton, J., Elbourne, D.R.: Systematic review of the Hawthorne effect: new concepts are needed to study research participation effects. J. Clin. Epidemiol. **67**(3), 267–277 (2014). https://doi.org/10.1016/J.JCLINEPI.2013.08.015
12. Nekar, D.M., et al.: Effects of augmented reality game-based cognitive-motor training on restricted and repetitive behaviors and executive function in patients with autism spectrum disorder. Healthcare (Switzerland) **10**(10), 1981 (2022). https://doi.org/10.3390/HEALTHCARE10101981/S1
13. Pereira, M.F., Prahm, C., Kolbenschlag, J., Oliveira, E., Rodrigues, N.F.: Application of AR and VR in hand rehabilitation: a systematic review. J. Biomed. Inform. **111** (2020). https://doi.org/10.1016/J.JBI.2020.103584
14. Phan, H.L., Le, T.H., Lim, J.M., Hwang, C.H., Koo, K.I.: Effectiveness of augmented reality in stroke rehabilitation: a meta-analysis. Appl. Sci. (Switzerland) **12**(4) (2022). https://doi.org/10.3390/APP12041848
15. Radianti, J., Majchrzak, T.A., Fromm, J., Wohlgenannt, I.: A systematic review of immersive virtual reality applications for higher education: design elements, lessons learned, and research agenda. Comput. Educ. **147** (2020). https://doi.org/10.1016/J.COMPEDU.2019.103778
16. Ren, X., Wu, Q., Cui, N., Zhao, J., Bi, H.Y.: Effectiveness of digital game-based trainings in children with neurodevelopmental disorders: a meta-analysis. Res. Dev. Disab. **133** (2023). https://doi.org/10.1016/J.RIDD.2022.104418
17. Romero-Ayuso, D., et al.: Effectiveness of virtual reality-based interventions for children and adolescents with ADHD: a systematic review and meta-analysis. Children **8**(2) (2021). https://doi.org/10.3390/CHILDREN8020070
18. Sabbadini, L.: APCM-2 - Abilità Prassiche e della Coordinazione Motoria - 2a Edizione. Hogrefe (2015)
19. Stander, J., et al.: Effect of virtual reality therapy, combined with physiotherapy for improving motor proficiency in individuals with down syndrome: a systematic review. South Afr. J. Physiother. **77**(1) (2021). https://doi.org/10.4102/SAJP.V77I1.1516
20. van de Wouw, C.L., Visser, M., Gorter, J.W., Huygelier, H., Nijboer, T.: Systematic review of the effectiveness of innovative, gamified interventions for cognitive training in paediatric acquired brain injury. Neuropsychol. Rehabil. 1–32 (2023). https://doi.org/10.1080/09602011.2023.2174561
21. Wuang, Y.P., et al.: Effectiveness of kinesthetic game-based training system in children with visual-perceptual dysfunction. IEEE Access **9**, 153838–153849 (2021). https://doi.org/10.1109/ACCESS.2021.3128109

Oriented Classroom Instructional Behavior Recognition Benchmark

Muxin Xu, Yingshan Shen(✉), Sizhu Wang, and Xiaofeng Yuan

South China Normal University, Guangzhou 510631, China
shenyingshan@scnu.edu.cn

Abstract. Classroom instruction behavior analysis is one of the effective methods to optimize methods and designs of classroom teaching, improving the quality and efficiency of classroom instruction, and enriching the practical knowledge of teachers. With the continuous breakthroughs in artificial intelligence technology, there is a growing body of research on instructional behavior analysis. Instruction behavior recognition algorithms face great challenges due to the lack of appropriate datasets as data support. Therefore, in this paper, we propose a dataset CIBR for classroom instructional behavior recognition. The dataset is based on real classroom teaching videos from primary and secondary schools, covering 14 instructional behaviors, with a total of 2, 380 video samples. We evaluated our CIBR dataset on five commonly used behavior recognition models, namely 3D-RESnet 50, I3D, R (2 + 1) D-RGB, S3D and Timesformer, and compared it with the mainstream behavior recognition datasets UCF101 and HMDB51. The results show that the CIBR dataset is reliable, feasible, and effective. The creation of the CIBR dataset provides a data base for AI techniques to automatically identify and analyze the behavior of teachers and students in primary and secondary schools.

Keywords: Classroom instructional behavior · CIBR Dataset · Behavior recognition

1 Introduction

In recent years, artificial intelligence and deep learning have made breakthroughs and have become the focus of public attention [1]. As one of the most important research directions in artificial intelligence, computer vision has gained a wide range of applications, such as image classification, image segmentation, video behavior recognition, and video description. Datasets are important for deep learning research, and some classical datasets are widely used, such as UCF101 [2], Kinetics [3], ActivityNet [4], AVA [5], etc. Some specific datasets have also been applied in different fields, such as MultiSports [6], which helps in sports research, and Distracted Driver Detection [7], which detects the driver's state. However, education-related datasets are still lacking. And, due to the complexity and specificity of classroom environments, it is difficult to achieve good results using classical datasets. Therefore, we construct a dataset of teacher and student behavior in a realistic teaching scenario.

Z. Kubincová et al. (Eds.): SETE 2023, LNCS 14606, pp. 130–141, 2024.
https://doi.org/10.1007/978-981-97-4243-1_11

Currently, there is no consensus on the definition of classroom instruction behavior in the field of instruction behavior research. Since teachers and students are the composite subjects of teaching activities, and the definition of instruction behavior by experts and scholars is summarized through research, we believe that classroom instruction behavior is the sum of teachers' teaching, students' learning and other related behaviors shown by teachers and students to achieve common teaching goals in the classroom environment [8]. The classroom instruction behavior includes the instruction behavior of the teacher and the learning behavior of the student, which is the primary representation of classroom teaching. The quality of classroom instruction behavior is directly related to the effectiveness of classroom instruction behavior analysis and research, which is one of the effective ways to improve classroom teaching quality. Classroom instruction behavior analysis is one of the effective ways to improve the objectivity of teaching evaluation, optimize classroom teaching methods and designs, improve the quality and efficiency of classroom teaching, enrich the practical knowledge of teachers, and serve as a reference for teacher behavior improvement and teacher training. Through the observation and analysis of classroom instruction behavior, teaching can be improved, and the professional skills and classroom quality of teachers can be enhanced.

Instruction behavior recognition algorithms face great challenges due to the lack of proper datasets as data support. In recent years, a growing number of scholars have started to study instruction behavior datasets. Most existing instruction behavior datasets are used to study the behavior and state of college students in the classroom. Since there is a big difference between middle and primary school students and college students' behavior in class, and the datasets of college students' behavior in class only contain students' behavior, it is impossible to evaluate and determine the influence of teachers' behavior in class on students by using data sets. Most of the existing datasets of instruction behavior in primary and secondary schools only focus on teacher behavior, which will split the integrity of classroom teaching. A small number of primary and secondary instruction behavior datasets include teacher behavior and student behavior, but some of the selected action categories in these datasets are not consistent with the reality of primary and secondary school classrooms. Therefore, the existing datasets on instruction behavior have certain limitations for us to study the behavior of teachers and students in primary and secondary schools.

In this study, we built a dataset for classroom instruction behavior recognition (CIBR). Based on real classroom teaching videos, we build a dataset of classroom instruction behaviors specifically for primary and secondary schools. It covers 14 kinds of behaviors, including teacher teaching, students answering questions, teacher touring, teacher asking questions, teacher-student interaction, students presenting on stage, students raising hands, teacher writing on the blackboard, students listening, students reading and writing, teacher pasting the teaching aids, students group activities, teacher displaying the teaching aids, and teacher operating the whiteboard, with a total of 2380 samples. To understand the impact of teacher teaching behavior on student learning, we collected classroom teacher and student behaviors in primary and secondary schools to make the CIBR dataset more comprehensive. The CIBR dataset includes teacher behavior, student behavior, teacher-student interaction, and student group behavior. Make the dataset richer in behavior types.

The rest of the paper is organized as follows: Sect. 2 describes the construction process of the CIBR dataset and the analysis of the CIBR dataset. Section 3 presents the CIBR dataset correlation experiments and analyzes the results. Section 4 summarizes our work and future research directions.

2 Data Processing and Analysis

In this section, we mainly introduce CIBR process of the construction of the data sets, including the determination of behavior category original video acquisition, data set behavior recognition and data set of samples. Figure 1 shows the construction flow chart of the CIBR dataset.

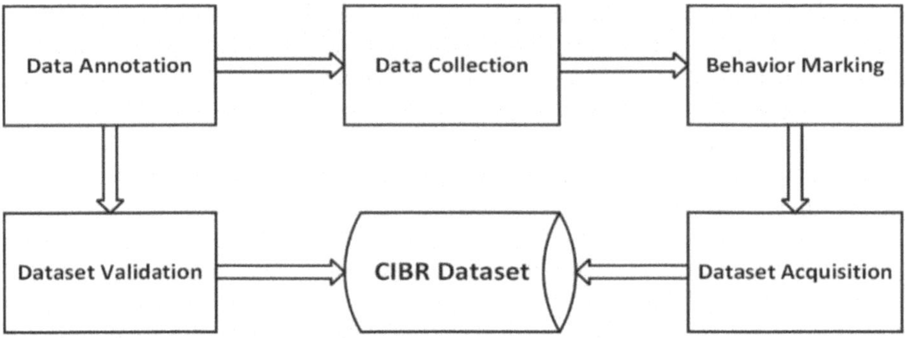

Fig. 1. The flowchart of CIBR dataset construction

2.1 Data Annotation

We use the improved S-T analysis method to classify the behavior of teachers and students [9]. Finally, 14 behavioral categories were identified.

We first obtained reasonable label vocabularies by reading the Teacher Code of Conduct and related literature. In addition, seven typical teacher behaviors were finally identified by observing videos of real teacher classes. With the rapid development of modern information technology, multimedia technology is also widely used in primary and secondary school classrooms. Using multimedia techniques, abstract and difficult knowledge points can be brought to life in front of students, effectively reducing the difficulty of learning a course and increasing the interest of students. Therefore, we add teacher operating the whiteboard into the teacher's behavior category. Questioning is an important means of teaching. In the classroom, teachers can guide students to systematic thinking under the guidance of question orientation, thereby improving the efficiency and quality of teaching. Therefore, we add the behavior category of teacher asking questions into the teacher behavior. Through classroom inspection, teachers can timely learn about the learning status of students, enhance emotional communication between teachers and students, identify deficiencies in classroom instruction, and adjust teaching strategies in a timely manner. In a quality class, appropriate classroom patrol is necessary, so we chose the behavior category of teacher touring. When explaining some abstract and difficult teaching difficulties, teachers can use teaching aids to motivate students to learn, improve teaching methods and improve the quality of education and teaching. Teaching aids is an effective way to convey teaching information. Therefore, we added two categories of teacher behavior, teacher displaying the teaching aids and teacher pasting the teaching aids. In addition, we select three categories of teacher behavior: teacher teaching, teacher touring, and teacher writing on the blackboard.

Since the behavior of students in primary and secondary schools can be spontaneous, many types of student behavior can be observed in the classroom. By answering questions, students can gain a deeper understanding of the points of knowledge, and they can also more easily accept the class, absorb the class and improve their concentration. Therefore, we added the two behaviors of students raising hands and students answering questions into the students' behaviors. Through student presentations, a positive and harmonious atmosphere is presented in the classroom. Students can effectively interact with each other and truly realize the purpose of mutual uplift and mutual promotion. Therefore, we have added this behavior category to the student behavior. Group cooperative learning is widely used in classroom teaching in primary and secondary schools. During group activities, students not only consolidate basic knowledge, but also cultivate student learning ability and a sense of cooperation, which then increases learning efficiency. Therefore, we chose the students group activities. Besides, we also add students listening, students reading and writing as students' classroom behavior.

Under the background of the new curriculum reform, the classroom teaching of primary and secondary schools has been greatly improved, and the teacher-student interactive teaching mode has been widely used in the classroom, which solves the problems of passive learning and low learning efficiency brought by the traditional teaching methods and can also promote the friendship between teachers and students in a sense. In the classroom, proper teacher-student interaction can help students better understand what they are learning, as well as give teachers an idea of how well students have mastered it, so that they can better carry out the teaching that follows. Therefore, teacher-student interaction is necessary in the classroom. In this dataset, we added the behavior category of teacher-student interaction.

Figure 2 shows 14 kinds of instruction behaviors selected from the CIBR dataset.

2.2 Data Collection

We obtained the original videos of the CIBR dataset from the National Public Service Platform for Educational Resources and the Guangdong Public Service Platform of Educational Resources. Teaching videos on these educational resources and public service platforms are publicly available. We reviewed nearly 10,000 instructional videos uploaded by teachers and selected those that fit the requirements. Chinese, mathematics and English are compulsory subjects for primary and middle school students, science is the best subject to foster good habits of inquiry in students. Therefore, we chose Chinese, Mathematics, English, and Science as the four subjects to study. Due to the small range of behaviors generated by lower grade students, they are not easy to identify, so in the grade selection, we selected grades 3 and above. We selected ministerial-level excellent

Fig. 2. Fourteen behavior categories in the CIBR dataset. (From top to bottom, actions are teacher teaching, students answering questions, teacher touring, teacher asking questions, teacher-student interaction, students presenting on stage, students raising hands, teacher writing on the blackboard, students listening, students reading and writing, teacher pasting the teaching aids, students' group activities, teacher displaying the teaching aids, teacher operating the whiteboard).

course transcripts with 5.0 scores and more than 10,000 page views. For each video, we download the class video in high definition such as 1080p etc. After downloading, cut each class video into several 5-min short videos to facilitate subsequent annotation. Table 1 shows some of the selected quality courses.

Table 1. The information of some of the selected quality courses.

Title	Teacher	Province	Subject	Grade	Duration
Baihuayuan	Liu Xiaohong	Liaoning	Chinese	3	40′04″
Junquan Heizi	Gu Min	Guangdong	Chinese	6	40′29″
How big is 100 million	Zhao Huan	Liaoning	Mathematics	4	35′58″
What can you do?	Pan Xianxia	Anhui	English	5	39′05″
Family of energies	Guan Han	Chongqing	Science	6	37′38″

2.3 Behavior Marking

After the generation of behavior labels, we obtain the instruction behavior dataset by performing behavioral labeling on videos. The taggers manually annotated the teacher and student actions and the temporal information occurring in the videos to be tagged. The label information consists mainly of participant, behavioral category, and behavioral time information. Based on the labeled information, the videos were cropped to obtain samples of teacher and student behavior. The detailed workflow is described below.

First, we numbered the original videos and distributed them to three qualified taggers for tagging. They watched videos of teachers in their classes and recorded 14 types of teachers and student behavior in the videos. Since the objects studied in this data set are teachers and classmates, the teachers and classmates may appear in the picture together at the same time, and the behaviors of students can be divided into single behaviors and multiple behaviors, so it is necessary to indicate the marking objects in the marking. We also need to label how many frames the behavior starts in the video and how many frames it ends in. Then, based on the label information, the original video is cropped using a video clipping tool to obtain samples of teacher and student behavior.

During the labeling process, the labels of each sample contain seven pieces of information, which are: dataset code, video number, behavior participant, behavior category code, behavior number, start frame number and end frame number. For example, in the class video numbered LiYing-UpandDown-1, the teacher asks questions to the students at frames 1139 to 1152, which is the 48th sample of questions to the students. Thus, it is labeled I_LiYing-UpandDown-1_1T_taq_0048_01139_01152. In the SunYing-PaperProducts-2 classroom video, several students have group discussions in frames 9291 to 9329, which is the 17th sample of group discussions. Hence, the label I_SunYing-PaperProducts-2_Ns_sga_0017_09291_09329.

3 Experiments and Analysis

3.1 Dataset Splits

Following the current popular dataset partitioning method, we randomly partition the dataset into training, validation, and test sets according to the 4:1:1 ratio. Table 4 shows the specific number of samples after division. Specifically, the number of sample videos in the training set is 1586, the number of samples in the verification set and the number of samples in the test set are 397.

3.2 Model and Setting

Five models, 3D-Resnet50 [10], I3D [11], R (2 + 1) D-RGB [12], S3D [13] and Timesformer [14], were used to conduct experiments on the CIBR dataset. All networks use the Cross Entropy Loss function and a numerical random gradient descent (SGD) optimizer, with weight attenuation and momentum set to 0.001 and 0.9, respectively. All networks were trained for 100 iterations with an initial learning rate of 0.003. After 10 consecutive iterations, the learning rate is updated when validation losses are no longer decreasing. In this study, 16 consecutive frames were extracted from each video as input, and the size of the original video frame was adjusted to 224 $\times$ 224. In addition, in this paper, data augmentation is performed by random horizontal flipping. Finally, the values of the RGB image three channels were normalized and the data were sorted into the interval [–1,1], and the frames*3*224*224 input were obtained. The difficulty of network training is further reduced by the above steps. Finally, the PyTorch framework is used to train the network under an Nvidia GTX 1080Ti GPU.

3.3 Evaluation and Analysis

Validation Accuracy for Each Behavior Category. We evaluated the performance of each behavior category of CIBR by using the R (2 + 1) D-RGB behavior recognition model. Figure 3 shows the validation accuracy for each behavior category. Most of the behavior categories are up to 70% accurate. Of these, the accuracy of the categories of behavior shown by students on stage and by students listening to lectures was as high as 100%. The accuracy of showing teaching AIDS, students raising hands, students group activities, teacher-student interaction, students answering questions, teachers walking around, students reading and writing, pasting teaching AIDS and teachers teaching all reached more than 80%. However, the teacher asking questions accuracy was only 39.29%. The confusion matrix in Fig. 4 shows the ambiguity between teacher asking questions, teacher teaching and students raising hands, resulting in low verification accuracy. In a real class, the teacher asking questions and the students raising hands are accompanied by each other, and the two behaviors are mutual. In the sample, we can also find cases of students raising their hands in the sample of teachers asking questions. Because the teacher stands at the front of the room while asking questions and teaching, and does not move around, only the hand changes. However, due to the camera shooting Angle, the behavior is blocked and for other reasons, the R (2 + 1) D-RGB model cannot accurately classify them.

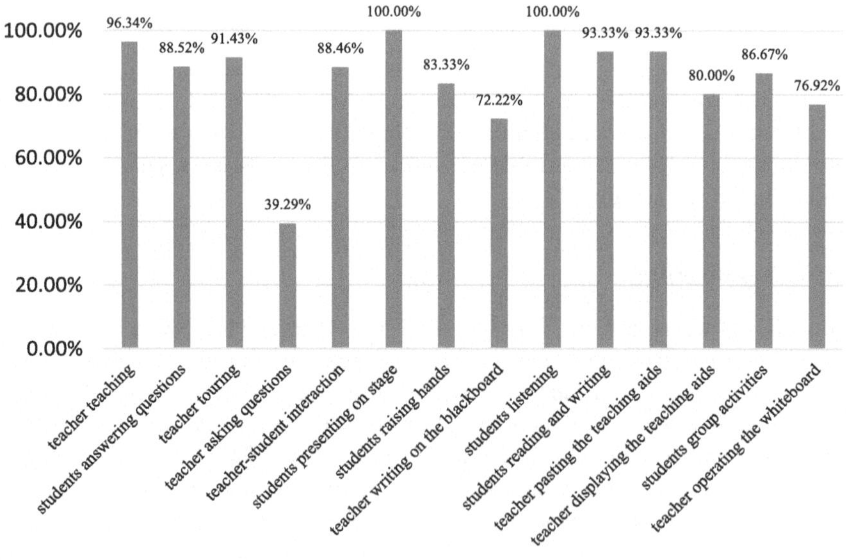

Fig. 3. The Validation accuracy for each behavior category

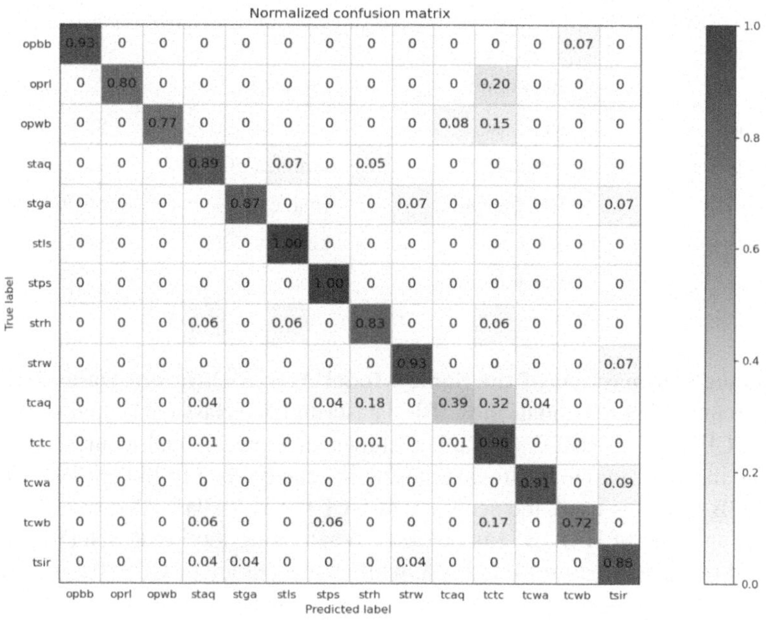

Fig. 4. The confusion matrix

Performance Comparison of Each Model on CIBR Dataset. Table 2 shows the performance comparison of the models on the CIBR dataset. As can be seen from the table, the accuracy rate of both R (2 + 1) D-RGB model and Timesformer model reaches more than 80%, which are 84.17% and 82.67% respectively. Although the accuracy of 3D-ResNet50 model and S3D model is not as high as that of R (2 + 1) D-RGB model and Timesformer model, it still reaches more than 75%, which are 77.33% and 76.35% respectively. The I3D model had the lowest accuracy of 66.70%. We analyze the performance results. First, in the domain of behavior recognition, 2D CNNs have shown promising results on single-frame videos. R (2 + 1) D-RGB model refers to the decomposition of 3D convolution into a 2D spatial convolution and a 1D time convolution, which will not only improve the nonlinear ability of the network but also significantly improve the accuracy. The Timesformer model is based on the self-attention mechanism in Transformer, allowing it to capture the temporal and spatial dependencies of the entire video. Therefore, Timesformer has greater learning power and higher accuracy compared to modern 3D convolutional neural networks. Because the I3D, S3D and 3D-Resnet50 models all use a 3D convolution kernel to extract features. The 3D convolution operation can extract spatial and temporal features from video data for behavior recognition, thus capturing motion information in video streams. However, because the classroom environment limits the behavior of teachers and students, the range of behavior change, and movement of teachers and students is small. We believe that the time factor is not important for accurate behavior recognition in the CIBR dataset. Therefore, the performance of R (2 + 1) D-RGB model and Timesformer model is superior to 3D-ResNet50, S3D, and I3D.

Table 2. Performance comparison of each model in CIBR dataset.

Methods	Backbone	Pre-train	Accuracy
Timesformer	ViT-base	kinetics-600	82.67%
3D-ResNet50	ResNet50	kinetics-700	77.33%
I3D	BN-Inception	Imagenet	66.70%
R (2 + 1) D-RGB	R3D-34	kinetics-700	84.17%
S3D	BN-Inception	None	76.35%

Performance Comparison of the Same Model Across Different Datasets. We use three different models to validate the CIBR dataset and two classical behavior recognition datasets, UCF101 and HMDB51. Table 3 shows the experimental results for the CIBR dataset and the other two mainstream datasets. As can be seen from the table, when R (2 + 1) D-RGB model is used, the accuracy of UCF101 is 88.94%, that of CIBR data set is 84.17%, and that of HMDB51 is 60.58%. When using the 3D-ResNet50 model, the accuracy of the CIBR dataset is 77.33%, while the accuracy of UCF101 and HMDB is 83.63% and 59.69%, respectively. When using the I3D model, the accuracy of UCF101 is 83.57%, CIBR dataset is 66.70% and HMDB51 is 54.59%. The results show that the CIBR dataset is feasible and efficient, and the existing algorithms can adapt well to the CIBR dataset.

Table 3. Performance comparison of the same model among different datasets.

Methods	Dataset		
	UCF101	CIBR	HMDB51
R (2 + 1) D-RGB	88.94%	84.17%	60.58%
3D-ResNet50	83.63%	77.33%	59.69%
I3D	83.57%	66.70%	54.59%

3.4 Discussion

Through the results obtained by the selected models, we can find that the average accuracy of each behavior category of the CIBR dataset is higher than the accuracy of the dataset. Next, we discuss the factors that may influence our experiments and propose corresponding solutions.

Objective Factors Influencing Experimental Results. Due to the particularity and complexity of teaching research scenarios, there are great challenges for the analysis of teaching behavior. First of all, in the real classroom, the number of students in each class is large. For example, there are 48 students in Chen Jiahui's "Watching Cattle Race in

Snow Plateau" class. For this case, it is very difficult to identify and detect. Secondly, in the classroom teaching process, there are many kinds of teaching behaviors coexisting, which brings great challenges for subsequent analysis and identification. Finally, in order not to disturb the state of teachers and students in class, the fixed position of the camera makes the size of students sitting in different positions very different, and even the behavior of some teachers and students will be occluded, which is not conducive to the subsequent recognition and analysis of teaching behavior.

In view of the above challenges, we can appropriately place more cameras in different positions without affecting teaching activities, so that the behaviors of teachers and students cannot be blocked as far as possible, and the teaching behaviors can be shown from different angles.

Subjective Factors Affecting Experimental Results. In the labeling process, we found that there were some deviations in the judgment of teaching behaviors when each person faced with the coexistence of multiple teaching behaviors, which led to the fact that there may be multiple sample videos with the same or similar scenes in the dataset and they were stored in different behavior categories. During the experiment, we found that the CIBR dataset has the problem of uneven sample distribution, which has a large impact on the recognition accuracy.

Therefore, when multiple teaching behaviors coexist, we use the judgment of the behavior in the improved S-T analysis method. If the teacher behavior is dominant in the sample, the sample will be divided into teacher behavior. If student behavior dominates the sample, the sample is classified as student behavior. If there is a dialogue between teachers and students, it is considered as teacher-student interaction. If none of them can be determined, the sample video is discarded. We will also continue to supplement the sample size to solve the problem of uneven sample distribution.

Technical Factors Influencing Experimental Results. By analyzing the selected models, we believe that there are several reasons that affect the experimental results. Firstly, since most of the actions we selected are persistent, randomly selecting 16 frames from each sample as input can greatly save resource utilization while ensuring that most of the actions are selected. This also carries the risk of individual actions not being selected. Secondly, we should note that due to the ambiguity between teacher questioning, teacher teaching, and student hand raising, the selected model cannot be accurately identified, resulting in a low validation accuracy. Finally, due to the complexity and comprehensiveness of classroom teaching, teachers, and students in the teaching process not only through movement, but also use a large number of languages, words and other ways to express, communicate and exchange. We only used the video data modality as input in the feature extraction process, and its information source is relatively single, which may lack key information to judge the behavior category.

In the follow-up research, we will use the object detection algorithm to determine the participants of the behavior, and then use the trained model to fine-tune the training, correct the parameters of the teacher's questions and the teacher's teaching judgment basis, and take all frames of the sample as input to participate in the training. Multi-modal learning can aggregate the information of multi-source data, making the representation learned by the model more complete. We will also try to integrate the teaching behavior video with the text and so on to improve the recognition accuracy.

4 Conclusion and Future Research

In this study, we construct a primary and secondary school classroom instruction behavior dataset called CIBR, which mainly contains 14 common classroom instruction behaviors with a total of 2, 380 samples. First, we obtained the original videos of the dataset from the National Public Service Platform for Educational Resources and the Guangdong Public Service Platform of Educational Resources. Then, we used the modified S-T analysis method to classify the behaviors of teachers and students, and finally identified 14 instruction behavior categories, such as teacher teaching, students answering questions, teacher touring, teacher asking questions, teacher-student interaction, students presenting on stage, students raising hands, teacher writing on the blackboard, students listening, students reading and writing, teacher pasting the teaching aids, students group activities, teacher displaying the teaching aids, and teacher operating the whiteboard. Subsequently, we label the videos with instruction behavior to obtain instruction behavior dataset. Finally, we evaluate our CIBR dataset on five commonly used behavior recognition models, 3D-Resnet50, I3D, R (2 + 1) D-RGB, S3D, and Timesformer, and through qualitative and quantitative analysis, the results show that the CIBR dataset achieves the best results among the five models on R (2 + 1) D-RGB with an accuracy rate of 84.17%. The results support the reliability of the CIBR dataset. The three models, 3D-Resnet50, I3D, and R (2 + 1) D-RGB, are also used to compare with two other mainstream behavior recognition datasets, UCF101 and HMDB51, and the results show that the CIBR dataset is feasible and effective, and the existing algorithms can be better adapted to the CIBR dataset. The establishment of the CIBR dataset provides a data basis for automatic identification and analysis of instruction behavior in the classroom through artificial intelligence techniques, thereby effectively reducing the cost of instruction behavior research using traditional methods such as questionnaire surveys and interviews.

Our plan for future research is described as follows: we will use CIBR as a data base and actively investigate an algorithm that can be used to assess excellence in primary and secondary schools, and therefore apply it to improve the quality of education. In addition, we will also investigate the commonality of classroom behavior between college students and primary and middle school students in the future, and create a dataset of classroom behavior with applicability, universality, and consensus.

References

1. Bertasius, G., wang, H., Torresani, L.: Is space-time attention all you need for video understanding? In: International Conference on Machine Learning (2021)
2. Carreira, J., Zisserman, A.: Quo vadis, action recognition? A new model and the kinetics dataset. In: 2017 IEEE Conference on Computer Vision and Pattern Recognition (CVPR), pp. 4724–4733 (2017). https://doi.org/10.1109/CVPR.2017.502

3. Gu, C., et al.: Ava: a video dataset of patio-temporally localized atomic visual actions. In: 2018 IEEE/CVF Conference on Computer Vision and Pattern Recognition, pp. 6047–6056 (2018). https://doi.org/10.1109/CVPR.2018.00633
4. Hara, k., Kataoka, H., Satoh, Y.: Can spatiotemporal 3d CNNs retrace the history of 2d CNNs and ImageNet? In: 2018 IEEE/CVF Conference on Computer Vision and Pattern Recognition, pp. 6546–6555 (2018). https://doi.org/10.1109/CVPR.2018.00685
5. Hassan, S.A., Akbar, S., Rehman, A., Saba, T., koliva, H., Bahaj, S.A.: Recent developments in detection of central serous retinopathy through imaging and artificial intelligence techniques-a review. IEEE Access **9**, 168731–168748 (2021). https://doi.org/10.1109/ACCESS.2021.3108395
6. Heilbron, F.C., Escorcia, V., Ghanem, B., Niebles, J.C.: Activitynet: a large- scale video benchmark for human activity understanding. In: 2015 IEEE Conference on Computer Vision and Pattern Recognition (CVPR), pp. 961–970 (2015). https://doi.org/10.1109/CVPR.2015.7298698
7. kay, w., et al.: The kinetics human action video dataset. Arxiv abs/1705.06950 (2017)
8. Kim, w., Choi, H.k., Jang, B.T., Lim, J.: Driver distraction detection using single convolutional neural network. In: 2017 International Conference on Information and Communication Technology Convergence (ICTC), pp. 1203–1205 (2017). https://doi.org/10.1109/ICTC.2017.8190898
9. Kuehne, H., Jhuang, H., Garrote, E., Poggio, T., Serre, T.: HMDB: a large video database for human motion recognition. In: 2011 International Conference on Computer Vision, pp. 2556–2563 (2011). https://doi.org/10.1109/IccV.2011.6126543
10. Li, Y., Chen, L., He, R., wang, Z., Wu, G., wang, L.: Multisports: a multi- person video dataset of spatio-temporally localized sports actions. In: 2021 IEEE/cVF International Conference on Computer Vision (ICCV), pp. 13516–13525 (2021)
11. Lin, Z., Xu, L.: Recognition of the research on teachers, behavior. Teach. Educ. Res. **2**, 23–26 (2006)
12. Soomrom, K., Zamir, A.R., Shah, M.: ucf101: a dataset of 101 human actions classes from videos in the wild. arxiv https://arxiv.org/abs/1212.0402 (2012)
13. Xie, S., Sun, C., Huang, J., Tu, Z., Murphy, K.P.: Rethinking spatiotemporal feature learning: speed-accuracy tradeoffs in video classification. In: European Conference on Computer Vision (2017)
14. Xue, X.: Application of s-t analysis method in teaching. Jiangsu Educ. Res. **29**, 4–8 (2019)

An Approach to Teach Text Analysis to Digital Humanists, a Qualitative Evaluation

Silvia Baldiris[1](✉), Jorge Cahiotis[2], and González Almarcha Patricia[3]

[1] Fundación Universitaria Tecnológico Comfenalco, Sede C Barrio Zaragocilla, Cartagena de Indias, Colombia
sbaldiris@tecnologicocomfenalco.edu.co

[2] Universidad Nacional de Colombia, Oficina Nacional de Gestión y Patrimonio Documental, Bogotá, Colombia
jcachiotis@unal.edu.co

[3] Universidad Complutense de Madrid, Madrid, Spain
glykofilussa@gmail.com

Abstract. Students from Digital humanities frequently face big challenges while they learn technically-based topics as text analysis due they never had practiced programming before. In this paper, we introduce an approach to facilitate teachers to teach text analysis using R to Digital Humanists. The manuscript provides qualitative results from an exploratory research study that show students obtain good result following the approach guidelines.

Keywords: R language · text analysis · digital humanities · teaching R · qualitative analysis

1 Introduction

Digital humanities have become an enthusiastic growing research area with a wide range of related topics, such as literature, music, heritage, etc. that promise to bring citizens closer to the different kind of heritage goods. In this context, text analysis become a novel technique with the capacity to discover knowledge in a hug amount of literature from different ages, contexts or authors. However, text analysis demands specific technical skills in humanists to be able to take text mining into their own hands to exploit it properly [1].

Teaching a programming language to non-programmers as humanists is really challenging and although R is recognized as an effective statistical computing and graphics software, because it is powerful, flexible, and open source, its teaching is not an easy task. In fact, when reflecting regarding their teaching practices, teacher that teach data analysis using R frequently argue on the following difficulties [2, 3]: 1) R have a steeper learning curve compared to some other commercially available software such as IBM SPSS Statistics (SPSS), STATA, and Microsoft Excel (Excel); 2) R is not considered beginner-friendly, being this one of the most important reasons due undergraduate students are not often taught R [4]; 3) "the syntax of R can be difficult for students to acquire, and students often report that they spend many hours debugging simple problems" [5].

Z. Kubincová et al. (Eds.): SETE 2023, LNCS 14606, pp. 142–154, 2024.
https://doi.org/10.1007/978-981-97-4243-1_12

On the other hand, data analysis for digital humanists should be focused more on interpretation than in the use of a tool or formulas, and sometimes teaching practices fails on achieving a real intertwined of the concepts, formulas, and data analysis procedures. As a result, "the knowledge students are left with at the end of the course does not easily transfer to new situations" [6, 7].

In same line, Books as A new companion to Digital Humanities reflects the big academic literature with a big range of topics which represent digital humanities [8], however, as argue by Hirsch et al. [9], the gap between the available literature on pedagogy and research on the ground is, paradoxically, widening. To close the gap, more research is needed to consolidate efforts regarding how to offer students a satisfactory educational experience not only on text analysis but also on the different braches of digital humanities.

In this study, we introduce our approach to support learning when student from Digital humanities learn text analysis using R, that include peer-review of the code their partners generate to solve concrete and real problems. Reviewing code by a peer could benefit students in both, learning the tool functionalities but also emphasizing in the data interpretation [10], as well, feedback could be more effective if more attention is given to the social situations within which feedback is offered and received [11].

Previous results of the approach implementation was report in the study Peer-Review to Support Teaching Text Analysis to Digital Humanists Using R [12]. However, evaluation in the mentioned publication was focused on a quantitative analysis based on the score achieved by the students. In this manuscript, a qualitative evaluation is presented in detail providing evidence regarding the process follow by the students more than in the resulting score.

This manuscript is structured as follow. Second section, describe the approach to qualitative content analysis of literary text. Third section describe the evaluation carried out, while Sect. 4 describes the conclusions and future work.

2 An Approach to Quantitative Content Analysis of Literary Texts

This study is focused on the activity named Quantitative Content Analysis of Literary Texts. The activity proposes students to develop a content analysis using R to response previously defined questions with respect to selected literature. The activity evaluate the knowledge and skills acquire by the students in the use of basic R functions to analyse long text but also the skills acquire for the construction of scatter plots in R, as techniques to visualize text analysis.

Students should follow the next elaboration guidelines:

- Select a text of the students' interest from the Project Gutenberg portal.
- Define interesting questions to be answered by the text analysis of the literature.
- Select words to support the analysis, indicating why the chosen words are relevant to your analysis.
- To build scatter plots in R to visualize the behaviour of the words choose from the text.
- Interpret the obtained results of the text analysis.

Once students have develop the activity, a peer review activity take place, in the following way:

- The teacher assign to each students the solution of the activity from two partners. It means each student review the work of two colleagues.
- Each student review the activity of the partners, following a specific rubric, and providing comments in each evaluation criteria.
- The reviewer assign a score to the partner according with the analysis carried out based on the rubric.
- The review provide by each student is sent to the student who developed the activity.
- Students use the feedback provide by their partner to improve their work.
- The professor also review the work done by each student and assign a score.
- Finally, students were asked to fill out a survey with the purpose to analyse their perception regarding the activity and its results.

3 Evaluation

Evaluation was focused on the analysis of some cases study to observe the efficacy of the approach to guide a text analysis using R by students.

3.1 Participants

Participants in the intervention were 17 students which were enrolled in the Master's Degree in Digital Humanities from The international university of La Rioja during the courses 21/22. Table 1 show the sample's distribution by gender, showing a remarkable tendency to woman participants.

Table 1. Sample by Gender

	Frequency	%
Man	4	
Woman	13	
Total	17	

During the course, the teacher use the instrument by Pascual et al. [13] to measure the self-perception of the participants regarding their digital competences.

The questionnaire consist of 5 dimensions that refer to competences in five areas, Information and data literacy, Communication and collaboration, Digital content creation, Safety and Problem solving.

Figure 1 shows the results obtained regarding the students perception of their programming competence, competence of special interest for the present study.

Results show a low level of programming according to the students' perception of their own programming skills.

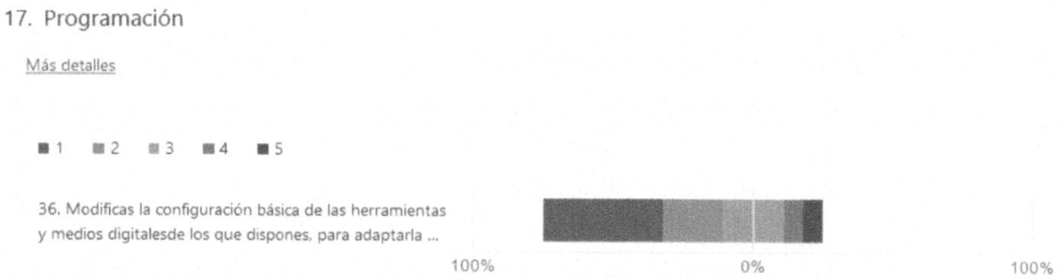

Fig. 1. Results of Programming competences according to DigCom Instrument.

3.2 Method

The steps follow for this study were:

1. The first action of the teacher was to carry out a quantitative analysis considering the text Moby Dick by Herman Melville [14], visualizing different words of the novel through dispersion plots using R. Simultaneously, the students followed the instructions, on their computer. It allowed them to acquire the competences to develop their own quantitative analysis as proposed in the activity described in Sect. 3.
2. Students carried out their own quantitative analysis as proposed in the activity during three weeks following the approach. Teacher was able to help and guide the students when doubts emerged.
3. Next, students carried out the peer review of two partners.

3.3 Instruments

Two works carried out by the students were analysed as cases studies, evaluating their consistency in following the methodology and the quality of the achieved analysis. The analysis allow us to identify if it was possible by the students to carry out the process following the approach as well as to provide insights regarding the quality of the achieved analysis.

3.4 Case Studies Analysis

In this section, we described two qualitative description of the work done by two individual participating in this study.

Crime and Punishment
Text selection

The student selected the plain text version of the work "Crime and Punishment" by Fiódor Dostoyevski, translated into Spanish by Pedro Pedraza y Páez, taken from the Gutenberg project [15]. Students used this portal because the files of the literary texts contain both the literature and the metadata.

Question definition

The student used the literary analysis proposed by Wikipedia, which states that in "Crime and Punishment", the author creates a complete chaos in the mind of the protagonist Raskolnikoff, due to his financial situation. This chaos worsens at the moment when the protagonist commits the crime by murdering an old woman[1]. The student's intention was to validate the argument found in Wikipedia through a quantitative textual analysis using R, analyzing words that could give clues about of the mental chaos and the feelings the protagonist was living in this novel.

Selection of words for analysis, indicating why they are relevant

Table 2 shows the list of word selected by the student for analysis.

Table 2. Words selected by the student regarding Crime and Punishment

Word	Relevance
"No"	The student proposed that the repeated presence of this adverb represents the protagonist's guilt before, during and after committing the crime. The scatterplots in Fig. 1 show that the word "no" is recurrent throughout the novel. It is the only word in which the scatter diagram appears almost 100% in black, which shows that it is one of the most important words for quantitative analysis
"Doubt"	By relating this word to the adverb of negation, the student explores the protagonist's hesitation when planning, carrying out and denouncing the crime committed. In addition, he proposes that it represents insecurity, the confrontation between good and evil, and the uncertainty of wanting to justify the murder. He also states that it is like a feeling of guilt that alters the mood of the protagonist, (see Fig. 2.) The word "doubt" allows a first approach to the analysis of feelings from a qualitative point of view to interpret the qualitative
"Voice"	When contrasting the word "voice" with the term "doubt", the student observes in Fig. 3, that the greatest recurrence of the word "voice" occurs in the second half of the novel, while the term " doubt" is presented in the first part. He interprets that after the crime, a "voice" that speaks to the mind intensifies, facing the "doubt" before committing it—which proves his weak mental state. Which allows us to affirm that the machine's analysis coincides with what we know about the protagonist's mental health status
"Mother"	Although the student finds that the word "mother" appears only in some moments, however, in these, its appearance is intense as Fig. 4 shows. He interprets it as milestones in the work or a call from the protagonist in his loneliness to cling to a direct psychological referent. Furthermore, he goes out of his way to argue that this word symbolizes an umbilical cord between madness and sanity and when it appears it may possibly represent moments of mental crisis. Another example that allows us to interpret quantitatively in a psychological context and reinterpret a literary work

(*continued*)

[1] Wikipedia (2022). February 10, 2022 https://es.wikipedia.org/wiki/Crime_y_punishment.

Table 2. (*continued*)

Word	Relevance
"House" "Room" "Exterior" "Town", "Park" "City"	The student groups these words to contrast exterior environments, represented by the terms "exterior", "village", "park" and "city", versus interior environments with the words "house", and "room". He shows that interior spaces appear more frequently and that they are recurrent throughout the work. For the student, this situation denotes the author's intention to create an environment of closed spaces, dark tones and cold colors directly related to the protagonist's mental health. Furthermore, the student argues that "spaces" can be approached as axes of analysis that enrich the interpretation as well as the temperature of the text, whether it is warm or cold based on quantitative analysis

Student constructs scatter diagrams in "R" to visualize the behavior of the chosen words in the text.

Figures 2, 3, 4, 5 show the dispersion plots created by the student using R.

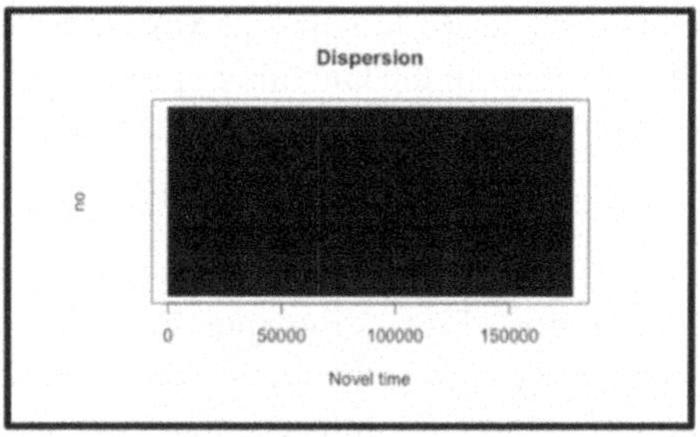

Fig. 2. Scatterplot of the word "No"

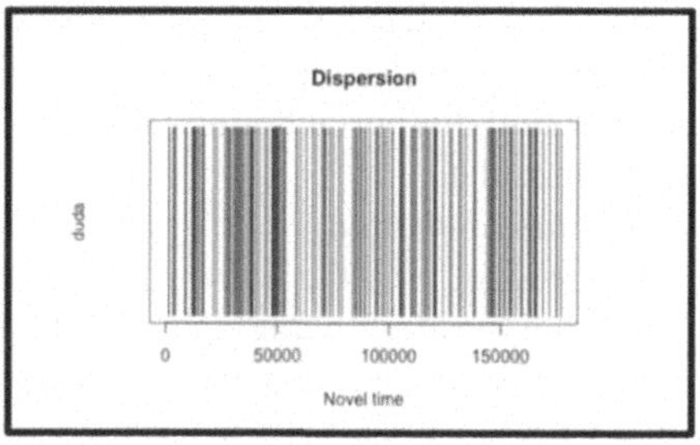

Fig. 3. Scatterplot of the word "Doubt"

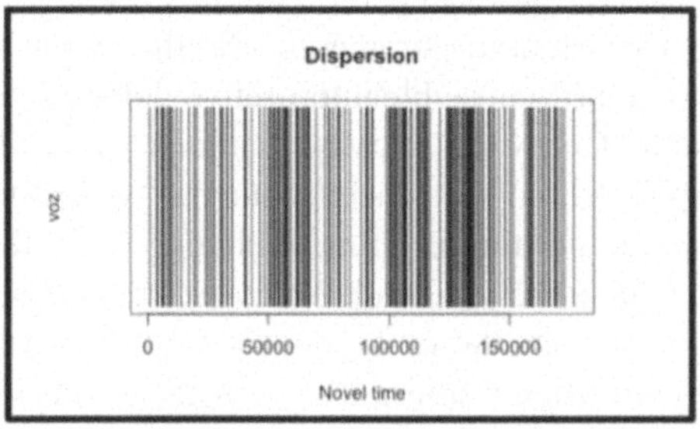

Fig. 4. Scatterplot of the word "Voice"

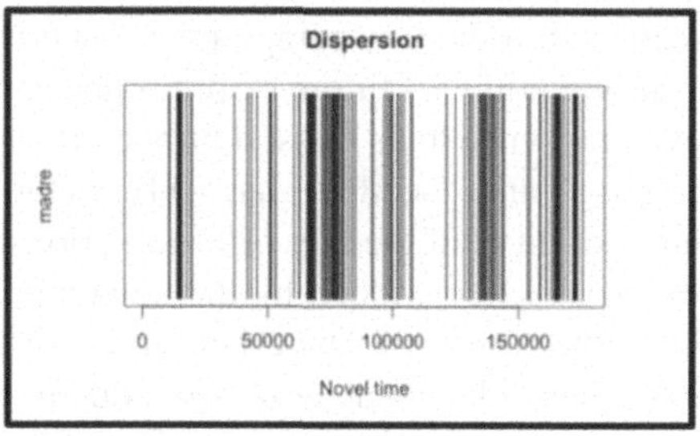

Fig. 5. Scatterplot of the word "Mother"

Interpretation of the Crime and Punishment's Results

The student presents his analysis of the mental problems of the protagonist Raskolnikoff, as a quantitative experiment that confirms 100% of the Wikipedia approach.

The student concludes that the repetitive use of the adverb of denial regarding planning and executing the crime, and then seeking forgiveness, the "voice" that he hears in his mind, the guilt that affects his mental health expressed through the word "doubt", and the call to the "mother", show the weak mental health of the protagonist. The greater reference to interior spaces, in contrast to exterior environments, allows us to perceive that the protagonist remains more in closed places and, therefore, is an additional indication of his feverish state of mind.

The student is surprised to find that from quantitative analysis and with the help of a technological tool he can undertake a qualitative analysis. Actually, the most important student's conclusion was that the statistical exercise allowed him to understand how "feelings analysis" could work in a particular context of Digital Humanities.

The peer review made it possible by the student to identify weaknesses or strengths in their text analysis. In case of finding weaknesses, the peer made comments from their own experience regarding how to address the identified issues. Otherwise, reading someone else's work allowed student to self-assess and recognize their own shortcomings as well as ways to improve their own work. On the other hand, discussed the general results of the activity on plenary sessions allow students to enrich their work.

Metamorphosis

Text selection

The student selected the plain text version of the work Metamorphosis by Franz Kafka, translated into English by David Wyllie, taken from the Gutenberg project [15]. Students used this portal because the files of the literary Ctexts contain both the literature and the metadata.

Question definition

The student used the literary analysis proposed by Kautman [16], which states that the initial expository paragraph of "The Metamorphosis" refers to expressionist poetics, but, above all and nonetheless, Kafka's creative gesture is the one in which Kafka works with the so-called "materialized metaphor", where, by himself, the short story transcends "pure" expressionism, in the direction of a "surrealism, which spins dreams and fantastic events". The theories of reception of Metamorphosis proposed by Černý [17] are also followed. The researcher suggests to the reader three options on how to treat the introductory paragraph of the novel; These reading strategies offer the recipient a starting point for future readings and help to identify possible interpretive fields of the text: (1) Samsa finds himself turned into a beetle (Černý specifically mentions the words "bedbug" and "beetle"): has truly metamorphosed, so that, faced with the "objective impossibility" of the fact of its mutation as a fact, nothing is going to change, so, if the reader is not convinced by the situation, he can simply go read Walter Scott, with its dark objections; (2) The entire initial situation reflects the protagonist's mental imbalance: Samsa has gone crazy and, due to difficult life circumstances, considers himself a bedbug, behaves like one and feels like these parasites feel.; (3) Samsa has not transformed into a bedbug, nor is he taken for a bedbug, but has developed the knowledge or awareness that he is a "human, lazy, stinking, parasitic bedbug." In his analysis, attempts to reveal the biblical symbology and imagination in Kafka's text, thus finding parallels between the suffering and death of Christ, and the fate of Gregor Samsa. Holland [18], even goes so far as to propose that Gregor's transformation and the reaction of those around her constitute the misunderstood and ignored second coming of Christ.

Selection of words for analysis, indicating why they are relevant .

Table 3 shows the words selected fort the analysis.

Table 3. Words selected by the student regarding Metamorphosis

Word	Relevance
"Vermin"	Relevant word in the analysis refers to the newly created condition (real or allegorical) of the protagonist as a bug. The semantic void of the word "insect" is not "allegorical" in the sense that it refers to a specific use, but rather the term shows an "allegorical structure" that encourages semantic closure, concretization. Its occurrence in the text is rare (Fig. 6)
"Gregor"	Kafka's choice of the main character's first name. Gregor stands as a nickname of Greek origin derived from the term grégoros, "watchman." Doesn't the fact that Gregor's transformation is preceded by the hero's betrayal of his own name, that is, Samsa falling asleep, prove this subtle irony of Kafka? Furthermore, according to the Christian calendar, the festival of Saint Gregory is celebrated on March 12, namely the month in which the story of The Metamorphosis ends. The incidence is maximum in the text (Fig. 7)
"Samsa"	The thematic-ideological background of the term lies in the theme of human suffering, vanity and the meaninglessness of life. Kafka would take this low and dark chord from the German philosopher Schopenhauer that inspires him, on one hand, in the general pessimistic tone of the story, and, on the other, in the allusions and references to Eastern philosophy, contained mainly in the choice of the surname of the story. Kafka's protagonist Samsa is a slightly distorted but still identifiable variation on the key concept of Hindu philosophy, Samsára. According to Ryan [19], Schopenhauer's inspiration is also present in the often analyzed scene at the end of the third part, in which Gregor's sister plays the violin in front of three tenants. According to Ryan, here a reference is made to Schopenhauer's valuation of the art of music, which he places above other artistic forms, since the musical stands as the most immediate emanation of the will itself, and, therefore, of the essence of the world; In music the deepest substance of man and all things supposedly speaks. The word Samsa occurs with high frequency (Fig. 8)

(*continued*)

Table 3. (*continued*)

Word	Relevance
"Family"	Kafka's subtlety in this word is captured in the irony that Samsa actually ends up as a victim, as a sacrificed on the altar of newly renewed family harmony, which is evident in the last paragraphs of the story. In this sense, the number of occurrences of the sema "family" also becomes crucial (Fig. 9)
"Harm", "Danger", "People"	The notions of insectivorous plague or threat and social scourge are present in the English vermin translation of the German Ungeziefer, which has a connotative power in other words of the work that contain the roots of harm, danger and the people (people). They only occur once (Fig. 10)
"Transformation"	The transformation is the result of a violation of absolutely binding responsibility and order in the sense of unity between man and the world. With Gregorio Samsa, a conflict occurs between his external and internal existence, which in a moment of crisis culminates in a "transformation", a final alienation, a loss of inner existence: the theft takes the intricately metaphorical form of a disgusting insect. It occurs twice (Fig. 11)

Student constructs scatter diagrams in "R" to visualize the behavior of the chosen words in the text.

The student builds diagrams in R to visualize the behavior of the chosen words in the text. Figures 6, 7, 8, 9, 10, 11 show the dispersion plots created by the student using R.

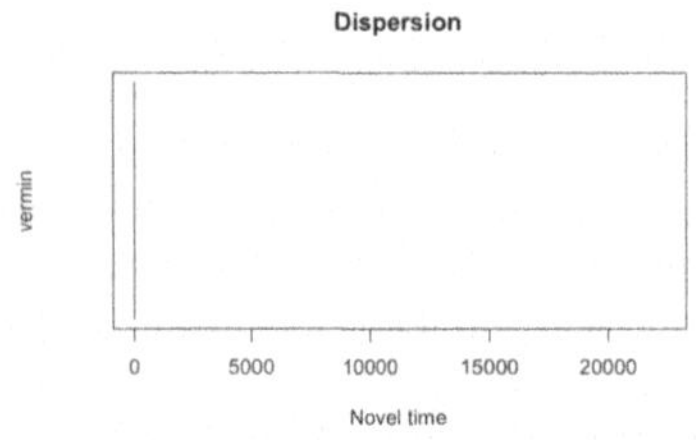

Fig. 6. Scatterplot the word "Vermin"

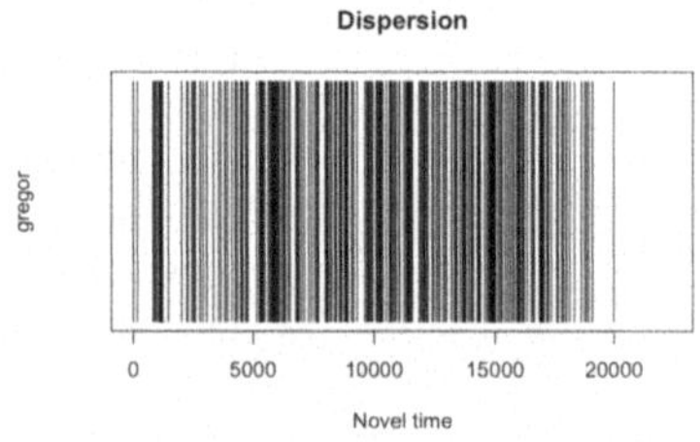

Fig. 7. Scatterplot the word "Gregor"

Interpretation of Metamorphosis

In line with Stromšík [20], the student concluded that the logical model of Kafka's prose lies in the fact that specific poetics generate texts whose field of interpretation is so unlimited that the potential analysis is, therefore, applicable to different situations; and if the interpretation is fixed on only one of the lexical junctures, "we narrow the radius

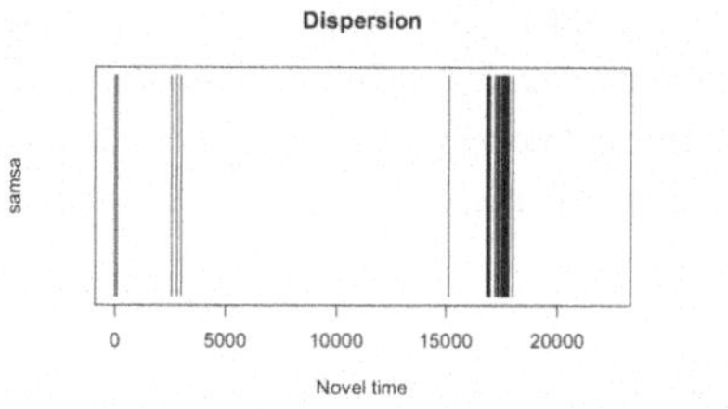

Fig. 8. Scatterplot of word "Samsa"

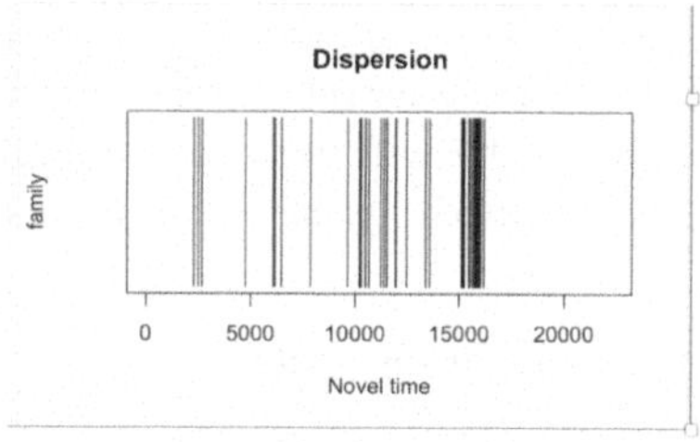

Fig. 9. Scatterplot of word "Family"

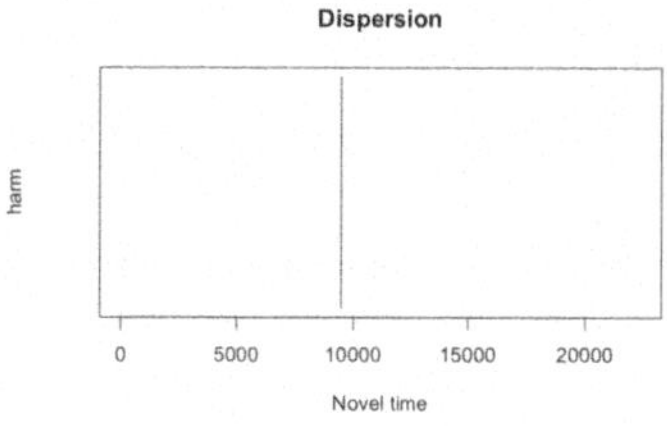

Fig. 10. Scatterplot of word "Harm"

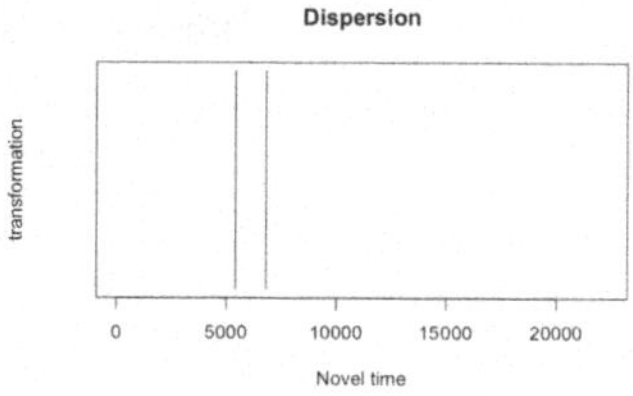

Fig. 11. Scatterplot "Transformation"

of action [of the text] and impoverish it, or rather ourselves, in a substantial part of what is reported."

In line with the words of low appearance, student identified the existentially influential Marxist allegories, which consist of the thesis that transformation is the result of a violation of responsibility and order absolutely binding in the sense of unity between man and the world. Samsa becomes a missing link in the mechanism of the commercial-industrial world, in which it is integrated and which it does not challenge. Hence the importance of the quantitative results in reference to the terms that return the insectivorous repugnance and the circularity of the entrapment from which there is no escape, the Hindu samsara.

Černý [17] is inclined to accept the initial premise of the plot as a "fact", which is the most difficult for the reader, but at the same time the most adventurous alternative on the imaginary scale of "experience" and "interpretability" of the story. But there are also interpretations that involve, to a certain extent, various riddles and a relative sophistication when it comes to giving a balance to the narrative exposition at the beginning of the work, interpreting it as an allegory, perhaps a more comfortable tool for approaching understanding. In summary and in light of Černý's ideas, relevant words in the analysis that student proposed would be those that allude, on the one hand, to the newly created condition (real or allegorical) of the protagonist as a bug (in English, vermin) and, on the other hand, to his customary anthroponymic identity (his first name and his surname, that is, Gregor Samsa), although they show a very dissimilar frequency of appearance.

Finally, the protagonist focus mainly on the surname Samsa, either pointing out that it is a variant of the word Kafka, or emphasizing the phonetic similarity with the Czech word, sam, "alone". Schopenhauer's inspiration is also present in the often analyzed scene at the end of the third part, in which Gregor's sister plays the violin in front of three tenants. Here reference is made to Schopenhauer's valuation of the art of music, which he places above other artistic forms, since the musical stands as the most immediate emanation of the will itself, and, therefore, of the essence of the world; In music the deepest substance of man and all things supposedly speaks.

3.5 Case Studies Results

Table 4 shows the analysis of the cases studies according with the criteria defined in the methodology.

Table 4. Results of case studies analysis

CRITERIA	Crime and Punishment	Metamorphosis
Select a text of the students' interest from the Project Gutenberg portal	Successfully developed	Successfully developed
Define interesting questions to be answered by the text analysis of the literature	Successfully developed	Although student does not define questions, student starts with the analysis of pre-defined analysis which guide the selection of interesting words and sit the discussion
Select words to support the analysis, indicating why the chosen words are relevant to your analysis	Successfully developed	Successfully developed
To build scatter plots in R to visualize the behaviour of the words choose from the text	Successfully developed	Successfully developed
Interpret the obtained results of the text analysis	Student developed an excellent analysis of the text, concluding with a deep interpretation guided by the questions	Student developed an excellent analysis of the text, concluding with a deep interpretation guided by the starting point over pre-defined analysis

4 Conclusions and Future Work

In this article, we introduce an approach to facilitate text analysis to digital humanities students while they are learn, focusing the evaluation on analyzing the process followed by the students with a qualitative point of view.

According to results, students were able to carry out the text analysis using R successfully considering the suggested process.

Study confirms that the use of quantitative analysis using R allows the generation of new interpretations of texts from a qualitative perspective.

Students considered peer review as a good alternative that enrich their learning process. Peer comments were treated with greater interest than the score itself, since students considered it allowed them to establish a dialogue between peers, respectfully enriching the exercise, by pointing out aspects that could have been addressed or also praising their peers' work.

The use of ChatGPT or other generative artificial intelligences to support the work of the students while they program are an interesting option to continues in next steps of this study.

References

1. Wiedemann, G., Niekler, A.: Hands-On: A five day text mining course for humanists and social scientists in R. In: Bockwinkel, P., Declerck, T., Kübler, S., Zinsmeister, H. (eds.) Workshop on Teaching NLP for Digital Humanities (Teach4DH 2017) (2017)
2. RStudio Homepage: https://rstudio.com/. Last accessed 6 Feb 2022
3. The R Foundation, https://www.r-project.org/. Last accessed 6 Feb 2022
4. Dae-HeeKim, C.: Teaching R to undergraduate business students. Bus. Educ. Innov. J. **11**(1), 37–43 (2019)
5. Eglen, S.J.: A quick guide to teaching R programming to computational biology students. PLoS Comput. Biol. **5**(8) (2009)
6. Fries, L., Son, J.Y., Givvin, K.B., Stigler, J.W.: Practicing connections: a framework to guide instructional design for developing understanding in complex domains. Educ. Psychol. Rev. **33**(2), 739–762 (2021)
7. Son, J.Y., Blake, A.B., Fries, L., Stigler, J.W.: Modeling first: applying learning science to the teaching of introductory statistics. J. Stat. Data Sci. Educ. **29**(1), 4–21 (2021)
8. Schreibman, S., Siemens, R., Unsworth, J.: A new companion to Digital Humanities, 1st edn. Wiley-Blackwell US (2016)
9. Hirsch, B.D., et al.: Digital Humanities Pedagogy: Practices, Principles and Politics, vol. 1. Open Book publishers, UK (2012)
10. Lipnevich, A.A., Panadero, E.: A review of feedback models and theories: descriptions, definitions, and conclusions. Front. Educ. 6 (2021)
11. Wiliam, D.: Feedback. In: Lipnevich, A.A., Smith, J.K. (eds.) The Cambridge handbook of instructional feedback, pp. 3–28. Cambridge University Press, Cambridge (2018)
12. Baldiris Navarro, S.M., Cachiotis Salazar, J.E.: Peer-review to support teaching text analysis to digital humanists using R. In: Chen, N., Rudolph, G., Sampson, D., Chang, M., Kuo, R., Tlili, A. (eds.) IEEE International Conference on Advanced Learning Technologies (ICALT 2023), pp. 149–151. IEEE (2023)
13. Pascual, M.A., Ortega-Carrillo, J.A., Pérez-Ferra, M., Fombona, J.: Competencias Digitales en los Estudiantes del Grado de Maestro de Educación Primaria. El caso de tres Universidades Españolas. Formación Universitaria **12**(6), 141–150 (2019)
14. Melville, H.: Moby Dick. Richard Bentley, UK (1851)
15. Project Gutenberg Literary Archive Foundation, https://www.gutenberg.org/, last accessed 2022/02/06
16. Kautman, F.: Franz Kafka. Academia Bruylant, Belgium (1996)
17. Černý, V.: Nad Kafkovou Proměnou. In TÝŽ: Tvorba a osobnost **2**, 305–316 (1991)

18. Holland, N.N.: Realism and unrealism: Kafka's metamorphosis. Mod. Fiction Stud. **4**(2), 143–150 (2009)
19. Ryan, P.M.: Samsa and samsara: suffering, death and rebirth in the metamorphosis. Ger. Quart. **72**(2), 133–152 (1999)
20. Stromšík, J.: Kafkovy modely. Literární Noviny **5**(26) (1994)

Artificial Intelligence and Learning of Students with Dyslexia: A Brief Review

Karma Dabaghi[1], Stefano D'Urso[2], and Filippo Sciarrone[2](✉)

[1] Lebanese American University, Beirut, Lebanon
karma.dabaghi@lau.edu.lb

[2] Faculty of Technological Sciences and Innovation, Universitas Mercatorum, Piazza Mattei, 10 00186 Rome, Italy
stefano.durso@studenti.unimercatorum.it,
filippo.sciarrone@unimercatorum.it

Abstract. In the new global reality, distance learning has grown exponentially, and students with Specific Learning Disorders (SLD), i.e., those with dyslexia, dysorthographia, or dyscalculia, struggle to learn. Because they have no direct contact with the teacher, they resort to using suitable tools and instruments, together with personalised learning plans. In addition, students with SLDs who take in-person courses must also follow an adapted didactic strategy. This problem affects millions of people around the world, and Technology Enhanced Learning currently proposes instruments and tools to help learners during their learning process. In this paper we propose a brief review of the literature about the use of Artificial Intelligence from 2018 to 2023 in the educational field specifically for dyslexic students in the post-transformer era. We aim to baseline the contribution of the use of generative and classic AI to help learners, highlighting possible strengths and weaknesses. The results of our inquiry show that in the specified years, the AI community has offered little to this field.

Keywords: Artificial Intelligence · Dyslexia · Learning

1 Introduction

In recent years, especially during and after the COVID-19 pandemic, the number of courses students have taken by distance learning has grown exponentially at all levels of education [1]: schools, universities, and companies have radically changed the way they make didactic materials available and interact with learners. A significant example of this are the Massive Open Online Courses (MOOCs), that is, distance learning courses characterised by a large number of enrolled students. Consequently, new didactic strategies of teaching and learning have made it possible to overcome the classical barriers of space and time and have launched new challenges for all stakeholders involved in educational processes. One of the challenges stems from the fact that in a distance education

Z. Kubincová et al. (Eds.): SETE 2023, LNCS 14606, pp. 155–169, 2024.
https://doi.org/10.1007/978-981-97-4243-1_13

context it is difficult, if not impossible, for the teacher to follow students in a personalized way and still ensure students' learning happens faster and is more profitable [2–5]. Unfortunately, in this new global scenario, students with Specific Learning Disorders (SLD), such as students with dyslexia, with dysorthographia or with dyscalculia, having no direct contact with the teacher, struggle to learn if they are not using suitable tools and instruments together with personalised learning plans. Additionally, students with SLD who take an in-person course must also follow an adapted didactic strategy. This problem affects millions of people around the world. In Italy it is estimated that there are almost three million people with SLD. Moreover, in schools, what emerges from the latest report issued by the Ministry of Education is that there is a progressive increase in the number of students diagnosed with SLD: over the last two years, students diagnosed with a SLD were 318,678 and 326,548, respectively, that is 5.3% and 5.4% of the total number of Italian students. Mainly these students were in years III, IV and V of primary school, and years I and II of high school, all with appropriate medical certification. According to the *European Dyslexia Association*[1] (EDA), other European countries' epidemiological estimates of SLD are between 5% and 12% of the entire population. Furthermore, the latest revision of the *American Psychiatric Association's*'s Diagnostic and Statistical Manual (APA, DSM V, 2013) raised the prevalence estimates for these disorders from 2–10% [6] to 5–15% [7,8]. Worldwide, dyslexia is the most common of all SLDs; the EDA describes it thus: *No matter which country - No matter which language - Dyslexia is everywhere.* It is for this reason that we chose dyslexia from among all SLDs as the focus of our review as the best place to begin our investigation, considering that it is the most prevalent. Among the assistive technologies for students with dyslexia, those based on Technology Enhanced Learning (TEL) are certainly the most widely used [9,10]. In TEL, Artificial Intelligence has been contributing to the improvement of learning support systems for years, from the Intelligent Tutoring Systems (ITS) to the latest generation of intelligent chatbots such as ChatGPT[2] [11]. In this article, we present a brief study of the literature concerning works dealing with AI, dyslexia, and education in order to construct an initial analysis of gaps that exist between these three disciplines in terms of publications where all of themes are involved. The rationale of this study in the context of existing knowledge is to reflect on and give indications about the state of the art in this mixed field. We have analysed a large set of papers, guided by the *Preferred Reporting Items for Systematic Reviews and Meta-Analyses* PRISMA method[3] [12], as the methodological approach, first selecting almost 400 papers and then classifying them by means of an accurate content analysis. The results show that, at present, the contribution of AI to students with dyslexia is minimal.

The remainder of the paper is organized as follows. Section 2 provides background on Dyslexia. Section 3 describes the process of selecting the set of papers

---

[1] https://eda-info.eu/.
[2] https://chat.openai.com/.
[3] http://www.prisma-statement.org/.

using the PRISMA method, while in Sect. 4 the results are evaluated. In Sect. 5 we discuss the results giving some useful indications about the relevance of this review. Finally, in Sect. 6 we present our conclusions and plans for future studies.

2 Dyslexia

Dyslexia is a common learning disability with a rate of prevalence that varies anywhere between 5 to 20% of the population depending on how it is defined [13–15]. It often is the most self-declared disability in higher education [16]. Though defined in different ways [17], one characteristic of the many descriptions stays constant, which is the difficulty identifying and pronouncing words accurately [18, 19]. Dyslexia is used as a term for a disorder that is mainly characterized by severe difficulties in acquiring reading, spelling and writing skills across languages [20–23]. The distribution of dyslexics in various regions of the world, based on an estimated prevalence, is 7.5%. It is important to keep in mind that these numbers are purely hypothetical and are based on general estimates. The actual prevalence of dyslexia can vary greatly depending on the region, culture and diagnosis methods used. Dyslexia is an essentially neurological disorder [24] and is the most common of all neuro-cognitive disorders [17]. This renders it incurable. Yet, with appropriate interventions and support, individuals with dyslexia can learn to manage their challenges and achieve success in academic and professional settings. Early diagnosis and intervention are key to helping individuals with dyslexia develop the skills they need to succeed. With early screening, diagnosis, evidence-based reading intervention, and appropriate accommodations, dyslexic individuals can become highly successful students and adults performing as well as anyone else - and sometimes even better [22, 25]. Some common interventions include specialized tutoring, assistive technology, and accommodations, such as extended time on tests or audio-books. The challenge is knowing which accommodations work best [13]and understanding what schools and workplaces are required to provide under the law [13] or according to practices and policies [16]. Being neuro-biological in origin [17, 24], genetic factors may be identified [25] and some environmental factors may be recognized as contributing to its impact on individuals. Dyslexia is explained as a deficit in the manner phonological information gets processed [26, 27], which affects the manner with which students recognize words and read as well as the way they produce words or spell [21, 25] The most widely accepted theory is that it is caused by difficulties in phonological processing, but verbal working memory, rapid naming, and sequencing skills are also affected [26]. Across Europe, the diversity of languages and the multilingual demands may pose particular challenges for dyslexic children and adults given their language learning difficulties.

There is no relationship between a person's level of intelligence [23, 28], individual effort, or socio-economic position [16] and the presence of dyslexia. The cognitive difficulties that cause dyslexia and different learning disorders can also affect other aspects of verbal learning including arithmetic [29, 30] Difficulties in organizational skills and motor coordination are frequently observed but these are not core to the condition [16]. On account of this, it is an ongoing challenge for people with dyslexia to navigate through life[4]. But while dyslexia cannot be cured, it is possible for individuals with dyslexia to make significant progress and improve their reading, writing, and spelling skills. And with ongoing support and practice, many individuals with dyslexia are able to overcome their challenges and achieve their goals.

3 Methods

In this section, we illustrate the procedure of collecting and analysing relevant papers retrieved from the corpus of literature. As mentioned in the introduction, we followed the PRISMA method. The following paragraphs present all elements of the method.

3.1 The Eligibility Criteria

Here we specify the inclusion and exclusion criteria for the review and how studies were grouped for the syntheses. The rationale behind our review is to construct the state of the art of the literature dealing with the contribution of AI in the educational field for students with dyslexia from 2018 to the present. Therefore, we considered articles that proposed help for students with dyslexia, both on a theoretical level and on a practical level, i.e., through intelligent support systems, as important for our research. We thus decided to group the search results into several categories, all related to the three initial macro-categories (AI, education, and dyslexia):

- *Research:* articles primarily engaged in research discussions on the theme;
- *Help:* articles centered on the development and usage of tools aiming at assisting learners with dyslexia;
- *Medical:* articles with a medical orientation, exploring the physiological aspects of dyslexia;
- *Review:* Articles offering a review of existing literature and studies on the topic;
- *Education:* Articles reporting on experimentation or application in the educational sector, be it at the school or university level;
- *Game:* Articles exploring gamification approaches to support individuals with dyslexia;
- *Detection:* Articles focused on innovative methods and techniques to detect dyslexia.

[4] https://eda-info.eu/what-is-dyslexia/.

3.2 The Information Sources

In this step we specify all databases, registers, websites, organisations, reference lists and other sources searched or consulted to identify our studies, specifying the date when each source was last searched or consulted. For our research, we used the following sources: IEEE, Springer, Arxis, Elsevier, and Google Scholar. The time frame in which this research was conducted runs from 2023-7-1 to 2023-8-31. We searched for papers in English only and coming from both conferences and journals.

3.3 The Search Strategy

Because of our focus on dyslexia as the most prominent SLD, and to select and retrieve relevant articles that are situated at the intersection of AI, dyslexia, and education, we used the following query for all the search engines introduced in the previous paragraph: *artificial intelligence AND dyslexia AND education*. We used the AND logic operator to retrieve papers matching all our categories of interest. Each paper has a group of related meta-data, but each publisher has its own way to tag papers.

3.4 The Selection Process

The methods used to decide whether a study met the inclusion criteria of the review was based on the reading of the title, the abstract, the keywords, and the meta-data associated with each paper, with the aim of conducting a binary initial screening of each paper into categories of good or not good. Each of us reviewed one-third of the retrieved papers. Each record was first analyzed and subsequently discussed in a plenary session. Each of us worked independently and then collaboratively. Moreover, we used Google drive as the working area and Google Sheets as the tool to build graphs and statistics.

3.5 The Data Collection Process

The data collection process was based on the construction of a shared worksheet where for each paper in our assigned lot, one of us worked independently to store the following data in separate columns and in the same row: ID_Paper, Year of publication, Authors, abstract, number of citations, type of publication (conference, journal, technical report, and so on), link to the article, publisher, keywords.

3.6 Data Items

For articles with incomplete information, such as articles lacking meta-data or missing citation numbers, after a more thorough search, an attempt was made in most cases to store the same. In other cases, each author marked as "Missing" the field in the appropriate row of the paper corresponding to the missing variable.

3.7 The Risk of Bias Assessment

We assessed the risk of bias about the included studies, especially during the categorization process. First each reviewer worked independently, classifying each paper based on the target categories. During several plenary sessions we discussed the papers at risk by analyzing in a deeper way their relevant variables of interest.

3.8 Effect Methods

As described in the introduction, the aim of this review is to illustrate the state of the art of the literature concerning articles on AI, dyslexia and education. To synthesise the results, we used the semantic categories of each article as a measure of effectiveness and then summarised the results by means of Venn diagrams. We then intersected the different sub-categories of each article.

4 Results

Figure 1 illustrates the process of identification, screening and inclusion of papers, following the PRISMA flow diagram. In the following sections each of them is described.

4.1 Identification

In this first phase, we first identified the databases we would use for our research. We started by consulting Google Scholar, used as an initial hub in order to discover the richest sources. Thus, by entering our query (i.e.: "Artificial Intelligence AND education AND Dyslexia"), we catalogued the richest sources of articles, both from conferences and journals. As a result, we determined to use: IEEE, Elsevier, Springer, and of course Google Scholar. This search led us to identify $n = 436$ papers from these databases. From this initial set we removed $n = 55$ duplicated records that appeared in more than one source.

4.2 Screening

We start screening $n = 383$ records in order to check and validate their eligibility. As described in Sect. 3, we considered some not eligible because their content did not match our requirements. Consequently, we excluded $n = 96$ papers. For example some papers came from medical reports or from non-official sources or were not written in English. At the end, we sought for retrieval $n = 287$ records, as shown in Table 1.

All records were retrieved so having $n = 0$ records not retrieved. During screening, we excluded two sets of papers belonging to *Review* or *Out of Scope papers*: $n = 30$ Reviews and 87 Out of Scope. We decided not to consider the category of review articles, as they are not relevant to our analysis, which aims

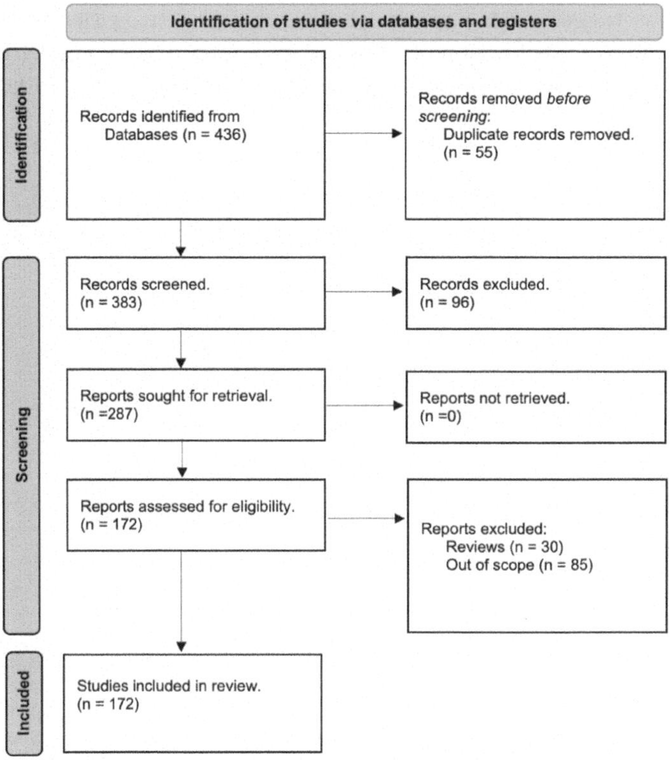

Fig. 1. The PRISMA flow showing the screening and eligibility process.

Table 1. The categories of papers after screening.

Category	# Papers
Out of scope	85
Research	59
Help	47
Medical	39
Detection	9
Review	30
Game	18
#	**287**

to propose an analysis of articles taken at the sources and not mediated by other reviewers. Other articles were deemed not relevant to our interests, and we declared papers out of scope that, after review, did not match our interests. Thus $n = 172$ records were assessed for eligibility. Subsequently, again in the screening phase, we first tagged each paper with one or more categories of interest and then processed all classifications to find articles that had two or three semantic categories in common, obtaining the distribution shown in Fig. 2 and Fig. 3.

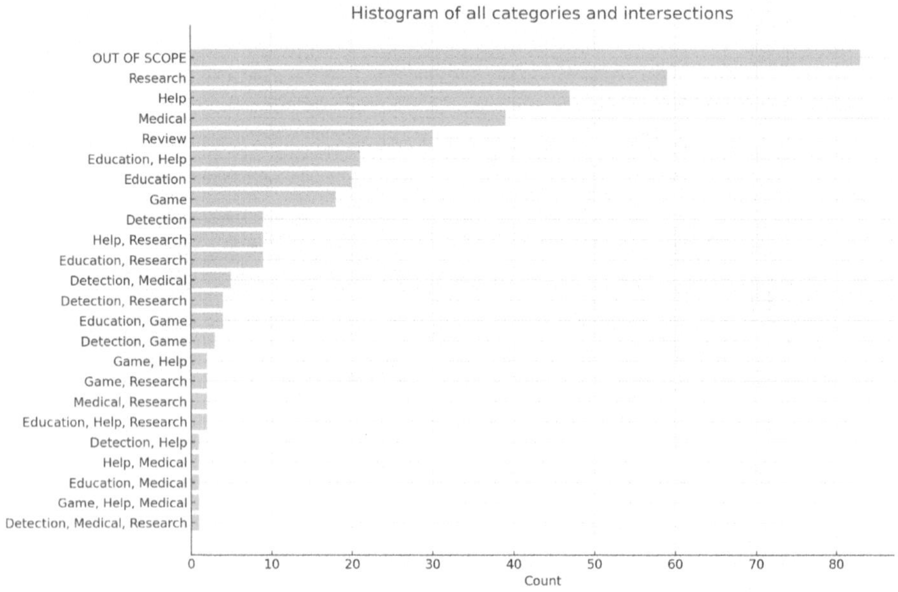

Fig. 2. The distribution of the different categories on the paper set.

In particular, we screened for the intersection between the most representative categories, i.e., those categories with the largest number of papers, represented in Fig. 4, Fig. 5 and Fig. 6.

4.3 Inclusion

At the end of the process, we included $n = 172$ papers in this review. Here we propose the most significant of them, i.e., the four papers that lie at the intersection of three categories, grouped as shown in Table 2 and Table 3.

5 Discussion

In this section, we attempt to draw conclusions by discussing the results obtained and summarised in the previous section. Limits of this research include potential biases inherent in the literature search and selection process, as well as the exclusion of non-English language studies, which could potentially have provided additional perspectives on the topic. The period of focus for our research, commencing from 2018, was chosen strategically to analyze the developments

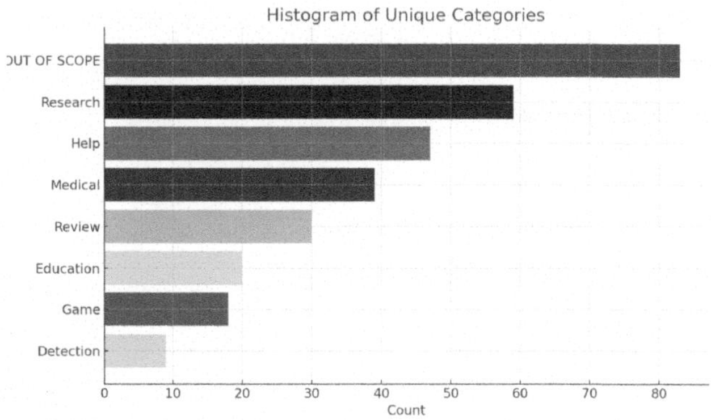

Fig. 3. The distribution of the papers with respect to the target categories.

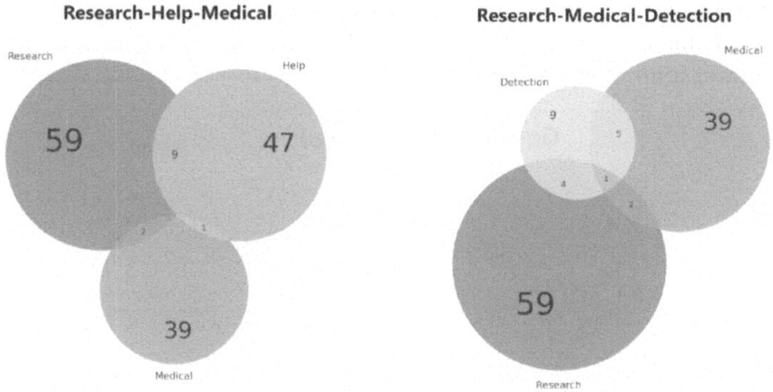

Fig. 4. The intersections among the categories: Research-Help-Medical (left) and the categories: Research-Medical-Detection (right), having respectively zero and one paper in common among the sets.

in the post-transformer era, a phase marked by the advent of generative AI technologies that have revolutionized various fields including natural language processing, computer vision, and more. It is somewhat surprising, therefore, to note a conspicuous absence of substantial research exploring the confluence of generative AI with educational strategies tailored for individuals with dyslexia. Our meticulous selection process, adhering to the PRISMA guidelines, brought to the fore a limited number of studies that genuinely intersect at the junction of AI, dyslexia, and education. This highlights not only a gap but perhaps an opportunity for researchers and educators to delve deeper into the uncharted territories where the transformative potential of generative AI can be harnessed to facilitate learning experiences for individuals grappling with dyslexia. Given the groundbreaking capabilities of transformer-based AI models in understanding and generating human-like text, we can envision a range of applications in the educational sphere. From personalized tutoring systems that adapt to

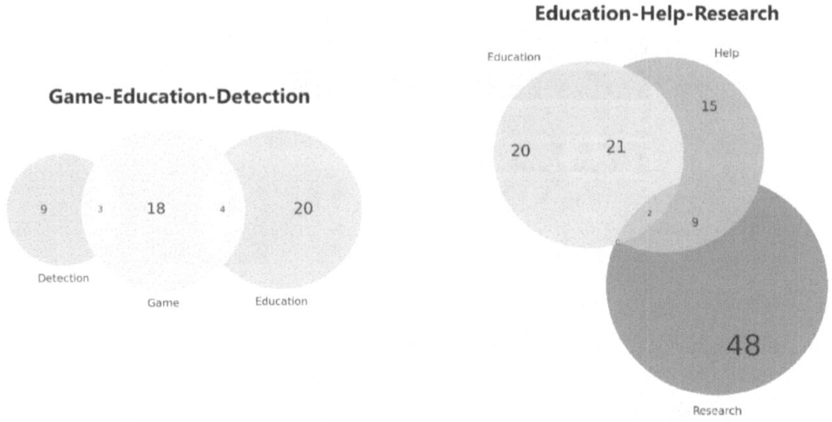

Fig. 5. The intersections among the categories: Game-Education-Detection (left) and the categories: Education-Help-Research (right), having respectively zero and two papers in common among the sets.

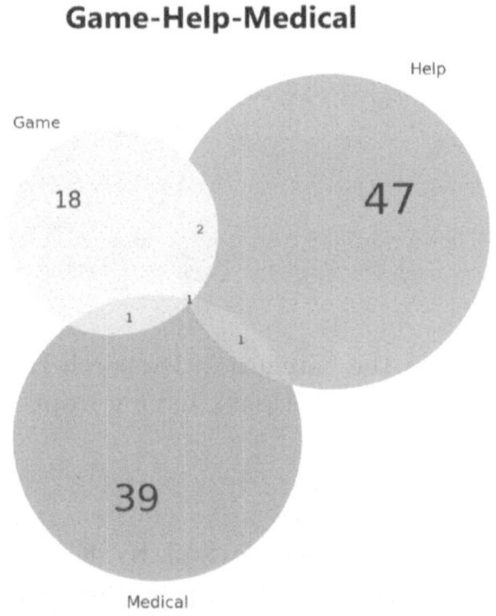

Fig. 6. The intersections among the categories: Game-Help-Medical, having two papers in common.

individual learning curves to intelligent content generation tools that can aid in creating customized learning materials, the scope is indeed vast and largely untapped. Moreover, the nuanced understanding of language facilitated by these AI models could potentially play a pivotal role in developing diagnostic tools with heightened sensitivity and specificity, enhancing the early detection of dyslexia and thereby paving the way for timely interventions. As we forge ahead, it is imperative to foster collaborations that are truly interdisciplinary, encouraging a synthesis of insights from the domains of AI technology, educational theory,

Table 2. The most relevant papers: Help, Education

Year	Ref.	Year	Ref.
2018	[31]	2020	[32]
2019	[33]	2020	[34]
2019	[35]	2020	[36]
2020	[37]	2021	[38]
2020	[39]	2021	[40]
2020	[41]	2021	[42]
2020	[43]	2021	[44]
2020	[45]	2023	[46]
2020	[47]	2023	[48]
2020	[32]	2023	[49]
2020	[34]	2023	[50]
		2023	[51]

Table 3. The most relevant papers: 3 categories

Year	Categories	Ref.
2019	Help, Education, Research	[35]
2019		[52]
2012	Medical, Help, Game	[53]
2023	Detection, Medical, Research	[54]

and medical research. The objective should be to cultivate a rich tapestry of knowledge that can guide the development of AI-driven solutions rooted in a deep understanding of the complex needs and nuances associated with dyslexia. In conclusion, our research serves as a clarion call to the academic and technological communities to leverage the transformative potential of post-transformer generative AI in crafting innovative solutions for education. The journey ahead should be marked by explorations that are both deep, to understand the intricacies of dyslexia, and broad, to encompass the expansive capabilities of AI, forging pathways to a future where every learner, irrespective of their learning challenges, can find avenues to thrive.

6 Conclusions and Future Plans

In this article, we proposed a brief review on the relationship, expressed in publications, between Artificial Intelligence, Dyslexia and Education. To set up the work properly, we used the PRISMA method, a methodological standard for structuring a review article as the frame for our work. Our search constraints included finding articles published only in the English language, as long as those articles were published between the years 2018 to 2023 and the subject of the article was the application of AI to education when considering dyslexic students. The results show that to date, there are few proposals that take into consideration all aspects related to the relationship between Artificial Intelligence in the educational field to support dyslexic students. This first and brief analysis indicates that there is still considerable effort to be devoted to this direction. This review has shown that our future work, which will continue to use the PRISMA methodology, needs to expand the breadth of research we consider, and to include categories of SLDs other than dyslexia, such as dysgraphia and dyscalculia. We will also examine literature published in languages other than English. Our expectation is that our review efforts will lead to experimental studies on the use of AI that best assists students with these particular SLDs to function successfully in an academic environment.

Acknowledgements. This work was supported by the funding project AI4DIX-16-FIN/RIC from Universitas Mercatorum.

References

1. Kara, A.: COVID-19 pandemic and possible trends into the future of higher education: a review. J. Educ. Educ. Dev. **8**(1) (2021)
2. Peng, H., Ma, S., Spector, J.: Personalized adaptive learning: an emerging pedagogical approach enabled by a smart learning environment. Smart Learn. Environ. **6**(9) (2019)
3. Limongelli, C., Gasparetti, F., Sciarrone, F.:Wiki course builder: a system for retrieving and sequencing didactic materials from Wikipedia. In: 2015 International Conference on Information Technology Based Higher Education and Training (ITHET), pp. 1–6 (2015)
4. Limongelli, C., Marani, A., Sciarrone, F., Temperini, M.: Measuring the similarity of concept maps according to pedagogical criteria. IEEE Access **10**, 27655–27669 (2022)
5. Polito, G., Temperini, M.:A gamified web based system for computer programming learning. Comput. Educ. Artif. Intelli. **2** (2021)
6. American, Psychiatric, Association: DSM-5, Task, Force: Diagnostic and Statistical Manual of Mental Disorders: DSM-4^{TM}, 4th edn. American Psychiatric Publishing Inc. (2000)
7. American, Psychiatric, Association: DSM-5, Task, Force: Diagnostic and Statistical Manual of Mental Disorders: DSM-5^{TM}, 5th edn. American Psychiatric Publishing Inc. (2013)
8. Mazefsky, C., McPartland, J., Gastgeb, H., Minshew, N.: Brief report: comparability of DSM-IV and DSM-5 ASD research samples. J. Autism Dev. Disord. **43**, 1236–1242 (2013)
9. Richardson, U., Lyytinen, H.:The graphogame method: the theoretical and methodological background of the technology-enhanced learning environment for learning to read. Hum. Technol. **10**(1) (2014)
10. Caute, A., Cruice, M., Marshall, J., Monnelly, K., Wilson, S., Woolf, C.: Assistive technology approaches to reading therapy for people with acquired dyslexia. Aphasiology **32**(supl), 40–42 (2018)

11. Abrusci, L., Dabaghi, K., D'Urso, S., Sciarrone, F.: AI4Architect: an intelligent help system to support students in the design domain. In: Milrad, M., et al. (eds.) MIS4TEL 2023. LNNS, vol. 764, pp. 65–72. Springer, Cham (2023). https://doi.org/10.1007/978-3-031-41226-4_7
12. Page, M.J., et al.: The PRISMA 2020 statement: an updated guideline for reporting systematic reviews. BMJ **372** (2021)
13. Knight, C.: What is dyslexia? an exploration of the relationship between teachers' understandings of dyslexia and their training experiences. Dyslexia **24**(3), 207–219 (2018)
14. Shaywitz, S.E.: Overcoming Dyslexia: A New and Complete Science-Based Program for Reading Problems at Any Level. A.A. Knopf, New York (2012)
15. Siegel, L.S.: Perspectives on dyslexia. Paediatr. Child Health **11**(9), 581–587 (2006)
16. Mortimore, T., Crozier, W.R.: Dyslexia and difficulties with study skills in higher education. Stud. High. Educ. **31**(2), 235–251 (2006)
17. Frith, U.: Paradoxes in the definition of dyslexia. Dyslexia **5**(4), 192–214 (1999)
18. Hancock, R., Richlan, F., Hoeft, F.: Possible roles for Fronto-Striatal circuits in reading disorder. Neurosci. Biobehav. Rev. **72**, 243–260 (2017)
19. Tanaka, H., et al.: The brain basis of the phonological deficit in dyslexia is independent of IQ. Psychol. Sci. **22**(11), 1442–1451 (2011)
20. El Kah, A., Lakhouaja, A.: Developing effective educative games for Arabic children primarily dyslexics. Educ. Inf. Technol. **23**(6), 2911–2930 (2018)
21. Ruberto, N., Daigle, D., Ammar, A.: The spelling strategies of francophone dyslexic students. Read. Writ. **29**(4), 659–681 (2016)
22. van der Leij, A.: Dyslexia and early intervention: what did we learn from the Dutch dyslexia programme? Dyslexia **19**(4), 241–255 (2013)
23. Tunmer, W., Greaney, K.: Defining dyslexia. J. Learn. Disabil. **43**(3), 229–243 (2010)
24. Kearns, D.M., Hancock, R., Hoeft, F., Pugh, K.R., Frost, S.J.: The neurobiology of dyslexia. Teach. Except. Child. **51**(3), 175–188 (2019)
25. Hayiou-Thomas, M.E., Carroll, J.M., Leavett, R., Hulme, C., Snowling, M.J.: When does speech sound disorder matter for literacy? the role of disordered speech errors, co-occurring language impairment and family risk of dyslexia. J. Child Psychol. Psychiatry **58**(2), 197–205 (2016)
26. Tijms, J.: Verbal memory and phonological processing in dyslexia. J. Res. Reading **27**(3), 300–310 (2004)
27. Beitcmann, J.H., Young, A.R.: Learning disorders with a special emphasis on reading disorders: a review of the past 10 years. J. Am. Acad. Child Adolescent Psychiatry **36**(8), 1020–1032 (1997)
28. Aaron, P.G.: The impending demise of the discrepancy formula. Rev. Educ. Res. **67**(4), 461–461 (1997)
29. Simmons, F.R., Singleton, C.: Do weak phonological representations impact on arithmetic development? A review of research into arithmetic and dyslexia. Dyslexia **14**(2), 77–94 (2008)
30. Vukovic, R.K., Lesaux, N.K., Siegel, L.S.: The mathematics skills of children with reading difficulties. Learn. Individ. Differ. **20**(6), 639–643 (2010)
31. Ati, M., Abdullahi, H., Kabir, K., Ahmed, M.: Implementation of augmented reality in the teaching of young children. In: Al-mamory, S.O., Alwan, J.K., Hussein, A.D. (eds.) NTICT 2018. CCIS, vol. 938, pp. 287–297. Springer, Cham (2018). https://doi.org/10.1007/978-3-030-01653-1_18

32. Simonetti, M., Perri, D., Amato, N., Gervasi, O.: Teaching math with the help of virtual reality. In: Gervasi, O., et al. (eds.) ICCSA 2020. LNCS, vol. 12255, pp. 799–809. Springer, Cham (2020). https://doi.org/10.1007/978-3-030-58820-5_57
33. Satapathy, A.: Applications of assistive tools and technologies in enhancing the learning abilities of dyslexic children. TechnoLearn: Int. J. Educ. Technol. **9**(2), 117–123 (2019)
34. Tayal, A.: An interactive alphabet and number learning system using OpenCV and CNN. In: 2021 Asian Conference on Innovation in Technology (ASIANCON), pp. 1–4. IEEE (2021)
35. Della Ventura, M.: Exploring the impact of artificial intelligence in music education to enhance the dyslexic student's skills. In: Uden, L., Liberona, D., Sanchez, G., Rodríguez-González, S. (eds.) LTEC 2019. CCIS, vol. 1011, pp. 14–22. Springer, Cham (2019). https://doi.org/10.1007/978-3-030-20798-4_2
36. Ripalda, D., Piedra, M., Cobos, M.: Multimedia tool for the treatment of dyslexia and dyscalculia
37. Mehringer, H., et al.: (swiss) Grapholearn: an app-based tool to support beginning readers. Res. Pract. Technol. Enhanc. Learn. **15**, 1–21 (2020)
38. Sharif, M.S., Elmedany, W.: A proposed machine learning based approach to support students with learning difficulties in the post-pandemic norm. In: IEEE Global Engineering Education Conference (EDUCON), pp. 1988–1993. IEEE (2022)
39. Soiffer, N., Larson, J.L.: Rainbow math: a case study of using colors in math for students with moderate to severe dyslexia. In: Miesenberger, K., Manduchi, R., Covarrubias Rodriguez, M., Peňáz, P. (eds.) ICCHP 2020. LNCS, vol. 12376, pp. 401–409. Springer, Cham (2020). https://doi.org/10.1007/978-3-030-58796-3_47
40. Mateos-Sanchez, M., Melo, A.C., Blanco, L.S., García, A.M.F.: Chatbot, as educational and inclusive tool for people with intellectual disabilities. Sustainability **14**(3), 1520 (2022)
41. Hauwaert, H., Ghesquière, P., Tordoir, J., Thomson, J.: Karaton: an example of AI integration within a literacy app. In: Miesenberger, K., Manduchi, R., Covarrubias Rodriguez, M., Peňáz, P. (eds.) ICCHP 2020. LNCS, vol. 12376, pp. 91–96. Springer, Cham (2020). https://doi.org/10.1007/978-3-030-58796-3_12
42. Wang, M., Muthu, B., Sivaparthipan, C.: Smart assistance to dyslexia students using artificial intelligence based augmentative alternative communication. Int. J. Speech Technol. 1–11 (2021)
43. Sowmiya, J., Kalaiselvi, K.: Instructor performance evaluation through machine learning algorithms. In: Smys, S., Tavares, J.M.R.S., Balas, V.E., Iliyasu, A.M. (eds.) ICCVBIC 2019. AISC, vol. 1108, pp. 751–767. Springer, Cham (2020). https://doi.org/10.1007/978-3-030-37218-7_84
44. Shardlow, M., Sellar, S., Rousell, D.: Collaborative augmentation and simplification of text (coast): pedagogical applications of natural language processing in digital learning environments. Learn. Environ. Res. 1–23 (2022)
45. Delić, V., et al.: Central audio-library of the university of Novi sad. In: Kotenko, I., Badica, C., Desnitsky, V., El Baz, D., Ivanovic, M. (eds.) IDC 2019. SCI, vol. 868, pp. 467–476. Springer, Cham (2020). https://doi.org/10.1007/978-3-030-32258-8_55
46. Mcvey, S.M., Chew, E., Carroll, F.: Educational robotics and dyslexia: investigating how reinforcement learning in robotics can be used to help support students with dyslexia. In: Garcıa-Peñalvo, F.J., Garcıa-Holgado, A. (eds.) TEEM 2022. LNET, vol. 1, pp. 43–49. Springer, Singapore (2022). https://doi.org/10.1007/978-981-99-0942-1_4

47. Dcruz, F., Tiwari, V., Soni, M.: Using machine learning to help students with learning disabilities learn. In: Karrupusamy, P., Chen, J., Shi, Y. (eds.) ICSCN 2019. LNDECT, vol. 39, pp. 262–269. Springer, Cham (2020). https://doi.org/10.1007/978-3-030-34515-0_27
48. Lhafra, F.Z., Abdoun, O.: Towards an adaptive learning process using artificial intelligence technologies. In: Motahhir, S., Bossoufi, B. (eds.) ICDTA 2023. LNNS, vol. 668, pp. 23–32. Springer, Cham (2023). https://doi.org/10.1007/978-3-031-29857-8_3
49. Guo, J.V., Francis, P.A., Tan, G.: D-pen-personalised practice with assistive pen for young dyslexic learners using machine learning. In: Guo, H., et al. (eds.) IRCSET 2022, pp. 209–243. Springer, Singapore (2023). https://doi.org/10.1007/978-981-19-7222-5_18
50. Pazmiño, K.L., Guerrero, E.J., Aguilar E, F.D., Arellano G, P.R., Garcés Cobos, F.: Presyllabic method to correct dysorthography in elementary school students. In: Botto-Tobar, M., Gómez, O.S., Rosero Miranda, R., Dıaz Cadena, A., Luna-Encalada, W. (eds.) ICAETT 2022. LNNS, vol. 619, pp. 325–336. Springer, Cham (2022). doi:https://doi.org/10.1007/978-3-031-25942-5_26
51. Al Yaari, S., et al.: Employing smart educational aids and multimedia to teach reading skill to students with specific learning difficulty: effectiveness identification and task specificity. In: Kang, DK., Alfred, R., Ismail, Z.I.B.A., Baharum, A., Thiruchelvam, V. (eds.) ICCST 2022. LNEE, vol. 983, 259–272. Springer, Singapore (2022). https://doi.org/10.1007/978-981-19-8406-8_19
52. Benmarrakchi, F., Ouherrou, N., Elhammoumi, O., El Kafi, J.: An innovative approach to involve students with learning disabilities in intelligent learning systems. In: Ezziyyani, M. (ed.) AI2SD 2018. AISC, vol. 914, pp. 39–50. Springer, Cham (2019). https://doi.org/10.1007/978-3-030-11884-6_4
53. Lyytinen, H., Ronimus, M., Alanko, A., Poikkeus, A.M., Taanila, M.: Early identification of dyslexia and the use of computer game-based practice to support reading acquisition. Nordic Psychol. **59**(2), 109–126 (2007)
54. Subudhi, A., Hasan, N., Nene, M.J.: Deen: deep ensemble framework for neuroatypicality classification. In: 2023 3rd International Conference on Intelligent Technologies (CONIT), pp. 1–6. IEEE (2023)

Workshop CLNN

Proficiency Effect on the Development of L2 Derivational Knowledge

Xingcheng Wang(✉) and Helen Zhao

University of Melbourne, Melbourne, Australia
{xingchengw1,helen.zhao}@unimelb.edu.au

Abstract. The present study examines second language (L2) learners' development of English derivational morphology and its relation to L2 proficiency. There is a limited number of empirical studies on L2 derivational morphology, particularly regarding relational, syntactic, and distributional aspects of derivational knowledge. Little is known about how these sub-aspects of derivational knowledge develop over time and how each aspect correlates to L2 proficiency. Fifty-four Chinese learners of English at three proficiency levels (intermediate, upper-intermediate, and advanced) were tested on their knowledge of morphological relatedness, syntactic categories, and distributional constraints. Results showed that L2 learners demonstrated a native-like pattern of acquiring relational, syntactic, and distributional knowledge. Learners' relational knowledge tended to stabilize once they reached and went beyond upper-intermediate proficiency, while their syntactic and distributional knowledge continued to grow. However, only intermediate learners showed moderate to strong correlations between L2 proficiency and overall derivational knowledge and between L2 proficiency and subcomponents of derivational knowledge (relational and distributional knowledge). L2 proficiency had statistically significant effects on each aspect of derivational knowledge and learners tended to score higher on well-formed than pseudo-formed derivatives. The findings provide important pedagogical implications to instruction on derivational morphology for learners at different stages of L2 learning.

Keywords: morphological awareness · derivational awareness · derivational knowledge · language proficiency

1 Introduction

Word knowledge plays a key role in learners' understanding of texts (Perfetti & Stafura, 2014) and literacy development (Marinova-Todd et al., 2013). Perfetti (2007) argued that with refined morphological awareness learners had a high-quality inventory of words. The facilitative effect of morphological awareness on vocabulary acquisition has been revealed in both L1 and L2 empirical studies (e.g., Cheung et al, 2010; Kieffer & Box, 2013; Ramirez et al., 2011; Sparks & Deacon, 2015; Zhang & Koda, 2012). Morphological awareness develops due to the increasing knowledge of word-formation processes in language emergence (Zhang, 2017). In particular, derivational awareness, a subdomain

Z. Kubincová et al. (Eds.): SETE 2023, LNCS 14606, pp. 173–187, 2024.
https://doi.org/10.1007/978-981-97-4243-1_14

of morphological awareness, enables learners to infer the meaning of an unfamiliar morphologically complex word (e.g., *unreasonable*) through decomposition (the prefix *un-*, the base *reason*, and the suffix–*able*). Additionally, knowledge of derivational morphology allows learners to infer syntactic information of a derivative through its suffix (*-able* indicates an adjective). More importantly, learners, with sufficient derivational knowledge, can generalise the use of morpheme components and to produce novel derivatives that follow orthographic and phonological constraints (Diessel, 2004).

Despite its utility, derivational knowledge was observed to be acquired later than some other word components such as form-meaning association and collocation (González-Fernández & Schmitt, 2020). Some L1 studies reported the cross-sectional development of morphological awareness including derivational awareness among English-speaking children (e.g., Carlisle, 2000; Nagy et al., 2006; Tyler & Nagy, 1989). While there are some studies that have addressed the same question in L2 acquisition (e.g., Lam et al., 2012; Ramirez et al., 2011; Zhang, 2017; Zhang & Koda, 2014), much less research has specifically focused on the L2 development of derivational knowledge and recognised the multilayered complexity of this construct (Tyler & Nagy, 1989).

2 Literature Review

2.1 Derivational Awareness and Three Aspects of Derivational Knowledge

Apel (2014) elaborately presented that derivational awareness includes the awareness of words in both spoken and written forms, the meaning of morphemes (the base and affixes), the grammatical class of the base and suffixes (e.g., nominal suffix *-er* causes a verb to be a noun, such as in *work-worker*), the orthographic and phonological changes that affixal concatenation may bring (e.g., *divide-division*), and the relation between the base and affixes, i.e. there is an authentic morphological relation between *teach* and *teacher*, but a pseudo relation between *corn* and *corner*. In short, derivational awareness serves as a global construct of derivational morphology that includes strategic manipulation of morpheme constituents and different aspects of derivational knowledge, e.g., morphological relatedness, syntactic functions, and distributional constraints.

Derivational knowledge is demonstrated as a separate construct from vocabulary breadth (Leontjev et al., 2022). According to Tyler and Nagy (1989), derivational knowledge can be operationalized into three main aspects, namely relational, syntactic, and distributional knowledge. Relational knowledge refers to the ability to identify the genuine morphological relatedness between two or more words (e.g., *general-generally* as opposed to *read-ready* or *cent-centre*). Syntactic knowledge is the ability to perceive the syntactic categories that derivational suffixes assign to the stem (Lieber, 2015). Without knowing the meaning and syntactic category of an unknown stem (e.g., *glottal*), a learner can make inference on the part of speech of a derivative (e.g., *glottalize* as a verb or *glottalization* as a noun). Distributional knowledge is the perception of constraints that affect how stems and affixes concatenate. A given derivational affix can only attach to stems that fit specific phonological, morphological, semantic, or syntactic properties (Dixon, 2014; Plag & Baayen, 2009). For example, the verbal suffix–*ify* attaches to adjectives (e.g., *solid*) but not to verbs (e.g., *hit*), so *solidify* is well-formed while **hitify* is ill-formed. Although derivational affixation is relatively predictable, the productivity of individual affixes varies due to the aforementioned linguistic restrictions.

To date, L1 studies on derivational morphology have shown that native English-speaking learners start to acquire relational knowledge at as early as Grade 2 to 3 (Carlisle, 2000; Mahony et al., 2000; McBridge-Change et al., 2005; Nagy et al., 2006; Sparks & Deacon, 2015). Tyler and Nagy (1989) reported that 4th grade children started to apply some syntactic knowledge to infer the parts of speech of unknown derivatives, whereas distributional knowledge was found to be acquired even later. Distributional knowledge is more cognitive demanding than relational and syntactic knowledge as it is a more sophisticated construct on how various properties of the stem and the affix interact under concatenation constraints. They also indicated that learners' derivational knowledge in all three aspects improved over years, although the acquisition of distributional constraints apparently fell behind those of relational and syntactic knowledge.

2.2 L2 Derivational Knowledge and L2 Proficiency

L2 learners of English are often instructed to use their derivational knowledge as a strategic tool to determine syntactic and semantic properties of unknown derived words. However, only a few studies have investigated the growth in L2 derivational knowledge cross-sectionally. Among those, most used masked priming methods to examine how learners acquire relational knowledge. To date, little research has been done to investigate how L2 learners develop all three aspects of derivational knowledge (relational, syntactic, and distributional) as their proficiency increases in a target language (except Menut et al., 2023).

Most of these priming studies conclude that knowledge of morphological relatedness develops along with the increase of L2 proficiency. More competent learners tended to show full priming effects when processing morphologically related word pairs, whereas less competent learners showed less or no such priming effects and were more likely to react to form-based priming or pseudo prime-target pairs. For example, Li et al. (2017) employed a masked priming lexical decision task to investigate Chinese-English bilinguals' sensitivity to derivational relation in English. The participants were assigned to a high–and a low-proficiency group on the basis of a paper-and-pencil English vocabulary test and their estimated weekly use of English. The bilinguals of both proficiencies showed full priming effects in all three conditions: transparent priming (e.g., *hunter-HUNT*), opaque priming (e.g., *corner-CORN,* in which–*er* is not attached as a derivational suffix and thus is a pseudo pair), and form priming (e.g., *freeze-FREE,* merely an orthographic overlap). The less proficient learners had stronger form priming (i.e., relying more on orthographic than derivational information). Also using priming but neuro-imaging techniques, Liang and Chen (2014) recorded the brain activities for event-related potentials (ERPs) when Chinese learners of English did online lexical decision on morphologically complex words. Scores of College English Test Band 6 (CET-6) administered by China's Ministry of Education was used to differentiate high–versus low-proficiency learners. The ERP data indicated that only high-proficiency L2 learners showed transparent priming, while form priming and semantic inhibition (e.g., *laughing-smile*) were observed in both high–and low-proficiency groups. Both Li et al. (2017) and Liang and Chen (2014) demonstrate that less proficient L2 learners, strongly affected by the surface orthography of prime-target pairs, tended to rely more on lexical storage during online processing of derived words and had not yet developed rule-based decomposition as high-proficiency learners.

Deng et al. (2017) found that learners with the same general L2 proficiency but differing in the domain specific competence of morphological knowledge showed different masked priming effects. Chinese learners of English were matched on L2 proficiency measured by the Oxford Placement Test (OPT) (Allan, 1992) and were divided into a high and a low morphological knowledge group. The results revealed a full priming effect on derived suffixed primes in the high-knowledge group, but no priming effect in the low-knowledge group. Meanwhile, only the high-knowledge group exhibited a significant processing cost (i.e., caused by rule-based decomposition) in the online processing of derived words.

In contrast, evidence from other priming studies provides counterevidence. Kraut (2015) investigated the relationship between gains in L2 morphological awareness and growth in L2 proficiency with a masked priming lexical decision task and a derivation task (i.e., to derive the stem of a morphologically complex word). They benchmarked participants' L2 proficiency against the Common European Framework Reference (CEFR) (Council of Europe, 2001). Advanced learners (B2 level) outperformed intermediate learners (A2 level) in the derivation task. But neither group showed any effect of morphological priming. Silva and Clahsen (2008) reported an only partial priming effect (instead of full priming) when advanced Chinese and German learners of English processed derivatives with deadjectival nominalizations (i.e. *-ness* and–*ity*). They also used the OPT (Allan, 1992) to measure L2 proficiency.

Menut et al. (2023) investigated how well French-English speakers at different proficiency levels (proficiency measured by a translation task and a lexical task) performed in three tasks that measured lexical semantic knowledge, syntactic knowledge, and distributive knowledge. Results confirmed that scores significantly improved with increased L2 proficiency in all three tasks and strongly associated with the lexical task, which is consistent with the results observed by (Iwaizumi & Webb, 2022), which suggested that learners' L2 vocabulary levels can to some extent indicate L2 derivational knowledge but in production tasks.

In short, despite the limited number of previous studies, most of them supported that learners with higher L2 competence showed a more nativelike sensitivity to the English derivational structure than less competent learners. Apparently, no clear standard has been established to define L2 proficiency among studies. Different proficiency measures were used by researchers, e.g., CET-6 in Liang and Chen (2014), a self-designed vocabulary test in Li et al. (2017), OPT in Deng et al. (2017) and Silva and Chen (2008), and translation and lexical tasks in Menut et al., (2023). This makes it difficult to compare and generalise the findings across them. In addition, most studies focused on investigating learner sensitivity to morphological relatedness. We need more empirical studies to explicate the complex interface between L2 proficiency and other aspects of derivational knowledge including syntactic and distributional knowledge.

3 The Present Study

The overall trend indicates that learners of higher L2 proficiency demonstrated a stronger sensitivity to derivational relations in online lexical processing than that of learners with lower proficiency. While some insights on this issue have been provided, the current study attempts to fill a few important gaps. First, there are a very limited number of studies on this topic and almost all of them only focused on the investigation of learners' derivational knowledge on morphological relatedness, with unvarying priming paradigms implemented in lexical decision tasks. L2 learners were benchmarked against the adult native speaker norm and were scrutinized for non-native-like behaviours in decomposing morphologically complex words (e.g., Diependaele et al., 2011; Li et al., 2017). As previous L1 studies have shown, derivational knowledge is a multidimensional construct with its sub-components playing different functions at different stages of language development (Tyler & Nagy, 1989). But little has been done to comprehensively capture the development of different aspects of L2 derivational knowledge, particularly in terms of syntactic functions and distributional constraints, with the growth of L2 competence (except Menut et al., 2023). Also, there is a great inconsistency in the determination of L2 proficiency levels among the previous studies on derivational knowledge. Probably due to lack of feasibility, very few of them could use widely-recognised standardized proficiency tests to measure participants' L2 proficiency. In some studies, the division of proficiency levels could be rather arbitrary and relative. This makes it difficult to compare, synthesize and generalise across findings of different studies.

Therefore, the current study aims to investigate how Chinese-speaking EFL learners at three L2 proficiency levels acquire the relational, syntactic, and distributional knowledge of English derivational morphology. We focus on the examination of receptive derivational knowledge and test learners on the processing of well-formed and pseudo-formed derivational relations. Specifically, the study addresses the following research questions:

1. What are the relationships between learners' L2 proficiency and their relational, syntactic, and distributional aspects of L2 receptive derivational knowledge?
2. How does L2 proficiency influence learners' relational, syntactic, and distributional knowledge of well-formed and pseudo-formed derivational relations?

4 Methodology

4.1 Participants

Fifty-eight (30 male and 28 female) Chinese learners of English in a major city in China participated in the study. Their average age was 16 years old and eighteen participants were in the 10th grade, 32 were in the 11th grade, and 8 were in the 12th grade. Participants' L2 proficiency was indexed by their IETLS scores. The mean overall score, mean reading score, and mean writing score were 5.6 (SD = .53), 5.7 (SD = .79), and 5.5 (SD = .43) respectively. On average, their L2 proficiency corresponds to CEFR B1 to B2 levels. Participants were divided into three proficiency groups according to their overall IELTS scores: 4.5 to 5 as the intermediate group (n = 20), 5.5 to 6 as the upper-intermediate group (n = 26), and above 6.5 as the advanced group (n = 12).

Their language background was collected using the simplified Chinese version of the Language History Questionnaire Version 3.0 (Li et al., 2019). Participants generally started English learning at the age of 6 (SD = 1.46), with the earliest at 3 and the latest at 9. Participants spent more than three-quarters of daily time on speaking their L1 (Mandarin) (SD = .12), while they used L2 (English) mainly in the classroom or when doing English assignments (25%, SD = .15). Seven participants were studying a third language (4 Japanese, 2 Spanish, 1 German), but they barely used the third language outside class hours. Four participants from the intermediate learner group were removed from the dataset due to their incompletion of all tasks. Therefore, 54 participants' data were valid and processed for the subsequent analyses presented in this study.

4.2 Research Design

The study adopted a mixed model design to investigate learners' multifaceted derivational knowledge at different proficiency levels. The current design included L2 proficiency (intermediate, upper-intermediate, advanced) as a between-subjects variable, and aspect of derivational knowledge (relational, syntactic, distributional) and formedness of derivational relation (well-formed, ill-formed) as within-subjects variables. Formedness was operationalised as whether the word stem and the derivational suffix formed a genuine derivational relation. Well-formed derivatives indicate a conventionalised stem-suffix relation, while "ill-formed" (pseudo-formed) derivatives violate this relation.

Stimuli. *Suffixes* – The current study only examined derivational suffixes. The target suffixes were selected from Bauer and Nation's (1993) affixes list in which affixes were stratified into a graded set of 7 levels. Multiple factors were considered to establish the hierarchical levels: affix frequency, affix productivity to produce novel words, affix predictability of the word meaning, regularity of the written and spoken form of the base, regularity of the written and spoken form of the affix, and regularity of function. The current study only used frequent derivational suffixes at Levels 3, 4, and 6, since Level 1 regards each word form as an independent word (e.g., *car* vs. *cars*), and Levels 2, 5, and 7 include only inflectional suffixes, infrequent affixes, and classical stems and affixes, respectively. In addition, the lexical stimuli were controlled for affixal neutrality (i.e., whether the concatenation of a suffix causes orthographic and/or phonological changes to its base). The target suffixes (Table 1) included 5 neutral suffixes and 5 non-neutral suffixes that carry different parts of speech. Note that the effect of affixal neutrality on L2 derivational knowledge is not within the scope of the current study.

Real words and pseudowords – the British National Corpus (BNC) word family lists (Nation, 2017) were used to select the real word stimuli in the derivational knowledge tasks. Only high-frequency words, i.e., at the first 1,000 and second 1,000 word-frequency levels, were used to form the target words (base and derived words) and test sentences. Four additional criteria were adopted in the stimuli selection:

- The word stems and their derivatives must belong to different parts of speech to allow for the testing on the knowledge of syntactic functions and distributional restrictions.
- Each word stem must have at least three derivational forms which make it possible to create sufficient answer choices in the syntactic knowledge task.

Table 1. Target derivational suffixes

	Part of speech			
	Nominal	Adjectival	Verbal	Adverbial
Neutral	*-ness, -er*	*-ful, -less*		*-ly*
Non-neutral	*-ion, -ity*	*-ic, -ial*	*-ify*	

- Suffixation includes minimal orthographical and phonological shifts (e.g., *face* → *facial*) to control for a potential intervening effect on cognitive loading that morphological complexity may cause (Tyler & Nagy, 1989).
- Suffixal stacking is averted by allowing only one layer of suffix concatenated to each stem. For instance, one stimulus used was *'general-ly'*, which is derived from *'general'*. Although *'general-iz(e)-ation'* is a possible derivative, it was not used as the targeted item.

Pseudowords were created with *Wuggy* (Keuleers & Brysbaert, 2010), a pseudoword generator, with anchor words (words used to generate nonwords) from the first 1,000 and second 1,000 word-frequency levels in the BNC word family list (e.g., *leace* comes from *lease*). All pseudowords followed English orthographical and phonological criteria, and all derived pseudowords followed English phonotactic constraints (e.g., *rin-ful, fool-ity, mun-ion*).

Instruments. Three separate tasks were designed to examine learners' relational, syntactic, and distributional knowledge, following Tyler and Nagy's (1989) framework of definition. All tasks in the study were programmed and implemented online via Qualtrics, and test items presented to participants were randomised.

Relational knowledge test. This test was modelled on the morphological relation judgement task (Nagy et al., 2006). Participants were asked to judge whether the second word in a word pair (e.g., *awareness*) forms a genuine derivational relation with the first word (e.g., *aware*). Ten pairs such as *aware-awareness* contained a well-formed derivational relation, whereas the other 10 pairs such as *corn-corner* formed a pseudo-formed derivational relation since the word *corner* is not derived from the word *corn.* In the pseudo-formed pairs, *'-y'* (neutral) and *'-th'* (non-neutral) were added as additional filler suffixes. The Cronbach's α was .72.

Syntactic knowledge test. This test was formulated as a sentence completion task modelled on Nagy et al. (2006) that measured participants' understanding of the syntactic properties of derivational suffixes. Participants read sentences each of which contains an empty slot that requires an obligatory suppliance of a derived word with the correct part of speech. Each slot was given three answer choices (derivatives) that shared a common stem. The lengths of the test sentences were controlled to offer sufficient but succinct information for participants to judge the syntactic function of the derivative. The target derived word was either a real word (well-formed) or a pseudoword (ill-formed). As an example of a pseudoword item, in the sentence '*He is a good ___ of the company*', participants chose among three pseudo-derivatives, *moller* (the correct choice due to the nominal suffix), *mollic* and *mollize*. Participants could only rely on the syntactic information carried by the suffixes in order to make a judgment. Only the syntactically correct answer would fit the context sentence. There were 10 real-word target items and 10 pseudoword items, both with an equal number of phonologically neutral and non-neutral suffixed derivatives. The Cronbach's α was .82.

Distributional knowledge test. This test was carried out in the form of a simple lexical decision task (Meyer & Schvaneveldt, 1971). The task required participants to judge as fast as possible whether a lexical stimulus visually presented on the screen was a real word (well-formed derivative) or a pseudoword (ill-formed derivative). There were 20 real-word items and 20 pseudoword items with an equal distribution of items with phonologically neutral and non-neutral suffixes. All stimuli were chosen or formed within a similar word length (8 to 10 letters), with an average length of 9 letters for both well-formed and pseudo-formed items. The Cronbach's α was .83.

4.3 Data Collection Procedures

The study was administered in three language training schools, and one self-study session was used for data collection. All tasks and the LHQ3.0 were completed online during the session. All participants were first guided to finish the LHQ via a Qualtrics link, and then they were instructed to take the tests in the following sequence: from the on-line processing task (distributional knowledge test) to recognition tests (relational knowledge test) and finally to the more analytical test (syntactic knowledge test). During all tasks, only one item was shown to participants on the screen each time. Once a response was logged, the webpage automatically moved to the next screen with no going-back available. All responses were automatically scored for accuracy of response and stored in the university's web server.

4.4 Data Analysis

Descriptive and inferential statistics were performed using SPSS (version 26.0, IBM Corp.). A Pearson's correlation analysis was implemented to answer RQ1, which investigated the relationships between L2 proficiency and the three aspects of receptive derivational knowledge. A three-way mixed model ANOVA was used to address RQ2 which was to analyse the main effects and interactions among L2 proficiency, aspect of derivational knowledge, and formedness of derivational relation. Follow-up step-down analyses were carried out to unveil identified interaction effects. Data normality had been assessed prior to parametric analyses and no significant departures were revealed.

5 Results

5.1 Relationships Between L2 Proficiency and Three Aspects of L2 Derivational Knowledge

Descriptive statistics (Table 2) show that overall participants scored the highest in relational knowledge (mean = .84), followed by syntactic knowledge (mean = .66) and distributional knowledge (mean = .61). Table 2 also reveals a steady development in L2 learners' derivational knowledge. With increasing L2 proficiency, participants showed continued growth in all three aspects of derivational knowledge (advanced > upper-intermediate > intermediate). Learners consistently performed better in the relational and syntactic knowledge tasks than in the distribution task, except that intermediate learners scored lower on syntactic knowledge than on distributional knowledge. Interestingly, compared to the larger growth in learners' understanding of morphological relatedness (.74 to .94) and syntactic properties (.48 to .89) of derivatives as a function of the proficiency increase, the improvement in distributional knowledge lagged behind (.55 to .70).

Results of Pearson's correlations between L2 proficiency (indicated by participants' IELTS scores) and the other variables are presented in Table 3. L2 proficiency and overall derivational knowledge were strongly correlated ($r = .76, p < .01$), which demonstrated an approximately 60% shared variance. L2 proficiency showed moderate to strong correlations with all aspects of derivational awareness (all *ps* < .01). L2 proficiency had a stronger correlation with syntactic knowledge ($r = .71$) than with relational and distributional knowledge ($r = .60$ and $r = .54$, respectively). Also, correlations among the three aspects of derivational knowledge were moderate (.45 to .51, all *ps* < .01), which indicates that relational, syntactic, and distributional knowledge shared a certain degree of variance but are sufficiently different from each other to be independent constructs.

Table 2. Mean accuracy of response in derivational knowledge tests by proficiency

Proficiency	**Relational**	**Syntactic**	**Distributional**	**Overall**
	Mean (Standard Deviation)			
Intermediate (n = 16)	.74 (.16)	.48 (.18)	.55 (.12)	.58 (.12)
Upper-intermediate (n = 26)	.85 (.09)	.68 (.16)	.61 (.10)	.68 (.07)
Advanced (n = 12)	.94 (.06)	.89 (.11)	.70 (.06)	.81 (.04)
Total (N = 54)	.84 (.13)	.66 (.22)	.61 (.11)	.68 (.12)

Note. The overall score is the sum of correct responses divided by the total number of items in relational, syntactic, and distribution knowledge tests

A breakdown analysis on Pearson's correlations between variables by proficiency. Only the intermediate group showed a significant correlation between L2 proficiency and overall derivational knowledge ($r = .63, p < .01$). Intermediate learners also showed a strong correlation between L2 proficiency and relational knowledge ($r = .78, p < .01$) and a moderate correlation between L2 proficiency and distributional knowledge ($r = .50, p < .05$). However, neither advance learners nor upper-intermediate learners showed significant correlations between L2 proficiency and their overall derivational knowledge or any aspect of knowledge.

Table 3. Correlations among variables across all proficiency groups

All Participants		1	2	3	4
1	L2 Proficiency				
2	Relational Knowledge	.60**			
3	Syntactic Knowledge	.71**	.51**		
4	Distributional Knowledge	.54**	.47**	.45**	
5	Derivational Knowledge (Overall)	.76**	.75**	.82**	.83**

5.2 Effects of L2 Proficiency, Aspect of Knowledge, and Well-Formedness on L2 Derivational Knowledge

A three-way mixed ANOVA analysis was performed to investigate the influence of one between-subjects variable (L2 proficiency: advanced, upper-intermediate, intermediate proficiency) and two within-subjects variables (aspect of derivational knowledge: relational, syntactic, distributional knowledge; formedness: well-formed vs. ill-formed derivational relation) on the mean accuracy of learner responses. The analysis yielded main effects of L2 proficiency ($F(2,51) = 26.85$, $p < .001$, partial $\eta^2 = .51$), aspect of knowledge ($F(2,102) = 62.84$, $p < .001$, partial $\eta^2 = .55$) and formedness ($F(1,51) = 19.65$, $p < .001$, partial $\eta^2 = .28$). There were also significant interactions between L2 proficiency and aspect of knowledge ($F(4,102) = 5.86$, $p < .001$, partial $\eta^2 = .19$) and between aspect of knowledge and formedness ($F(2,102) = 4.08$, $p < .05$, partial $\eta^2 = .07$). The proficiency × formedness interaction and the proficiency × aspect of knowledge × formedness three-way interaction were not statistically significant ($p >$ .05).

Step-down analyses were implemented to explicate the main effects and the interactions. L2 proficiency was found to have a significant influence on all aspects of derivational knowledge. The proficiency effect was most salient in syntactic knowledge in which all three proficiency groups performed differently. The group difference and the interaction are illustrated in Fig. 1. Specifically regarding the processing of relational knowledge, both advanced learners and upper-intermediate learners were significantly different from intermediate learners, with $t(20) = 4.53$, $p < .001$ and $t(22) = 2.43$, $p <$ .05 respectively, whereas there was no significant group difference between advanced and upper-intermediate learners ($p >$ .05, indicated by Bonferroni adjustment). For syntactic knowledge, L2 proficiency was significant in all group comparisons: advanced vs. upper-intermediate ($t(36) = 4.21$, $p < .001$), advanced vs. intermediate ($t(26) = 7.10$, $p < .001$), and upper-intermediate vs. intermediate learner groups ($t(40) = 3.79$, $p < .01$). For distributional knowledge, there were significant group differences between advanced and intermediate learner groups ($t(26) = 3.71$, $p < .01$) and between advanced and upper-intermediate learner groups ($t(36) = 2.78$, $p < .01$). No significant effect of L2 proficiency was found between upper-intermediate and intermediate learners' distributional knowledge. Figure 2 illustrates the interaction between aspect of derivational knowledge and formedness. Participants consistently performed better on well-formed than ill-formed derivatives in both syntactic and distributional knowledge tasks (t(53)

= 2.04, $p < .05$ and $t(53) = 4.97$, $p < .001$ respectively), whereas they achieved a fairly equal amount of accuracy on well-formed and pseudo-formed derivatives in the relational knowledge task ($p > .05$).

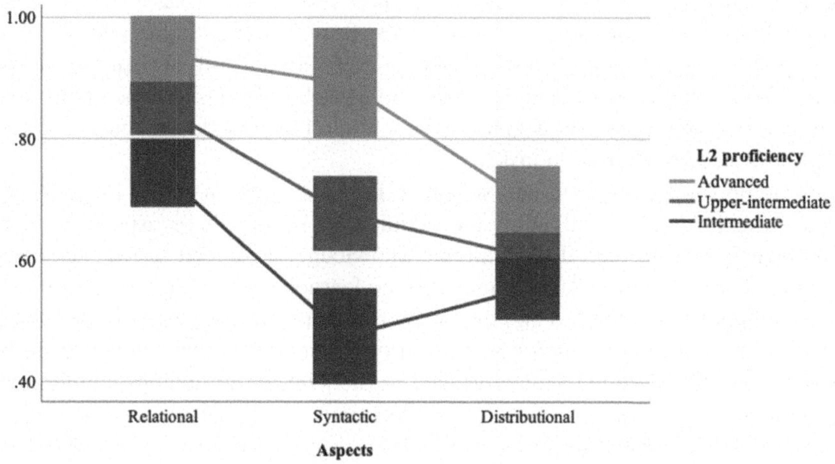

Fig. 1. Interaction between L2 proficiency and aspect of derivational knowledge

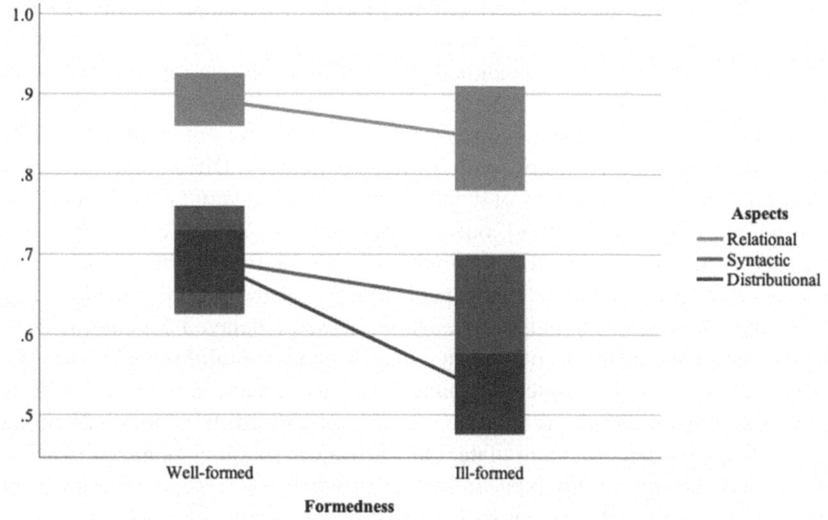

Fig. 2. Interaction between aspect of derivational knowledge and formedness of derivational relation

6 Discussion

Aligned with findings in L1 studies on derivational knowledge (Tyler & Nagy, 1989), L2 learners experienced a similar difficulty hierarchy in the acquisition of relational, syntactic, and distributional knowledge. It requires less effort for L2 learners to understand morphological relatedness between words. But mastering and manipulating syntactic properties and distributional constraints of derivational suffixes is more strenuous for them. The finding concurs with Hayashi and Murphy (2011), in which intermediate Japanese learners of English showed limited manipulation of syntactic and distributional knowledge in an affix elicitation task.

The finding on the acquisitional sequence is further demonstrated in the ANOVA results on the proficiency effect in the acquisition of the three aspects of derivational knowledge. With regard to relational knowledge, advanced learners and upper-intermediate learners outperformed intermediate learners, but no significant difference was revealed between advanced and upper-intermediate learners; learners showed continuous development of syntactic knowledge throughout the three proficiency levels; with regard to distributional knowledge, advanced learners outperformed upper-intermediate and intermediate learners, but no difference between upper-intermediate and intermediate learners. As indicated by Pienemann's Processability Theory (1998), L2 learners need to cultivate their processing abilities progressively to accommodate the increasing complexity of a linguistic operation. As the easiest, relational knowledge was the earliest acquired type of derivational knowledge. Exposure to L2 input with support from classroom instruction on frequent derivational morphemes enabled learners to develop the ability to recognize the internal structure of a derivative. They honed their skills in recognizing whether there exists an authentic morphological relation in complex words (e.g., *worker* vs. **corner*). Once they became adept at rule-based decomposition, the development of relational knowledge reached the ceiling and got stabilized. Syntactic knowledge was difficult for learners with limited proficiency. Differentiation and memorization of the syntactic functions of derivational suffixes are cognitive demanding and require time and effort. But to work out the grammatical role that a derivative assigns in a sentence is a common type of grammar exercise for EFL learners. Learners continued to develop competence in this aspect. Finally, distributional knowledge as the most difficult type of derivational knowledge witnessed a delayed development. By its nature, distributional constraints of concatenation depend on multilayered metacognitive awareness including morphological, semantic, syntactic, and phonological awareness. Distributional constraints are predictable, but less organised, thus are challenging for lower-proficiency learners to manipulate. Only advanced learners managed to achieve a significant breakthrough in this type. In fact, even advanced learners only achieved 70 percent accuracy on the 10 frequent suffixes in the distributional knowledge test.

We also examined whether formedness of derivational relation had an influence on the performance of all three distributional knowledge tasks across proficiency groups. Results demonstrated that all learner groups scored higher on well-formed than pseudo-formed derivatives in the syntactic and distributional knowledge tasks, but not in the relational knowledge task. A possible explanation is that learners could well-differentiate real words (well-formed) from pseudowords (ill-formed) in the syntactic and distributional knowledge tasks. But pseudo-formed pairs used in the relational knowledge task were formulated by highly frequent real words with pseudo morphological relations (e.g., *corn-corner*). In terms of learner familiarity with the lexical stimuli, the contrast between real words and pseudowords is much larger than the contrast between the real word pairs with real vs. pseudo morphological relations.

7 Conclusion

As inflectional morphology has drawn vast attention in the fields of first and second language acquisition, the present study contributes to the much-needed research on derivational knowledge in SLA. The findings of the study revealed the rich nature of how learners with varied L2 proficiency processed derivational morphology. Learners' derivational knowledge developed as their language abilities enhanced; more precisely, relational knowledge stabilized once learners' decoding ability matured, while syntactic knowledge and distributional knowledge continued to grow. Learners at earlier stages of acquiring an additional language may benefit more from derivational morphology. More advanced learners' development of derivational knowledge may be contributed more by metacognitive skills beyond word decoding. We acknowledge the limitation of a relatively small sample size in our advanced learner group, which may impact the generalizability of the findings to a broad population. Further studies are needed to address this issue.

Such findings provide important implications for language instructors to design pedagogy that will cater for learners' demands at different learning stages. Comprehensive derivational knowledge will benefit learners in vocabulary building (González-Fernández & Schmitt, 2020), reading comprehension (Zhang & Koda, 2013), and writing (McCutchen & Stull, 2015). Its benefit for vocabulary learning may be most effective at the relatively earlier stages of L2 development (intermediate or below), during which learners are most cognitively ready and active (Pienemann, 1998) in forstering derivational awareness. Thus, derivational knowledge can be optimally teachable at such phases. Beginner and elementary learners can start with learning how to identify morphological relatedness and gradually move to syntactic functions. Instruction at the earlier stages can prioritize high-frequency derivational affixes, the knowledge of which can facilitate the learning of words belonging to the same word family and help with sentence parsing. Intermediate to more advanced learners can focus on less frequent and irregular derivational affixes and the development of distributional knowledge. Instruction can further encourage productive use of a wider variety of derivational morphemes to enrich lexical use.

8 Funding Acknowledgement

The author(s) received no financial support for the research, authorship, and/or publication of this article.

References

Allan, D.: Oxford Placement Test. Oxford University Press (1992)

Apel, K.: A comprehensive definition of morphological awareness: Implications for assessment. Top. Lang. Disord. **34**(3), 197–209 (1992)
Bauer, L., Nation, P.: Word families. Int. J. Lexicogr. **6**(4), 253–279 (1993)
Carlisle, J.F.: Awareness of the structure and meaning of morphologically complex words: Impact on reading. Read. Writ. **12**(3), 169–190 (2000)
Cheung, H., Chung, K.K.H., Wong, S.W.L., McBride-Chang, C., Penney, T.B., Ho, C.S.H.: Speech perception, metalinguistic awareness, reading, and vocabulary in Chinese-English bilingual children. J. Educ. Psychol. **102**(2), 367–380 (2010)
Council of Europe.: Common European framework of reference for languages: Learning, teaching, assessment. University of Cambridge (2001)
Deng, T., Shi, J., Bi, H., Dunlap, S., Chen, B.: The relationship between the morphological knowledge and L2 online processing of derivational words. Int. J. Biling. **21**(4), 402–418 (2017)
Diependaele, K., Duñabeitia, J.A., Morris, J., Keuleers, E.: Fast morphological effects in first and second language word recognition. J. Mem. Lang. **64**(4), 344–358 (2011)
Diessel, H.: The acquisition of complex sentences (Vol. 105). Cambridge University Press (2004)
Dixon, R. M.: Making new words: Morphological derivation in English. Oxford University Press (2014)
González-Fernández, B., Schmitt, N.: Word knowledge: Exploring the relationships and order of acquisition of vocabulary knowledge components. Appl. Linguis. **41**(4), 481–505 (2020)
Hayashi, Y., Murphy, V.: An investigation of morphological awareness in Japanese learners of English. Language Learning Journal **39**(1), 105–120 (2011)
Iwaizumi, E., Webb, S.: Measuring L1 and L2 productive derivational knowledge: How many derivatives can L1 and L2 learners with differing vocabulary levels produce? TESOL Q. **56**(1), 100–129 (2022)
Keuleers, E., Brysbaert, M.: Wuggy: A multilingual pseudoword generator. Behav. Res. Methods **42**(3), 627–633 (2010)
Kieffer, M.J., Box, C.D.: Derivational morphological awareness, academic vocabulary, and reading comprehension in linguistically diverse sixth graders. Learn. Individ. Differ. **24**, 168–175 (2013)
Kraut, R.: The relationship between morphological awareness and morphological decomposition among English language learners. Read. Writ. **28**(6), 873–890 (2015)
Lam, K., Chen, X., Geva, E., Luo, Y.C., Li, H.: The role of morphological awareness in reading achievement among young Chinese-speaking English language learners: A longitudinal study. Read. Writ. **25**(8), 1847–1872 (2012)
Leontjev, D., Huhta, A., Tolvanen, A.: L2 English vocabulary breadth and knowledge of derivational morphology: One or two constructs? Lang. Test. **40**(2), 300–324 (2022)
Li, J., Taft, M., Xu, J.: The processing of English derived words by Chinese-English bilinguals. Lang. Learn. **67**(4), 858–884 (2017)
Li, P., Zhang, F., Yu, A., & Zhao, X.: Language History Questionnaire (LHQ3): An enhanced tool for assessing multilingual experience. Bilingualism: Language and Cognition, 1–7 (2019)
Liang, L., Chen, B.: Processing morphologically complex words in second-language learners: The effect of proficiency. Acta Physiol. (Oxf) **150**, 69–79 (2014)
Lieber, R.: Introducing morphology. Cambridge University Press (2015)
Mahony, D., Singson, M., Mann, V.: Reading ability and sensitivity to morphological relations. Reading and Writing: An Interdisciplinary Journal **12**(3), 191–218 (2000)
Marinova-Todd, S.H., Siegel, L., Mazabel, S.: The association between morphological awareness and literacy in English language learners from different language backgrounds. Top. Lang. Disord. **33**(1), 93–107 (2013)
McCutchen, D., Stull, S.: Morphological awareness and children's writing: accuracy, error, and invention. Read. Writ. **28**(2), 271–289 (2015)

Menut, A., Brysbaert, M., & Casalis, S.: Derivational awareness in late bilinguals increases along with proficiency without a clear influence of the suffixes shared with L1. Bilingualism: Language and Cognition, 26(1), 138–151 (2023)

Meyer, D.E., Schvaneveldt, R.W.: Facilitation in recognizing pairs of words: Evidence of a dependence between retrieval operations. J. Exp. Psychol. **90**(2), 227–234 (1971)

Nagy, W., Berninger, V.W., Abbott, R.D.: Contributions of morphology beyond phonology to literacy outcomes of upper elementary and middle-school students. J. Educ. Psychol. **98**(1), 134–147 (2006)

Nation, I.S.P.: The BNC/COCA Level 6 word family lists (Version 1.0.0) (2017)

Perfetti, C.: Reading ability: Lexical quality to comprehension. Sci. Stud. Read. **11**(4), 357–383 (2007)

Perfetti, C., Stafura, J.: Word knowledge in a theory of reading comprehension. Sci. Stud. Read. **18**(1), 22–37 (2014)

Pienemann, M.: Language processing and second language development: Processability theory. John Benjamins (1998)

Plag, I., Baayen, H.: Suffix ordering and morphological processing. Language **85**, 109–152 (2009)

Ramirez, G., Chen, X., Geva, E., Luo, Y.: Morphological awareness and word reading in English language learners: Evidence from Spanish-and Chinese-speaking children. Appl. Psycholinguist. **32**(3), 601–618 (2011)

Silva, R., & Clahsen, H.: Morphologically complex words in L1 and L2 processing: Evidence from masked priming experiments in English. Bilingualism: Language and Cognition, **11**(2), 245–260 (2008)

Sparks, E., Deacon, S.: Morphological awareness and vocabulary acquisition: A longitudinal examination of their relationship in English-speaking children. Appl. Psycholinguist. **36**(2), 299–321 (2015)

Tyler, A., Nagy, W.: The acquisition of English derivational morphology. J. Mem. Lang. **28**(6), 649–667 (1989)

Zhang, D., Koda, K.: Contribution of morphological awareness and lexical inferencing ability to L2 vocabulary knowledge and reading comprehension among advanced EFL learners: Testing direct and indirect effects. Reading and Writing: An Interdisciplinary Journal **25**(5), 1195–1216 (2012)

Zhang, D., Koda, K.: Morphological awareness and reading comprehension in a foreign language: A study of young Chinese EFL learners. System **41**(4), 901–913 (2013)

Zhang, D., Koda, K.: Awareness of derivation and compounding in Chinese-English biliteracy acquisition. Int. J. Biling. Educ. Biling. **17**(1), 55–73 (2014)

Zhang, D.: Derivational morphology in reading comprehension of Chinese-speaking learners of English: A longitudinal structural equation modeling study. Appl. Linguis. **38**(6), 871–895 (2017)

Mental Simulation of Implied Orientation Information in Chinese Sentences

Huili Wang[1], Wei Li[2], Beixian Gu[2], Yang Fu[1], Xin Chang[3], and Wei Liu[4](✉)

[1] School of Foreign Languages, Hangzhou City University, Hangzhou, China
[2] School of Foreign Languages, Dalian University of Technology, Dalian, China
[3] Department of English Teaching, Shenyang Normal University, Shenyang, China
[4] School of Education Sciences, Shenyang Normal University, Shenyang, China
liuwei53719@163.com

Abstract. The traditional theory amodal symbol system was challenged by Barsalou's Perceptual Symbol System theory. The Perceptual Symbol System theory indicates that perceptual symbols will be mentally simulated and automatically activated in the human brain in the process of language comprehension. Based on this theory, many empirical studies have provided evidence for mental simulation during language comprehension. However, object orientation, a critical part of perceptual information, has received less attention compared to other visual object attributes such as shape, color, and size. Furthermore, most studies in this field focused on English and other Indo-European languages, and the less research focused on Chinese to demonstrate the effectiveness of mental simulation. Therefore, the current paper aims to explore the mental simulation of object orientation information and its relationship with mental imagery in Chinese sentence comprehension. The classic sentence-picture recognition task was employed in the present research. Results showed that participants' responses were more accurate and faster in the match condition than in the mismatch condition and in the vertical direction task than in the horizontal direction task. Additionally, the results of the Vividness of Visual Imagery Questionnaire showed no significant correlation between mental simulation and mental imagery. Therefore, it can be concluded that in the process of Chinese sentence comprehension, the human brain activates the perceptual symbol of the object orientation information and conducts corresponding mental simulation. The findings agree with the Perceptual Symbol System theory and provide further empirical evidence for the mental simulation of sentence comprehension and embodied cognition.

Keywords: Sentence Comprehension · Mental Simulation · Implied Orientation · Perceptual Symbol System

1 Introduction

Much attention has been paid to a question in psycholinguistics, namely, how linguistic information is represented in the human brain. The amodal system theory was once popular, assuming that language processing is achieved through abstract, amodal, and

Z. Kubincová et al. (Eds.): SETE 2023, LNCS 14606, pp. 188–203, 2024.
https://doi.org/10.1007/978-981-97-4243-1_15

arbitrary symbols and the arbitrary relationship between language and its referents [1, 2]. Language meaning is derived from the connection between the signifier and the signified and has no relationship with the sensor and motor system. However, the embodied view of language comprehension challenges it for its unexplainable grounding problem [3] and provides numerous empirical supports. The embodied view claims that language processors will automatically simulate their experience and re–experience the event state as described in conversation through mental simulation [4]. In contrast to the traditional view, the embodied view believes that a word's meaning is embedded in the sensorimotor system. One would unconsciously trigger a relevant sensorimotor memory from a past experience while inferring a word's meaning. Consider a classic situation of a nail in the study of Stanfield and Zwaan [5], "The carpenter hammered the nail into the wall" and "The carpenter hammered the nail into the floor plank" Based on our sensorimotor experience, when participants were asked to judge the orientation of the nail in these two sentences, the answer would be horizontal or vertical. Therefore, they proposed that language speakers unconsciously simulate the situation in their minds when comprehending language.

Sentence-picture verification task serves as a classic paradigm to verify the mental simulation of object orientation, shape, color, size, and motor information, respectively. As for the object orientation, the results are mixed with match or mismatch advantages. However, most of them were confined to English or Indo–European languages. Thus, based on previous studies, this current research replicated the study of Stanfield and Zwaan [5], and attempted to investigate the mental simulations of object orientation across Chinese sentences and provide evidence for the embodied view of language comprehension. However, some researchers have suggested that people may apply the mental imagery strategy in language comprehension due to its similar processing mechanisms to mental simulation [6, 7] while others hold that conscious mental imagery is not equivalent to the conceptual representation [5]. Based on that, this paper employed a Vividness of Visual Imagery Questionnaire (VVIQ) as a post-test to explore the relationship between mental simulation and mental imagery.

The present study employed a sentence-picture verification paradigm to investigate whether mental simulations are activated across Chinese sentences with implied orientation information. As stated, the majority of previous research on mental simulation has taken English and other alphabetic languages as targets. Different from previous studies, the current paper extended the research into the embodiment effect of mental simulation on sentence comprehension in Chinese. Specifically, with Chinese-speaking participants, the present study aimed to enrich empirical evidence and analyze the influencing factors on the mental simulation of object orientation.

The following research questions are proposed in light of research objectives:

1) What is the effect of mental simulation of orientation information on Chinese sentence comprehension?
2) Does mental imagery share the same mechanism of language processing with mental simulation?

2 Literature Review

It is necessary to discuss words, the essential level of language, which has attracted much attention in linguistic circles, before proceeding to sentences. A number of studies have been conducted to prove that perceptual representations can be activated when reading or listening to isolated words. In the study of Zwaan and Yaxley [8], they attempt to explore whether the shape information would be activated during semantic processing. An experiment was designed to verify whether objects shape was activated during information processing. Participants were instructed to judge whether a target word is related to a prime word. Even when the prime and target words were not directly related, if they share similar shapes (e.g., Spoke versus Pin), participants took longer to respond "no" compared to unassociated prime-target pairs. The results indicate that shape information is indeed activated. In further studies of verifying the word's activation of perceptual representations, according to Guan, the core of mental simulation is the connection between the word and the memory trace of sensorimotor experience [4].

In terms of object shape, Zwaan, Stanfield, and Yaxley [9] found a matching effect by applying pictures that match or do not match the implied shape of an object (e.g., The ranger saw the eagle in the sky, followed by a picture of an eagle with folded wings or with outstretched wings). These shapes were implied by the context in the way of manipulating the location of the object. Immediately following the sentence, a picture was presented, and the participants were required to decide whether the depicted object had been mentioned in the preceding sentence. According to their results, participants were faster and more accurate to recognize the object when the shape of the picture matches the orientation implied by the sentence than when it does not match. Their study disclosed that people activate perceptual symbols of referents during language comprehension, even when the perceptual characteristics are merely implicit expressions in the context rather than explicitly stated. The sentential context has a strong and rather immediate impact on the nature of the mental representation. Based on Zwaan's experiment, a number of replications have been conducted showing the match effect. For instance, Zwaan and Pecher [10] designed six revisiting experiments to re-test mental simulation and found a significant effect on object shape than that in orientation. In addition to alphabetical languages, scholars have paid attention to Chinese. Li and Wang's results [11] also supported the perceptual symbols theory rather than the amodal theory and showed that the activation of perceptual symbols is a strategic process, which depends on whether the activation is meaningful to the current understanding. Perceptual symbols corresponding to object features are activated only when the activation is conducive to understanding. Similarly, Chang and Ling [12] investigated the effect of sentence features on the representation of the object's shape during language comprehension across primary school students. Their results support the opinion that no matter whether sentences are logical or illogical, participants can activate the perceptual representation of objects' information associated with language comprehension and their characteristics. Chang and Ling suggest that language comprehension encompasses the perceptual representation, which is a priority and a modal representation. Mental simulation lies in the process of language comprehension when participants view and process illogical sentences. When illogical sentences are present to the subjects, the simulation process exists in language comprehension. Li and Chang's studies provide convincing evidence for the impact of mental simulation in Chinese and further add positive support for the Perceptual Symbol System and embodied view of language comprehension. Previous research on object shape has drawn a common and well accepted conclusion that people will mentally represent object shape during language comprehension and exert a significant match effect in language processing.

Research has revealed that mental imagery and perception share a mechanism which is specific to certain senses [16] and conceptual features and the image activates the brain areas overlapping with the image of the perceived activity. Conceptual representations and mental imagery activate brain regions which are the same as those activated during perception [17, 18]. Mental imagery refers to the ability to create and manipulate images, even without current sensor and motor stimulation or explicit motor behavior. This function can be chained to mental activities and subjective feelings of people. It is widely believed that perception and action have similarities with mental representations, which are triggered by the sensorimotor system. Some researchers claim that the process of sensory movement's engagement in cognitive activities shares many similarities with mental imagery. For instance, most of the simulation process is based on mental simulation, performed unconsciously without costing cognitive resources [19]. Empirical data related to this issue vary in a small scope. Some studies have concluded that there is no natural connection between sensory representations and mental imagery in language comprehension. However, other scholars have verified the relationship between imagery ability and cognitive tasks through scores on imagery tests, particularly when facing the same mechanisms [7]. Pecher experimented on the subjects' spatial and visual imagination ability. The results showed that the effect of modality transformation is unrelated to imagination, which means that mental representation is not related to imagination and that concept is not represented by conscious imagination [20]. Additionally, one psychological test was designed by Zwaan and Pecher, concerning the subjects' mental imagery in the way of VVIQ. A vivid description was carried out by their correlation analysis with the match effect of object shape, color and orientation, namely, the mental simulation was not equal to mental imagery [14]. Consequently, concepts can be activated automatically by the sensor-motor system. And the activation process has nothing to do with an individual's ability to imagine objects. According to the view of embodied cognition theories, the role of the sensorimotor system is quite fundamental. Most likely, only the simulation of sensory actions is the main trigger. There are also more abstract and symbolic mechanisms involved in mental simulation, though. Indeed, some results that supported the mental simulation involved a mixture of sensorimotor and other effects. When the average was set, these effects may still include slight sensorimotor effects. In view of the previous studies, more research needs to be done on the relationship between mental image and mental simulation targeting Chinese speakers.

As reading Chinese characters requires a totally different transformation process compared to reading English words, that is, a grapheme-to-phoneme conversion rules versus the orthography-to-phonology transformation [21]. Considering the semantic representation of language comprehension may be influenced by mental imagery, this research designed a post-test to further clarify the correlation between mental imagery and mental simulation using the VVIQ. As mentioned above, sufficient studies can serve as evidence for the embodied view rather than the amodal view. Based on previous studies, conclusions can be drawn that mental simulation will be activated during language processing. Some representative studies of mental simulation in language comprehension were presented at the level of word processing and language comprehension from five aspects of the representation of implied shape, size, color, movement information and orientation. Apart from object orientation, it is fair to say scholars have reached a common ground through behavioral and ERP experiments, that is, a match advantage. While for object orientation, except for English as the target language, others such as German and Dutch all found a mismatch effect. Meanwhile, few studies have explored mental simulation at the level of object orientation. Hence, the combination of controversial conclusions about orientation and insufficient studies inspired the present study to conduct a behavioral experiment by taking Chinese speakers as target participants. Considering the unique characteristics of Chinese compared to alphabetic languages like English, the present study aimed to find a significant match effect and add positive support for the embodied view of language comprehension. As stated, Zwaan's experimental model would be adopted in the current study with proven and sufficient effectiveness. In a word, by taking Chinese native speakers as targets, this present research intended to investigate whether participants mentally simulate objects' implied orientation information in the process of understanding Chinese sentences on the basis of the Perceptual Symbol System.

3 Methodology

3.1 Participants

Forty participants were recruited for the pre-test, including 25 females and 15 males. For the main test, another eighty participants were recruited, which were all healthy, right-handed Chinese native speakers from a university in China majoring in different disciplines. All 120 participants were informed that data collected were only for academic use and their privacy information such as real names would not be recorded.

3.2 Pre-test

To make sure the validity of all materials, a pre-test was designed. In the pre-test, participants were asked to read Chinese sentences with a certain implicit orientation instead of expressed in an explicit way. Most of the experimental sentences were from the original study and they were translated into the natural Chinese version. Considering that there would be cultural differences and distinct language habitual use between English and Chinese, and to make sure that the validity of the experimental sentences, a pre-test was conducted by forty participants from a university in China.

It is important to ensure that the two sets of experimental sentences (horizontal and vertical) equally constrained the potential orientations of their respective objects. In other words, it is undesirable to have a vertical object be a plausible representation of a horizontal sentence and vice versa. Therefore, a four-alternative forced-choice experiment was conducted on each trial, with one of the experimental sentences and the corresponding horizontal and vertical pictures. Participants' task was to choose among the following options: (a) the vertical picture best matched the sentence, (b) the horizontal picture best matched the sentence, (c) the two pictures equally matched the sentence, and(d) neither picture matched the sentence. Sentence-picture pairs could remain in the main test only when over 90% of participants chose them. In this pre-test, among the 68 sentence-picture pairs, 8 of them were excluded. The best 60 pairs were applied in the following experiment based on the results of pre-test. In this method, the pre-test could ensure that participants can activate the desired implied orientation information as we expected through experimental stimuli, and the quality of stimuli is valid. 50 females and 30 males were included in the participants for the main test with age ranging from 18 to 27 (average = 23.2; SD = 1.912), of which most were 24. To the study, the participants would be excluded if the accuracy scores were below 80%. All participants had normal visual acuity and no difficulties in language comprehension or image recognition. The whole process of the experiment was conducted in a quiet classroom provided by the university to make sure no interruptions and lasted approximately 30 min. Participants were rewarded with a small gift for their kind support and participation.

3.3 Materials

Experimental materials consisted of 60 sentences (40 of them were translated from the original study and 20 were newly designed) and 60 black and white line drawings for each experimental block. In the current study, for the purpose of language comprehension, much attention was paid to adjusting the language's habitual use of natural Chinese in the process of translation. As for the tense, this current research replicated "着" and "了" from was/were doing something in the original ones. Table 1 described the features of experimental stimuli in English and Chinese. Also, sentence lengths were controlled. All sentence pairs implied a certain object orientation that is either horizontal or vertical. The experimental objects should be reversible in orientation. For instance, a nail can be hammered into the floor plank (implies vertical) and the wall (implies horizontal). The stimuli consisted of 30 sentence-picture pairs for each of the four versions, with half of the pairs having matched orientations and the other half having mismatched orientations. Each condition had an equal number of vertical and horizontal items, and all items were equally distributed across the matched and mismatched conditions. Since all experimental items required a "yes" response, 30 additional sentence pairs were used as fillers to achieve a counterbalancing effect (all of them are translated from the original experiment). The filler sentences were similar in length and object noun position to the experimental sentences, but were followed by an unrelated picture, thus requiring a "no" response.

An additional set of 6 sentence-picture pairs (3 related, 3 unrelated) were used as warm-up trials, which were not included in the experiment. In the experiment process, each sentence pair was followed by an object picture with implied object orientation either in match or mismatch condition, which needs two reversible pictures of a certain object. Most pictures came from Zwaan's open sharing. For those newly designed sentence pairs, highly related pictures were selected from the Baidu Image search engine, and then edited with PS software to be presented as grayscale and without any background (the color effect and background information would influence the results). Table 2 illustrated an example of experimental sentence pair.

Table 1. Features of experimental stimuli in English vs. Chinese

	English	Chinese
Verb tense expression (imperfective verb)	was / were doing	“当时 / 正在”, “着”, “了”, “过”
Typological word order	“S + V + Pre + NP”	“S + Pre + NP + V”
Sense	positive / negative	positive / negative (can omit)

Table 2. Example of one-sentence pair.

Orientation	Sentence	Match	Mismatch
Horizontal (Block 1)	木匠将钉子钉入了墙壁。		
Vertical (Block 1)	木匠把钉子钉入了地板。		

3.4 Design and Procedure

Four versions of sentence-picture pairs were produced. A given sentence-picture pair could occur in one of four conditions: vertical-vertical, horizontal-horizontal, vertical-horizontal, and horizontal-vertical. Each participant was exposed to each condition randomly, but each item appeared in only one condition per list, and each participant was required to complete one list only. It was thus a 2 (match vs. mismatch) * 2 (picture orientation) design with matching conditions and orientations as within-participant variables and experimental lists as a between-participant variable.

Six warm-up trials were designed to get participants familiar with the task, and the experiment would not start until all the required bars were pressed correctly in the practice. During each trial, participants first saw a left-justified and vertically centered fixation point for 500 ms; next, a sentence appeared. Participants were required to press the space bar once they understood the sentence. Following that, a fixation point occurred in the center of the screen for 500 ms, and then a picture appeared. Participants then had to determine if the pictured item had been mentioned in the previous sentence, by pressing the “J” key for “yes” responses and the “F” key for “no” responses. Participants were instructed to respond as quickly as possible since their reaction times were being measured automatically.

In regarding to the responses, all 30 experimental sentence-picture pairs (i.e., both match and mismatch conditions) viewed by participants required a YES response, while all of the 30 filler pairs required a NO response for the purpose of counterbalance. Furthermore, to ensure all participants’ full concentration and effective data collection, half of the filler sentences were followed by a reading comprehension question, and the J key was also pressed for a YES response and the F key for a NO response. The trials were presented in random order. Figure 1. & Fig. 2. Illustrated the experimental trial with and without comprehension questions.

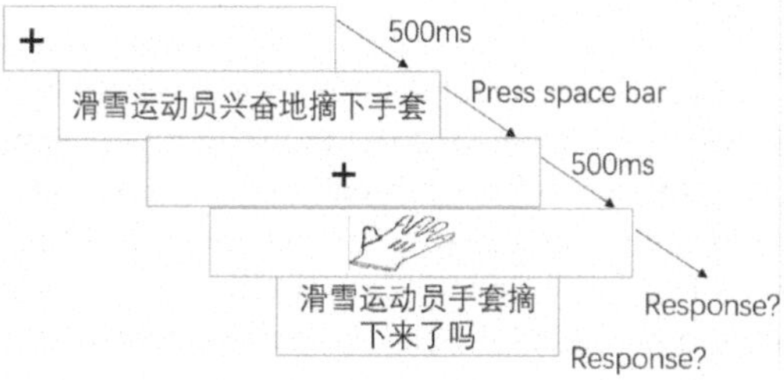

Fig. 1. Illustration of the experimental trial without a comprehension question

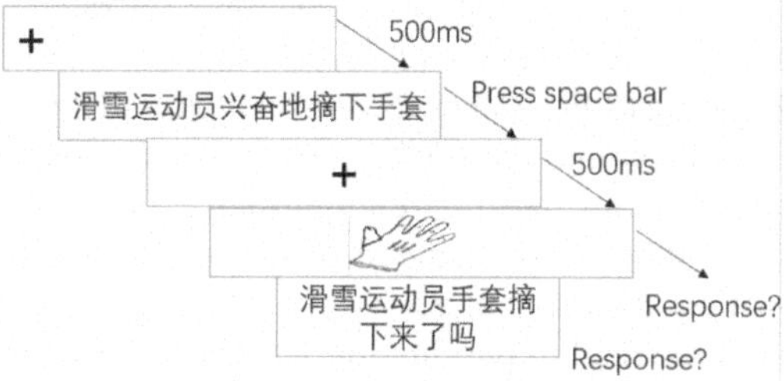

Fig. 2. Illustration of the filler trial with a comprehension question

The experiment was a single-factor design: prime type. The study mainly aimed to investigate whether matching or mismatching orientation, namely the vertical or horizontal direction implied by the sentence, could facilitate language comprehension or not. Therefore, during the experimental process, both RT and RA were collected. RT refers to the time of pressing the space bar after comprehension, while RA refers to the accuracy of participants' response defined by pressed space bar. At the end of each sentence in the experiment, participants were asked to press the space key as soon as they understand these sentences. Notably, to make sure the validity of the results, the whole experiment was observed. The experiment was run on the E-prime 2.0 software, with the reaction time being automatically recorded. Prior to the analysis, experimental data with response time shorter than 300 ms or longer than 3000 ms were excluded as outliers [22]. Also, incorrect responses were eliminated as those were not deemed as a representation of mental simulation in the process of sentence-picture verification task. For any participant, outliers were defined as response time that exceeded their respective means by more than 2 standard deviations; outliers were replaced with the cut-off value (2*Standard Deviation + Mean). Although filter data were not analyzed in view of the experiment purpose, the outlier part was still held to make sure that participants behaved as instructed. During data exclusion, all 80 participant's data was retained as their accuracy rates were all over 80%. As for remaining valid data, the dependent variables, including reaction time and the mean score of VVIQ, were analyzed by SPSS 17.0 software.

3.5 Post-test of Mental Imagery

To ensure the effect occurred due to mental simulation rather than the purposeful imagination strategy, a post-test was designed. After completing the experiment on the computer, participants were required to have a break and fill out a questionnaire including 32 questions in total. They could choose to fill it on their own cellphone or the computer in the experiment room. The questionnaire was applied to investigate the relationship between mental simulation and mental imagery, an adapted version of Zwaan's Vividness of Visual Imagery. To balance the effect, all the questions were translated into Chinese with accessible and available objects mentioned. This part, in general, would cost participants 5–10 min to complete. This questionnaire instructed participants to think of four different situations and then specified four aspects of the situation that they should try to visualize. Vividness of the mental picture was rated on a five-point scale in regarding to personal experience in the real world (1 means no image at all, you only "aware" that you are thinking of the object; 2 means vague and dim; 3 means moderately clear and lively; 4 means clear and reasonably vivid; 5 means perfectly clear and vivid as real seeing). In addition, items 9 to 12 were questions about a familiar store (shop in the original version), and these were changed so that they corresponded more to contemporary experiences than the original version (9. The overall appearance of the store from the opposite side of the road or parking lot. 10. The store's name sign including its location, colors, and shape. 11. You are near the entrance. The color, shape, and details of the door. 12. You enter the store and walk into an aisle. You look at the items and pick something you want.)

4 Results

4.1 Effects of Mental Simulation on Language Comprehension

First and foremost, the response accuracy in two conditions is analyzed. In the matched condition, the accuracy rate was high at 95.01%, whereas in the mismatched condition, it came to 91.83%. This indicated that responses were more accurate when object orientation implied by the sentence was consistent with the picture. Furthermore, a T-test was conducted to compare the two conditions, which reveals a significant effect ($t = 1.808$, $p = 0.043$, < 0.05) for response accuracy, with responses being significantly more accurate in the matched condition.

In addition, to make a comparison of the average response time, a paired sample T test was conducted. The mean reaction time in the matched condition was 997.86 ms, and the standard deviation was 504.19 ms. Nevertheless, in the mismatched condition, the mean reaction time was 1045.02 ms and the standard deviation was 620.93 ms. It can be concluded that a significant match effect on reaction time occurred. In other words, during this judgement task, participants tended to make choices much faster when the object orientation was consistent with the picture. What's more, the T-test result revealed that between two conditions, $t(1, 79) = -1.978$, $p = .048 < 0.05$, therefore, there was a significant difference between the matched condition and mismatched condition. The rmANOVA for response time (only focused on correct responses) found a main effect for match, that is, participants responded significantly faster when the picture matched the orientation implied by the final sentence than when it was mismatched. Such a match effect indicates that the implied orientation can activate our sensorimotor system and then facilitate language comprehension. Accordingly, in the mismatch condition, the inconsistent orientation in sentence-picture pairs cost more time to respond and showed interference in language comprehension.

The experiment introduced a comprehension question recall task to ensure that participants read sentences and completed the sentence-picture verification task attentively. Ten comprehension questions were designed and balanced in the experiment. We strictly followed the standards of the original experiment, making these ten questions focused on the filter sentences. Average comprehension accuracy was high at 85.12% (SD = 15.2%) for questions. Such a high accuracy proved that participants concentrated on the experiment and that their data were valid and meaningful to be analyzed.

Through an ANOVA, participants' behavioral differences between horizontal and vertical trials were found. In the horizontal condition, the percentage of accuracy was 93.3%, while in the vertical condition, the percentage was 93.7%. Therefore, the responses were slightly more accurate in the vertical condition. The p–value of 0.74 for ACC showed that there was no significant accuracy difference between the two conditions. Nevertheless, the p-value of 0.043 for RT indicated that there was a significant difference between response times. The mean response time was 1096.54 ms and the standard deviation was 662.60 in the horizontal condition; the mean response time was 1006.82 ms and the standard deviation was 577.37 in the vertical condition. Therefore, from the perspective of types of cognitive language comprehension, participants tended to respond faster to vertical trials. Since vertical and horizontal conditions in match and mismatch conditions were assigned equally, the types of materials could not be counted as an influencing factor for the different results between matched and mismatched tasks. However, it could be concluded that different types of languages and mental simulations could lead to differences in language comprehension in Chinese.

However, according to the p-value, it can be concluded that there was no significant gender difference ($p > 0.05$), which could prove gender is not a significant factor of language comprehension in the current experimental context and the inequality of gender distribution in the experimental design has no significant influence on the results. This nonsignificant result is in line with Zwaan's, indicating that gender differences do not exert an influence on orientation effect in the context of Chinese.

4.2 Explorations of Mental Imagery

For each participant, we calculated the effect size of the match effect using the data based on Connell's outlier criteria (as we could not use the medians to calculate individual effect sizes). The effect size, according to Stanfield and Zwaan was calculated as the difference between the means in the match and mismatch conditions, divided by the pooled standard deviations of the match and mismatch conditions [5]. We also calculated each participant's mean score on the VVIQ. The correlation between the VVIQ scores and effect size was marginally significant, ($r = -0.21$, $p = 0.058$). Effect size did not correlate with age and education level. Pearson Correlation Coefficient was used to correlate match effect size during response time and mental imagery score, and the results showed no significant correlation between them either. These results suggested that the match effect is derived from mental simulation rather than mental imagery. For instance, if participants had used an image-generation strategy, the VVIQ should have had a greater influence on the results. Individuals with better spatial cognition would be more likely and more capable of generating such images than individuals with poorer spatial cognition. However, as stated, the pattern of results was the same for participants with low and high spatial abilities.

5 Discussion

The present research aimed to explore whether subjects mentally simulate object orientation during language comprehension in Chinese, consisting of vertical and horizontal square pictures. As expected, the results in the present study achieved a match advantage, which aligns with previous research applying English materials like Zwaan and his student Standfield's original experiment [5]. However, the results were inconsistent with De Koning [13], whose experiment utilized Dutch materials and employed L2 learners. In a word, findings in this paper align with the predictions of the Perceptual Symbol Systems [2], but not with those of amodal symbol systems.

In the current research, first of all, response accuracy and response time were calculated. We obtained a similar result to the study of Stanfield and Zwaan [5]. Participants tended to perform the right behavior in a shorter time in the matched condition than in the mismatched condition, indicating that a match advantage occurred during the experiment. In this current research, we also speculated that responses in the sentence-picture judgment task were more accurate and shorter once the object mentioned in the sentence had the same orientation with the following picture. The shorter response time in the match condition supported the idea that participants mentally simulated the object's implied orientation information during sentence comprehension. For instance, participants were shown an image of a pencil with a vertical orientation after reading the sentence "He stuck his pencil in the coffee mug". Since the sentence implies a vertical orientation that matches the given picture, a match advantage appears. Faced with this phenomenon, the traditional amodal view of language comprehension fails to illustrate it. Under the rule of amodal representation, the sentence above is constructed as "Stuck (He, Pencil, Mug), with implied orientation information left behind. Different from the amodal view, the embodied view can provide convincing explanations. As a part of a strong embodied view of language comprehension, the perceptual symbol system proposes that output of simulations should mimic the output of operations performed during actual perception [5]. That is to say, participants' simulations are supposed to cover or share some features with that object in real life. For instance, if the "pencil" is shown as vertical, the simulations should be vertical accordingly. Although the orientation is implicit rather than explicit, the idea of affordance to some extent ensures participants recognize the right orientation [2]. Often, the affordance of a pencil is long, and the associated simulation can only be vertical, since its "length" is not available to be presented horizontally in a mug. Participants obtain the concept of "pencil" from the regular experience in daily life with sensor and motor systems. During language comprehension, mental simulation and sensorimotor representation are combined and activated. In addition, a comprehensive situation model is constructed, which causes the identical or similar perceptual activation just as the described in the event.

According to the Perceptual Symbol System theory, once subjects were shown the picture during the verification task in the formal experiment, a visual trace was generated. To be specific, after seeing the picture, a trace of "a pencil" was generated in subjects' minds. At the same time, visual traces stored in minds before were also reactivated automatically to understand the meaning of sentences. For example, when people try to understand a sentence like "He stuck his pencil in the desk drawer", the trace of a horizontal pencil was reactivated. Obviously, the triggered trace was more similar in the matched condition than that in the mismatched condition. Hence, it is reasonable for subjects to respond and make choices more quickly in the matched condition. According to the faster response in the matched condition, it can be found that the implied orientation information in the sentence would have an influence on the speed of subjects' comprehension of the sentence, which suggests that orientation information as an important feature of an object will exert an influence on language comprehension.

In addition, it was found that the overall accuracy of participants was very high (more than 95%), and the responses of participants were more accurate when the picture matched object orientation in the preceding sentence. Prior to the experiment, participants were required to respond as quickly and accurately as possible to whether the object picture was mentioned in the previous sentence. They were told that their response time is of great importance and would be measured by the computer. The accuracy pattern of sentence-picture verification is consistent with that in the study of Stanfield and Zwaan [5]. As for the prerequisites of constructing a simulation, scholars have explored the relationship between processing mechanisms and language comprehension. Two factors, temporal overlap and integrability, are important in determining whether a match or mismatch effect occurs in mental simulation. Temporal overlap refers to the timing of the sentence to be read and stimulus. While integrability means the extent to which the stimuli can be integrated into the simulation [23, 24]. If subjects try to understand a sentence and see a picture, a match effect will appear with the integrable text and picture. For example, when participants see a picture of a key in a vertical orientation while trying to understand the sentence "She put the key to the monkey cage on the hook", the picture of a key can be integrated with the sentence. Accordingly, a mismatch effect will occur when they are hard to integrate. For instance, when subjects see a picture of a vertical key while reading the sentence "She put the key to the cage in the lock". In addition, when the sentence and the stimulus are presented sequentially, there is also a match advantage under if the perception and the sentence are integrable (e.g., When participants see an image of an eagle outstretched as if in flight in the sky after reading and processing the sentence "The ranger saw an eagle in the sky"). The findings in the present study are consistent with the claim that there is a match advantage when the object orientation in the picture is integrable with the object's orientation implied by the sentence and the picture of the object is presented sequentially after the sentence. For instance, in this research, faster response latency occurred when a picture of a vertical book was shown after the sentence "The librarian put the book back on the shelf" compared to the sentence "The librarian put the book back on the table".

Some studies have discussed the relationship between mental simulation and mental imagery [6, 10, 32], but it still lacks Chinese evidence. Importantly, the representation of perception derived from mental simulation stated in this thesis differs from mental imagery, although they are both related to cognitive processes [33]. Generally speaking, mental imagery is a conscious process. For example, when people are required to think of a classmate or a teacher to whom they are close, they may visualize specific details of those people like the exact cheek line, head, shoulders, dress, usual facial expression, and so on. Integrating these details into a full mental image could cost extra cognitive effort. Different from the intentional attempts to construct conscious representations, mental simulation often occurs automatically and unconsciously. Hence, when people try to understand a sentence like "The librarian put the book back on the table.", a simulation of a horizontal book will occur without costing extra cognitive resources. Language comprehension is closely linked to one's perception of the condition illustrated in the sentence. If one has experienced that event before, the related experiences stored in memory will be reactivated. In addition, as an ability to imagine, the level of mental imagery differs from person to person, [7, 34, 35] while one's perceptions of an object are quite effortless to be produced as long as they have regular cognitive capacities.[6] In other words, mental imagery is a conscious ability to use cognitive resources to deal with complex tasks; while mental simulation, as an unconscious activity, results from the embodied effect, without extra cost of cognitive resources. Concepts may rely on the automatic activation of modality-specific systems independent of an individual's ability or tendency to use mental imagery. Grounded cognition theories propose that sensory-motor systems play a fundamental role in conceptual knowledge. To sum up, the match advantage of perceptual information on concept representations has resulted from unconscious mental simulation, supporting the idea that perceptual simulation is crucial to understanding concepts.

6 Conclusion

To conclude, the results of the present paper support the opinion that a match effect will occur when the pictured object corresponds with the object orientation implied by the sentences, facilitating language comprehension.

First and foremost, participants' native tongues may have an impact on how they simulate language in their minds. The original study by Stanfield and Zwaan and its direct replications by Zwaan and Pecher presented the stimuli in English with natives. The current study obtained a similar result, namely, match advantage, which was ensured by all participants are native Chinese speakers who have no trouble understanding Chinese. Those researchers who obtained a mismatch effect, are employed native speakers of Dutch and L2 German speakers [13, 15, 25]. It is partially caused by language influencing mental simulations, and utilizing a foreign language reduces the vividness of mental imaging compared to speaking in one's tongue [26]. As a result, when participants employ a foreign language, their mental models may be turned off to some extent, which affects their decision-making in the experiment. Moreover, in order to construct the mental images, participants must reactivate and rebuild their memories to produce new mental representations [27]. Hence, those who use L2 would cost extra cognitive resources that may lessen the vividness of mental images [28, 29]. In regarding to Koster's mismatch result, it can be attributed to the second language' interference.

Secondly, the orientation effect may be absent in Dutch languages since enough empirical studies can serve as evidence. It suggests that the orientation effect may not always be as regular as we think to generalize effects from one language to another language and from one task to another task [30]. De Koning concluded that the main reason for the mismatch effect is caused by orientation's extrinsic property in object information [13]. Rather than an object's color, shape and size, orientation's role in simulation is less important than previously thought. However, previous research has shown that spatial information is an important part of the memory representation constructed from discourse and that the linguistic expression of spatial relations helps determine accessibility [31]. The present study obtained a match effect in Chinese sentences, further supporting the idea of orientation's mental simulation.

Lastly, deviations from original designs will admittedly influence results. Unlike Stanfield and Zwaan's original experiment, Rommers et al. failed to design a recall trial, including comprehension questions to ensure participants' concentration. In addition, sentence materials in Rommers et al.'s study combined shape and orientation indication together. Mixing different categories could have affected the results, leading to a natural inconsistency in the original study. The shape sentence pairs were manipulated by changing a single word (e.g., "a cigarette out of the pack", "a cigarette out of the ashtray") and they were less complex and implicit than the orientation sentences [15]. As for replication works, it is significant to be precise with the original experiment.

Funding. Funded by Youth Project of Liaoning Province Social Science Planning Fund (L18CYY001).

References

1. Newell, A., Simon, H.A.: Computer science as empirical inquiry: symbols and search. Commun. ACM **19**(3), 205–211 (1976)
2. Barsalou, L.W.: Perceptual symbol systems. Behavioral & Brain Sciences **22**(4), 577–609 (1999)
3. Harnad, S.: The symbol grounding problem. Physica D **42**(1–3), 335–346 (1990)
4. Guan, Q.: A new interpretation of embodied cognition for language understanding: psychological simulation as a means of language comprehension. Psychol. Sci. **28**(5), 1252–1256 (2007)
5. Stanfield, R.A., Zwaan, R.A.: The effect of implied orientation derived from verbal context on picture recognition. Psychol. Sci. **12**, 153–156 (2001)
6. Kozhevnikov, M., Kosslyn, S., Shephard, J.: Spatial versus object visualizers: A new characterization of visual cognitive style. Mem. Cognit. **33**(4), 710–726 (2005)
7. Blajenkova, O., Kozhevnikov, M., Mote, M.A.: Object-spatial imagery: A new self-report imagery questionnaire. Wiley **20**(2), 239–263 (2006)

8. Zwaan, R., Yaxley, R.: Lateralization of object-shape information in semantic processing. Cognition **94**(2), 35–43 (2004)
9. Sato, M., Bergen, B.K.: Does implicit grammatical person influence perspective in mental simulation? J. Med. Syst. **28**(28), 321–333 (2009)
10. Zwaan, R.A., Pecher, D.: Revisiting mental simulation in language comprehension: six replication attempts. PLoS ONE **7**(12), e51382 (2012)
11. Li, Y., Wang, R., Mo, L.: The impact of implied object shape information on picture recognition. Psychol. Sci. **28**(3), 588–590 (2005)
12. Chang, X., Ling, X.: The influence of sentence features on object shape representation in language comprehension. Northwest. Normal Univ. J. Soc. Sci. Ed. **3**, 138–144 (2017)
13. De Koning, B.B., Wassenburg, S.I., Bos, L.T., Van Dijk, S.M.: Mental simulation of four visual object properties: similarities and differences as assessed by the sentence-picture verification task. Theor. Exp. Plant Physiol. **29**(4), 420–432 (2017)
14. Zhang, P., Lu, Z.: The psychological representation of color information in sentence comprehension. Acta Psychol. Sin. **45**(4), 406–415 (2013)
15. Rommers, J., Meyer, A.S., Huettig, F.: Object shape and orientation do not routinely influence performance during language processing. Psychol. Sci. **24**(11), 2218–2225 (2013)
16. Bos, L.T., De Koning, B.B., Van Wesel, F., Boonstra, A.M., Van Dijk, S.M.: What can measures of text comprehension tell us about creative text production? Read. Writ. **28**, 829–849 (2015)
17. Borst, G., Kosslyn, S.M.: Visual mental imagery and visual perception: Structural equivalence revealed by scanning processes. Mem. Cognit. **36**(4), 849–862 (2008)
18. Bergen, B. K. (2007). Experimental methods for simulation semantics. Methods in Cognitive Linguistics, 277–301
19. Vermeulen, N., Corneille, O., Niedenthal, P.M.: Sensory load incurs conceptual processing costs. Cognition **109**(2), 287–294 (2008)
20. Pecher, D., Zeelenberg, R., Barsalou, L.W.: Verifying different-modality properties for concepts produces switching costs. Psychol. Sci. **14**(2), 119–124 (2003)
21. Wu, C.Y., Ho, M.H.R., Chen, S.H.A.: A meta-analysis of fMRI studies on Chinese orthographic, phonological, and semantic processing. Neuroimage **63**(1), 381–391 (2012)
22. Connell, L.: Representing object color in language comprehension. Cognition **102**(3), 476–485 (2007)
23. Kaschak, M.P., et al.: Perception of motion affects language processing. Psychol. Sci. **94**(3), B79–B89 (2005)
24. Kaschak, M.P., Zwaan, R.A., Aveyard, M., Yaxley, R.H.: Perception of auditory motion affects language processing. Cogn. Sci. **30**(4), 733–744 (2006)
25. Koster, D., Cadierno, T., Chiarandini, M.: Mental simulation of object orientation and size: A conceptual replication with second language learners. J. Eur. Second Lang. Assoc. **2**(1), 38–48 (2018)
26. Hayakawa, S., Keysar, B.: Using a foreign language reduces mental imagery. Cognition: Int. J. Cogn. Psychol. **173**, 8–15 (2018)
27. Schacter, D.L., Addis, D.R.: Remembering the past to imagine the future: A cognitive neuroscience perspective. Mil. Psychol. **21**(1), S108–S112 (2009)
28. Baddeley, A.D., Andrade, J.: Working memory and the vividness of imagery. J. Exp. Psychol. Gen. **129**(1), 126–145 (2000)
29. Baba, S., Joel, H.: The impact of anticipating satisfaction on consumer choice. Journal of Consumer Research **27**(2), 202–216 (2000)
30. Wheeler, K.B., Greenspan, S.L.: Non-native language processing engages mental imagery. In Proceedings of the Annual Meeting of the Cognitive Science Society **28**, 882–887 (2006)
31. Morrow, D.G., Greenspan, S.L., Bower, G.H.: Accessibility and situation models in narrative comprehension. J. Mem. Lang. **26**(2), 165–187 (1987)

32. Pecher, D., van Dantzig, S., Schifferstein, H.N.J.: Concepts are not represented by conscious imagery. Psychon. Bull. Rev. **16**(5), 914–919 (2009)
33. Rouw, R., Kosslyn, S.M., Hamel, R.: Detecting high-level and low-level properties in visual images and visual percepts. Cognition **63**, 209–226 (1997)
34. Laws, K.R.: Category-specific naming and modality-specific imagery. In 12th Annual Meeting on Tennet –Theoretical and Experimental (pp. 418–420) (2002)
35. Marks, D.F.: Visual imagery differences in the recall of pictures. Br. J. Psychol. **64**(1), 17–24 (2011)

Workshop DLCCE

Reliability of Effort Indicators for Human Translation and Post-editing of Machine Translation: An Eye Tracking and Keylogging Study Involving Student Translators

Ying Cui[1], Xiao Liu[2], and Wei Wang[1](✉)

[1] Guangdong University of Foreign Studies, Guangzhou 510420, China
wwei@gdufs.edu.cn
[2] Shandong University, Weihai 264209, China

Abstract. Evaluating student translators' effort in translation and post-editing of machine translation provides valuable reference for translation training and learning. The effort indicators currently used such as those based on eye-tracking and key-logging data are variant. This study investigates the reliability of those effort indicators. It focuses on student translators working on the English-Chinese language pair. An eye-tracking and key-logging experiment was conducted to capture participants' fixation, pause, translation time, and edit data. Thirty-three students participated in the experiment and did translation and post-editing tasks. Data analyses have revealed the following characteristics of effort indicators: indicators based on the source text (ST) word count are more reliable than those based on the target text (TT) word count; indicators based on pause count are more reliable than those based on pause duration; indicators based on ST fixation are more reliable than those based on TT fixation; and the indicator of edit number is applicable to post-editing but not human translation. The findings are intended to facilitate the more precise evaluation of student translators' effort.

Keywords: Effort · Human Translation · Machine Translation · Post-editing

1 Introduction

A proper evaluation of students' effort in doing human translation (HT) tasks can provide valuable insight for instructors. With the progress of machine translation (MT) technologies and their extensive application in the language service sector (Castilho 2016; Moorkens et al. 2018; Yamada 2019), it is also of significance to measure students' effort in doing post-editing (PE) tasks. Effort can be assessed via subjective methods, such as translators' self-ratings, but it is pointed out that subjective ratings are not always reliable (Moorkens et al. 2015: 282). Apart from subjective methods, objective data also provide evidence for translators' effort. In particular, fixation duration and count data recorded via the eye-tracking technique have been found to be correlated with one's effort (Miquel-Iriarte et al. 2012: 263–264; Koponen 2016: 25; Szarkowska et al. 2018:

Z. Kubincová et al. (Eds.): SETE 2023, LNCS 14606, pp. 207–218, 2024.
https://doi.org/10.1007/978-981-97-4243-1_16

189; Walker 2018: 227). Besides, pause duration and count data recorded via the key-logging technique have also been proven to indicate effort (Daems et al. 2015; O'Brien 2006; Vieira 2017). However, researchers have been applying different methods to process eye-tracking and key-logging data and selecting different indicators based on such data, which often lead to inconsistent findings (Daems et al. 2015; O'Brien 2006; Vieira 2017). Therefore, it is essential to explore the reliability of effort indicators in order to ensure the accurate evaluation of translators' effort. This study focuses on student translators of the English-Chinese language pair and intends to explore the reliability of effort indicators based on eye-tracking and key-logging data in the hope of providing a practical reference for the assessment of students' translation effort.

2 Selection of Effort Indicators

Translators' fixation and pause data need to be processed and analyzed in relation to the length and style of the source text (ST) and target text (TT) because the fixations and pauses that translators make are attributable to the textual complexity and style to a great extent. As mentioned earlier, the selection of effort indicators is not always consistent, and the reliability of effort indicators has been understudied. Actually, to the best of our knowledge, there is only one study exploring this issue (Vieira 2017). We will briefly mention the effort indicators studied by Vieira (2017), which we have further extended in this research. The indictors that Vieira (2017) explores cover the following:

- Fixations per Word (FPW), namely the total number of fixations normalised by ST word count to avoid sentence-length effects;
- Average Fixation Duration (AFD), namely total fixation time divided by the total number of fixations;
- Pause-to-Word Ratio (PWR), namely total number of pauses divided by the number of ST words;
- Average Pause Ratio (APR), namely average time per pause divided by the average time per source word;
- Pause Ratio (PR), namely total pause time in a sentence divided by the total time spent post-editing that sentence;
- Seconds per Word (SPW), total post-editing time divided by the TT word count;
- and Subjective Ratings (SR), namely the subjective choice of a scale that indicates one's effort (Vieira 2017: 48–49).

The results of factor analysis show that there is correlation between those effort indicators, with APR and PR negatively correlated to other indicators (Vieira 2017: 50), and the rest positively correlated with each other (Vieira 2017: 57). The study also finds that SPW, PWR and FPW have stronger correlations between themselves, while AFD, PR, and SR show weaker correlations (Vieira 2017: 50). Such difference implies that SPW, PWR and FPW are more reliable as effort indicators.

All in all, the findings of Vieira (2017) suggest that the effort indicators based on fixation and pause data divided by the number of words in a text are more reliable, while those based on such data divided by translation time are less reliable. There is often difference between translators in terms of their translation speed and the time they spend on a translation task; however, the text which translators fixate on and make pauses in is constant. Therefore, our study focuses on the effort indicators that are based on the fixation and pause data divided by the number of words in a text.

Meanwhile, there are two more issues to be further studied. First, it remains to be explored whether effort indictors should be based on ST word number or TT word number. The indictors explored by Vieira (2017) cover both. Some are based on ST word number such as PWR, and some on TT word number such as SPW. Theoretically, both make sense. ST word number represents the workload of a task assigned to translators, and TT word number represents the output of translators. This study intends to further explore the difference between effort indicators based on ST or TT word number. Second, the indicators analyzed by Vieira (2017) can be further refined. Fixation data are not analyzed according to the area of interest (AOI) in Vieira (2017). This study distinguishes between ST fixation and TT fixation, because the two types of fixation carry different implications, with the former more concerned with ST difficulty and comprehension and the latter more related to the organization of TT. Besides, the indicators of Vieira (2017) mainly cover the temporal and cognitive dimensions of effort. There is a third dimension, namely the technical one, outlined in the framework of Krings (2001), which is well-established and extensively applied (Moorkens et al. 2015: 270). It is worth noting that the three dimensions of effort are inter-connected with each other. For example, translators' cognitive processing takes time, which is the temporal dimension, and involves operations with the keyboard and mouse, which is the technical dimension. It is suggested that cognitive effort be explored with reference to temporal and technical effort (Vieira 2014). This study also includes the technical dimension. Considering that the edits are made to produce TT, this indicator refers to TT word count.

To sum up, this research aims to investigate the reliability of objective effort indicators and has selected the following ones:

- Seconds per Target Word (STW), namely translation time divided by TT word count;
- Seconds per Source Word (SSW), namely translation time divided by ST word count;
- Edits per Target Word (ETW), namely edits divided by TT word count;
- Pause Count per Source Word (PCSW), namely pause count divided by ST word count;
- Pause Count per Target Word (PCTW), namely pause count divided by TT word count;
- Pause Duration per Source Word (PDSW), namely pause duration divided by ST word count;
- Pause Duration per Target Word (PDTW), namely pause duration divided by TT word count;
- Source Fixation Duration per Source Word (SFDW), namely fixation duration on ST divided by ST word count;
- Target Fixation Duration per Target Word (TFDW), namely fixation duration on TT divided by TT word count;
- Source Fixation Count per Source Word (SFCW), namely fixation count on ST divided by ST word count;
- and Target Fixation Count per Target Word (TFCW), namely fixation count on TT divided by TT word count.

3 The Eye-Tracking and Key-Logging Experiment

This study analyzes the same set of data generated from the eye-tracking and key-logging experiment of Cui et al. (2023), but excludes the data of participants' self-ratings and translation scores and applies different effort indicators. For readers' convenience, we will briefly recount the experiment.

3.1 Participants

Thirty-three Chinese postgraduate students specializing in translation participated in the experiment, including 26 females and 7 males, aged between 22 and 28 (M = 23.93, SD = 1.61). Twenty-eight of them were right-handed, and five were left-handed. All of them had normal or corrected-to-normal vision, with no history of neurological or psychological impairment and no current medication. We informed them of the detailed experiment procedure and the anonymization of data in advance. They signed the Consent Form and took part in the experiment voluntarily. After the experiment, we gave each of them a souvenir to thank them for their participation.

3.2 Tools

We used Gazepoint GP3 HD Desktop Eye Tracker for the experiment. It provides binocular eye-tracking, with a sampling rate of 150 Hz and a visual angle accuracy of 0.5–1 degree. To ensure the accuracy of eye-tracking, we prepared a chin-and-forehead rest which was placed 60 cm in front of a monitor with 1920 × 1080 resolution. We used Translog-II to record key-logging data, which runs in the background and does not interfere with the translation process (Carl 2012: 155). We used Google Translate (March 2021) to generate MT output.

3.3 Experiment Procedure

We selected eight English passages for HT and PE tasks, which were of similar length, varying from 44 to 51 words, and self-contained in meaning. Using short passages would be appropriate for eye-tracking research (Saldanha & O'Brien 2013: 140). The experiment covered four steps. Step 1 was a training session for participants to get familiar with the Translog window. We did not set any time limit but asked participants to finish the HT and PE tasks as quickly as they could, transferring the meaning accurately and presenting it fluently in accordance with the original stylistic features. An electronic dictionary was put on the right of the Translog window to provide external sources for participants and ease up the possible tension caused by the experiment. In Step 2, we calibrated the eye tracker, and participants translated four passages assigned to them randomly. In Step 3, the participants did PE tasks. In Step 4, participants filled out an online questionnaire and rated their effort on a five-point scale.

4 Data Analyses and Discussion

4.1 Processing of Data

Two participants' eye movement data were incomplete due to the malfunctioning of the eye tracker. We deleted their data. Then we further processed fixation data, as not all fixations are concerned with cognitive processing. Considering that translation involves reading, which is the basis for transferring between languages, and fixations in reading last from 100 ms to over 500 ms (Pavlović & Jensen 2009: 97), we set the threshold at 100 ms and deleted the fixations lasting less than 100 ms. We did not set an upper limit for fixation, for translation is complex than reading and longer fixations are also valid.

The user activity data captured by Translog in this study are all valid, including translation time, total edits, and pauses. Similar to fixation, not all pauses are associated with cognitive processing. We set the threshold of significant pauses at 300 ms which has been empirically validated (Lacruz et al. 2014: 82).

Having processed fixation and pause data, we calculated the measures of effort according to the indicators summarized in Sect. 2 and carried out statistical analyses.

4.2 Correlation Tests

We conducted Spearman's rank correlation tests on HT and PE effort indicators. The results are summarized in Tables 1 and 2 respectively.

As shown in Table 1, the indicators of HT effort are significantly correlated, and the correlation coefficients mostly fall between .60 and .90 ($p < .001$). Such positive and significant correlation shows that the effort indicators are relatively reliable and can reflect participants' effort objectively. Meanwhile, there are three groups where the correlation is insignificant. The correlation coefficient between SFCW and PCSW is .150 ($p = .095$). Such insignificant correlation may actually be valid because participants might be fixating on ST or TT when making pauses. In other words, pauses might be attributed to TT instead of ST, hence insignificant correlation between SFCW and PCSW. The other two groups of effort indicators with insignificant correlation are both concerned with ST fixation and the technical effort of edits. The correlation coefficient between SFDW and ETW is .065 ($p = .474$), and that between SFCW and ETW is -.006 ($p = .948$). Such insignificant correlation between ST fixation and edits is related to the cognitive mechanism of HT. The TT window was empty during the experiment, and participants had to fixate on TT and type their translations from scratch, which could lower their fixation on ST. No matter how effortful it was for participants to comprehend ST, they would have to operate the keyboard and mouse to produce TT. For this reason, whether ETW is suitable for measuring HT effort remains to be further explored.

The correlation between PE effort indicators is stronger and more consistent than that between HT effort indicators. As demonstrated in Table 2, the PE effort indicators are all significantly and positively correlated with each other without any exception. It shows that the indicators are reliable. Further examination of the results in Tables 1 and 2 shows that the same HT and PE effort indicators based on ST word count and TT word count are highly correlated. The correlation coefficients between SSW and STW, PCSW and PCTW, and PDSW and PDTW can reach .90. As discussed in Sect. 2, there is ground to

Table 1. Correlation of HT Effort Indicators

	STW	SSW	ETW	PCSW	PCTW	PDSW	PDTW	SFDW	TFDW	SFCW
SSW	.927									
p	.000									
ETW	.411	.354								
p	.000	.000								
PCSW	.508	.609	.520							
p	.000	.000	.000							
PCTW	.647	.601	.618	.898						
p	.000	.000	.000	.000						
PDSW	.934	.990	.288	.584	.591					
p	.000	.000	.001	.000	.000					
PDTW	.993	.920	.337	.494	.626	.944				
p	.000	.000	.000	.000	.000	.000				
SFDW	.739	.760	.065	.211	.233	.771	.754			
p	.000	.000	.474	.018	.009	.000	.000			
TFDW	.759	.756	.641	.580	.643	.721	.720	.513		
p	.000	.000	.000	.000	.000	.000	.000	.000		
SFCW	.690	.696	-.006	.150	.191	.714	.709	.947	.444	
p	.000	.000	.948	.095	.034	.000	.000	.000	.000	
TFCW	.782	.745	.555	.492	.590	.723	.752	.540	.947	.531
p	.000	.000	.000	.000	.000	.000	.000	.000	.000	.000

choose ST word count or TT word count as reference when measuring HT and PE effort, and the significant and positive correlation between ST-based indicators and TT-based ones provides evidence that both are reasonable. Still, there may be nuanced difference between the indicators based on ST or TT word count, as the two sets of indicators are not 100% correlated. To further investigate the relations between and the inner structure of effort indicators, we carried out exploratory factor analyses on the data.

4.3 Factor Analyses

This study includes 11 HT or PE effort indicators. Thirty-one participants' HT and PE data are valid, each of whom finished 4 HT tasks and 4 PE tasks. Therefore, the total sample size reaches 124, which can meet the basic requirement for factor analysis.

HT Effort Indicators

We first carried out the Kaiser-Meyer-Olkin (KMO) Test on HT effort indicators, and the result is .651. Barlett Test of Sphericity shows $p = .000$. It suggests that the 11 HT

Table 2. Correlation of PE Effort Indicators

	STW	SSW	ETW	PCSW	PCTW	PDSW	PDTW	SFDW	TFDW	SFCW
SSW	.977									
p	.000									
ETW	.793	.749								
p	.000	.000								
PCSW	.828	.808	.975							
p	.000	.000	.000							
PCTW	.836	.798	.983	.994						
p	.000	.000	.000	.000						
PDSW	.967	.995	.695	.765	.754					
p	.000	.000	.000	.000	.000					
PDTW	.997	.977	.752	.794	.801	.974				
p	.000	.000	.000	.000	.000	.000				
SFDW	.726	.732	.341	.379	.382	.755	.745			
p	.000	.000	.000	.000	.000	.000	.000			
TFDW	.911	.885	.842	.858	.866	.862	.896	.592		
p	.000	.000	.000	.000	.000	.000	.000	.000		
SFCW	.635	.651	.229	.279	.278	.681	.657	.950	.460	
p	.000	.000	.010	.002	.002	.000	.000	.000	.000	
TFCW	.918	.916	.779	.825	.823	.904	.909	.650	.935	.587
p	.000	.000	.000	.000	.000	.000	.000	.000	.000	.000

effort indicators are highly correlated and suitable for factor analysis. Then, we did an exploratory factor analysis using varimax rotation and identified three factors.

As summarized in Table 3, the three factors correspond to the three effort dimensions outlined in Sect. 2. As noted earlier, the three dimensions are interconnected. The results of the factor analysis corroborate such connection. Factor 1 mainly shows the temporal effort. This factor covers indicators related to translation time, pause duration, and ST fixation, namely STW, SSW, PDSW, PDTW, SFDW, and SFCW. The time spent on translation also involves ST fixation which is concerned with ST comprehension and pauses which translators make when they need more cognitive processing in translation. These indictors can account for 43.91% of the variation in data. The Cronbach's α coefficient stands at .934, which implies that this factor is highly reliable. Factor 2 is mainly about the technical effort. It covers the indictors related to pause count and edits, namely PCSW, PCTW, and ETW. These indicators can account for 25.64% of the variation in data. The operations on the keyboard and mouse generate translators' output, while pauses show that such operations are interrupted and translators may be having difficulty. The Cronbach's α coefficient for this factor is .836, which implies that

Table 3. Factor Analysis on HT Effort Indicators

	Factor 1	Factor 2	Factor 3	Uniqueness	α
STW	.746			.000	.934
SSW	.784			.000	
PDSW	.799			.000	
PDTW	.763			.000	
SFDW	.969			.027	
SFCW	.959			.042	
ETW		.520		.212	.836
PCSW		.939		.009	
PCTW		.881		.008	
TFDW			.771	.046	.701
TFCW			.803	.053	

it is highly reliable. Factor 3 mainly shows the cognitive effort related to the production of TT. It covers the indicators related to TT fixation, namely TFDW and TFCW. This factor accounts for 20.39% of the variation in data. The Cronbach's α coefficient for this factor is .701, implying that it is reliable.

An examination of the loadings reveals the following characteristics of HT effort indicators. First, the loadings of most indicators fall between .746 and .969, which is higher than the acceptance level of .70, but the loading of ETW is .520, which is lower than the acceptance level. The uniqueness value of ETW is .212, while the uniqueness values of other indicators are below .053. The higher uniqueness value stands for the lower correlation with other indictors in the factor model. This result lends support for our inference that ETW may not be suitable for measuring HT effort. As analyzed earlier, translators need to type out their translations from scratch when doing HT tasks regardless of their actual effort in processing ST and organizing TT. For this reason, the number of edits cannot reflect translators' effort accurately. However, it may be different with PE, where translators do not need to type out the whole text and the number of edits can indicate translators' effort more precisely. More discussion in this regard will be provided later.

Second, the same indicators have higher loadings when they are based on ST word count than on TT word count. The loading of SSW (.784) is higher than that of STW (.746), the loading of PDSW (.799) is higher than that of PDTW (.763), and the loading of PCSW (.939) is higher than that of PCTW (.881). This result implies that the effort indicators based on ST word count are more reliable. It can be attributed to translators' variant styles. The word count of ST is constant, while the word count of TT is up to translators. Those who prefer concise wording may produce a shorter TT, and those who tend to be wordier may produce a longer TT. Therefore, TT word count is not only concerned with translators' effort but also their style, and, comparatively speaking, the effort indicators based on ST word count are more accurate. Still, as the difference between the two sets of indicators is small, and more explorations in this aspect are needed.

Third, for the indicators involving pauses, those based on pause count have higher loadings than those based on pause duration. The loading of PCSW (.939) is higher than that of PDSW (.799), and the loading of PCTW (.881) is higher than that of PDTW (.763). This result corroborates the view that pause count is more enlightening than pause duration (Vieira 2017: 54). It is mainly because there are different types of pauses. Not all pauses represent effort such as those unproblematic pauses which consist of reading MT output and leaving it unedited (Vieira 2017: 55), and sometimes shorter yet more intensive pauses stand for more effort on the part of translators.

Fourth, for the indicators involving fixation, those based on ST fixation have higher loadings than those based on TT fixation. The loading of SFDW (.969) is higher than that of TFDW (.771), and the loading of SFCW (.959) is higher than that of TFCW (.803). It may be related to the fact that translators tend to devote more attention to TT (Castilho 2016: 46). In other words, regardless of translators' actual effort, they would fixate on TT longer and more frequently because their goal is to produce TT. In contrast, ST fixation may indicate translators' effort more accurately.

PE Effort Indicators

We did the KMO test on the PE data, and the result is .686. Barlett Test of Sphericity shows $p = .000$. Therefore, the 11 PE effort indicators are highly correlated and suitable for factor analysis. Then, we did an exploratory factor analysis using varimax rotation and also identified three factors (Table 4).

Table 4. Factor Analysis on PE Effort Indicators

	Factor 1	Factor 2	Factor 3	Uniqueness	α
STW	.687			.000	.964
SSW	.720			.000	
PDSW	.752			.000	
PDTW	.721			.000	
TFCW	.638			.056	
TFDW	.638			.049	
ETW		.937		.017	.914
PCSW		.901		.002	
PCTW		.919		.002	
SFCW			.935	.041	.597
SFDW			.898	.040	

Factor 1 is mainly about temporal effort, including translation time, pause duration, and TT fixation. This factor covers such indictors as STW, SSW, PDSW, PDTW, TFDW, and TFCW, and it can account for 31.75% of the variation in data. The Cronbach's α

coefficient is .964, which shows that the factor is highly reliable. Factor 2 is concerned with technical effort, including pause count and edits. This factor covers such effort indicators as PCSW, PCTW, and ETW, and it can account for 38.76% of the variation in data. The Cronbach's α coefficient is .914, which suggests that the effort indicators under this factor are highly consistent. Factor 3 mainly shows the cognitive effort associated with ST comprehension and includes the indicators of ST fixation, namely SFDW and SFCW. This factor can account for 26.54% of the variation in data. The Cronbach's α coefficient is .597. It is lower than the acceptable value of .70 in applied research (Mellinger and Hanson 2017: 202). However, considering that the sample size in this study is small, and there is considerable individual difference in participants' fixation behavior (Rayner 1998: 376), which may have been complicated by the co-existence of ST and MT output in the case of PE, we believe that the .597 result still shows internal consistency between the effort indicators under this factor. Actually, the interpretation of Cronbach's α coefficient is not that simplistic, and some researchers set the acceptance level of 0.50 for newly developed items (Maat et al. 2015).

The three factors identified in PE effort indicators mostly correspond to those in HT effort indicators, and the major difference between the two lies in Factor 3. For HT effort measurement, the indicators of TT fixation are highly correlated and form a separate factor, while for PE the indicators of ST fixation form a factor. This difference is largely attributable to the different work mode of HT and PE. Translators can devote most of their attention to TT production after comprehending ST when doing HT tasks. They may refer back to ST when coming across difficulties, but their attention is mostly assigned to fixating on and editing TT (Castilho 2016: 46). PE involves a different scenario, for translators may need to refer back to ST and make comparison between ST and MT output constantly in order to revise it. Such differences in the mode of work may have contributed to the difference in factor analyses.

The loadings of the PE effort indicators fall between .720 and .937 except for STW, TFCW, and TFDW whose loadings are below .70. Analyses of the loadings reveal the following features. First, the loading of ETW (.937) is higher than that in HT effort measurement (.520). It shows that ETW is suitable for measuring PE effort. Different from HT where translators have to type TT from scratch, the keyboard and mouse operations in PE reflect translators' effort more accurately, as PE is based on the MT output and translators do not need to type from scratch. Second, similar to HT effort measurement, the indicators based on ST word count tend to have higher loadings. The loading of SSW (.720) is higher than that of STW (.687), and the loading of PDSW (.752) is higher than that of PDTW (.721). However, the loading of PCTW (.919) is higher than that of PCSW (.901). Considering that the difference between the two sets of indicators is small, it calls for more exploration. Third, similar to HT effort measurement, the indicators based on pause count have higher loadings than those based on pause duration. The loading of PCSW (.901) is higher than that of PDSW (.752), and the loading of PCTW (.919) is higher than that of PDTW (.721). This result again provides evidence that pause count can be more reliable in revealing translators' effort (Vieira 2017: 54). Fourth, indicators concerned with ST fixation have higher loadings than those related to TT fixation. The loading of TFCW (.935) is higher than that of TFCW (.638), and the loading of SFDW (.898) is higher than that of TFDW (.638). It suggests that ST fixation data can reflect translators' effort more accurately.

5 Implications and Conclusion

To conclude, this study explores the reliability of HT and PE effort indicators based on the data collected in an eye-tracking and key-logging experiment. The major findings and implications regarding the measurement of student translators' HT and PE effort include the following. First, the effort indicators suitable for HT and PE can be different. Particularly, ETW is not suitable for measuring HT effort, as translators need to type translations from scratch and the number of edits cannot distinguish the different degrees of effort experienced by student translators. Second, there is similarity between HT and PE effort indicators. The indicators based on ST word count are more reliable than those based on TT word count, indicators based on pause count are more reliable than those based on pause duration, and indicators based on ST fixation are more reliable than those based on TT fixation. We are aware that this remains to be further explored. This study involves translation into participants' native language, and such directionality may have an impact on their cognitive processing (Chou et al. 2021). Participants would need to process ST in their foreign language but produce TT in their native language, and their effort might have lied with ST processing. Therefore, further research is needed in this regard. Third, fixation and pause data need to be properly processed to ensure accurate measurement of effort. Since the effort indicators covered in this study show significant and positive correlation with each other, it implies that the threshold applied in this research are valid for measuring HT and PE of the English-Chinese language pair. To be more specific, fixation data can be processed at the 100 ms threshold, and pause data can be processed at the 300 ms threshold. Meanwhile, this study has the following limitations. First, the number of participants is limited. Although more than 30 students took part in the study, their background were homogeneous and there was gender imbalance. In future studies, recruiting participants from more diverse background and comparing the translation behavior of different groups may generate more enlightening findings. Second, as the workload to process and analyze eye-tracking data is huge, the length, number, and directionality of experiment materials are limited. In future studies, we will enlarge the sample size and explore different directions of HT and PE to further test the validity of current findings.

Acknowledgements. This work was supported by Center for Scientific Research and Development in Higher Education Institutes, Ministry of Education of China under Grant [2022IT218], by Humanities and Social Science Fund of Ministry of Education of China under Grant [23YJC740007], and by the Innovation Project of Graduate Education of GDUFS under Grant [24GWYJSCX-04].

References

Carl, M.: Translog-II: a program for recording user activity data for empirical translation process research. IJCLA **3**(1), 153–162 (2012)

Castilho, S.: Measuring Acceptability of Machine Translated Enterprise Content. Dublin City University (2016)

Chou, I., Liu, K.L., Zhao, N.: Effects of directionality on interpreting performance: evidence from interpreting between Chinese and English by trainee interpreters. Front. Psychol. **2021**, 1–11 (2021)

Cui, Y., Liu, X., Cheng, Y.: A comparative study on the effort of human translation and post-editing in relation to text types: an eye-tracking and key-logging experiment. SAGE Open **13**(1), 1–15 (2023)

Daems, J., Vandepitte, S., Hartsuiker, R., Macken, L.: The impact of machine translation error types on post-editing effort indicators. In: Proceedings of the Fourth Workshop on Post-Editing Technology and Practice, pp. 31–45. Association for Machine Translation in the Americas (2015)

Lacruz, I., Denkowski, M., Lavie, A.: Cognitive demand and cognitive effort in post-editing. In: Proceedings of the Third Workshop on Post-Editing Technology and Practice, pp. 73–84. Vancouver (2014)

Koponen, M.: Machine Translation Post-editing and Effort Empirical Studies on the Post-editing Process. The University of Helsinki (2016)

Krings, H.P.: Repairing Texts: Empirical Investigations of Machine Translation Postediting Processes. The Kent State University Press, Kent, OH (2001)

Maat, S.M., Adnan, M., Abdullah, M.F.N.L., Ahmad, C.N.C., Puteh, M.: Confirmatory factor analysis of learning environment instrument among high performance school students. Creat. Educ. **6**, 640–646 (2015)

Mellinger, C.D., Hanson, T.A.: Quantitative research methods in translation and interpreting studies. Routledge, London (2017)

Miquel-Iriarte, M., Vilaro, A., Orero, P., Serrano, J., Delgado, H.: Entitling: a way forward for accessibility. In: Eye Tracking in Audiovisual Translation. ARACNE, Rome (2012)

Moorkens, J., O'Brien, S., Silva, I.A.L., Fonseca, N., Alves, F.: Correlations of perceived post-editing effort with measurements of actual effort. Mach. Transl. **29**(3), 267–284 (2015)

Moorkens, J., Toral, A., Castilho, S., Way, A.: Translators' perceptions of literary post-editing using statistical and neural machine translation. Translation Spaces **7**(2), 240–262 (2018)

O'Brien, S.: Pauses as indicators of cognitive effort in post-editing machine translation output. Across Lang. Cultures **7**(1), 1–21 (2006)

Pavlović, N., Jensen, K.T.H.: Eye tracking translation directionality. In: Translation Research Projects 2, pp. 93–109. Intercultural Studies Group, Tarragona (2009)

Rayner, K.: Eye movements in reading and information processing: 20 years of research. Psychol. Bull. **124**(3), 372–422 (1998)

Saldanha, G., O'Brien, S.: Research Methodologies in Translation Studies. Routledge, London (2013)

Szarkowska, A., Dutka, Ł., Szychowska, A., Pilipczuk, O.: Visual attention distribution in intralingual respeaking: an eye-tracking study. In: Eye Tracking and Multidisciplinary Studies on Translation, pp. 185–204. John Benjamins Publishing Company, Amsterdam (2018)

Vieira, L.N.: Indices of cognitive effort in machine translation post-editing. Mach. Transl. **28**(3), 187–216 (2014)

Vieira, L.N.: How do measures of cognitive effort relate to each other? a multivariate analysis of post-editing process data. Mach. Transl. **30**, 41–62 (2017)

Walker, C.: Towards a quantitative measurement of equivalent effect and a tentative conceptualisation of cognitive equivalence. In: Eye Tracking and Multidisciplinary Studies on Translation, pp. 225–258. John Benjamins Publishing Company, Amsterdam (2018)

Yamada, M.: The impact of google neural machine translation on post-editing by student translators. J. Specialised Transl. **31**, 87–106 (2019)

Translation Practice and Competence Enhancement in the Age of AI: Applying ChatGPT to Translation Education

Fangyuan Li and Lu Tian(✉)

School of Interpreting and Translation Studies, Guangdong University of Foreign Studies, Guangzhou, China
ivytianlu@gdufs.edu.cn

Abstract. Various advanced tools and technologies have had a significant impact on the practice and education of translation. In this era of AI, the emergence of generative technology has introduced an advanced conversational work mode that involves closer coordination between humans and machines. ChatGPT, as a representative of generative AI technology, holds significant potential for further advancements in the field of translation. Against this background, this study aims to investigate the utilization of this new generative AI technology in the context of translation education. As an invaluable resource for translation students, ChatGPT can offer them valuable guidance and support throughout the translation task. The article first explores how ChatGPT can effectively aid translation learners at different phases of the translation process, encompassing pre-translation, machine translation, and post-editing stages. Then, drawing on the influential PACTE model of translation competence, it explicates how ChatGPT can contribute to the enhancement of translation students' competence, particularly their bilingual, extra-linguistic, and strategic sub-competences.

Keywords: Translation Competence · Translation Education · Translation Process · Generative AI · ChatGPT

1 Introduction

In this era of blossoming artificial intelligence (AI), the rapid advances of technology have significantly influenced the work mode of translation and offered users possibility and flexibility to customize their work. Within this evolving landscape, it is imperative for translation education to adjust to the new situations and circumstances by precisely reorienting its training objectives and teaching methods. In addition, translation education must remain updated and adapt to the needs of society and the changing work mode of translation. This article reports the authors' experience of applying ChatGPT to translation practice and explores its implications on translation education. It particularly focuses on the changes the AI tool has brought to the translation process and its function in facilitating the enhancement of translation competence for translation learners.

Z. Kubincová et al. (Eds.): SETE 2023, LNCS 14606, pp. 219–230, 2024.
https://doi.org/10.1007/978-981-97-4243-1_17

2 Translation Education in the Age of AI

2.1 Translation Education and Technologies

The advancement of technology has had a substantial influence on translation education. First and foremost, the internet has facilitated convenient access to a vast array of online resources including online dictionaries and specialized terminology databases. Translation teachers, therefore, started to play a crucial role in guiding students to navigate the abundance of information available online, to critically evaluate and select reliable resources, and to effectively utilize these materials in their teaching. In addition, various corpus tools and computer-aided translation platforms have been widely embraced in academic settings as they can enrich students' lexical resources and enhance their translation efficiency [1, 2].

Technological advancements have also facilitated remote learning, lifting translation education from the restrictions of time and space, and bringing quality education resources to more translation learners and interested groups. Online courses such as Massive Open Online Courses (MOOCs) and Small Private Online Courses (SPOCs) have enabled students to participate in classes regardless of their geographical locations. This has paved the way for the creation of an online learning community that encourages peer support and feedback, transcending language and cultural barriers and exposing students to diverse perspectives and challenges [3, 4]. Specialized online platforms dedicated to translator training leverage big data and efficient information retrieval to offer professional guidance to translation teaching and learning. For instance, *Textwells* features a rich knowledge network that enables students to engage in meaningful exercises and provides possibility for designing customized computer-assisted translation courses [5, 6]. Moreover, these online platforms offer effective methods for teachers to monitor students' performance, enabling them to provide more scientific and reliable formative evaluation [7].

The appearance of machine translation (MT), including popular tools such as Google Translate and various other neural machine translation models, has also become a concern in translation education and brought about heated discussions. Attitudes towards MT vary among scholars. Some argue that MT can assist non-native speakers in reducing language errors and improving translation quality, while others express worries that excessive reliance on MT may hinder students' motivation to enhance their translation competence [8, 9]. Like it or not, MT and AI tools have been changing the work mode of translators. Translation education has inevitably to face up to such changes and make proactive adjustments.

2.2 ChatGPT and Its Potential in Translation Education

Since its initial launch in November 2022, ChatGPT has experienced a surge in popularity, attracting millions of users within a few weeks. One of the remarkable features of ChatGPT is its ability to generate conversations that resemble human-like interactions. Figure 1 shows ChatGPT's (version 3.5) own explanation of how it works.

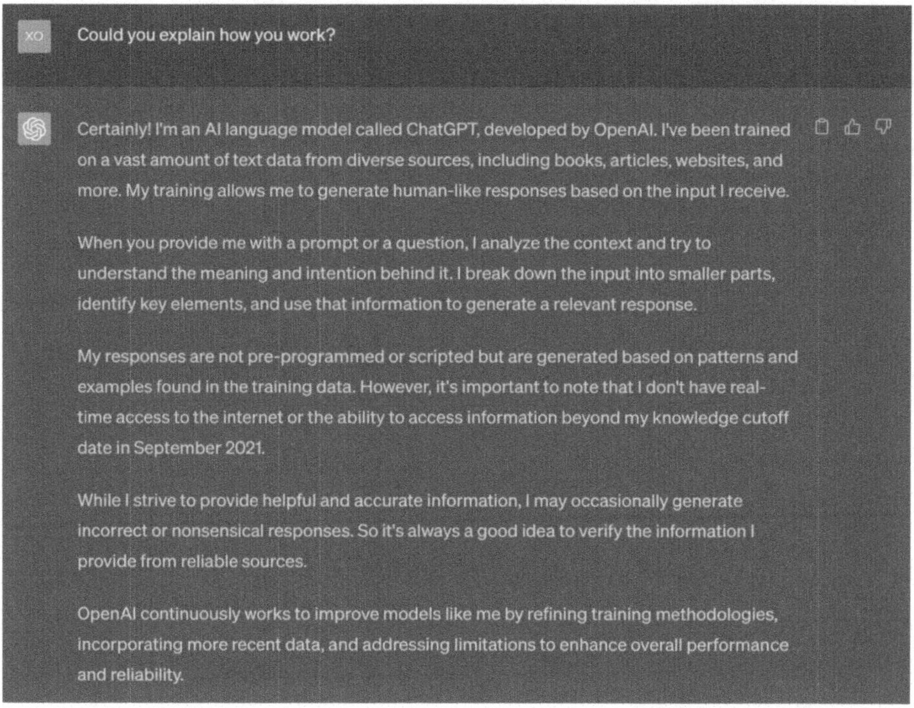

Fig. 1. ChatGPT's Self-explanation of Its Functioning (access date: 2023.07.18)

Through its self-explanation, we can find that ChatGPT operates within a conversational context rather than simply executing instructions passively. It generates intended outcomes by responding to prompts posed by the users. As its responses are not scripted, ChatGPT does not usually provide the same answer even to the same question, creating an illusion of originality. However, the responses generated by ChatGPT can hardly be considered as entirely original as they are derived from a vast pre-trained dataset containing extensive statistics gathered from the internet. Therefore, ChatGPT is unable to provide information or concepts that have not been included in its databank.

Like any other AI tools, ChatGPT can occasionally make mistakes, but it can correct itself within the conversational context. These features empower ChatGPT to function as a more accessible encyclopedia, a patient teacher, as well as an experienced translator, posing both opportunities and challenges to translation education. In fact, ChatGPT has demonstrated significant competence in the field of translation [10].

Due to the impressive capabilities of ChatGPT, there are urgent concerns in the academia about its impact on the education industry. While some people worry that AI may replace human teachers for good, others argue that teachers should embrace new technologies as reliable assistants in their teaching rather than viewing them as adversaries [11]. Considering that the primary objective of translation education is to foster students' translation competence [12], it is necessary and significant to discuss the impact of ChatGPT on the cultivation of translation competence for translation learners.

3 Translation Competence in the Age of AI

According to the widely acknowledged PACTE model, translation competence is composed mainly of five sub-competences—bilingual, extra-linguistic, instrumental, knowledge about translation, and strategic sub-competences [13, 14]. In addition, psycho-physiological components also affect translators' performance. Figure 2 demonstrates the PACTE model of translation competence.

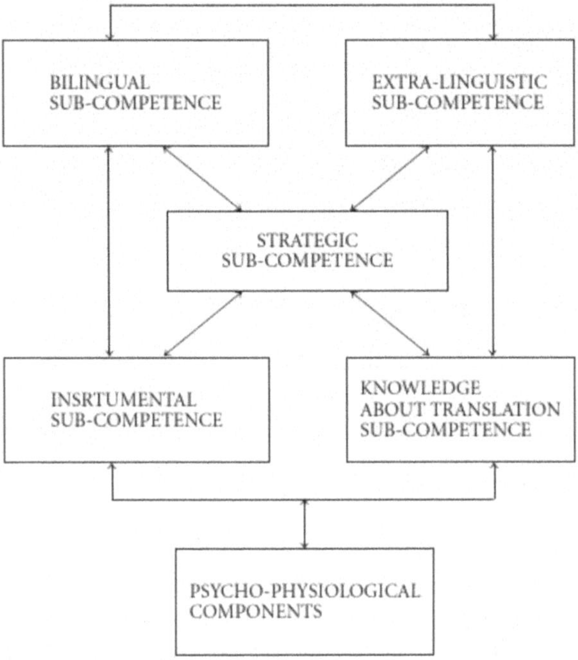

Fig. 2. PACTE Model of Translation Competence [13]

The bilingual sub-competence, as its name suggests, refers to the ability to communicate in two languages. It includes the lexical, grammatical, textual, pragmatic, and socio-linguistic knowledge of the two languages and is considered primarily procedural knowledge. Extra-linguistic sub-competence is predominantly declarative knowledge about the world. It is made up of bicultural knowledge, encyclopedic knowledge, and subject knowledge. Instrumental sub-competence is the ability to make use of various resources and tools such corpora, search engines, and MT. Knowledge about translation sub-competence is predominantly declarative knowledge about translation such as translation units, translation processes, translation methods, and the translation profession, for instance, the work market. Of all the sub-competencies, strategic sub-competence is considered the most essential. It functions throughout the whole translation process and coordinates between different sub-competencies. Moreover, strategic sub-competence also includes the ability to identify and solve problems during the translation process. Apart from these sub-competencies, psycho-physiological components also play a part in the system. They include cognitive components, attitudinal aspects, and abilities such as creativity, reasoning, and analysis.

The integration of AI into translation practices necessitates a reassessment of the composition of translation competence and the weighting of each sub-competence in the mechanism. Due to its nature as a large language model and its feature of interactivity, ChatGPT has proven to be more than mere an instrument for translators. If properly used, it can not only facilitate the enhancement of translators' competence but also compensate for the incompetence of human translators. In comparison to most translation learners, ChatGPT possesses more prominent bilingual and extra-linguistic competences, but it lacks professional knowledge and skills in translation and is incapable of making appropriate decisions in the translation process. In general, ChatGPT excels in declarative knowledge but is weak in procedural knowledge. Therefore, it is necessary to discuss how ChatGPT could facilitate translation practice and enhance translators' competence.

4 ChatGPT-Facilitated Translation Education

4.1 ChatGPT-Facilitated Translation Practice

In this section, a short paragraph extracted from *The Economist*, a prestigious English magazine in economics, is taken as the source text (ST) to be translated into Chinese. We will report how ChatGPT could help translators in different stages of the translation process. All the output generated by ChatGPT 3.5 in our demonstration was retrieved in July 2023.

> *There was a time when everyone thought the quants had figured it out. That is not the perception today. When it comes to the stockmarket, at least, automation has not been the winner-takes-all event that many fear elsewhere. It is more like a tug-of-war between humans and machines. And though the machines are winning, humans have not let go just yet.*
>
> (Retrieved from https://www.economist.com/finance-and-economics/2023/03/09/lessons-from-finances-experience-with-artificial-intelligence on 24 July 2023)

4.1.1 ChatGPT-Aided Comprehension

In translation practice, unfamiliar expressions and terms can pose significant challenges to translators. Traditionally, dictionaries and encyclopedias have been considered authoritative sources that provide definitions and explanations of the meaning and usage of such expressions and terms. However, dictionaries and encyclopedias can hardly include all specific contexts, and the rapid pace in creating new expressions and usages far surpasses the speed at which dictionaries are updated. In contrast, ChatGPT has been extensively trained on vast amounts of data, so it can provide easy access to relevant information within its existing database when prompted appropriately.

Upon initial inspection of the ST, expressions like "quant", "winner-takes-all", and "tug-of-war" might turn to be unfamiliar to Chinese students. Inquiries with ChatGPT provide an efficient way for them to get access to the detailed explanation, word history, and even metaphorical meaning of the relevant expressions.

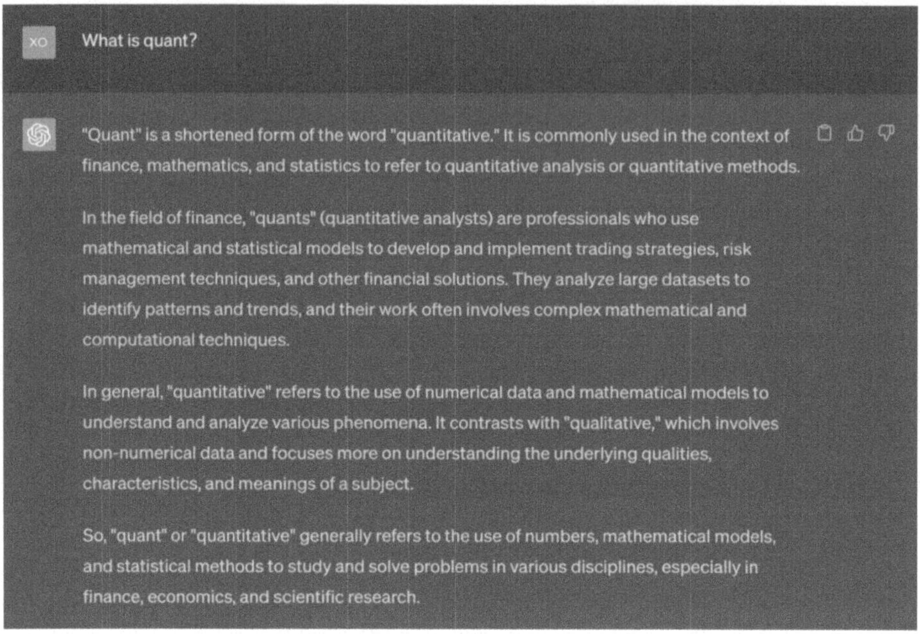

Fig. 3. ChatGPT-aided Comprehension

It can be observed that the response provided by ChatGPT is not limited to the definition of a certain concept. It extends to encompass specific domain knowledge as well. As Fig. 3 demonstrates, when asked about "quant", it specifically explains its meaning and usage in the field of finance. If needed, translators could pose further queries about the role of quantitative analysts or other information for their comprehension.

4.1.2 ChatGPT-Generated Translation

Although ChatGPT is not specifically designed for translation purposes, it possesses considerable potential to serve as a MT tool. A straightforward prompt such as "Translate this passage into Chinese" is sufficient for it to generate a translation version although an instruction with detailed requirements may stimulate more desirable results.

Like other MT tools, ChatGPT may inevitable produce inaccurate or inappropriate translation in its output. In this regard, human translators can proactively intervene in the translation process by specifying the desired options so that the generated output will align with the intended needs and requirements. As Fig. 4 demonstrates, the expression "tug-of-war" was translated by ChatGPT as 拔河比赛, its literal counterpart in Chinese, but this interpretation failed to fit in the financial setting of this context. In this case, preferred translation or expressions to be excluded can be specified in the prompt. In other words, when there are expressions or terms that already have acknowledged and fixed translation versions, it is desirable to include the information within the prompt. By explicitly providing the preferred option, human translators can to a certain extent

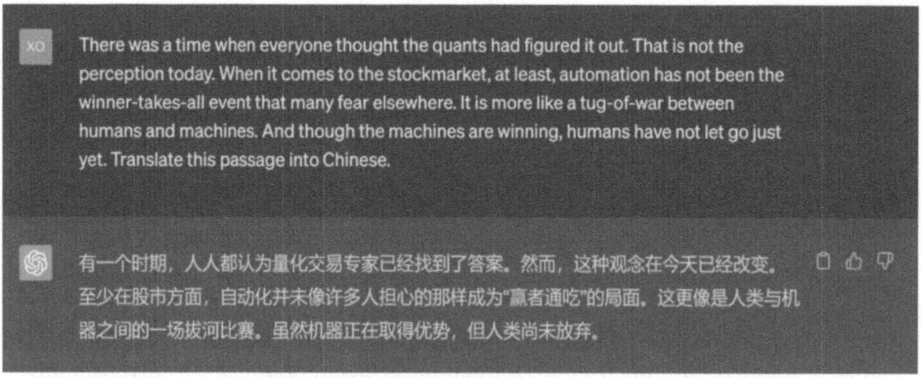

Fig. 4. ChatGPT-generated Translation

manipulate the response of MT and ensure the accuracy and consistence of the translation in specific contexts.

4.1.3 ChatGPT-Assisted Post-editing

With the advances in technology, MT has increasingly become a significant component in the translation workflow. However, the output of MT is not entirely reliable as it may contain potential errors or even factual inaccuracies. Therefore, it is essential to incorporate post-editing by human translators into the work process [15]. On the one hand, human translators excel in capturing the cultural and contextual nuances that might have been neglected by machines; one the other hand, human translators can also bring expertise and creativity to the translation, ensuring the quality and appropriateness of the final product. Therefore, a combination of MT and human post-editing (PE) has become an effective approach for translation practices in many sectors.

Given its nature of generativity and advantage of interactivity, ChatGPT can be used to post-edit translations done by human translators or by other machines. This operation can be particularly beneficial for translation learners as they can either compare their own translation with the machine-generated output or learn from machines' feedback on their translation. Both methods could help them find out grammatical errors, awkward expressions, or even mistranslations, thus helping in improving the accuracy and quality of their translations. ChatGPT is also eligible to assist translation learners in refining their language to improve the readability and comprehensibility of their works.

Furthermore, as Fig. 5 demonstrates, when provided with specific instructions regarding the desired register, ChatGPT has the capability to generate revised versions that align with the intended level of formality and adhere to the norms of specific domains. This usage can help translation students customize their translations according to the target audience and contextual requirements.

4.2 ChatGPT-Facilitated Translation Competence Enhancement

The employment of ChatGPT in translation practice and translator training is naturally related to the demonstration and cultivation of instrumental competence. At the same

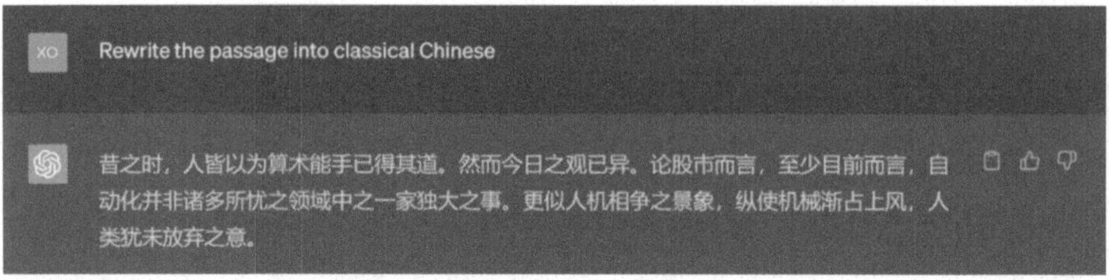

Fig. 5. ChatGPT-assisted Post-editing

time, it enables the enhancement of other translation competences. In this session, we will particularly focus on its function in facilitating bilingual competence, extra-linguistic competence, and strategic competence.

4.2.1 Bilingual Competence Enhancement

Bilingual competence is an essential prerequisite for translation. For most Chinese translation learners, the lack of foreign language environment poses a challenge for them to achieve language proficiency through adequate practice. Now ChatGPT can provide support for them to develop bilingual competence by providing language environment and interaction with native-like speakers. Students can engage in conversations with ChatGPT in the target languages, practicing reading and writing, even listening and speaking in a seemingly native context. ChatGPT can act as a language teacher to give feedback on their vocabulary, grammar, sentence construction, and other linguistic elements. ChatGPT can also act as a friend or other assigned roles to discuss various topics with the students.

ChatGPT is particularly useful in helping students enhance their writing skills as the AI tool can give feedback and suggestions on their written compositions. It can identify grammatical errors, suggest alternative phrasing, and provide explanations for any potential mistakes. It can also suggest improvements for clarity and coherence, evaluate passages based on the stipulated criteria, and provide insights into overall writing style.

By engaging in dialogue with ChatGPT, students can practice and refine their pragmatic skills, which are essential for effective communication in real-world situations. Such skills include understanding social cues and politeness conventions, and appropriate language use in different contexts. Furthermore, ChatGPT can assist students in developing their metalinguistic awareness, which involves reflecting on language structures, functions, and variations. Students can ask questions about grammar rules, language usage, and stylistic choices, and ChatGPT can provide explanations and examples to deepen their understanding of the language.

4.2.2 Extra-Linguistic Competence Complement

As a large language model, ChatGPT is equipped with vast knowledge database. Therefore, it can function as a super encyclopedia ready to provide users with information and cultural aspects of all kinds including professional knowledge of a specific area, customs and traditions, and idiomatic expressions specific to different regions. Although machines may not be able to truly comprehend cultural nuances, they can offer historical, geographical, and anecdotal information to help translators better comprehend the ST.

Thanks to its intelligent algorithm, ChatGPT can easily provide summaries of topics unfamiliar to human translators within seconds. This capability saves translators' valuable time from looking for and sorting out relevant information by themselves, and consequently helps enhance their work efficiency. In addition to generating overviews and summaries, ChatGPT can provide detailed information on specific objects or concepts within a certain field. It can assist translation learners in identifying the contextual and field-specific meanings of relevant expressions and in having a thorough understanding of technical terminologies, both of which can be crucial yet challenging for novice translators. In summary, the employment of ChatGPT in translation practice contributes to translation learners' accumulation of world knowledge and knowledge of specific areas and functions as a complement to their extra-linguistic competence.

4.2.3 Strategic Competence Reinforcement

As the core of translation competence, strategic competence is related to decision making and plan implementation in the workflow of translation. The skill of effectively organizing and managing tasks is crucial for ensuring both work efficiency and translation quality. Different from the traditional work mode of human translators whose strategic competence is evenly reflected in the translation process, the collaboration between human translators and ChatGPT enables translators to spend more time on post-editing and proofreading. In this new work mode, translators' strategic competence also lies in their effective interaction with the AI tool. Clear and proper prompts are more likely to induce accurate and disable results.

Apart from effective planning and execution capabilities, strategic competence in translation also encompasses problem detection and resolution. ChatGPT, despite its outstanding performance, does not always provide accurate and reliable output. Therefore, it is incumbent upon translators to discern and rectify any errors or inaccuracies that may arise from ChatGPT's output. This requires translators' competence in evaluating and refining the machine-generated translations so as to ensure satisfactory accuracy and desired translation quality. Moreover, as ChatGPT can generate multiple options in response to a prompt, choice-making turns to be another essential capability that translation learners need to master in the age of AI.

5 Discussion

Apart from the translation sub-competences mentioned in the previous session, ChatGPT could also facilitate the development of communicative competence, a key capacity for language learners. Given the lack of authentic environment to speak with native speakers, ChatGPT provides an opportunity for non-native speakers to have first-hand experience to communicate with a near-native AI net friend. As far as translation learners are concerned, their communicative competence can be sharpened when they request translations from ChatGPT. Only clear and effective instructions can entail accurate and desirable results.

It is worth noting that ChatGPT is designed to prioritize user satisfaction and to improve its performance based on the feedback. While this responsiveness is commendable, it can sometimes result in unnecessary adjustments or even inaccurate information in its responses. Hence, applying ChatGPT to translation practice highlights the crucial role of critical thinking for translation students. While ChatGPT can assist in providing relevant knowledge and generating translations, it is imperative for students to approach its output with a discerning and analytical mindset. Critical thinking enables students to evaluate and question the accuracy, coherence, and cultural appropriateness of machine-generated output. Instead of over relying on AI tools, they must have the awareness to seek validation from multiple sources to ensure the reliability of the generated information. Critical thinking also encourages students to explore alternative solutions and consider the limitations of MT. It guides them to delve deeper into the complexities of language and culture, fostering a deeper understanding of translation principles and the intricacies involved in producing high-quality translations.

Moreover, the ethical issues have always been a topic heated discussed in the academic field. As the mechanism of ChatGPT is to generate responses based on a pre-trained database that includes a vast collection of existing data, its output essentially involves reorganizing previously publicized materials to create a new composition, without obtaining permission from the original authors or providing proper citations. When requested to translate a text, it is possible that ChatGPT offers a translation done by a human translator but does not indicate its act of citation. This lack of traceability can lead to issues of plagiarism if users are not aware of these risks. This echoes Noam Chomsky's attitude toward ChatGPT as he related it to "hi-tech plagiarism" and considered it "a way of avoiding learning" [16]. Hence, it is crucial to address these concerns and find ways to mitigate the risk of plagiarism when applying AI tools in education or any other context. Promoting awareness among users about the limitations and potential ethical issues associated with these models can foster responsible usage of AI.

6 Conclusion

This study explores the application of ChatGPT in translation education, providing specific examples to illustrate its integration into the translation process. It also examines how this technology can facilitate the enhancement of translation competence for translation learners. The study demonstrates that ChatGPT can effectively assist student translators in improving their work efficiency and refining their translation competence. They can benefit from various forms of assistance at different stages of the translation process, including ST comprehension and terminology explanation before translation, customized MT output that meets specific requirements, and proofreading and suggestions for improvement during post-editing.

The study also reveals that ChatGPT can contribute to the development of translation learners' bilingual competence in a comprehensive manner and function as a complement to their extra-linguistic competence. On the one hand, ChatGPT can facilitate vocabulary acquisition, improve syntactic and grammatical accuracy, and refine students' overall language proficiency in both source and target languages. On the other hand, it can help expand students' cultural and contextual knowledge, as well as their familiarity with domain-specific terminologies, thus enabling them to produce translations that accurately reflect the intended meaning and cultural nuances of the ST. In addition, due to the generative nature of ChatGPT's operation, the strategic competence of translation learners can be particularly strengthened as they must make choices from the multiple options provided by the machine and exercise wise judgment to avoid errors and ethical issues. By using ChatGPT as a tool for problem-solving and decision-making, translation learners can enhance their ability to employ effective strategies to overcome translation challenges and make informed choices regarding their translation solutions.

The integration of AI technology into translation education is becoming a prominent trend in the field's future development. As technology continuously evolves and improves to achieve better performance, ongoing research and discussions are necessary to keep pace with its rapid advancement and explore the optimal balance in human and machine coordination.

Acknowledgements. The work presented in this article was supported by the 2022 Teaching Quality and Reform Project for Undergraduate Education in Guangdong Province entitled "Learning Journal-based Reform and Practice of Critical Thinking and Value Education in College English Teaching" and the 2022 Research Project of the Guangdong Undergraduate MOOCs Committee (2022ZXKC159, "The Construction and Application of a Digitally Intelligent Space for Translation Learning").

References

1. Akkoyunlu, A.N., Kilimci, A.: Application of corpus to translation teaching: practice and perceptions. Int. Online J. Educ. Teach **4**(4), 369–396 (2017)
2. Sikora, I.: The need for CAT training within translator training programmes. TRAlinea Special Issue: Challenges in Translation Pedagogy. 1–6. (2014)
3. Beaven, T., Comas-Quinn, A., Hauck, M., De los Arcos, B., Lewis, T.: The open translation MOOC: creating online communities to transcend linguistic barriers. J. Interact. Media Educ. **2013**(3), 18 (2013)
4. Liao, C., Tian, L.: An online English learning community for college students based on community of inquiry framework. In: Pang, C., et al. (eds.) Learning Technologies and Systems, pp. 370–379. Springer, Cham (2021)
5. Mu, Y., Tian, L., Yang, W.: Towards a knowledge management model for online translation learning. In: Hao, T., et al. (eds.) Emerging Technologies for Education, pp. 198–207. Springer, Cham (2018)
6. Tian, L., Zhu, C.: Making connections through knowledge nodes in translator training: on a computer-assisted pedagogical approach to literary translation. Int. J. Transl. Interpretation Appl. Linguis. (IJTIAL) **2**(2), 15–29 (2020)
7. Mu, Y., Yang, W.: Knowledge-network-based inter-institutional collaborative teaching of translation. In: Pang, C., et al. (eds.) Learning Technologies and Systems, pp. 411–419. Springer, Cham (2021)
8. Kenny, D.: Technology and translator training. In: O'Hagan, M. (ed.) The Routledge Handbook of Translation and Technology, pp. 498–515. Routledge, London & New York (2019). https://www.taylorfrancis.com/chapters/edit/10.4324/9781315311258-35/technology-translator-training-dorothy-kenny?context=ubx&refId=e596dd06-8dda-437e-a0cc-321edba62547

9. Lee, S.M.: The impact of using machine translation on EFL students' writing. Comput. Assist. Lang. Learn. **33**(3), 157–175 (2020)
10. Jiao, W., Wang, W., Huang, J.T., Wang, X., Tu, Z.P.: Is ChatGPT a good translator? Yes with GPT-4 as the engine (2023). https://arxiv.org/abs/2301.08745
11. Baidoo-Anu, D., Leticia, O.A.: Education in the era of generative artificial intelligence (AI): understanding the potential benefits of ChatGPT in promoting teaching and learning. J. AI **7**(1), 52–62 (2023)
12. Zhao, C., Feng, Q.: Translation competence in teaching guide for undergraduate translation major: connotation, component and training suggestion. Foreign Lang. World **198**(03), 12–19 (2020)
13. PACTE: Building a translation competence model. In: Alves, F. (ed.) Triangulating Translation: Perspectives in Process Oriented Research, pp. 43–66. John Benjamins Publishing Company, Amsterdam (2003). https://doi.org/10.1075/btl.45.06pac
14. PACTE: Investigating translation competence: conceptual and methodological issues. Meta Transl. J. **50**(2), 609–619 (2005)
15. Koponen, M.: How to teach machine translation post-editing? Experiences from a post-editing course. In: O'Brien, S., Simard, M. (eds.) 4th Workshop on Post-Editing Technology and Practice (WPTP4), pp. 2–15 (2015)
16. Chomsky, N., Roberts, I., Watumull, J.: The false promise of ChatGPT. New York Times (2023). https://www.nytimes.com/2023/03/08/opinion/noam-chomsky-chatgpt-ai.html. 24 July 2023

Designing an Integrated Teaching Model of College English Course Assisted by Digital Platforms

Jingjing He(✉)

School of Foreign Studies, Hefei University of Technology, Hefei, China
Sophiahe.good@163.com

Abstract. In this digital era, the integration of the internet and information technology has repainted the landscape of college English teaching in current China. This study aims to explore a comprehensive instructional approach that capitalizes on diverse information technology platforms to optimize and enhance personalized learning experiences. By synthesizing emerging pedagogical methods, such as blended teaching, second classroom teaching, self-learning of e-courses and formative assessment, and meanwhile by conducting a detailed examination of various new media and information technology platforms (e.g., Rain Classroom, Delta Reading, Pigai.org, and U Campus…), this research seeks to seamlessly integrate these digital tools with advanced teaching methodologies to design an intelligently integrated and smartly personalized teaching model for college English teaching. The trial model has been attempted by the majority of college English teachers in HFUT in recent two years with the primary objective to enhance the quality and efficiency of college English course, ensuring a more scientific and tailored approach to language instructions. The relevant questionnaire and data collected in the implementations of this teaching mode in this study promisingly reflect the validity of this model and yet offers insights and clues for further improvements.

Keywords: Integration · information technology · blended teaching · second classroom · formative assessment

1 Introduction

The advent of the internet + era with multitudinous advanced digital teaching technologies and ubiquitous learning resources on the networks has ushered in diversified teaching modes and facilitated personalized self-learning routes.

It is imperative for university-level English education to embrace and optimize the integration of the latest information technology and networks with the teaching curriculum, leveraging modern educational technologies, to correspond to the demands of college students' individualized and diversified learning. Particularly with the release of the 2020 edition of the University English Teaching Guidelines [1] issued by the Ministry of Education in China, the application of modern information technology in

Z. Kubincová et al. (Eds.): SETE 2023, LNCS 14606, pp. 231–241, 2024.
https://doi.org/10.1007/978-981-97-4243-1_18

college English teaching and the deep fusion of e-learning platforms and the face-to-face(F2F) classrooms has been explicitly emphasized to promote the setup of smart and modernized learning communities, and enhance the teaching quality and efficiency.

Based on the analyses of the current status of digital assistance in college English teaching in Hefei University of Technology(HFUT), this paper is oriented to further explore an integrated design of intelligent course construction in college English teaching by amalgamating various on-line learning resources, utilizing the digital elements and incorporating multifaceted teaching methodologies to enable the teachers and learners themselves to navigate learning routines, facilitating greater engagement of reciprocal teaching and learning, to make the course designing more interactive and adaptable to the individualized learning needs, and ultimately to enhance students' semantic competence, cultural learning, and moral development, and equip them with a well-rounded understanding of English language and its broader implications.

2 Integration of Internet and Information Technology in College English Course

2.1 Literature Review

The integration of internet and information technologies in college English course has been an extensive research. The authors has conducted a relevant survey of the research literature with CNKI (China National Knowledge Infrastructure) as literature sources by searching for core journals with the key concept"integrated education in college English" and this process has yielded about 386 papers to study. The retrieving results suggest that the underlying core theories and methodologies of the related studies revolve around expansions of constructionists' transferring of knowledge and strategies in collaborative settings and, in particular, in the context of learning undertakings (Brown,Collins & Duguid,1989) [2] for instance, through scaffolding teaching, random access teaching, anchor teaching and cooperative learning assisted by diverse apps and digital platforms [3]such as We-learn platforms[4], QQ learning groups[5]. Moreover, there are the blended teaching explorations and practices of constructions of the on-line and F2F classroom and flipped classroom teaching modules in the college English writing or translating course by assimilating various digital platforms such as the practical designing and scheduling of the online and offline hybrid teaching model of college English based on the WeChat official account[6]. Besides, there are some empirical studies of OBE(Outcome based education) model [7], and the POA oriented blended English writing assessment on the Pigai.org to explore self-study and self-assessment of college English writing [8, 9]. There is also an attempt to explore a deep integration between the multi-modal intelligent classroom based on scaffolding theory so as to explore the effective college English translation teaching mode to improve the quality of translation courses [10]. Additionally, there are some practical studies on the constructions of SPOC and MOOC to promote the deep fusion of on-line courses and off-line courses and to leverage technology for improved student engagement, personalized learning, and effective knowledge construction [11]. Among those on-line courses constructions, some basic framework and functions of mobile English learning platform are further proposed and researched to facilitate the effective integration of mobile learning into college English teaching [12, 13].

Among the previous studies and researches epitomized above, there are few essays specifically categorizing the newly emerging e-learning platforms and media channels to update and expand the integration of one-line learning resources and platforms and further sorting and classifying the digital platforms so as to scheme the concrete and feasible modules of profound integration and foster the more effective and profound fusion of digital elements in college English course.

2.2 Categorizing of Platforms Applied in HFUT

Accordingly, in this essay, the author categorizes and analyzes the various internet platforms currently applied by the majority of college English teachers at Hefei University of Technology in alignment with the instructional objectives of holistic competence cultivation of college English learning, encompassing listening, speaking, reading, writing, translating, inter-cultural communicating, and morality development emphasized in the 2023 course curriculum in HFUT. Through specific categorization and classification, as displayed in Table 1, these internet e-learning platforms, software and apps offer a broad range of updated resources and interactive practices tailored to specific and respective college English learning objectives, which integrate technology and multimedia to make English self-learning and blended learning more engaging and interactive.

For the speaking and listening, the U-Campus platform, in conjunction with the New Standard listening and speaking e-textbook resources, facilitates the development of listening and speaking skill; the FunDubbing app allows students to practice voice dubbing, enhancing pronunciation and fluency, and experiencing diverse genres of English movie cultures. For the vocabulary acquisition, the Word Master WeChat mini-app mainly aids in key vocabulary and phrase acquisitions and recycled memorization of the useful expressions through context-based exercises and quizzes which have been analyzed in the F2F integrated college English course, and its self-assessment feature and instant grading system ensures continual motivations and constant progresses, avoiding the monotony of vocabulary memorization. Delta Reading (WeChat mini-app) provides extensive reading materials, which are combined with cross-references to course content and overlapped with the topics of the college English textbooks, CET46 reading tests and current newspaper readings. Those updated reading resources promote comprehension and improve reading analytical skills and also extend the visions and expand the reading horizons. For writing and translation, Pigai.org network provides an instant self-assessment and a library of sentence examples, supporting repetitive self-polishing and promoting improvements in writing and translation abilities. Ethical and cross-cultural insights are ubiquitously shared via WeChat public accounts and QQ English learning group, fostering cultural awareness and cultivating moralities. There are also integrated SPOC such as College English Integrated Course 1, 2, 3, Innovation College English Course and Nucleus College English Course, which are designed and filmed by HFUT's College English teaching teams and released in the the HFUT Cloud Classrooms on the platform of MOOC of China's universities. Those on-line SPOC encompass diverse aspects of English learning such as fundamental grammar and structure analyse, rhetorical analyses, cultural extensions, academic English discussions and etc. In addition, the dynamic updating learning resources from some English learning influencers on the popular self-media platforms like TikTok, Xiaohongshu, and Bilibili are constantly recommended for the students to add an element of engagement and motivation.

Table 1. Diversified Newly-emerged Digital Learning Platforms

Learning Orientations	Platforms/Software	Features and Activities
Comprehensive Interactions and Communications	Rain Classroom	-Interactive functions of bullet-screen/comment and message submitting -Audio, video and PPT learning content
Listening&Speaking Competence	Campus Platform (New Standard Listening E-Course)	- Audio and video learning content - Graded listening tests
	FunDubbing App	- Dubbing exercises
Vocabulary Acquisition	Word Master WeChat Mini-App	- Vocabulary self-study and quizzes
Extensive Reading	Delta Reading (WeChat Mini-App)	- Extensive reading materials and compatible exercises
Writing and Translation	Pigai.org	- Self-assessment for translation and writing
Ethics and Cross-Culture Cultivation	WeChat Public Accounts QQ Learning Group	- Ethical and cultural insights
Comprehensive SPOCS	China's University MOOC Platform HFUT School SPOC in Cloud Classroom	- Integrated College English Course -Innovation College English Course -Nucleus College English Course
Self-Media Learning Channels on Social Media Platforms	TikTok, Xiaohongshu, Bilibili	- Dynamic recommendations from English learning influencers

3 Designing and Application of an Integrated Teaching Model in HFUT

In accordance with the 2020 edition of the University English Teaching Guidelines and 2023 college English course curriculum in HFUT, on the basis of the above specific categorizations of digital learning platforms and channels currently applied in HFUT's college English course by the author and her colleagues, this research focuses on the deep integration of college English teaching and digital technologies so as to further propel the construction of a well-organized and diversified integrated network to English language self-learning and blended teaching assisted by the digital platforms to cater to various learning objectives, and to further harness internet technology to make college English learning engaging, interactive, and accessible to a wide range of students.

In HFUT, the college English course as one of the compulsive courses of General Education, consists of the integrated English course and listening course. The former implements level-based English teaching of Level 1,2,3, which places emphasis on improving students' integrated English competences of speaking, reading, translating, writing, intercultural communication and morality development. This course is conducted by a blended teaching with a combination of F2F classroom teaching, blended teaching of rain classroom and online SPOC supplementary teaching, and etc. The latter attempts to improve students' listening ability realized by their autonomous learning on the internet platform---U Campus on computer or on the mobile phone.

3.1 Participants

The participants of this research were the non-English-major Sophomores(about 190 students from five classes; approximately 38 students per class) of Grade 2022 starting from fundamental learning stage---college English Level 1 in the author's college English course. They have participated in this integrated teaching model for three learning semesters and have overall offered positive feedback for the learning effect illustrated later in the questionnaire part of this research.

3.2 Procedures

Generally, this integrated English teaching model is predicated on the fusions of various teaching methodologies and integrated designing of internet platforms and media channels sorted and categorized in the previous part of this research on the bases of the diverse English learning orientations (Table 1). Subsequently, the specific designing and setting of those platforms and media channels with multiple tasks and tremendous learning resources will assist and facilitate the implementations of an integrated learning network consisting of the blended, interactive and communicative teaching of F2F classroom assisted by rain classroom, Delta Reading and Pigai.org; second classroom teaching aided by multiple internet media platforms such as WeChat public accounts, QQ learning group, self-media learning channels on social media platforms as well as self-learning E-courses on the China's University MOOC platform and U Campus platform. Ultimately there are formative statistics and clues to incorporate multiple assessments to help reflect and analyze the integrated teaching and learning effect.

Specifically, as displayed in Fig. 1, firstly, the detailed implementations of the integrated teaching model mainly rely on the blended teaching of communicative and interactive teaching in F2F classroom assisted by the on-line learning and practicing on rain classroom (a smart mobile teaching Wechat mini-app newly developed by Tsinghua University in 2016) and Delta Reading (a Wechat reading mini-app developed by an education and technology company in Beijing in 2018 supplying a multitude of specified and updated CET46 reading materials and news-reports to cater to graded English reading) and Pigai.org (an automatic assessing network of writing and translating). Students get access to instructional self-learning resources such as preview videos, PPT

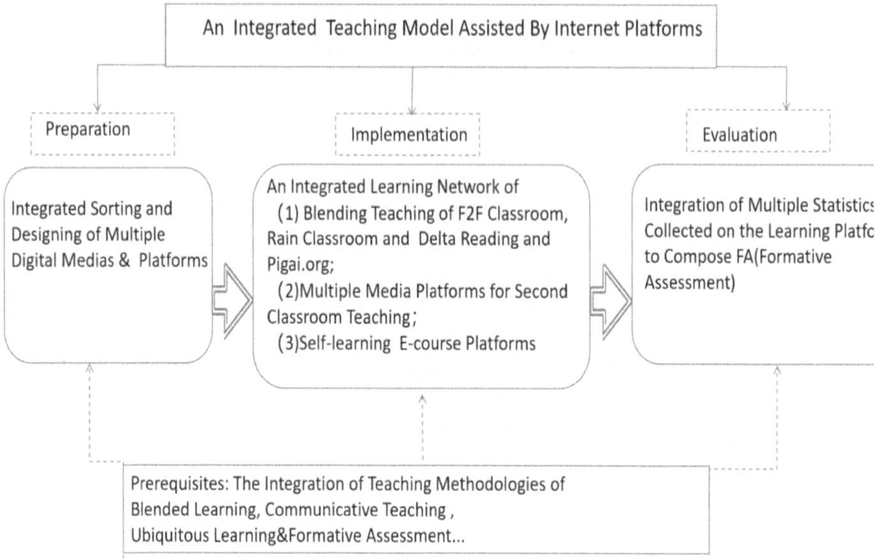

Fig. 1. Teaching Procedures

on the platforms of rain classroom before attending in-person classes, which promotes self-directed previewing and allows classroom time to be more interactive and engaging. Students can come to class prepared, ready to participate actively in discussions and activities through F2F communicative and interactive teaching also aided by the digital functions of rain classroom---bullet screen and message submission to improve the interaction frequency, which enables students to benefit from the flexibility of online resources while still enjoying face-to-face interactions with their peers and instructors. Compatibly, to help reinforce the learning effect in the above blended teaching, there are some monthly inter-related reading tasks and writing and translating tasks scheduled on the Delta reading and Pigai.org with an overlapping of the themes and discussions of the previous learning to further solidify the relevant linguistic competence. Some typical errors in reading tasks and the inaccuracy of the outputting in the writing and translating will be reanalyzed among the peers and instructor in the F2F classroom after the automatic correction on the platforms.

Secondly, through QQ learning group, the continuous information push of CET46-realted test strategies such as news-report listening and news reading resources, and recommendations of updated posts on multiple internet media platforms such as WeChat public accounts, and self-media learning channels on social media (TikTok, Xiaohongshu, Bilibili) help expand the teaching curriculum into the second extra-curriculum virtual classroom to facilitate an ubiquitous learning mode, which extend the cultural visions, cultivate the moralities, and ensure the freshness and timeliness of current learning information and resources. In this second classroom, there is also a variety of extra-curricular coaching or training(one-to-one coaching or team training) set for the diverse College English Contests on the previously-mentioned on-line platforms such as National College English Writing/Translating Contests on Pigai.org, National English Vocabulary Contest, National Academic English Vocabulary Competition on WeChat mini-apps, and etc., which targets the most prominent linguistic competences of some students and helps them demonstrate their skills and boosts their learning motifs. The competing and teaching components are reciprocally coordinated in the second classroom. Basically, the above extra-curriculum second classroom recognizes that every student is unique, and by integrating these diverse medias and platforms, this dynamic teaching can cater to a wide spectrum of learning preferences and needs and contribute to activating learning motivations.

Thirdly, each semester, the college English teachers in HFUT set the self-learning sections of E-courses on the U Campus platform(listening course) requested in the teaching curriculum. The orientations of improving intensive listening competence and cultivating self-listening routines are enforced through unit-based tasks with specific deadlines, ensuring students complete their coursework punctually. Moreover, on the U campus platform, students are subjected to regular self-assessments, involving listening comprehension tests two to three times per semester. These evaluations not only serve as monitoring tools but also encourage students to actively engage with the course materials. In tandem with this, other comprehensive English electronic courses including SPOCS of Integrated College English Course, Innovation College English Course and Nucleus College English Course are available on China's university MOOC platform. These digital courses serve as a valuable complement to traditional textbooks and classroom lectures. They provide students with a dynamic and interactive learning experience, which paper-based materials alone cannot offer. To further enrich the learning experience, an interactive Q&A section of these courses is respectively incorporated within China's university MOOC platform. This feature fills the gap left by the limitation of physical classroom time. It allows students to seek clarification, engage in discussions, and resolve doubts promptly, enhancing their understanding of the course materials. The implementation of the new self-study electronic course standards and the availability of comprehensive English courses on MOOC platforms represent a progressive approach to education. They empower students to take charge of their learning and provide valuable resources to supplement traditional classroom instruction, ultimately contributing to a more dynamic and effective learning environment.

Finally, a multifaceted evaluation approach is adopted for the integrated English teaching at HFUT, which rely on the consolidation of students' learning data from various online platforms, creating a diversified process of assessment labeled as FA (Formative Assessment). According to the teaching curriculum, the formative assessment accounts for 50% of the final grades of college English course in HFUT. Within this 50% evaluation, the oral English assessment takes 20%, which mainly consists of one-to-one oral test in the F2F class, and oral activities such as dubbing exercises on the the FunDubbing app or personal presentations in F2F class. Another aspect of this assessment process involves tracking students' performance in writing and translation through Pigai.org. Students' average scores in writing and translation are collected and evaluated among four to five delivered passages of writing or translating each semester. This component contributes to the process of assessment, accounting for 10% of the overall assessment. Another critical component is the classroom performance evaluation which also constitutes 10% of the formative assessment. This class performance evaluation mainly consists of the following three aspects displayed in Fig. 2: the learning data collected from rain classroom, which mainly includes previewing, interacting through bullet screen and message sending and some exercises in F2F class and and after-class reviewing tasks; the physical F2F classroom interaction data including brainstorming, conversations, discussions and etc.; the performance metrics from Delta Reading, which includes reading duration and accuracy. Additionally, data from U Campus electronic listening courses are incorporated into the formative assessment. The data of this part includes metrics related to the time spent on the courses, accuracy in completion, and listening test scores. It holds a 10% weight in the overall process of assessment (Fig. 3). Overall, these diversified evaluation methods for the university's integrated English teaching are intricate and comprehensive. They encompass data from various online platforms, each contributing a specific percentage to the overall assessment. This integrated approach ensures that students' progress and performance are evaluated from multiple angles, leading to a well-rounded assessment of their English language skills.

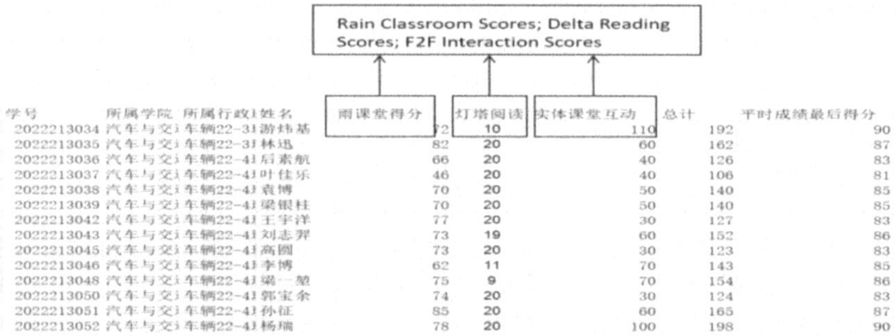

学号	所属学院	所属行政班	姓名	雨课堂得分	灯塔阅读	实体课堂互动	总计	平时成绩最后得分
2022213034	汽车与交通	车辆22-3班	游炜基	72	10	110	192	90
2022213035	汽车与交通	车辆22-3班	林迅	82	20	60	162	87
2022213036	汽车与交通	车辆22-4班	后素航	66	20	40	126	83
2022213037	汽车与交通	车辆22-4班	叶佳乐	46	20	40	106	81
2022213038	汽车与交通	车辆22-4班	袁博	70	20	50	140	85
2022213039	汽车与交通	车辆22-4班	梁银柱	70	20	50	140	85
2022213042	汽车与交通	车辆22-4班	王宇洋	77	20	30	127	83
2022213043	汽车与交通	车辆22-4班	刘志羿	73	19	60	152	86
2022213045	汽车与交通	车辆22-4班	高圆	73	20	30	123	83
2022213046	汽车与交通	车辆22-4班	李博	62	11	70	143	85
2022213048	汽车与交通	车辆22-4班	梁一楚	75	9	70	154	86
2022213050	汽车与交通	车辆22-4班	郭宝余	74	20	30	124	83
2022213051	汽车与交通	车辆22-4班	孙征	85	20	60	165	87
2022213052	汽车与交通	车辆22-4班	杨瑞	78	20	100	198	90

Fig. 2. Class Performance Score List Consisting of Data from Delta Reading, Rain Classroom and F2F Interactions

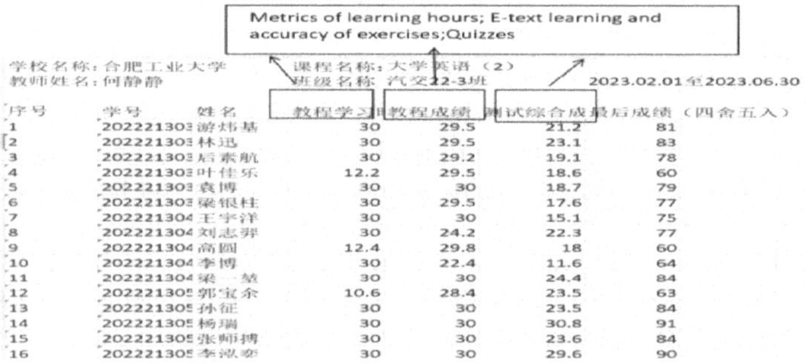

序号	学号	姓名	教程学习时	教程成绩	测试综合成	最后成绩（四舍五入）
1	20222130	游炜基	30	29.5	21.2	81
2	20222130	林迅	30	29.5	23.1	83
3	20222130	后素航	30	29.2	19.1	78
4	20222130	叶佳乐	12.2	29.5	18.6	60
5	20222130	袁博	30	30	18.7	79
6	20222130	梁银柱	30	29.5	17.6	77
7	20222130	王宇洋	30	30	15.1	75
8	20222130	刘志羿	30	24.2	22.3	77
9	20222130	高圆	12.4	29.8	18	60
10	20222130	李博	30	22.4	11.6	64
11	20222130	梁一楚	30	30	24.4	84
12	20222130	郭宝余	10.6	28.4	23.5	63
13	20222130	孙征	30	30	23.5	84
14	20222130	杨瑞	30	30	30.8	91
15	20222130	张师搏	30	30	23.6	84
16	20222130	李泓奕	30	30	29.6	90

Fig. 3. Listening Course Assessment on U Campus

4 Analysis of Questionnaire and One-to-One Interviews

The above studied and designed teaching model assisted by diverse digital platforms has been applied by the author and her colleagues since 2022–2023 academic year in HFUT. The following research-relevant questionnaire and one-to-one surveys are conducted among sophomores of non-English majors who have participated in this integrated teaching mode for three semesters. The questionnaire was devised on the Questionnaire Star Website and issued to students involved through QQ learning groups at random. This survey aimed to assess the opinions and preferences of users regarding this integrated teaching mode for further improvements. A total of 177 respondents provided valuable insights. Here's a concise summary of the key findings.

Firstly, a substantial portion (66.1%) found self-studying college English crucial and important, emphasizing the need for effective learning resources and supplementary support on-line and off-line and a significant majority (70.06%) of respondents reported having experience with self-studying college English, indicating a prevalent interest in autonomous learning. The effectiveness of utilization of the digital college English self-learning platforms in this teaching mode could be perceived that among users that over half of the respondents(57.06%)responded that the platforms either very helpful or helpful, demonstrating a positive feedback for the validity of the above digital self-learning platforms.

More specifically, from the statistics collected, the majority of learners desired for personalized learning plans (69.49%), emphasizing the need for accessible and customized learning experiences. And most learners appreciated the validity of this integrated teaching mode with diverse technical aids of internet platforms yet still proposed valuable suggestions for future improvements especially stressing on the smart interactions and flexible and routine designing of on-line team discussions and communications. Users expressed a high demand for video explanations (73.45%) and textual materials (66.67%), highlighting that these learning resources should be timely updated on the platforms. Moreover, a substantial number of respondents emphasized the importance of adaptive learning plans (80.23%) and real-time online support (63.28%), underlining the need for interactive and personalized features of the digital self-learning platforms. And for the levels of those relevant materials, respondents preferred intermediate (89.27%) and high-level content (76.84%), reflecting a demand for challenging materials for academic and professional advancement in the future.

Additionally, among these platforms, a statistical rating of point1–5 ranking level is further conducted to evaluate the user satisfaction, with point5 as the indicator of the top rank of satisfaction. It's noteworthy that the provided QQ learning community received a positive average rating of 4.37, indicating high user satisfaction. Meanwhile, some of the one-to-one interviewing surveys also reflected that the learning resources and strategy instructions provided by the teachers and the interactions among peers within the QQ learning community proved to be useful and compatible with the routine learning. The rain classroom interactive functions of bullet screen and message sending were also favored by the most of the respondents, having an average rating of 4.21. Comparatively speaking, the "Delta Reading" and "Pigai.org" apps for reading and writing self-learning and automatic assessment received an average of 3.93. Indicating medium satisfaction. Some of the interviewees in the face-to-face surveys reflected that though the Delta Reading as a WeChat mini-app offered abundant reading resources and designed some compatible reading and interpreting tasks, it didn't provide detailed relevant analyses and explanations for the tasks and sometimes the learners still felt puzzled after checking the answers and reading through some complex sentences. And "Pigai.org", as the on-line grammar and syntax checkers, though offering instant polishing advice, overly relied on the databases of vocabulary and syntax, while neglecting the polishing of the rhetorical applications and paragraph organizing. Therefore, self-revisions in most cases still centered around the enhancing of advanced vocabulary and sentence patterns while overlooking the structural and cultural perspectives and neglecting content-related corrections. Those reflections reminded the teachers that in the future utilization of the Delta Reading and Pigai.org, they should further foster the in-depth fusion and integration of the automated proofreading together with human assessment of teaches' analyzing and peers' assessing. The quality of feedback should be further optimized through regular in-class discussions and analyses.

The current integrated model is far from being perfect. These findings offer valuable guidance for optimizing the university English self-study platforms to better meet users' needs and preferences. More specific suggestions were put forward by some respondents in the individual F2F surveys, which reminds teachers to further polish and revise the model for reciprocal enhancement for teaching and learning. The suggestions are briefly summarized as the following: This integrated model should pay more attention to the learning needs of the fundamental learners and introduce more targeted learning strategies for them to follow in the different stages of learning; the model may further integrate the teachers' evaluations and peers' assessments with the automatic assessment and organize relevant discussions in the F2F class; the designing and setting of the tasks on the platform should be more smart and this mode may offer some personalized learning plans for the individual learners; the integrated mode could further enhance the interactions by designing some group debating activities on the platforms regularly through setting some on-line chatting rooms and etc.

5 Conclusion

The constant assimilation of information and network technologies to enhance college English teaching is undeniably the future trend and an inevitable tendency. As new information technologies and platforms continually emerge, they present renewed challenges to educators in the college English teaching and researching field. The teaching faculty will confront questions such as how to conduct more in-depth categorization of the functionalities and applications of these various online platforms and, more crucially, how to integrate them more profoundly into the college English teaching procedures. Furthermore, striking the right balance between human-computer interactions and collaboration in technology-enhanced teaching models is a pressing concern. The design of more smart and personalized integrated teaching models catering the dynamic learning demands of students will constantly propel the college English teachers to strive for a more dynamic and adaptable teaching mode to empower students to acquire language skills and cultivate cultural visions and develop ethnic values more intelligently.

Acknowledgements. The work was substantially supported by the Social Science Fund Project of Hefei University of Technology (Project No. JS2020HGXJ0013).

References

1. The Steering Committee of College Foreign Language Teaching: College English Teaching Guidelines. Chinese Higher Education Press, Beijing, China (2020)
2. Brown, J.S., Collins, A., Duguid, P.: Situated cognition and the culture of learning. Educ. Res. **18**, 32–42 (1989)
3. Zhao, Y., Dong, G.: Exploration and practice of organic integration of multiple teaching modes in online teaching based on Constructivist Learning Theory (基于建构主义学习理论的线上教学中多种教学模式有机融合的探索与实践). China J. Multimed. Netw. Teach. (2), 21–22 (2022)
4. Sun, L., Liu, D.: Research on the centralized purchasing management mechanism innovation of scientific research instruments and equipment in higher vocational colleges (基于"We learn"的大学英语混合式教学的促学作用研究). J. Qingdao Ocean Shipping Mariners College **43** (2), 64–79 (2022)
5. Zhou, Q.: Research on mobile teaching modes of college english based on QQ platform (基于QQ平台的大学英语移动学习模式研究). J. Overseas English **9**(5), 194–195 (2022)
6. Xu, X., Yang, Y.: The exploration of the online and offline hybrid teaching model of college english based on the wechat official account (基于微信公众号的大学英语线上线下混合式教学探索). Theory Pract. Innov. Entrepreneurship **6**(16), 160–162 (2023)
7. Yu, Y.: An empirical study on the blended teaching of college english course based on OBE approach (基于OBE的大学英语混合式教学模式实践研究). Insight·Shaanxi (9), 133–135 (2023)
8. Hu, Y.: A practical study of POA in college english writing teaching under the model of "Pigai.org". ("批改网"模式下POA在大学英语写作教学中的实践研究). J. Sichuan Minzu College **29**(2), 73–77 (2020)
9. Lv, H.: The application POA methodology in digital teaching of college english writing (" 产出导向法"在大学英语数字化写作教学中的应用). J. Harbin Vocat. Tech. College (6), 155–157 (2017)
10. Zhou, T., Bai, X.: Exploring a deep integration model of multi-modal intelligent teaching and college english classroom (多模态智慧教学与大学英语翻译课堂的深度融合模式探析). J. Chendu Normal Uni. **38**(12), 80–87 (2022)
11. Wang, Y., Zhi, W.: The construction of an open interactive multi-dimensional network platform of teaching，learning and researching of foreign languages (开放互动式外语教、学、研多维网络平台构建以MOOC理论与实践为借鉴). Technol. Enhanced Foreign Lang. **165**(9), 36–40 (2015)
12. Sun, N.: Construction of a mobile teaching mode based on learning functions of smartphones (基于智能手机的大学英语移动学习教学模式构建). J. Yanbian Inst. Educ. **34**(2), 85–87 (2020)
13. Zhao, Y.: New explorations on integration of mobile learning and new college english teaching modes (基于融合移动学习的大学英语教学新模式探索). Contemp. Educ. Res. Teachi. Pract. (11), 41–42 (2019)

Knowledge-Network-Based Translation Learning and Learners' Perception

Shuangshuang Zheng[1(✉)] and Yan Dong[2]

[1] Department of Chinese and Bilingual Studies, The Hong Kong Polytechnic University, Hong Kong, China
335294975@qq.com

[2] School of Foreign Studies, Chaohu University, Hefei, China

Abstract. In today's digitalized society, online platforms undoubtedly play a significant part in assisting translation education. Whereas it is the development of the core competence of the translation learners that can truly prompt the bright future of translation field. Hence this paper begins with an overview of a corpus-assisted and knowledge-network-based online translation learning platform, and then presents the application of it in practical translation (self-) learning and pays special focus on the perception of the learners of the system. By analyzing the data collected from the questionnaire survey, the paper aims to, from learners' perceptions of the system, further focus on the feedback of learners, and then explore whether the knowledge-network-based approach plays a more efficient part in the development of translation learning and if so, how as well as the potential improvement of the system to cater to the emerging needs of the users, thus aid users in developing more efficient mode in translation learning.

Keywords: Knowledge-network · Online Learning · Learners' Perception · Questionnaire Survey

1 Introduction

In the current era of digital humanities [1], resource reserves and technological support are the escorts of teaching reform [2]. "Digital education resources" even ranks as forefront of Implementing Actions in Education Informatization 2.0 Action Plan issued by The Ministry of Education. And advanced technologies, such as AI, big data and etc., has been widely applied and caused dramatic changes in education, including translation teaching and learning, which also booms a lot under such circumstances. However, while a greater number of translation materials tend to be more available, they still need "further practice and improvement", "especially insufficient in the textbooks that own the characteristics of the times, reflect the current reality, or are close to translation reality" [3]. Actually, Zhu and Wang [4] noticed increasing needs for corpus-based translation education and predicted that "Electronization and Networking will become a new trend in translation education". So, to optimize the learning resources and enhance the efficiency of learning effects in translation, an online translation learning platform,

Z. Kubincová et al. (Eds.): SETE 2023, LNCS 14606, pp. 242–252, 2024.
https://doi.org/10.1007/978-981-97-4243-1_19

ClinkNotes, which is corpus-assisted and knowledge-network-based, perfectly complements resources with emerging technology, has been designed and put into use with the help of emerging technologies.

2 Literature Review

In 1985, the concept "knowledge network" was first proposed by Gagne, and then a diverse range of researches were conducted in this field, which highlighted its interdisciplinary nature. To explore the research trends and hot topics related to knowledge networks, we conducted a bibliometric analysis. By using the Web of Science (including SCI-Expanded and SSCI) published by the American Institute of Scientific Intelligence (ISI) and CNKI (China National Knowledge Infrastructure) as the search strategy, we searched the papers whose topic is "knowledge network" and retrieved a total of 714 articles in the Web of Science, among which computer science, business economics and engineering ranked the top three research areas, whereas the ones concerning educational field is only 14. Whereas in CNKI, when "knowledge network" was searched as the only topic, 872 articles were retrieved in total, with enterprise economy, secondary education and library information and digital museums held the ahead three positions of the roll, and 267 in educational area. Then we added keywords "teaching and learning" as the other topic, and searched again, 6 articles were retrieved in the Web of Science, while 148 articles in CNKI, and most of these articles lying more emphasis on building macro framework, like constructing a learning model [5] or designing a teaching system [6].

Though some had observed interactive behavior throughout the entire learning process [7], it lacked follow-up research. Overall, up to now, though there have been more and more researches on "knowledge network" and built kinds of modes and platforms, not enough empirical studies are conducted to prove the feasibility and acceptability of learners themselves, that is, the learners' perception is seldom cared. While ClinkNotes sets a good example. At the very beginning, only a small number of pilot projects have been undertaken at the University of Hongkong since 2001, then a coinage ClinkNotes is created to refer to a knowledge-network-based and corpus-assisted online translation learning platform, which means to enables the users to "click to link to the notes" [8], and the basic concept served as the starting point and further developed in series studies [4, 8, 9]. In 2013, the ClickNotes Online Platform was updated to a web-based system, where tag words are firstly introduced as the knowledge web to form a roadmap of navigation [10], which stood for the maturity of the platform. During the process, this platform had been applied in 8 Chinese universities and a series of surveys are conducted, whose initial research purpose is to explore teaching models, course designs and learning strategies paired with the platform, then later more attention has been converted and paid to learners themselves, to explore how the users view and accept this kind of translating learning [11–15]. Therefore, this paper aims to, by analyzing the questions collected from the questionnaire survey, from learners' perceptions of the system, further evaluate the feedback of learners and then explore whether it can keep up with the on-going material and meet the current needs of translation learners and whether the knowledge-network-based approach plays a more efficient part in the development of translation learning, and if so, how as well as the potential improvement of the system to cater to the emerging needs of learners.

3 Applicability of ClinkNotes: Users' Perceptions

As mentioned above, the knowledge-network-based translation learning platform has been set up and launched in several universities in China, along with some relevant pedagogical research conducted and the platform reformed accordingly, hence this experiment is still centered on students' self-learning outcomes of the ClinkNotes Online Platform in the undergraduate practical translation courses in Chaohu University, to test out such a teaching and learning mode can be perceived and accepted by the students users, thus to explore the feasibility and acceptability in improving users' translation ability.

3.1 Participants

The participants were 46 undergraduates whose major is English. To ensure a better test result, the students first took two-semester translation courses, and then joined in the specialized teaching experiment. Therefore, these college students have mastered basic translation knowledge and skills. Besides, as a young generation, they are familiar with online information technology. To carry out the experiment as early as possible, at the beginning of the translation class, they are instructed to get used to the operation of the ClinkNotes, which lasted for one more semester. So, after a systematic training and practical operation, each student was well informed of the ClinkNotes Online Platform and developed their own perception towards this platform, like the platform's impact on their translation skills, knowledge acquisition, and overall learning experience.

3.2 Questionnaire

Based on the Likert Scale, the questionnaire was designed with 5 levels of points ranging from the highest 5 to the lowest 1 for different options. There are 12 questions that fall into two categories: the top 10 are close-ended questions, concerning perceptions of data annotation, retrieval as well as the translation learning mode, aiming to collect users' specific comments in a particular aspect; while the other 2 are open ones, asking for more "individualized" feedback on ClinkNotes, aiming to gather learners' overall valuable feedback about the software's strengths and weaknesses, as well as identify possible areas for improvement. All the information can be later used to make changes and updates to the software to better meet the needs of its users.

3.3 Procedures

Before conducting the questionnaire survey, the teacher helped students to get familiar with the platform. During the process, the tag-word network was especially introduced for its crucial function: not only served as a guidepost to describe and explain the language phenomena or translation techniques, but also functioned as a guideline in online navigation. There are 56 tag-words in all and divided into 6 categories, namely word level perspective, sentence level perspective, information perspective, discourse perspective, rhetorical perspective and inter-textual association.

After learning, the teacher guided students to carry out concrete textual analysis of the given corpus on the platform, and then asked themselves to check whether they had made the correct judgement by appreciating the given translation explanation. After class, post test translation assignment was given to each student.

One semester later, a questionnaire survey was conducted to collect students' self-perception, exploring if there is any inconvenient experience during the learning process and hoping to receive practical suggestions for further improvement towards the platform. This was the final standard to measure how feasible of this online translation teaching and learning model, which is valuable in refining and enhancing the platform. Figure 1 shows the detailed procedures.

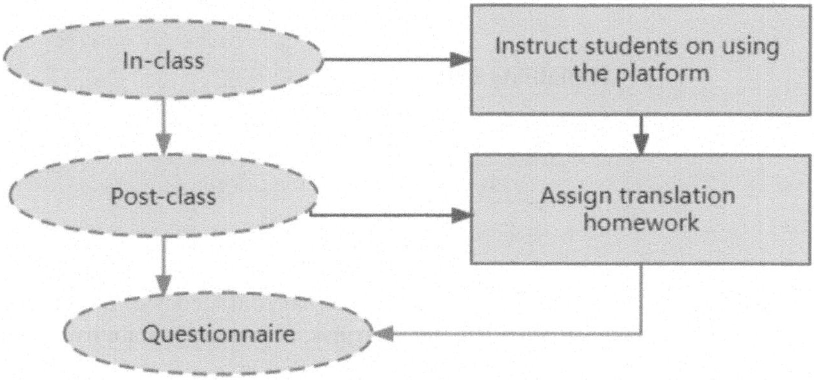

Fig. 1. Research procedures

4 Analysis of the Questionnaire

A total of 46 copies of questionnaire survey were sent out to students and all of them were collected with effective rate 100%. SPSS statistic software was used to analyze the data. The steps were shown as follows:

Step 1 Reliability

To test the reliability of the scale, Cronbach's Alpha is adopted. Generally speaking, if its coefficient is greater than 0.9, it means that the internal consistency of the scale is very high, and the higher the reliability coefficient, the more consistent, stable, and reliable the results; if between 0.7 and 0.9, a good one; and if below 0.7, it indicates a high degree of inconsistency among various items in the scale, and the scale needs to be revised.

As can be observed from Table 1, from "Case processing Summary", it can be seen that a total of 46 cases participated in the reliability analysis, and there were no missing values; from the measurement results of "Reality Statistics", the Crobach's alpha value

Table 1. Reliability of the questionnaire

Scale: ALL VARIABLES

Case Processing Summary

		N	%
Cases	Valid	46	100.0
	Excluded[a]	0	.0
	Total	46	100.0

a. Listwise deletion based on all variables in the procedure.

Reliability Statistics

Cronbach's Alpha	N of Items
.929	10

is 0.929, higher than 0.9, which means that the internal consistency of the scale is very high. Therefore, the analyzed data has high intrinsic consistency, stability, and strong reliability.

Step 2 Validity.

Table 2. Factor Analysis

KMO and Bartlett's Test

Kaiser-Meyer-Olkin Measure of Sampling Adequacy.		.761
Bartlett's Test of Sphericity	Approx. Chi-Square	378.391
	df	45
	Sig.	<.001

If KMO value is greater than 0.6, and significance value is less than 0.05, both meet the requirements, indicating that exploratory factors are suitable for evaluating validity. As can be seen in Table 2, KMO value is 0.761, greater than 0.6, and significance value is 0.01, less than 0.05, proving exploratory factor is a good way to test validity.

Table 3. Total Variance

Total Variance Explained

Component	Initial Eigenvalues			Extraction Sums of Squared Loadings			Rotation Sums of Squared Loadings		
	Total	% of Variance	Cumulative %	Total	% of Variance	Cumulative %	Total	% of Variance	Cumulative %
1	6.148	61.480	61.480	6.148	61.480	61.480	3.923	39.232	39.232
2	1.047	10.468	71.948	1.047	10.468	71.948	3.272	32.716	71.948
3	.823	8.228	80.176						
4	.643	6.426	86.602						
5	.510	5.097	91.699						
6	.308	3.076	94.775						
7	.198	1.983	96.758						
8	.181	1.814	98.572						
9	.085	.845	99.417						
10	.058	.583	100.000						

Extraction Method: Principal Component Analysis.

As Table 3 shows, 10 questions are divided into 2 components, whose total variance is 71.948 > 60.00, hence its reliability is confirmed. The following Table 4 tells which questions are specifically included in these two components and the validity of each question.

As can be seen from Table 4, Q4, Q1, Q9, Q2, Q10, Q3 and Q7 belong to component 1 while Q3, Q8, Q5 and Q6 are involved in component 2. Clearly, question 3 repeatedly occurs in the two components and each load is higher than 0.5, which means that it can reflect both, indicating that its specificity is not strong and its validity is not high. Therefore, question 3 is a question without validity, thus it should be deleted. The remaining questions only have a value higher than 0.5 on a single dimension, thereby they are considered valid, so they have passed the validity test and are retained. Based on all the above analysis and the content of questions, the first component contains Q4, Q1, Q9, Q2, Q10, and Q7, named "Perception on post-learning"; the second component contains Q8, Q5 and Q6, named "Perception on while-learning".
Step 3 the current situation of questionnaire data and the findings.

The mean value is used to reflects the current situation, that is, the users' current perception of the platform. As is shown in Table 5, the mean value of "Perception on post-learning" is 1.3297 and that of "Perception on while-learning" score is 1.2246. Both of them are close to point 1. In the original scale, 1 point = totally agree, which indicates that the learners totally agree that the platform is very helpful during their learning process and after learning.
Step 4 Correlations

The paired mean values above are then used to explore the correlation between "Perception on post-learning" and "Perception on while-learning".

Table 4. Rotated Component Matrix

	Component 1	Component 2
Q4	.898	
Q1	.887	
Q9	.700	
Q2	.695	
Q10	.620	
Q3	.599	.506
Q7	.554	
Q8		.912
Q5		.821
Q6		.816

Extraction Method: Principal Component Analysis.
Rotation Method: Varimax with Kaiser Normalization.

a. Rotation converged in 3 iterations.

Table 5. Descriptive Statistics

	N	Minimum	Maximum	Mean	Std. Deviation
postlearning	46	1.00	2.17	1.3297	.39983
whilelearning	46	1.00	2.00	1.2246	.38525

As Table 6 shows, the correlation value is a positive value 0.687, and $p = 0.000 < 0.05$. The two data confirms the significant correlation between "Perception on post-learning" and "Perception on while-learning". The results also provide a basis and guarantee for the subsequent research on influencing factors.

Table 6. Correlations

whilelearning	Pearson Correlation	1	.687**
	Sig. (2-tailed)		.000
	N	46	46
postlearning	Pearson Correlation	.687**	1
	Sig. (2-tailed)	.000	
	N	46	46

**Correlation is significant at the 0.01 level (2-tailed).

5 Findings

Based on all the calculation results of the data analysis, the statistical conclusion is as follows:

1. Both the reliability and validity of the survey are good, which means that the data obtained through the questionnaire can fully reflect the user's perception truthfully and reliably.
2. The survey results of the current situation of the questionnaire show that users are satisfied with the platform, and their attitudes towards the positive effect of the platform on translation learning range from "totally agree" to " relatively agree", and they are more inclined to "totally agree", which, from the perspective of learners' perception, demonstrated the superiority of the platform in translation learning.
3. There are two components divided by SPSS and there is a significant positive correlation between the two.

Besides that, the last two questions are open ones, one asking for their perception of advantages and disadvantages of the platform, and then the other collecting their suggestions on improvement. The main problems are concerned with the following three aspects.

1. Resources: insufficient, and not so updated. So the effect of practical ability may not be very obvious.
2. Interface: too mechanized, poor interactivity, and may easily be distracted
3. Technical problems: many platforms required and prone to cause errors

Some useful suggestions are also supplied for improvement:

1. Resources: add the ones with hot topics to improve the utilization of knowledge nods.
2. Interface: create specialized studies with relevant exams; upload some micro videos explained by teachers.
3. Technical problems: add an interactive platform that integrates listening, speaking, and writing.

As our survey shows, such a corpus-assisted and knowledge-network-based online translation learning mode was strongly appreciated by the majority of the participants, and its utility in contributing to the learning and teaching of translation is confirmed as well. This is consistent with our original goal in designing this platform. That is probably why all participants expressed their expectancy to use the platform in a long run for their further improvement, and showed their tendency to recommend it to their surrounding friends (even the several ones who posed some disadvantages of the platform). In addition, according to the learners' perception of practising the post-class exercise, the platform is also a welcome companion in self-study. Probably this is because after class, they are in a more free learning environment. Not only can they become their own masters, arranging their "customized" materials at their convenience, but also they are their own teachers, owing to the truth that they can check their exercise by themselves with the data retrieval and timely feedback. So, from this point, we can say that this online platform is a useful platform for bilingual learning both in and out of class. All in all, as an emerging way of teaching and learning in translation, this platform is designed to familiarize any users kinds of translation methodology and adopt the theories to explain the translation phenomenon in real translation practice, meanwhile, a self-assessment column is applied to ensure the correct direction of translation. All of them can be traced and here, though there still are some drawbacks, be confirmed its utility.

According to the feedback of the users, there are two main areas we can focus on to further develop the system. Firstly, enhance the user-friendliness of the design. This can include improving the layout and navigation of the system, making it more intuitive for users. Additionally, we can add guided exercises is available to help users effectively utilize the system's features. Furthermore, we can incorporate facilities for learner-tutor communication, such as chat or messaging features, to enable learners to seek clarification or guidance from tutors directly within the system. Secondly, expand the content offered in the system. The planned series stemming from this pilot project can be expanded to include a greater variety of text types, covering different subjects. This will provide learners with a more diverse range of materials to practice with. Additionally, more refined annotations of methodologies are needed to further aid learners in their understanding and language development.

By focusing on these two fronts, we can make the system more user-friendly and self-sufficient, while also broadening the range of content available to learners and improving the quality of annotations.

6 Conclusion

This article has analyzed the data collected from the questionnaire concerning undergraduates' perception towards the platform, getting the valid and positive feedback from the learners, which means that it is meaning to go on updating the platform. Though it is true that the web-based platform still need to streamline its on-line operations and update its resources, by integrating translation teaching and learning with bilingual listening components, along with engaging tools, multimedia content, and personalization features, this online platform is promising to provide learners with a well-rounded language learning experience, catering to both teachers and students' need by offering integrated bilingual listening, speaking, reading and writing.

Acknowledgements. The work was substantially supported by The National Social Science Fund of China (Project No. 19BYY125: A Data-Mining Driven Mode of Co- construction of Knowledge Network for Translation Learning and Its Application).

References

1. Wang, Y., Zhang, Z.: New path in translation research: new interpretation of digital humanities (翻译研究新路径:数字人文新释). Foreign Lang. Teach. **41**(2), 81–86 (2020)
2. Wu, Y.: Translation teaching and disciplinary innovation development in the context of the epidemic (疫情背景下的翻译教学改革与学科创新发展). Chin. Translators J. **06**, 61–65 (2020)
3. Tao, L., Huang, Y.Y.: On the construction of translation discipline and talent cultivation in the new era (论新时代翻译学科建设与人才培养). Foreign Lang. Teach. **1**, 10–14 (2021)
4. Zhu, C., Wang, H.: A corpus-based, machine-aided mode of translator training: clinknotes and beyond. Interpreter Translator Trainer **2**, 269–291 (2011)
5. Southard, K., Wince, T., Meddleton, S., Bolger, M.: Features of knowledge building in biology: understanding undergraduate students' ideas about molecular mechanisms. CBE-Life Sci. E **3**, 1–16 (2016)
6. Yang, Z., Wang, Y., Gan, J., Li, H., Lei, N.: Design and research of intelligent question-answering (Q&A) system based on high school course knowledge graph. Mob. Netw. Appl. **26**, 1884–1890 (2021)
7. Duan, J., Xie, K., Hawk, N., Yu, S., Wang, M.: Exploring a personal social knowledge network (PSKN) to aid the observation of connectivist interaction for high- and-low-performing learners in connectivist massive open online courses. Br. J. Edu. Technol. **1**(50), 199–217 (2019)
8. Zhu, C., Yip, P.: ClinkNotes: towards a corpus-based, machine-aided programme of translation teaching. Meta **2**, 387–408 (2010)
9. Wang, H., Zhu, C.: Annotation and application of translation teaching corpus-introduction to the "Chinese translation and annotation corpus of English Financial Reporting" (翻译教学语料库的标注及应用-"英文财经报道中文翻译及注释语料库"介绍). Foreign Lang. Teach. Res. **2**, 246–255 (2012)
10. Mu, Y., Zhu, C.: In-depth data processing in constructing an online platform for teaching/self-learning of E-C translation and bilingual writing (在线翻译与双语写作教学/自学平台建设中的语料精加工). Contemp. Transl. Stud. **1**, 56–62 (2013)
11. Mu, Y., Tian, L., Yang, W.: Towards a Knowledge Management Model for Online Translation Learning. In: Hao, T., Chen, W., Xie, H., Nadee, W., Lau, R. (eds.) SETE 2018. LNCS, vol. 11284, pp. 198–207. Springer, Cham (2018)
12. Mu, Y., Yang, W.: A teaching experiment on a knowledge-network-based online translation learning platform. In: Popescu, E., Hao, T., Hsu, T.-C., Xie, H., Temperini, M., Chen, W. (eds.) SETE 2019. LNCS, vol. 11984, pp. 319–328. Springer, Cham (2020). https://doi.org/10.1007/978-3-030-38778-5_35
13. Tian, L., Zhu, C.: Making connections through knowledge nodes in translator training: on a computer-assisted pedagogical approach to literary translation. Int. J. Trans. Interpret Appl. Linguist. **2**, 15–29 (2020)

14. Mu, Y., Yang, W.: Knowledge-network-based Inter-institutional Collaborative Teaching of Translation. In: Pang, C., et al. (eds.) SETE/ICWL -2020. LNCS, vol. 12511, pp. 411–419. Springer, Cham (2021). https://doi.org/10.1007/978-3-030-66906-5_39
15. Zhuang, Y., Zheng, S.: Developing translation abilities through knowledge network-based translator training. In: Gonzalez-Gonzalez, C., et al. (eds.) Learning Technologies and Systems. SETE 2022. LNCS, vol. 13869, pp. 513–524. Springer, Spain (2022). https://doi.org/10.1007/978-3-031-33023-0_48

The Influencing Factors of Learning Motivation in the Computer-Aided Speaking Course: An Empirical Approach

Beibei Lin(✉)

College of Foreign Languages, Zhejiang University of Technology, Hangzhou, China
linbeibei@zjut.edu.cn

Abstract. With the development of technology, online teaching systems are resorted to in the purpose of improving the teaching efficiency, which is closely related to students' participation in the aiding online systems. What are the factors influencing students' using of the online systems? To answer this question, this study, in the light of Dornyei's theory, proposed four hypotheses concerning the influencing factors of second language learning motivation. It introduced the Fif online speaking training system in the speaking course *Audio-Visual-Oral Business English*, and designed four tasks according to the four hypotheses to see students' participation in the tasks. By carefully examining the data collected, this study found that the hypothesized motivational factors, including the students' desire, positive feedback from the teacher, relevancy with the in-class learning content and the requirement of the course did work in their post-class autonomous learning which is seen through their completion of the online speaking task. It is observed that the students made efforts to narrow the discrepancy between the real self and the possible self of future as competent second language users. Besides, negative self-suggestion would lead to the poor performance in completing the online exercise. Based on the results and findings, how to better engage the learners in their online training is further discussed.

Keywords: Learning Motivation · Computer-Aided Teaching · L2 Motivational Self System

1 Introduction

The development of technology is exerting profound influence upon education, in which the application of information technology can be widely observed. The online teaching system is frequently used in an online-and-offline combined teaching mode. Many studies have found that it could bring vital benefits. Xiao, Cai and Su [1] found that with the aid of established online platform, the students performed well in their examinations. Mishra, Gupta and Shree [2] portrayed online teaching-learning modes and stated that the implementation of the modes could well facilitate students for the subsequent semester examination. Libre [3] discussed the implementation of an online discussion and observed a positive correlation between the students' interaction in the

Z. Kubincová et al. (Eds.): SETE 2023, LNCS 14606, pp. 253–267, 2024.
https://doi.org/10.1007/978-981-97-4243-1_20

online learning environment and their knowledge acquisition. Gunawan, Zulkarnain, Apriani, Baharudin, Prayoga, Kurniawati and Wardani [4] showed that online teaching with the online platform was effectively to support instructional activities. Lin [5] stated that using online teaching platform for the translation course could have a positive impact on the students' learning efficiency. All of these researches also suggest that the effect of online teaching systems is closely related to the students' participation in the online learning activities.

Considering that the students' higher participation in the online learning system could contribute to a more efficient teaching, looking into the factors influencing the students' learning motivation in the online activities would be of much necessity since the online teaching systems are more and more adopted with the development of technology. This study, in the light of Dornyei's second language motivation theory, came up with four hypothesized motivational factors for online learning and designed a four-task experiment to verify these factors in the FiF speaking training system.

2 Dornyei's Motivation Theory

Dornyei [6] defines motivation as a "process whereby a certain amount of instigation force arises, initiates action, and persists as long as no other force comes into play to weaken it and thereby terminate action, or until the planned outcome has been reached". It is a driving force for second language (L2) learners to participate in learning, which is key in influencing the success of L2 learning. According to Dornyei [7], there are different levels of the components of L2 learning motivation.

Table 1. The Components of Foreign Language Learning Motivation [7]

Level	Motivational components
Language Level	Integrative Motivational Subsystem
Instrumental Motivational Subsystem	
Learner Level	Need for Achievement
Self-confidence	
	•Language Use Anxiety
	•Perceived L2 Competence
	•Causal Attributions
	•Self-Efficacy
Learning Situation Level	
Course-Specific Motivational Components	Interest
	Relevance
	Expectancy
	Satisfaction
Teacher-Specific Motivational Components	Affiliative Motive
	Authority Type
	Direct Socialisation of Student Motivation
	•Modelling
	•Task Presentation
	•Feedback
Group-Specific Motivational Components	Goal-orientedness
	Norm & Reward System
	Group Cohesion
	Classroom Goal Structure

Table 1 presents a three-level framework of motivation, including language, learner and learning situation. The Language Level focuses on "ethnolinguistic, cultural-affective, intellectual, and pragmatic values and attitudes attached to the target language; these values and attitudes are, to a large extent, determined by the social milieu in which the learning takes place"; the Learner Level is related with "various fairly stable personality traits that the learner has developed in the past"; and the Learning Situation Level concerns "situation-specific motives rooted in various aspects of language learning in a classroom setting" [6]. It can be observed that Dornyei highlights the major role of L2 learners, whose interest and need should be taken into consideration in the learning. The situation of learning, which involves components of different aspects, matter in the learning. All elements of the course design should motivate learners. Donyei and Csizer [8] gives his advice for motivating language learner in this framework (Table 2).

Table 2. Ten commandments for motivating language learners: final version [6]

1 Set a personal example with your own behaviour.
2 Create a pleasant, relaxed atmosphere in the classroom.
3 Present the tasks properly.
4 Develop a good relationship with the learners.
5 Increase the learners' linguistic self-confidence.
6 Make the language classes interesting.
7 Promote learner autonomy.
8 Personalize the learning process.
9 Increase the learners' goal-orientedness.
10 Familiarize learners with the target language culture.

The above process-oriented commandments respond to the three levels of language, learner and learning situation. They are more specific teaching strategies advanced in the three levels while learner-situation-related strategies overwhelms others. The learner's L2 competence, characteristics, interest, autonomy and goals are also considered during the learning process.

This theory is further developed with self psychology and shifts to the socio-dynamic direction. Dornyei [9] took in the self theory and proposed the L2 Motivational Self System (L2MSS), of which there are three dimensions: the ideal L2 self (IL2S), the ought-to L2 self (OL2S), and the L2 learning experience (L2LE). The ideal L2 self is "the L2-specific aspect of one's ideal self"; the ought-to L2 self "refers to the attributes that one believes one ought to possess" and the L2 learning experience focuses on the learner's "present experience". These three components basically concern with the subjective intended effort of the learner, who is motivated to reduce the discrepancy between the current self and the ideal L2 self as well as ought-to L2 self. The learner's expectation of his/her future self as the target language user motivates him/her in L2 learning.

Dornyei's theory on motivation has laid the theoretical foundation for this study, which tried to discuss the motivating factors of L2 learners in the online learning system. According to Donyei [7], the components of foreign language learning motivation at the learner level include 1) Need for Achievement and 2) Self-confidence (Language Use Anxiety, Perceived L2 Competence, Causal Attributions, and Self-Efficacy). We assumed that the L2 learners participate the online system for the purpose of improving their second language competence, which can be evaluated in a certain form. The feedback to their online performance would influence their frequency of taking the online activities and completion of the online tasks. Positive feedback could be more encouraging. And on the other hand, considering the three-dimension L2 Motivational Self System (L2MSS), the feedback could also make the L2 learners aware of the discrepancy between the current self and the ideal L2 self as well as ought-to L2 self, which would urge them to take more online activities. In this case, four hypotheses were advanced:

(1) The students' desire to be competent L2 users works in motivating them to take the online exercises;
(2) The teacher's positive feedback on the online exercises could encourage students;
(3) Familiar learning materials which are of high relevancy with the classroom learning could better attract the students;
(4) The requirement of passing the course matters for the students.

3 The Experiment

Based on Dornyei's theory on motivation, this study conducted an experiment to examine the factors motivating students to take the speaking exercise in the online learning system – FiF speaking training system (https://www.fifedu.com/iplat/html/index.html), which is used to aid the teaching of the course Audio-Visual-Oral Business English that is a core course for the Business English major students in the mainland China.

3.1 Participants

This experiment was conducted in the speaking course *Audio-Visual-Oral Business English*, including 15 students, which is the all of Business English students in the university. 6 of them are male and others are female. They are young and energetic, with the age of around 21. The small number of participants allowed the teacher to have a close and timely observation of their online learning activities. Further one-by-one talks between the teacher and the participating students in the different given tasks were also part of this study. These students were all native speakers of Mandarin Chinese and studying English as the second language. As junior students of English major, they have already taken courses of English listening, Oral English, and business English, which prepare them for this experiment. According to Dornyei's *L2SMM* theory, these students are working to narrow the discrepancy between the real selves and *the ideal L2 selves and ought-to L2 selves. The ideal L2 self* is the self the students desire to become, who is capable of handling the daily communication with English-speaking people in Business, which corresponds to the integrative motivation. *The ought-to L2 self* of students is related with family influences, the requirement of the course, and so on, which matches with the instrumental motivation. *L2 learning experience* is rather complex: the function of the Fif system, the pre-taken courses, the influencing of peers, the teaching style of the teacher, and others all have impact on the L2 learning.

3.2 Procedure

We introduced the Fif speaking training system to the students who had already acquired some knowledge concerning Business English speaking in this course. FiF is a teaching and management system, developed by iFLYTEK and frequently adopted as an assisting online speaking tool for second language learning. It includes speaking traning materials covering different aspects of content, with their levels of difficulty marked. The registered learners can search for these training materials according to their learning needs and interests. They may speak after the given materials and take the correponding tests. Based on the intelligent voice and semantic evaluation technology, Fif is able to score the learners' speaking according to their pronunciation, fluency and completeness of the given material. And the management system in it further supports the teacher to observe the students' online learning activities as well as their performance in the speaking exercise. In this regard, the Fif online speaking system provides an operable platform for carrying this experiment. In this experiment, the students' performances in the assigned online tasks were automatically evaluted by the Fif with the Hundred Score system, with 100 as the highest score and 0 as the lowest score. And 15 English letters—A, B, C, D, E, F, G, H, J, K, L, M, N, O, P—were used to stand for these students in the collected data.

When assigning the first task, the teacher, after demonstrating the function of Fif system and teaching students how to make use of the speaking materials in it, emphasized that taking more speaking exercise could improve their oral English and help them coping with the communication in Business. Finding that there were fewer students than expected taking the exercise, the teacher extended the deadline, which seemed to fail to work. Although the task remained open for nearly three weeks, only 50% of all students took this exercise and the performance was not satisfactory with an average score of 44, as shown in Table 3 and Fig. 1.

Table 3. The statistical data of Task 1

The statistical data of Task 1 Period:2023–04-24 - 2023–05-12							
Total students	Students completing the task	Task completion	Students failing in completing the task	Recording duration per student(min)	Average score	Highest Score	Lowest score
15	7	50%	6	7	44	92	19

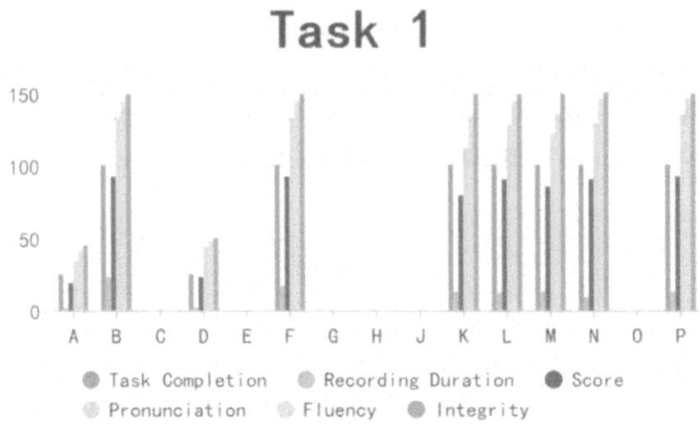

Fig. 1. The students' performance in Task 1

After the deadline of Task 1, the teacher made comments on the performance of the participating students and gave suggestions for further improvement. The following task was then assigned. 56% of all students completed Task 2 within two weeks and gained a better average score of 51, as shown in Table 4 and Fig. 2.

Table 4. The statistical data of Task 2

The statistical data of Task 2 Period:2023–05-12 - 2023–05-26							
Total students	Students completing the task	Task completion	Students failing in completing the task	Recording duration per student(min)	Average score	Highest Score	Lowest score
15	8	56%	6	12	51	93	33

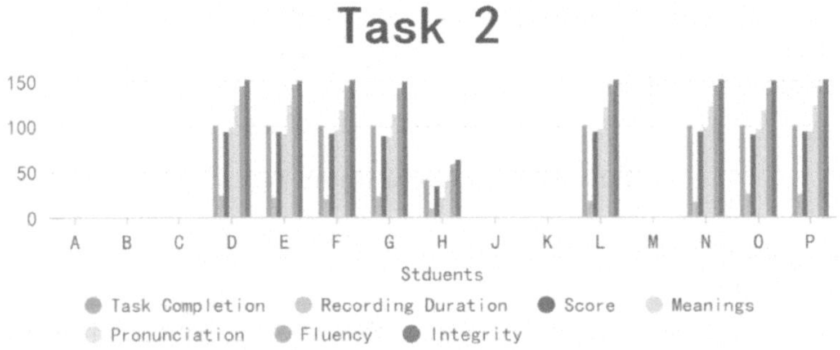

Fig. 2. The students' performance in Task 2

As for the third task, the teacher tried to further motivate students by adopting a topic which had just been explained in class and encourage them to practice what they have learned online after class. 62% of all students completed this task within nine days and the average score was 4 points higher than that of Task 2, as shown in Table 5 and Fig. 3.

Table 5. The statistical data of Task 3

The statistical data of Task 3 Period:2023–05-26 - 2023–06-03							
Total students	Students completing the task	Task completion	Students failing in completing the task	Recording duration per student(min)	Average score	Highest Score	Lowest score
15	6	62%	4	15	55	92	9

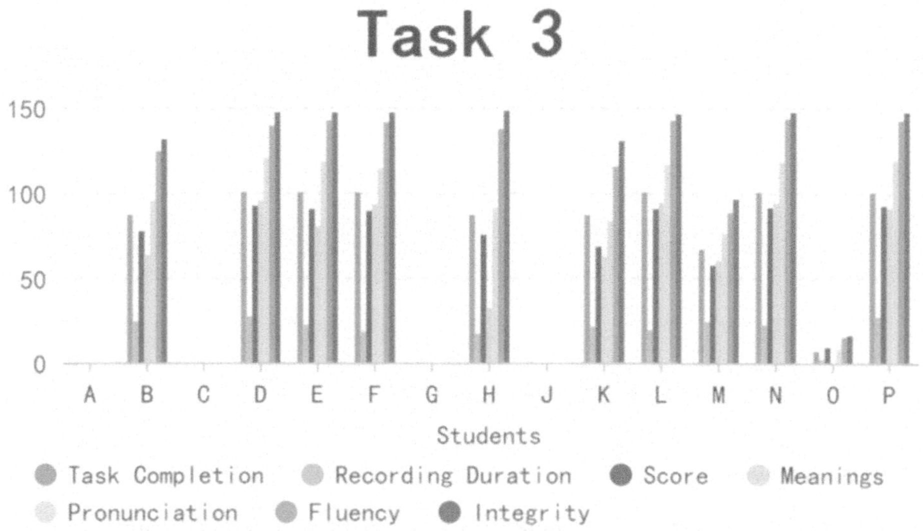

Fig. 3. The students' performance in Task 3

Task 4 was released upon the end of course and students were reminded that the participation in the online speaking exercise would be taken into account in their final assessment. 70% of all students completed the task within eight days and the average score was over the passing line, as shown in Table 6 and Fig. 4.

Table 6. The statistical data of Task 4

The statistical data of Task 4 Period:2023–06-02 - 2023–06-10							
Total students	Students completing the task	Task completion	Students failing in completing the task	Recording duration per student(min)	Average score	Highest Score	Lowest score
15	10	70%	4	13	64	97	41

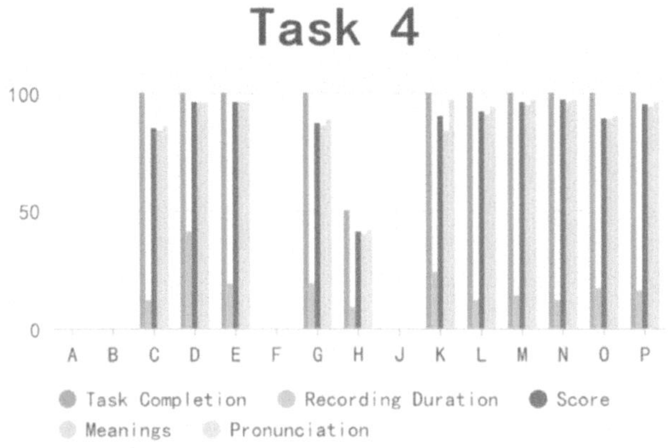

Fig. 4. The students' performance in Task 4

3.3 Data Analysis

Based on the data concerning the students' performance in the four tasks, which was automatically generated by the Fif training system, this study adopted the Matlab software to draw Figs 1, 2, 3, 4, 5, 6, 7, 8, 9 and 10.

The collected data shows that from Task 1 to Task 4, the increasing numbers of participating students, the improving average score, and the shortening time limit of task can be noticed, which could verify the four advanced hypotheses and suggested the factors, including the students' desire, the teacher's feedback, the relevancy with the in-class learning, and the requirement of the course, could motivate the students in taking the online speaking exercises. But different students would be motivated by different factors, as shown in Fig. 5 which presents the individual participation in the four tasks.

In Fig. 5, the capitalized English letters stands for the 15 students taking this course *Audio-Visual-Oral Business English* and different symbols are adopted to display the scores they obtained in the four tasks. This figure suggests another influencing factor of the students' learning motivation in the online system in the four-task experiment. It can be easily observed that there is a correlation between the scores of the students and the frequency of their taking the online exercise. Those students who gained higher scores tend to take more speaking exercise. It indicates that the perceived language competency

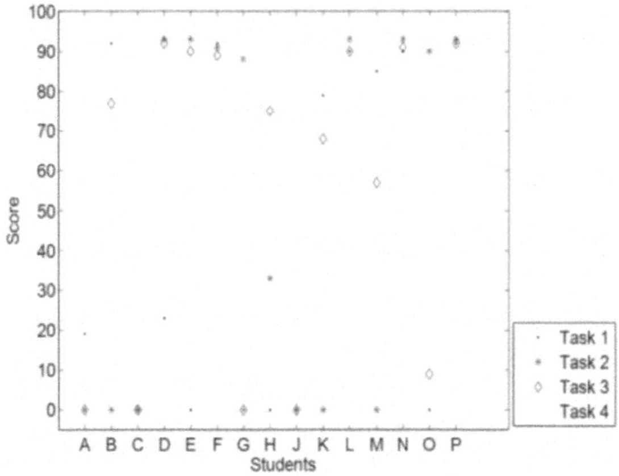

Fig. 5. The scores of the students in the four tasks

could help foster the self-confidence of students, which motivates them in taking more exercises. And the students who have relatively poor performance in meaning conveying, pronunciation, or fluency, either of which would lead to a lower score, took less online speaking exercises, as Figs. 6, 7 and 8 show.

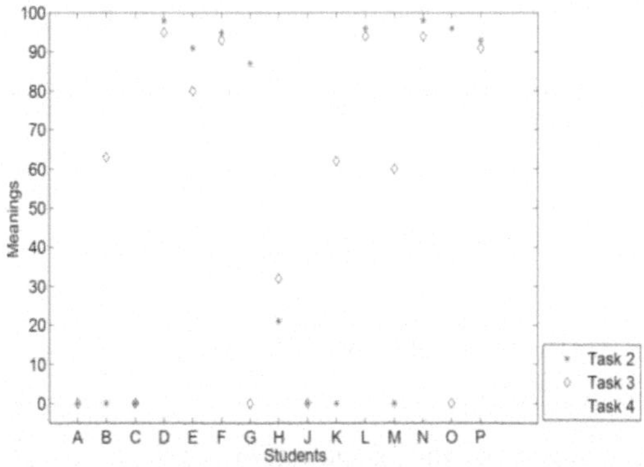

Fig. 6. The scores of the students' conveying of meanings in four tasks

Figure 6 shows the scores of the participating students, given by the Fif system, according to their conveying of meanings in their online speaking tasks. It can be found that the students had a better performance in Task 2, which was posted just after the teacher made detailed comments on their performance in Task 1.

Figure 7 shows the scores of the participating students, given by the Fif system, according to their pronunciation in their online speaking tasks. Generally speaking, the students performed better in Task 1 and their performance got worse in the later tasks. A possible reason could be that these students were asked to improve their conveying of meanings, fluency and the other aspects in the after-task comments.

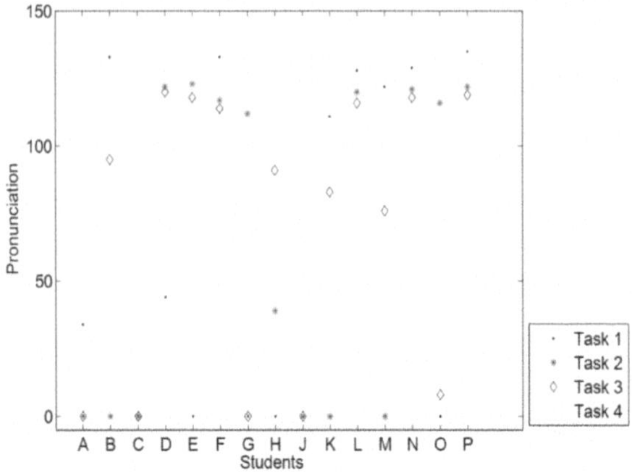

Fig. 7. The scores of the students' pronunciation in four tasks

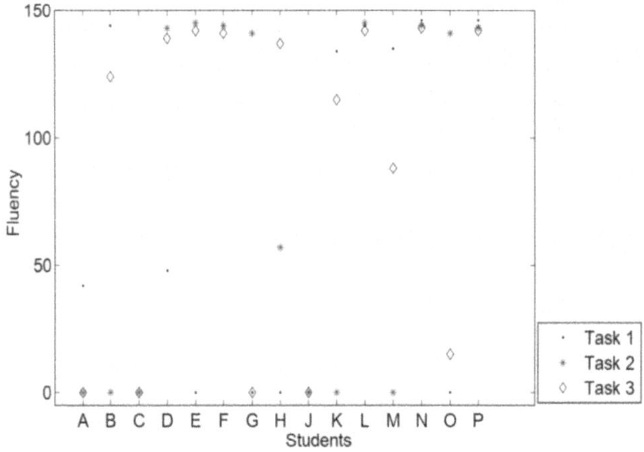

Fig. 8. The scores of the students' fluency in four tasks

Figure 8 shows the scores of the participating students, given by the Fif system, according to their fluency in their online speaking tasks. They basically did well in this aspect. As for those who got relatively lower scores, they failed to complete the tasks, according to the one-to-one talks with them. The factors that lead to their failure include their unfamiliarity with the system, they being busy with tasks of other courses, the unfriendly environment and so on.

That the higher perceived language competency could better motivate the students in taking more exercise is further supported by the degree of these students' completion of four tasks, as shown in Fig. 9.

These students with better performance in the tasks also tend to spend more time in completing the tasks, as the following Fig. 10 shows.

The recording duration does not have a close relation with the scores those students obtained. Between these two scales, there is lack of discriminant validity. But we may

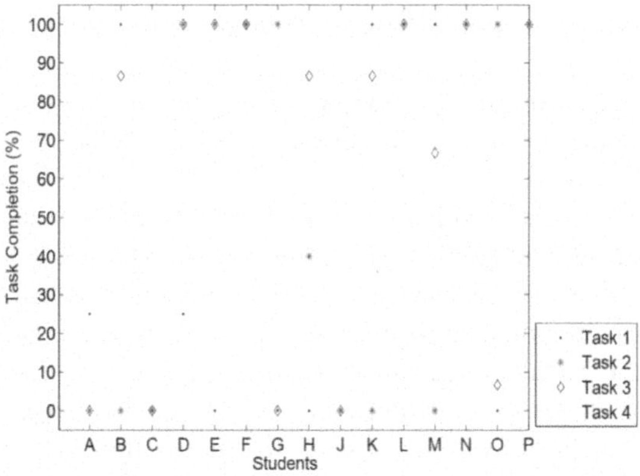

Fig. 9. The students' completion of four tasks

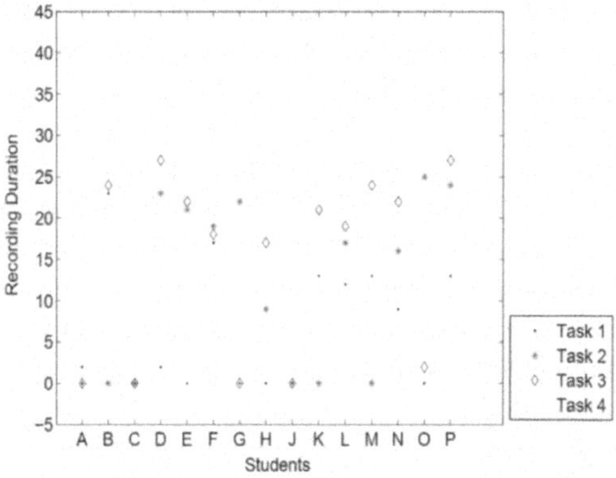

Fig. 10. The recording duration of the four tasks for different students

see that the majority of the students taking the online speaking exercise were willing to spend the time necessary to complete the tasks.

Another important point to mention is that although the students' participation in the four task is increasing, some students stopped to take the following task(s). With one-by one talks with the students, it is found that the frequently-mentioned reasons include the lack of spared after-class time, no obvious effect in improving the speaking, and the complicated operation of the system.

4 Discussion

Previous studies have discussed the technology adopted in developing the online teaching systems [10–12], the teaching mode designed to combine the online systems [13–15], the effect of adopting online teaching system [16–18], etc. Their studies pay more attention to the modification of the online learning systems to improve the learning efficiency as well as the advantages of adopting these systems to motivate learners to study at any time and any place.

This study focused on influencing factors of online learning motivations. The analyzed results are basically consistent with Dornyei [6, 7, 9], which can be explained with reference to his motivation theory. The course *Audio-Visual-Oral Business English* tried to improve the students' oral Business English and make them capable of handling the business communication with English-speaking people, which is *the ideal L2 self* that students desire to become. Emphasizing that taking the online speaking exercise could help them speak more fluently and pronouncing better in the business situations did persuade 50% students to take the 1st task. *The ideal L2 self* is related to the students' internalized aspiration to be a competent user of the target language.

Starting from the 1st task, we may observe the increasing participation rate and the students with a relatively high score tend to take more online exercises, which could suggest that the positive feedback from the teacher and the good performance of taking the exercise could induce or enhance such aspiration.

That Task 1 is of the lowest participation rate, of course, does not mean the influencing factor of the students' desire is less efficient in motivating students than other factors. The increasing participation rate from Task 1 to Task 4 allows us to see the stack effect of more influencing factors of motivation. Such stack effect does not work for all students since we can observe only 4 of the 15 students in the experiment took all of the 4 tasks and other students shows their different responses to the influencing factors of motivation. Such differences can be accounted by *L2 learning experience* of students. In individual talks with the students who were incompetent in or even shun from taking online speaking exercise, it is found that such ignorance can be caused by many factors, among which ANXIETY in using language/speaking English is frequently mentioned. The designing of the four tasks was intended to motivate students in L2 learning, but we observed negative effects on those whose oral English were poor and they had no confidence in improving it with the online exercises. It, together with the strong correlation between the obtained score and the participation rate, indicates that self-suggestion is vital in influencing students' taking the online exercises. However, the approaching of the final assessment upon the end of the course succeeded in urging the majority of the students to take the online Task 4. The requirements of passing the course is related to *the ought-to L2 self*, which concerns externally imposed obligation.

From the pedagogical perspective, the results and findings have vital implications for L2 learning. Based on these findings, this study advanced the following suggestions for enriching the classroom study with the online system: (1) fostering the self-confidence of the learners could promote autonomous learning, which would encourage them to make better use of the online resources; (2) personalizing the online exercises for the learners with different *L2 learning experience* could more efficiently cultivate their motivation; (3) establishing the relation between what is learned in off-line class and the post-class online exercise would better motivate the learners; and (4) highlighting the goal of taking the online exercise, for improving the oral English, which corresponds to the *ideal L2 self*, and meeting the requirement of the course, which is related to the *ought-to L2 self*, works well in motivating the learners.

These suggestions were adopted in other courses for English-major students, which were also aided by online teaching systems, and the rise of those students' pariticipating in online activities could be clearly observed. Since online teaching systems are more and more preferred to aid the classroom teaching, paying close attention to the students' online participation would be of necessity.

5 Conclusion

This study has examined the influencing factors of learning motivations of the students in the course Audio-Visual-Oral Business English by designing a four-task experiment. In the light of Dornyei's three-level framework of motivation, we hypothesized that the students' desire to be competent L2 users, positive feedback from the teacher, the connection with the in-classroom learning content and the need of meeting the course's requirements could motivate them to complete the online speaking tasks, which was verified by the analysis and discussion. Probing into every small detail concerning the students' performance in the online exercises, it further found that self-suggestion influences their motivations. The students gaining higher scores (showing they have better language competency) tend to participate in more online tasks than those less-confident ones whose scores are relatively lower. That the aforementioned factors are efficient in motivating the students to take the online exercises can be well explained by Dornyei's theory of L2SMM. The English-major students aspire/are expected to be competent English users who can sufficiently communicate with English-speaking people, which is the idea L2 selves/ought-to L2 selves. They were working to narrow the discrepancy between such possible selves of future and the current selves. But their efforts to do so would be influenced by their different L2 learning experience, as we can observe in the different degrees of the students' completing the tasks and their taking different tasks. These findings show that Dornyei's proposed strategies to motivate L2 learners work in the online exercise system that is used to aid the off-line teaching. Of course, this study is of limitations, which cannot examine all of the motivational components suggested by Dornyei. Although further researches are needed to reveal how those motivational components interact with others in motivating the L2 learners to take the post-class online exercise, this study shed some light upon the dynamic influence of the studied motivating factors in the online learning system aiding the L2 learning.

It is hoped that this study can shed light on the discussion of motivating online L2 learning in the era when the online teaching systems are frequently adopted. Although the sample was small, it has included all of the Business English students of 2020 in this university, which also suggested the students' reluctance of taking this major--yet, another topic to discuss. In most universities of China, there would not be many students of Business English. The findings of this study would potentially provide reference for the teaching in such universities. At the same time, it allows us to peep at the online learning of students in Business English in China. English is the most widely-adopted second language in the foreign trade in this country and Business English is quite an application-oriented major. Unlike those students who study English literature and linguistic and generally wish to pursue future study, Business English students are expected to work with foreign companies after graduation. Their oral ability is thus greatly emphasized. However, there are few studies concerning it. An attempt to look into their participation in online speaking tasks would be encouraging to launch more relevant researches.

However, there are some limitations concerning this study. Although the small number of learners participating in the experiment allows the teacher to closely observe their behaviors and have frequent talks with them, more generalized results can be missed due to limited number of participants. Besides, there are more possible factors that would influence learners' participation in the online activities according to Dornyei's theory. In this case, more researches, such as looking at more possible influencing factors of learning initiative in more learners, are needed to lay an effective pedagogical base for better adopting online teaching systems and improving students' learning initiative.

Acknowledgments. This research was funded by the Department of Education of Zhejiang Province.

Disclosure of Interests. The author has no competing interests to declare that are relevant to the content of this article.

References

1. Xiao, C., He, C., Su, Y.: Online teaching practices and strategies for inorganic chemistry using a combined platform. J. Chem. Educ. **97**(9), 2940–2944 (2020). https://doi.org/10.1021/acs.jchemed.0c00642
2. Mishra, L., Gupta, T., Shree, A.: Online teaching-learning in higher education during lockdown period of COVID-19 pandemic. Int. J. Educ. Res. Open **1**, 100012 (2020). https://doi.org/10.1016/j.ijedro.2020.100012
3. Libre, N.A.: A discussion platform for enhancing students interaction in the online education. J. Online Eng. Educ. **12**(2), 07–12 (2021)
4. Gunawan, I., et al.: D. Evaluation of online teaching with the SIPEJAR platform during the COVID-19 pandemic. In: 2022 2nd International Conference on Information Technology and Education (ICIT&E), pp. 374–377. IEEE (2022). https://doi.org/10.1109/ICITE54466.2022.9759547
5. Lin, B.: On the design of computer-aided translation teaching. In: Learning Technologies and Systems. ICWL 2022, SETE 2022. Lecture Notes in Computer Science, vol. 13869, pp. 460–470 (2023). Springer, Cham. https://doi.org/10.1007/978-3-031-33023-0_43
6. Dornyei, Z. What is motivation? In: AAAL 1998 Conference, Seattle, WA (1998)
7. Dornyei, Z.: Motivation and motivating in the foreign language classroom. Modern Lang. J. **78**, 273–284 (1994). https://doi.org/10.2307/330107
8. Dornyei, Z., Csizer, K.T.: Commandments for motivating language learners: results of an empirical study. Lang. Teach. Res. **2**(3), 203–229 (1998). https://doi.org/10.1177/136216889800200303
9. Dornyei, Z.: The L2 motivational self system. Motiv. Lang. Identity L2 Self **36**(3), 9–11 (2009)
10. Dawley, L.: The Tools for Successful Online Teaching. IGI Global (2007). https://doi.org/10.4018/978-1-59140-956-4
11. Kats, Y. (ed.): Learning Management System Technologies and Software Solutions for Online Teaching: Tools and Applications. IGI Global (2010). https://doi.org/10.4018/978-1-61520-853-1

12. Sun, Z., Anbarasan, M., Praveen Kumar, D.: Design of online intelligent English teaching platform based on artificial intelligence techniques. Comput. Intell. **37**(3), 1166–1180 (2021). https://doi.org/10.1111/coin.12351
13. Awal, N.M., Ho-Abdullah, I., Zainudin, I.S.: Parallel corpus as a tool in teaching translation: translating English phrasal verbs into Malay. Procedia – Soc. Behav. Sci. **112**, 882–887 (2014). https://doi.org/10.1016/j.sbspro.2014.01.1245
14. Huang, L.-S.: Taking stock of corpus-based instruction in teaching English as an international language. RELC J. **49**(3), 381–401 (2018). https://doi.org/10.1177/0033688217698294
15. Lin, B., Yip, P.: On the construction and application of a platform-based corpus in tourism translation teaching. Int. J. Trans. Interpret. Appl. Linguist. **2**(2), 30–40 (2020). https://doi.org/10.4018/IJTIAL.20200701.oa3
16. Bailey, C.J., Card, K.A.: Effective pedagogical practices for online teaching: perception of experienced instructors. Internet High. Educ. **12**(3–4), 152–155 (2009). https://doi.org/10.1016/j.iheduc.2009.08.002
17. Yue, T., Zou, Y.: Online teaching system of sports training based on mobile multimedia communication platform. Int. J. Mobile Comput. Multim. Commun. (IJMCMC) **10**(1), 32–48 (2019). https://doi.org/10.4018/IJMCMC.2019010103
18. Mu, Y., Du, L., Li, Q.: A study on knowledge network acceptability facilitated by a computer-based translation learning platform. In: González-González, C.S., et al. (eds.) Learning Technologies and Systems: 21st International Conference on Web-Based Learning, ICWL 2022, and 7th International Symposium on Emerging Technologies for Education, SETE 2022, Tenerife, Spain, November 21–23, 2022, Revised Selected Papers, pp. 445–459. Springer International Publishing, Cham (2023). https://doi.org/10.1007/978-3-031-33023-0_42

An Experiment on Translation Education Information System Driven-By Knowledge Network Management

Lizhen Du[1,2] and Yuanyuan Mu[1](✉)

[1] School of Foreign Languages, Chaohu University, Hefei, China
390842884@qq.com

[2] Center for Research on the Theory and Practice of Multilingual Terminology, Anhui University, Hefei, China

Abstract. Considering the rapid development of artificial intelligence and the transformation of learning behavior, the researchers have designed a translation education information system to provide a platform for translation educators and learners in the experiment. All translation phenomena or nodes are annotated by knowledge nodes in 6 categories, which form a knowledge network in the system. There are 56 translation node types, 165 translation terms, 235 translation texts and 2,519 pieces of annotated knowledge nodes. The research invites 26 junior undergraduates majoring in translation and interpretation in Anhui Province (China) to learn translation knowledge with the guidance of professors. The paper reveals that the system has a positive influence on the translation education process according to students' translation scores and questionnaire results, and this conclusion is based on systematic research and concrete data, instead of impressionistic summary as used to be provided by old fashion translation teaching. Therefore, this also proves that knowledge-network driven translation teaching assisted by information technology should be widely adopted. Based on the analysis of statistical tools, the study finds that the system should be updated another 5 important translation node types.

Keywords: Translation education · knowledge network · e-learning system

1 Introduction

The first available Massive Open Online Courses (MOOC) platform was designed by Stanford University in 2012 as the first formal Small Private Online Course (SPOC) platform, which was studied and analysed by Harvard University in 2013 [1]. Since then, multifarious online education systems and software emerge around the world. The project researchers in Chinese and English translation field considered to develop a professional online translation education system, Textwells, in view of the mature information technology and systematic translation knowledge nodes and terms. Textwells 1.0 was firstly designed and harnessed in traditional classes in 2019, whose designers were mainly professors and experts in the field of translation studies, and the system has been

Z. Kubincová et al. (Eds.): SETE 2023, LNCS 14606, pp. 268–282, 2024.
https://doi.org/10.1007/978-981-97-4243-1_21

used in translation courses in The Chinese University of Hong Kong(Shenzhen), Hefei University of Technology, Chaohu University and University of Science and Technology of China [2–4]. The theoretical support is chiefly provided by Chunshen Zhu and Yuanyuan Mu, who have played a critical role in every system upgradation, particularly in Textwells 3.0 design [5]. The 3.0 version is driven by knowledge network, which connects 56 knowledge nodes with 165 knowledge terms annotated.

The experiment aims to comprehensively assess the scientific nature, stability, pertinence and practicality of Textwells 3.0 from the perspective of statistics and semi-structured questionnaire. Textwells 1.0 utilizes several theories in fields of computer science, translation studies, language acquisition, functional linguistics, and corpus linguistics [3]. In Textwells 3.0 version, novel approaches endow the system wondrous functions, which are natural language processing, data mining, and machine learning. This interdisciplinary design makes the system versatile as it can not only provide a platform for students to complete translation self-learning activities, but also build a bridge for teachers and students to attend SPOC courses.

The experiment chooses 26 junior undergraduates majoring in translation and interpretation in Anhui Province, Hefei, China, with the method of systematic sampling, whose translation scores, node recognition and questionnaire are analyzed [6]. The paper intends to adopt sample data to testify the system's universality on a large scale and the positive significance of translation network in translation education field. The analytical results reveal that Textwells 3.0 is innovative to undertake tasks of translation education and self-learning or e-learning in the whole world.

2 Translation Education Information System

The wide application of electronic equipment demands that bilingual or multilingual translators should be proficient in computer. To be more specific, translation educators usually impart computer knowledge in normal education activities with the help of electric devices or computer-aided technology, such as computer-aided translation and machine translation. Having a good master of related computer skills have positive effect on students' potential favorable jobs, translation standardization and productivity [7]. Nevertheless, there is not a correlative connection between computer competence and translation quality, particularly in abundant culture-loaded texts. The great majority of papers in translation education technology fields pays attention to design framework, implementation method and algorithms in terms of computer-aided translation. Research is seldom recorded about how to improve students' translation competence or ability by the aid of education system.

The paper draws a general outline of translation education information system research in order to form a whole and comprehensive concept, whose data come from Web of Science (WOS) and China National Knowledge Infrastructure (CNKI) [8, 9]. In WOS Core Collection, the retrieval query is set as TS = (translation education AND (technology OR digitalization OR platform OR computer-aided tool OR computer-assisted tool OR system)), where 1,072 pieces of records are searched (retrieval date: 3/9/2023). According to the results, there is an unexpected interdisciplinary research domain in translation education, which is health care science services with 136 papers counted. The findings reveals that the papers or articles from WOS database prefer to discuss translation education and health care science services together [10]. In other words, translation education platforms or systems are broadly adopted in health care science field compared with other disciplines. The first related article is mainly written in 2005 by Darrell J. Solet and J. Michael Norvell, whose title is *Lost in translation: Challenges and opportunities in physician-to-physician communication during patient handoffs* [11] (Fig. 1). Darrell designs an experiment to discuss the translation challenges and opportunities of a computer-assisted patient handoff system. It is worth mentioning that translation in health care science field usually means communication between machine and users, which is different from communication between source text and targeted text in translation and interpretation field. The common research subjects in translation education are public environmental occupational health, educational research, education scientific disciplines, nursing, medicine general internal, medical informatics, health policy services, and linguistics, whose paper results are 112, 104, 79, 79, 69, 47, 46 and 46. The first bar chart is publication number per year, showing gradual increase from 2003 to 2022 as a whole. Its sum is 1,072 as variation is from 2 to 158. The following discussion is detailed descriptions about information system in educational and linguistic fields. The trend of second bar chart is the same as the first one, where the subjects are translation education and linguistics (Fig. 1). Its total publication number is 270, range from 1 in 2003 to 45 in 2022. Arthur Tatnall and Bill Davey wrote the paper entitled *Modelling the Adoption of Web-Based Mobile Learning – An Innovation Translation Approach in 2003, which discusses mobile e-learning and educational management* [12]. The earliest paper can be retrieved in WOS Core Collection is *An e-learning platform for guideline implementation – Evidence- and case-based knowledge translation via the Internet*, which is written by Horst Christian Vollmar in 2006 [10]. Its research fields are similar to this study, which are continuing medical education (CME), knowledge translation and e-learning platform. From the second chart, the research topic in translation system is not unambiguous prior to 2018, most of which put emphasis on various fields, such as medicine and computer. Since 2018, increasing articles study translation system, linguistics and education management together. Qiuyan Zhu puts forward an innovative English translation learning approach in 2023, whose topic focuses on various English translation learning system [13].

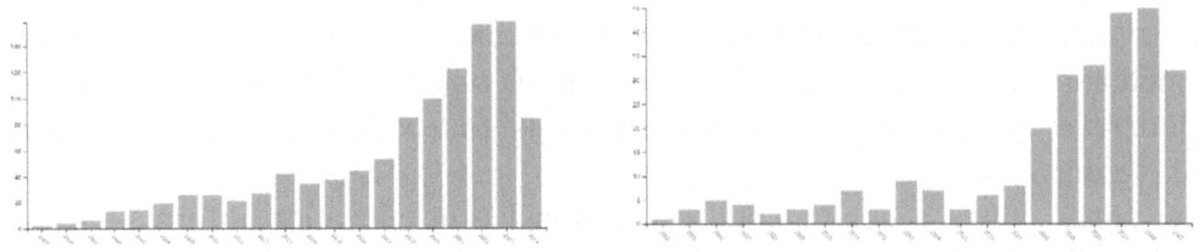

Fig. 1. Publication number per year (TS = translation education and linguistics)

Chinese research also plays key roles in translation education domain. As the query is written as SU% ='翻译教学系统' +'翻译教学平台' +'翻译教学技术' +'翻译教学电子化' +'计算机辅助翻译教学' in CNKI database, 1,161 pieces of papers and articles are searched (retrieval date: 3/9/2023). The following pie graph shows the percentage of research topic, where 6 topics account to 50%, namely translation education, translation technology, computer-aided/assisted translation, education model, education application and translation education pattern (Fig. 2). The number of records is respectively 394, 136, 97, 97, 76 and 72 as percentage is 23.73%, 8.19%, 5.84%, 5.84%, 4.58% and 4.34%. The line chart displays publication number per year (time line from 1919 to 2023) (Fig. 2). Although there are several papers mentioned translation education or system prior to 2003, most of them cannot provide valuable information. In 2003, Chinese scholar, Baolin Wan, discusses the role of translation teaching in translation teaching through *Feasibility of Modern Educational Technology Application in Translation Teaching* in 2003 [14]. From 2008, relate professional papers are released online and offline, reaching its peak (111 pieces) in 2021. Many papers study MOOC and SPOC in translation education field since 2015, whose research adopts open system or platform, such as Moodel and iSmart [15]. And some papers study simple or single translation technology in translation, for example corpus, online dictionary, TRADOS, SDL, Transmate and Wordfast [16]. It is worth mentioning that domestic articles lay more emphasis on theory and framework rather than system realization.

In general, related research number is increasing and relativity is closer in translation education information system topic from the retrieved data. It is noted that overall amount is inadequate when it is unavailable for teachers and students to communicate translation knowledge and complete courses simultaneously in existed translation education system. Under these circumstances, the paper upgrades Textwells from version 1.0 to 3.0 in order to provide translation educators and learners an alternative channel, which is innovative in translation field.

Fig. 2. Percentage of research topic, and publication number per year of SU

3 Textwells and Knowledge Network Management

The knowledge theory framework is driven by knowledge network, terms and nodes, which connect translation educators and learners in Textwells 3.0. The platform provides two main functions as illustrated in the figure, namely translation education system and online bilingual courses (Fig. 3). The preparation is finished by commentators or experts in/between Chinese and English translation field, who annotate knowledge nodes, elaborately design objective and subjective questions. The platform engineers develop

5 management options for teachers and students' communication in traditional classes, which are homework, translation workshop, exercise, Q&A, and translation knowledge teaching. In the fifth option, they utilize 56 translation knowledge nodes (6 genres) and 165 knowledge terms to impart general translation knowledge [17, 18]. Then educators can upload and download courseware in the second option. It's possible for students to discuss or communicate with each other on the platform at the same time although they are absent from desks. The first function is usually used in conventional classes as Textwells is one of tools for teachers to teach. Students should attend the first and second tests at the beginning and end of the course when their instructors require. After the tests, each student is invited to fill in a semi-structured questionnaire. Each test text is simultaneously marked by two professional teachers according to translation standard of TEM-8 (Test for English Majors, Band 8) [19]. The two scores are averaged directly as the gap is less than 6, or else lecturer marks for the third time before three scores are averaged. Average towards on test is regarded as the as the final result. The above is an overall description of options and knowledge system about the first function.

The online bilingual course is similar to SPOC in view of course timeline and procedure. Course providers release course plan on Textwells before they prepare teaching materials and test the stability and fluency of system. The difference is that Textwells 3.0 offers an existed translation knowledge system annotated by experts as other online course platform couldn't. In other words, most SPOC lecturers in the experiment know well about translation knowledge network, nodes and terms. The premise is an advantage for researchers to optimize knowledge system in future as lecturers discuss and feedback. After designers upgrade the system, MOOC resources will be also available in future.

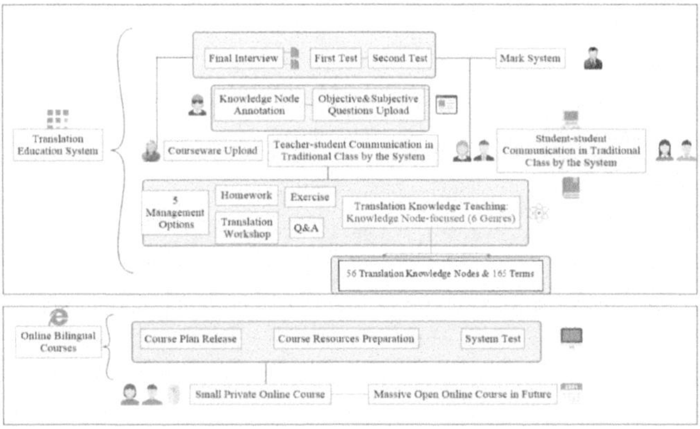

Fig. 3. Two main functions of Textwells 3.0

There are 2,610 pieces of objective questions and 31 pieces of subjective questions (Fig. 4). All questions have specific references, which can be found in books, articles or papers. These questions are additional tests for students' understanding of knowledge nodes and terms. Default contents should be filled in blank as shown in the figures. As students click submission option, answers and annotation will appear automatically.

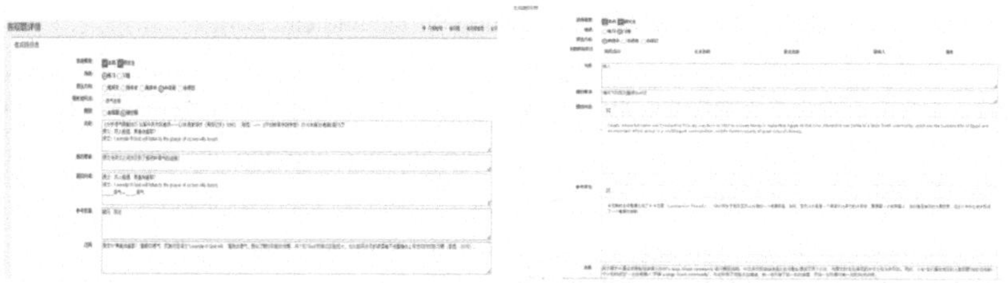

Fig. 4. Objective questions and subjective questions, and annotated texts

Texts that contain translation phenomena are annotated with knowledge terms as one phenomenon reflects one kind of knowledge nodes (Fig. 4). As the red-colored words in the above figure, the conversion between source and target texts embodies alliteration, one kind of rhetorical devices. Thus, this part is tagged with the node, rhetorical device alteration as the annotated content is described with knowledge terms, alliteration, onomatopoeia, parallelism and rhythm. When users open one text, he or she can look through whole nodes.

When learners plan to discuss with teachers or other users in extracurricular periods, they can write issues in accordance to question genre in Q&A part. As can be seen in the figure, users would make comments on the topic.

In Textwells 3.0, 56 items of translation knowledge nodes are categorized into 6 genres, namely information-level, intertextuality-level, lexical, rhetorical, syntactical and textual knowledge nodes (Table 1). However, five knowledge nodes are never annotated in the system, which are function word repetition, image retention, allusion alteration, allusion retention and tense omission. This phenomenon reflects that more texts need to be annotated to enrich the node types. According to the data from system, 2,519 pieces of knowledge nodes are annotated in 235 texts, which is analyzed by Tableau 2019. According to the table, 87% nodes are quoted more than 20 times, suggesting rationality of frequency. 6 nodes frequently quoted are semantic matching, word class alteration, sequence alteration, rank alteration, syntactic matching and voice alteration, accounting to 63%. Among 6 genres, lexical knowledge nodes appear 932 times, accounting to 37% while information-level knowledge nodes are annotated 61 times, accounting to 2% as shown in the following pie graph (Table 2, Fig. 5). It indicates that more text should be annotated from the perspective of information-level and intertextuality-level knowledge nodes.

In view of annotated texts, 92.34% of total texts are annotated with less than 20 pieces of knowledge nodes (Table 3, Fig. 6). There are 6 texts which contain one item of nodes. This obvious shortcoming verifies that quantitative analysis is beneficial for researchers to choose more appropriate passages in future as rational knowledge distribution helps students build a relatively whole knowledge network.

165 items of translation knowledge terms also can be divided into 6 genres, namely information-level, intertextuality-level, lexical, rhetorical, syntactical and textual knowledge terms. Howbeit the items of term in 6 genres are not corresponding to the ones of nodes in 6 genres. For example, noun, in lexical knowledge term can be used to in

Table 1. Annotated knowledge node and categories

Category	Knowledge Node	Annotated Number in the System	Percentage
Lexical Knowledge Node	Semantic Matching	374	14.85%
Lexical Knowledge Node	Word Class Alteration	357	14.17%
Syntactical Knowledge Node	Sequence Alteration	297	11.79%
Textual Knowledge Node	Rank Alteration	260	10.32%
Textual Knowledge Node	Syntactic Matching	167	6.63%
Lexical Knowledge Node	Voice Alteration	137	5.44%
Syntactical Knowledge Node	Sentence Component Alteration	89	3.53%
Rhetorical Knowledge Node	Rhetorical Device Addition	81	3.22%
Rhetorical Knowledge Node	Rhetorical Device Retention	71	2.82%
Rhetorical Knowledge Node	Logical Relation Retention	65	2.58%
Rhetorical Knowledge Node	Positive-Negative Alteration	48	1.91%
Rhetorical Knowledge Node	Notional Word Addition	43	1.71%
Rhetorical Knowledge Node	Rhetorical Device Alteration	40	1.59%
Syntactical Knowledge Node	Sentence Component Addition	39	1.55%
Rhetorical Knowledge Node	Rhetorical Device Omission	39	1.55%
Intertextuality-level Knowledge Node	Register Matching	39	1.55%
Textual Knowledge Node	Context Matching	26	1.03%
Textual Knowledge Node	Perspective Alteration	22	0.87%
Others	Others	325	23%

Table 2. Knowledge node category and percentage

Category	Annotated Number	Percentage
Information-level Knowledge Node	61	2%
Intertextuality-level Knowledge Node	75	3%
Lexical Knowledge Node	932	37%
Rhetorical Knowledge Node	387	15%
Syntactical Knowledge Node	492	20%
Textual Knowledge Node	572	23%

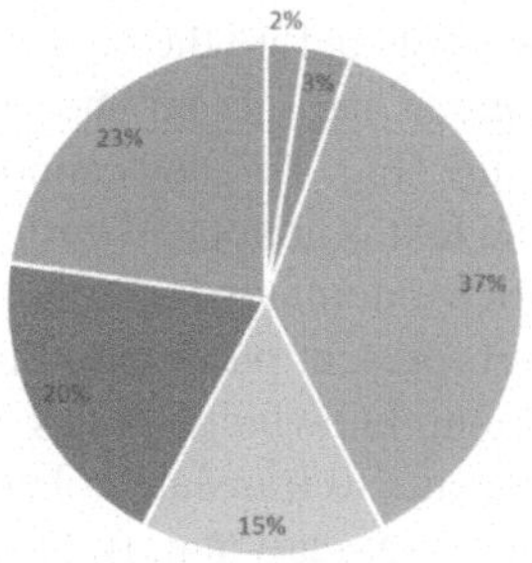

Fig. 5. Pie graph of knowledge node category

Table 3. Annotated knowledge node number and percentage

Knowledge Node Number Annotated in One Same Text	Text Number	Percentage
75	1	0.43%
53	1	0.43%
> 30	4	1.70%
> 20	12	5.11%
> 10	84	35.74%
≤ 10	133	56.60%
total	235	100.00%

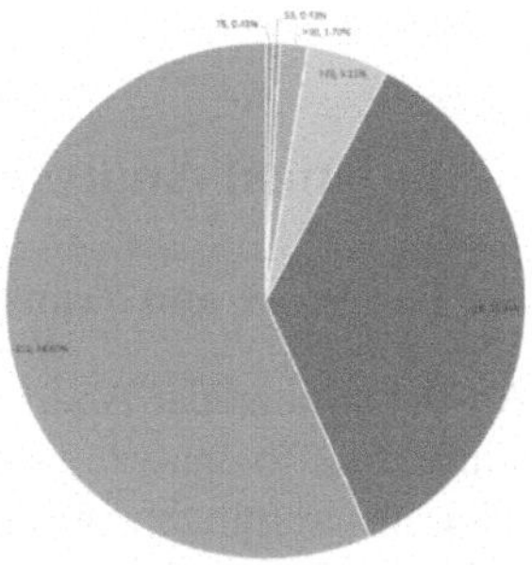

Fig. 6. Pie graph of annotated knowledge node number

syntactical or other 5 knowledge nodes. The following table covers 165 items and 6 genres of terms, most of which can also be found in publications.

4 An Experiment on Textwells

4.1 Translation Course Design

The participants in translation course include one lecturer, two test commentators and 26 junior undergraduates majoring in translation and interpretation. 26 students are elaborately chosen from 130 junior undergraduates with the help of systematic sampling [6]. Students are ascendingly sequenced by Student ID as sample distance is 5. And they have attended machine translation course in the second year of college, which is the basis for them to operate the system and learn knowledge nodes. 26 students are required to finish two tests before they learn and after the course is completed. The first test content is the same as the second one, which is a 281-word-Chinese source text shown in the fourth figure (Fig. 4). They cannot use other tools besides paper dictionary during examination. The text is annotated with ten knowledge nodes, namely intertextuality, repetition, classifier, onomatopeia, echo, noun-pronoun, transferred epithet, rhythm, alliteration and verb-present participle. Students need to learn the definitions, features and differences among knowledge nodes and terms. And the connection among nodes is beneficial for students to translate coherently in one text. The effect of translation teaching through the system are mainly analyzed from translation scores and node recognition.

4.2 Semi-construction Questionnaire

In order to evaluate the system in a comprehensive way, a semi-structured questionnaire is designed, whose form is Likert-scale [20]. The online questionnaire in the following figure is released to students on the website, https://www.wjx.cn/. WJX website is renowned in Chinese questionnaire field [21]. There are 6 Likert-scale questions and 2 open questions. The answers, 1, 2, 3, 4 and 5, respectively represent strongly disagree, disagree, agree, agree more and strongly agree. The related results are analyzed in the 5.2 section.

5 Statistical Analysis and Findings

5.1 Test Score and Translation Knowledge

SAS 9.4 (Statistical Analysis System 9.4), a software developed by SAS Institute, is mainly used to analyze students' test scores in the study [22]. Unlike Excel or SPSS, SAS is programmable instead of operable. After 26 students submit their first and second test in the system, the researcher will collect 52 score records and prepare data in certain file. Then data analyst reports and exports results by means of SAS programming applications. The following figure is a screenshot of SAS code, which can generate statistical results, charts and figures, such as mean, standard deviation, skewness, three-line table and normal distribution (Fig. 7).

T-test is a representative type of hypothesis test, indicating there is an obvious difference between the first scores and second scores or not [23]. In general, H_0 is regarded as the invalid hypothesis as H_1 is considered the alternative hypothesis. Concretely speaking, the acceptance of H_0 in the study indicates that there is no difference between the first scores and second scores, which doesn't conform to the purpose of Textwells. Otherwise, the result approves H_1, which proves the difference and testify that the system and translation knowledge nodes are beneficial for translation education. According to the results, when standard α ($Pr > |t|$) is less than 0.05 the study will accept H_1. Contrarily, H_0 would be accepted [23].

The normal distribution of paired sample data is the foundation of t-test, which is proved by SAS. In the following figures, the numerical difference of first and second scores conforms to normal distribution as the curve is symmetrical and the observed values scatter around the straight line ($Y = X$) in the Q-Q plot [24] (Fig. 8). The third

Fig. 7. Codes of SAS 9.4

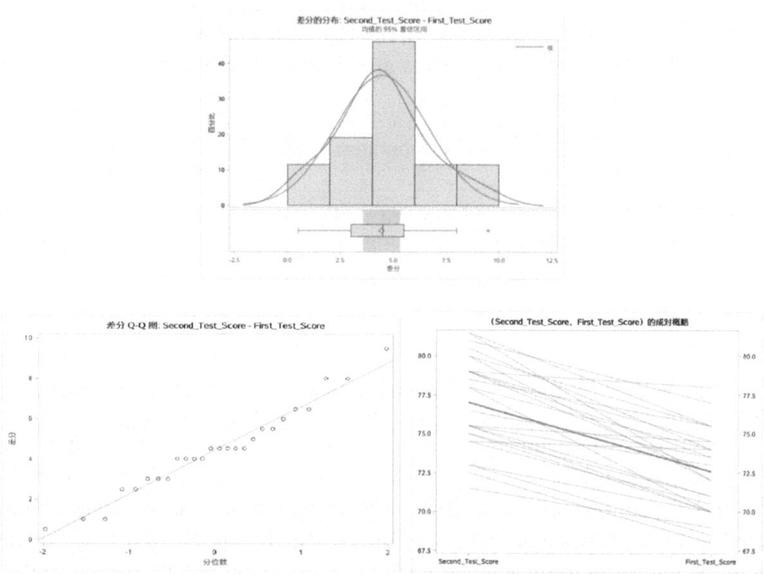

Fig. 8. Normal distribution, Q-Q plot, and scores changes of two tests

figure clearly describes the changes from first scores to second scores. These positive results allow the study to furtherly testify t-test and hypothesis.

This table contain basic statistical information of first and second test scores. Value in the table means numerical difference of first and second scores (Table 4). As can be seen, the mean of the first test scores in 72.58 as the second mean is 77.02, uprising 4,44 (mean of value). The score improvement reveals that the education system has a positive effect on students' translation competence as a whole. The value of skewness in the first test is 0.12, indicating the normal distribution tilts right [25]. Similarly, the normal distribution tilts left in the second test. As the values of kurtosis in two tests are both negative, the peak of normal distribution is gentle instead of steep [25].

Table 4. Statistical information of first and second test scores

	Mean	Std. Deviation	N	Std. Error Mean	Skewness	Kurtosis
First Test	72.58	2.66	26	0.52	0.12	−0.76
Second Test	77.02	2.96	26	0.58	−0.13	−1.12
Value	4.44	2.17	26	0.43	0.32	0.21

In the t-test table, the value (of Pr > |t|) is less than 0.0001 (Table 5). The study accepts H_1 and rejects H_0 as the standard α is far less than 0.05. The value of t is 10.4 in the table, which shows there is a comparatively obvious difference between the first and second test scores. The values of t and α again prove the positive influence of Textwells in translation education field. According to the features of systematic sampling, it can be considered that 130 junior undergraduates approve the positive influence of Textwells.

Table 5. T-test result (second test score – first test score)

Lower & Upper 95% Mean		Lower & Upper 95% Std. Deviation		Df	T	Pr > |t|
3.5642	5.3204	1.7050	3.0011	25	10.4	< .0001

In order to guarantee the rigor of experiment, study also verifies the system from the perspective of knowledge recognition. The following table is an analysis about students' recognition number of translation knowledge term in the first and second test as well as student percentage (Table 6). Student percentage of first test is the result of second column divided by 26. For example, 50% in the third column and second row indicates that 13 among 26 students can recognize intertextuality in the first test. According to the table, students can recognize more terms in the second test than ones in the second test. The study concludes that it's feasible for students to learn translation knowledge by recognizing terms. Combined with the test score findings, the new conclusion is that students can accept Textwells 3.0 driven by translation knowledge network or nodes, and improve their translation ability by grasping them.

5.2 Questionnaire Data

Among 6 Likert-scale questions, there are 3 (the first, fourth and sixth) questions toward knowledge network recognition and 3 (the second, third and fifth) questions toward efficacy (Fig. 9). Knowledge network recognition refers that students can memorize the definition and features of terms and nodes as knowledge network efficacy means that

Table 6. Recognition number of translation knowledge terms

Terms	Recognition Number of First Test	Student Percentage	Recognition Number of Second Test	Student Percentage
Intertextuality	13	50%	17	65%
Repetition	4	15%	17	65%
Classifier	20	77%	25	96%
Onomatopedia	4	15%	21	81%
Echo	7	27%	17	65%
Noun-Pronoun	6	23%	14	54%
Transferred Epithet	3	12%	14	54%
Rhythm	4	15%	16	62%
Alliteration	1	4%	6	23%
Verb-present Participle	10	38%	18	69%
Total	41		164	

students approve the significance of knowledge network or nodes. 26 students complete the semi-structured questionnaire. In the figure, question N (%) mean the percentage of student number as the value of mean describes the Likert-scale score. For example, 43.9% students (11 students) strongly agree the first structured question. And 4.27 is more than 4, indicating 26 students agree more toward the first question as a whole. As a conclusion, students considers that it's significant for them to memorize knowledge network or nodes.

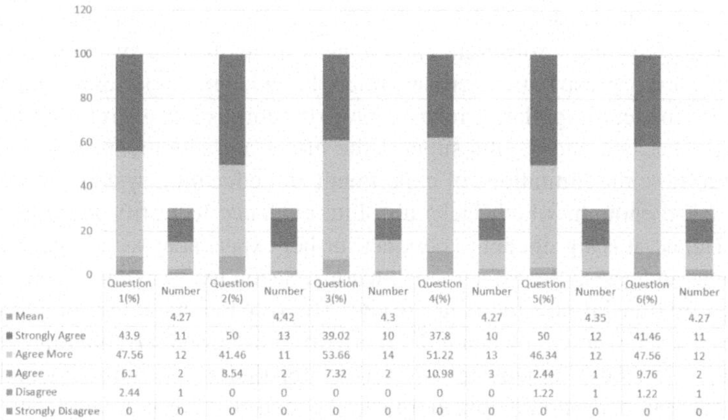

Fig. 9. Means and results of semi-structured questionnaire

2 open questions are: (1) After learning the knowledge nodes and annotations on the platform, and translating the same text again, do you feel that the quality of your translation has been improved compared with the previous one? Please give an example of improvements. (2) What is your evaluation of the platform and knowledge network learning methods and do you have any comments or suggestions to help the platform improve? Some students comment that the system is very helpful for translation studies, and compared to traditional translation learning methods, this online learning method of translation knowledge has two main advantages. Firstly, the knowledge related to translation on the Textwells platform is very systematic and comprehensive, and it is also classified according to different categories. It helps form a systematic knowledge network, and clearly grasp both macro and micro knowledge. Secondly, the translation knowledge online learning platform has a powerful corpus and exercise option.

According to the questionnaire data, the study finds that students hold a positive attitude towards Textwells 3.0 and translation knowledge network or nodes. Importantly, it's essential to improve system and enrich translation knowledge in future.

6 Conclusion

The paper analyzes translation education information system from the perspective of system design, knowledge network, translation tests, knowledge node recognition and questionnaire. With the assistance of Tableau 2019, SAS 9.4, WJX, and machine learning, experiment data are fully anatomized to explore the effect of education system and knowledge nodes on translation ability. The research finds that Textwells plays a positive role in translation education field according to T-test. During the translation node recognition test, students deem that they can accept Textwells 3.0 driven by translation knowledge network or nodes, and improve their translation ability by grasping them. By analyzing the questionnaire content, it is concluded that students hold a positive attitude towards Textwells 3.0 and translation knowledge network or nodes. Students believe that "Compared with traditional translation learning methods, the knowledge related to translation on the Textwells platform is very systematic and comprehensive, and it is also classified according to different categories. It helps form a systematic knowledge network, and clearly grasp both macro and micro knowledge. Importantly, the translation knowledge online learning platform has a powerful corpus and exercise option."

Although the data and results support the effect and significance of Textwells, it is essential to note the limitations of experiment and education system. Firstly, sample size is not large enough, which lacks absolute evidence to testify the universality of Textwells. Hence, it is significant to conduct further experiment with larger sample size to supplement and revise the existed conclusions. Secondly, translation texts and nodes are prepared by translation experts at present. The researchers are willing to design an option for students, where they can upload or edit translation texts, annotate translation phenomena, and make comments in order to develop their critical thinking and practical ability. And researchers should upload translation texts that are annotated with another 5 important translation node types. Consequently, there are a lot of work for researchers to compare Textwells with other translation education system and optimize system options.

Acknowledgements. The work was substantially supported by the project entitled "A Data-Mining Driven Mode of Co-construction of Knowledge Network for Translation Learning and Its Application" sponsored by The National Social Science Fund of China, 2019 (Project No. 19BYY125).

References

1. Mahajan, R., Gupta, P., Singh, T.: Massive open online courses: concept and implications. Indian Pediatr. **56**(6), 489–495 (2019). PMID: 31278230
2. Tian, L., Mu, Y., Yang, W.: Designing a platform-facilitated and corpus-assisted translation class. In: Hao, T., Chen, W., Xie, H., Nadee, W., Lau, R. (eds.) SETE 2018. LNCS, vol. 11284, pp. 208–217. Springer, Cham (2018). https://doi.org/10.1007/978-3-030-03580-8_22
3. Mu, Y., Tian, L., Yang, W.: Towards a knowledge management model for online translation learning. In: Hao, T., Chen, W., Xie, H., Nadee, W., Lau, R. (eds.) SETE 2018. LNCS, vol. 11284, pp. 198–207. Springer, Cham (2018). https://doi.org/10.1007/978-3-030-03580-8_21
4. Mu, Y., Yang, W.: Knowledge-Network-Based Inter-institutional Collaborative Teaching of Translation. In: Pang, C., et al. (eds.) Learning Technologies and Systems: 19th International Conference on Web-Based Learning, ICWL 2020, and 5th International Symposium on Emerging Technologies for Education, SETE 2020, Ningbo, China, October 22–24, 2020, Proceedings, pp. 411–419. Springer International Publishing, Cham (2021). https://doi.org/10.1007/978-3-030-66906-5_39
5. Zhu, C., Mu, Y.: Towards a textual accountability-driven mode of teaching and self-learning for translation and bilingual writing: with special reference to a CityU online teaching platform. Chin. Translators J. **2**, 56–62 (2013)
6. Khan, Z., Shabbir, J., Gupta, S.: A New sampling design for systematic sampling. Commun. Stat. – Theory and Methods **42**(18), 3359–3370 (2013). https://doi.org/10.1080/03610926.2011.628771
7. Wu, H.: Multimedia interaction-based computer-aided translation technology in applied English teaching. Mob. Inf. Syst. **2021**, 1–10 (2021)
8. Vera-Baceta, M.A., Thelwall, M., Kousha, K.: Web of Science and Scopus language coverage. Scientometrics **121**, 1803–1813 (2019)
9. Qiua, Z., Suna, M.: Analysis of reclaimed water irrigation research based on China National Knowledge Infrastructure. Desalination Water Treat. **281**, 103–111 (2023)
10. Vollmar, H.C., Schuerer-Maly, C.C., Frahne, J., Lelgemann, M., Butzlaff, M.: An E-learning platform for guideline implementation. Methods Inf. Med. **45**(04), 389–396 (2006)
11. Solet, D.J., Norvell, J.M., Rutan, G.H., Frankel, R.M.: Lost in translation: challenges and opportunities in physician-to-physician communication during patient handoffs. Acad. Med. **80**(12), 1094–1099 (2005)
12. Tatnall, A., Davey, B.: Modelling the adoption of web-based mobile learning – an innovation translation approach. In: Zhou, W., Nicholson, P., Corbitt, B., Fong, J. (eds.) Advances in Web-Based Learning – ICWL 2003, pp. 433–441. Springer Berlin Heidelberg, Berlin, Heidelberg (2003). https://doi.org/10.1007/978-3-540-45200-3_40
13. Zhu, Q.: Empowering language learning through IoT and big data: an innovative English translation approach. Soft. Comput. **27**, 12725–12740 (2023). https://doi.org/10.1007/s00500-023-08850-1
14. Baolin, W.: Feasibility of modern educational technology application in translation teaching (翻译教学应用现代教育技术的可行性研究). Technol. Enhanced Foreign Lang. **4**, 55–57 (2003)

15. Jun, Y.: Construction and application of a translation teaching platform based on moodle (基于Moodle的翻译教学平台构建与应用). J. Chongqing Coll. Electron. Eng. **26**(04), 125–127 (2017). https://doi.org/10.13887/j.cnki.jccee.2017(4).31
16. Yufan, J.: A Practical report on english chinese translation based on trados computer aided translation (基于Trados计算机辅助翻译的英汉翻译实践报告). Xi'an Univ. Technol. (2020). https://doi.org/10.27398/d.cnki.gxalu.2020.000719
17. Zhuang, Y., Zheng, S.: Developing translation abilities through knowledge-network-based translator training. In: González-González, C.S., et al. (eds.) Learning Technologies and Systems: 21st International Conference on Web-Based Learning, ICWL 2022, and 7th International Symposium on Emerging Technologies for Education, SETE 2022, Tenerife, Spain, November 21–23, 2022, Revised Selected Papers, pp. 513–524. Springer International Publishing, Cham (2023). https://doi.org/10.1007/978-3-031-33023-0_48
18. Mu, Y., Yang, W.: Knowledge-network-based inter-institutional collaborative teaching of translation. In Learning Technologies and Systems: 19th International Conference on Web-Based Learning, ICWL 2020, and 5th International Symposium on Emerging Technologies for Education, SETE 2020, Ningbo, China, October 22–24, 2020, Proceedings 5, pp. 411–419. Springer International Publishing (2021)
19. Chen, H., Cai, Y., de la Torre, J.: Investigating second language (L2) reading subskill associations: a cognitive diagnosis approach. Lang. Assess. Q. **20**(2), 166–189 (2023)
20. Kriksciuniene, D., Sakalauskas, V., Le, R.: Evaluating the interdependent effect for Likert scale items. In: Abramowicz, W., Corchuelo, R. (eds.) BIS 2019. LNBIP, vol. 373, pp. 26–38. Springer, Cham (2019). https://doi.org/10.1007/978-3-030-36691-9_3
21. Yanqiu, C., Ynfang, H., Lisheng, L.: Construction and application of functional experiment question bank based on questionnaire star (基于问卷星的机能学实验题库建设与应用). Basic Med. Educ. **23**(09), 628–630 (2021). https://doi.org/10.13754/j.issn2095-1450.2021.09.09
22. Talsma, P.A.: Estimation of median survival time and its 95% confidence interval using SAS PROC LIFETEST. J. Biopharmaceut. Stat. **34**, 366–378 (2023)
23. Cronbach, L.J.: Coefficient alpha and the internal structure of tests. Psychometrika **16**(3), 297–334 (1951)
24. Zhao, Q., Liang, J.: A Q-Q plot for detecting non-multinormality based on a normal characterization and the S–W statistic. Commun. Statist.-Theory Methods **51**(5), 1367–1378 (2022)
25. De Bastiani, F., Stasinopoulos, D.M., Rigby, R.A., Heller, G.Z., Silva, L.A.: Bucket plot: a visual tool for skewness and kurtosis comparisons. Braz. J. Probability Stat. **36**(3), 421–440 (2022)

Chinese Students' Perception and Demand on AI Assisted Interpretation Technology and Its Implication on Education of Interpreters

Haiqin Sun[1] and Yujia Han[2](✉)

[1] Graduate Institute of Interpretation and Translation, Shanghai International Studies University, Shanghai, China

[2] School of Languages, Shanghai University of International Business and Economics, Shanghai, China

anna_han1@163.com

Abstract. In order to understand student interpreters' use and awareness of AI-assisted interpreting technology, this study conducted a questionnaire survey on the use and perception of AI assisted interpreting technologies among student interpreters and the development of technology-related courses in interpretation teaching in universities. The survey results show that student interpreters are at a relatively basic stage in terms of technology use, and they have not yet formed a clear understanding of the relevant technology. There is still a lot of room for universities to educate interpreters with technology awareness and skills. Based on the findings, this paper further discusses how interpreters should establish a correct concept of technology to cope with the changes in the future interpretation industry under the impact of technology; and discusses the direction and possibilities of technology competence cultivation in interpretation teaching beside the key skills of interpretation in translation and interpretation programs.

Keywords: AI-assisted interpreting technology · key skills of interpretation · interpreters' perception of technology

1 Introduction

The rapid development of Internet technology and the promotion and application of artificial intelligence provide technical conditions for the development of language service industry. After years of technological development, people are no longer focused on whether machine translation will replace interpreters; instead, a more efficient man-machine collaborative model has become the general trend [1]. According to NAATI (National Accreditation Authority for Translators and Interpreters) Annual Report 2019–2020, the digital transformation continues with a strong focus on using industry-standard software to improve collaboration across the organisation and improve customer experience [2].

At the same time, companies continue to advance large language models. Taking the example of ChatGPT (Chat Generative Pre-trained Transformer), developed by OpenAI, serves as an important component of the AIGC (AI Generated Content) product

Z. Kubincová et al. (Eds.): SETE 2023, LNCS 14606, pp. 283–294, 2024.
https://doi.org/10.1007/978-981-97-4243-1_22

application framework. With its powerful capability of text generation, deep learning, and user-friendly interactivity, education researchers and practitioners have begun to explore its application in the field of education. Currently, technology giants in China and many other countries such as Google, iFlytek, and Baidu are actively deploying the AIGC industry and launching products similar to ChatGPT. Artificial intelligence technology is entering a stage of deep development, continuously empowering educational innovation [3].

As a fundamental condition for the development of the language service industry and an important guarantee of service quality, language service talents are receiving increased attention. How should universities integrate artificial intelligence technology with translation education as the main source of language service talents? What adjustments should be made to the traditional translation teaching model? How will professional translation education adapt to the new industry demands? These are all urgent topics that need to be explored in the field of language services. This study focuses on the perception, usage, and learning needs of interpreting-related technology among student interpreters, and further explores the direction for universities to carry out targeted teaching of using technology.

2 Development of AI-Assisted Interpreting Technology and Its Application in Interpreting Teaching

2.1 Development of AI-Assisted Interpreting Technology

Artificial intelligence is a new science that involves the development and research of methods, theories, and application systems to simulate and extend human intelligence. Its essence is an attempt to understand the nature of human intelligence and produce a new kind of intelligent machine that can react in a way similar to human intelligence.

Natural Language Processing (NPL) is a key technology in the cognitive process of artificial intelligence, including natural language interaction and understanding, semantic analysis, morph syntactic analysis, and sentiment analysis. The American Translators Association (ATA) defines machine translation as "the translation of a text from one language into another language by a computer without any human involvement during processing [4]." The technology of machine translation has long been in existence and has undergone three stages of development: rule-based machine translation, statistical machine translation, and neural machine translation [5]. Nowadays, artificial intelligence is applied in various aspects of the translation field, such as speech translation, VR translation, and text translation. With the development of artificial intelligence, its integration with interpreting will bring interpreting technology into an intelligent stage. The interaction between users and machine translation designers is valued. Machine translation was previously seen as a threat to the translation profession, but now translators are more deeply involved in the operation of machine translation [6]. With the support of data storage, data mining, and other related technologies, machine can play an important role in terminology prompts and vocabulary retrieval. The nature of interpreting is a communication process that interpreter helps the speaker inform, explain, persuade, and influence the audience. Human interpreters have a natural advantage in recognizing emotions and logics. Combining the advantages of human and machine in different aspects, the "assistance" rather than "replacement" role of machine has become a consensus in the language service academics and industry. Machines equipped with AI speech recognition, transcription, and translation systems can provide assistance to human interpreters [7]. A large number of AI-assisted technologies are being applied in the process of interpreting, such as ChatGPT, VR-assisted translation, and speech recognition.

2.2 Application of AI-Assisted Interpreting Technology in Interpreting Education

Stimulated by the development of the language service industry, interpreting education both domestically and internationally is continuously evolving. The European Union, leveraging the rich resources in the ELISA and BACKBONE corpora, has established the Virtual Reality Interpreting (IVY) resource library [8]. Additionally, the University of Manchester's Centre for Translation and Intercultural Studies has established the Translational English Corpus, providing students with a wealth of interpreting practice materials. In China, interpreting learner corpora based on actual interpreting learning scenarios are also continually being developed and improved. For example, Professor Hu Xianyao at Southwest University has established the Contemporary Chinese Translated Fiction Corpus, and Professor Hu Kaibao's team at the Corpus Institute of Shanghai International Studies University has developed the multi-language database platform for "Xi Jinping: The Governance of China" (http://imate.cascorpus.com/) [9]. In addition, online interpreting teaching resources are being more widely utilized. Virtual simulation laboratories with functions such as scenario-based teaching, micro-lecture recording, classroom recording, and virtual reality training have been established. With the support of information technology, the teaching modes for interpreting in both Chinese and Western contexts continue to innovate. The introduction of flipped classrooms and blended teaching has expanded the time and space for teaching and learning, reconstructing the traditional classroom teaching structure [8].

3 Research Design

This study focuses on AI-assisted interpreting technology, aiming to investigate the following issues: the current usage, perception and attitudes of AI-assisted technology among student interpreters; the implementation of related technological teaching in universities; and the suggestions and expectations of student interpreters regarding technological development.

The research utilized the "Wenjuanxing" platform to design a questionnaire, comprising a total of 27 questions, including 17 single-choice questions (including 9 Likert scale questions), 8 multiple-choice questions, and 2 open-ended questions. The survey was conducted from December 19, 2022, to January 11, 2023, and a total of 212 valid responses were received.

Prior to the official release of the questionnaire, the author invited 6 student interpreters (2 second-year graduate students and 4 third-year graduate students) and 3 university interpreting instructors who are also experienced interpreters (with over 200 interpreting service experiences) to conduct a primary test. Based on their feedback, the structure and content of the questionnaire were refined and optimized.

The questionnaire link was distributed through the WeChat platform, and the participants were able to submit their responses using a mobile phone or computer. The author utilized the "Wenjuanxing" platform's function of "statistics and analysis" to collect the data.

4 Research Results and Analysis

4.1 Basic Information of Participants

This research distributed questionnaires in the form of a "Wenjuanxing" link to all current graduate students majoring in interpreting in Shanghai. A total of 212 valid responses were collected, covering all four universities in Shanghai that offer master's programs in interpreting. The response rates were 97.56% (Shanghai University of International Business and Economics), 88.30% (Shanghai International Studies University), 63.64% (East China Normal University), and 50% (Fudan University). Specific participant information is detailed in Table 1.

Table 1. Participants' Basic Information

Grade	First-year graduate school student	Second-year graduate school student		Third-year graduate school student
	89（41.98%）	56（26.42%）		67（31.6%）
University	Fudan University	East China Normal University	Shanghai University of International Business and Economics	Shanghai International Studies University
	7（3.3%）	14（6.6%）	40（18.87%）	151（71.23%）
Language Pair	Chinese-English	Chinese-French/Spanish	Chinese-Japanese/Korean	Chinese-Russian/Afghan
	129（60.85%）	26（12.26%）	45（21.23%）	12（5.66%）
Interpreting Practical Experience	0 times	1-20 times	20-50 times	50 times
	54（25.47%）	140（66.04%）	13（6.13%）	5（2.36%）

4.2 Current Use of AI-Assisted Interpreting Technology Among Student Interpreters

The survey results indicate that auxiliary tools are widely used in the interpreting process by the participants. The tools used can be broadly categorized into two types: traditional tools (paper dictionary, paper-based study notes, reference books, etc.) and machine-based tools (online dictionary, search engines, CAT, etc.). The main purposes of usage include information retrieval, note-taking, text acquisition, and comparison and evaluation.

Compared to the during-interpretation stage, participants reported higher frequencies of tool usage in the pre- and post-interpretation stages. The multiple-choice questions revealed that participants used a total of 14 different tools in the pre- and post-interpretation stages (11 machine-based and 3 traditional tools). During the interpretation stage, participants reported using a total of 11 different tools (8 machine-based and 3 traditional paper-and-pen tools). Refer to Table 2 for more details.

Table 2. Use of Interpretation Assistance Tools Among Student Interpreters.

Before/After Interpreting Stage: Which of the following tools have you used? [Multiple Choice Question]		
Tool	Subtotal	Usage Rate
OnlineDictionary/ChatGPT*	206	97.17%
Search Engine/Online Resources*	167	78.77%
Paper-based Study Notes	144	67.92%
Office Software*	133	62.74%
Voice Transcription*	95	44.81%
Paper-based Reference Books	72	33.96%
Vocabulary Management Software*	61	28.77%
Paper Dictionary	58	27.36%
Machine Translation*	35	16.51%
CAT Tools*	29	13.68%
Text Comparison System*	15	7.08%
Machine Interpreting*	10	4.72%
Voice Comparison System*	7	3.30%
Interpretation Evaluation System*	4	1.89%
Other	0	0.00%
During Interpretation Process: Which of the following tools have you used? [Multiple Choice Question]		
Tool	Subtotal	Usage Rate
Online Dictionary/ChatGPT*	180	84.91%
Search Engine/Online Resources*	156	73.58%
Traditional Note-taking Tools (Paper + Pen)	134	63.21%
Recording Pen*	84	39.63%
Consecutive/Simultaneous Interpreting Equipment*	82	38.68%
Paper-based Terminology Materials	67	31.60%
Electronic Terminology Materials*	63	29.72%
Electronic Note-taking Devices*	36	16.98%
Paper Dictionary	30	14.15%
Voice Transcription*	30	14.15%
Machine Interpreting*	5	2.36%
Other	0	0.00%
Note: Tools related to machine assistance are marked with "*"		

4.3 Student Interpreters' Perception of AI-Assisted Interpreting Technology

The overall understanding of the participants is vague. As seen in Table 3, in the Likert scale questions assessing the level of understanding of this technology, a total of 90.56% of participants chose "quite vague," "not very clear," or "do not understand," while 9.43% of participants chose "4 points - somewhat clear." None of the participants chose "5 points - clear."

Table 3. How well do you know about "machine-assisted interpreting" technology?

Option	Subtotal	Percentage
1 point - Not understanding	60	28.30%
2 points - Not very understanding	91	42.92%
3 points - Somewhat unclear	41	19.34%
4 points - A little understanding	20	9.43%
5 points - Understanding	0	0.00%

Additionally, the participants have a narrow understanding of the scope of this technology. Combining the data from Table 2, it is evident that more than 50% of machine-based auxiliary tools were used in the pre- and post-interpretation stages (3 types) and during the interpretation stage (2 types). However, only 8.02% and 7.08% of the participants agreed with the statements "I have used AI-assisted interpreting technology in the pre- and post-interpretation stages" and "I have used AI-assisted interpreting technology throughout the entire interpreting process," respectively (a total of 32 participants). Refer to Table 4 for details.

Table 4. Have you ever used "machine-assisted interpreting" technology?

Option	Subtotal	Percentage
No	180	84.91%
Only before/after interpreting	17	8.02%
Before/during/after interpreting	15	7.08%

Among the 32 participants who acknowledged using AI-assisted interpreting technology, 78.13% provided predominantly negative feedback on their usage experience, with only 21.88% believing that technology has a positive impact on improving interpreting performance.

4.4 The Learning and Teaching of Student Interpreters Regarding Machine-Assisted Interpreting Technology

The participants have a practical and strong willingness to learn about technology, with the most desired training being "the cultivation of methods for using technology-related applications and software" (87.74%). They are also willing to learn computer basics (61.79%), understand the future development trends of machine-assisted interpreting (51.89%), and the technical principles of machine-assisted interpreting (45.28%). However, the participants' subjective initiative for learning is relatively weak, with only 27.36% of participants stating that they have autonomously studied technology-related content.

Over 70% of the participants agree on the necessity of introducing technology-related teaching in MTI (Master of Translation and Interpreting) education, and explicitly express their hope for related training to be conducted in their own universities. However, at the current stage, there is insufficient teaching of relevant technology in universities, with few courses offered, and mainly through lectures, seminars, and other forms to introduce students to the latest technological developments. The standardization and participation of the existing teaching activities related to technology are also relatively low.

As shown in Table 5, there is a significant difference in the participants' understanding of teaching activities in their universities, both in terms of "whether the university has conducted relevant teaching activities" and "the form in which the teaching activities are conducted". In addition, more than half of the participants stated that although the university has conducted relevant teaching, they have not participated in the learning.

Table 5. Does your university have any teaching contents to Machine Aided Interpreting?

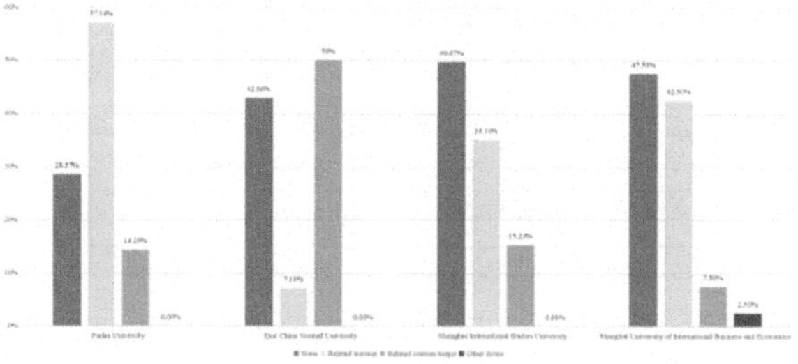

4.5 Attitude of Student Interpreters Towards Interpreting-Assisting Technology

Overall, the participants have an open attitude towards technology: 77.36% of the participants are willing to use machine-assisted interpreting during the interpreting process. The main driving factors for their willingness to use technology include recognition of its practicality, curiosity, and agreement with the future trend of "machine-assisted interpreting mode" (all three factors were chosen by more than 50% of the participants). Regarding the practicality of the technology, the participants are most concerned about its help in relieving the pressure of listening, note-taking, and short-term memory (all three factors were chosen by over 60% of the participants).

A small minority of participants (13.68%) hold a negative attitude towards the technology, questioning its practicality and its interference in the interpreting process. Some participants also explicitly state their aversion to the promotion and advertising behavior of related technology companies. The concerns of the participants about the use of technology are mainly concentrated in the interpretation stage, with two prominent points: technology use leading to distraction (80.19%) and increasing additional cognitive burden (63.21%).

In response to open-ended questions such as "What is your opinion or evaluation of machine-assisted interpreting?" and "What suggestions do you have for relevant technology development companies?" 155 and 144 participants respectively provided specific answers. To understand the participants' focus and thoughts, the author extracted high-frequency keywords from the detailed responses to the two questions and sorted them by frequency of occurrence, as shown in Tables 6 and 7.

Table 6 shows that the participants generally acknowledge the future trend of machine-assisted interpreting in the interpreting industry, affirming the helpful role of assistive technology. However, they also raise issues regarding the current immature development stage of the technology, believing that although the technology has prospects, it still needs further development and improvement. At the same time, the participants generally believe that "machines" cannot replace human interpreters and the two should be combined for mutual development. A small minority of participants hold a pessimistic attitude towards the technology.

Table 6. Views on machine-assisted interpretation

Frequently used words	Number	Percentage
Cannot be replaced	41	26%
Inevitable trend	30	19%
Helpful	29	19%
Immature/Not ideal	27	17%
Need time	20	13%
Auxiliary	16	10%
Promising	13	8%
Human-machine coupling/combination	12	8%
Utilization	7	5%
Unpromising	5	3%

Table 7. Advice to relevant technology companies

Frequently used words	Number	Percentage
Practical	35	24%
Interpreter participation	26	18%
Against replacement	15	10%
Actual	14	10%
Expand the corpus/database	14	10%
Convenient	13	9%
Understand the requirements	12	8%
Excessive/False publicity	11	8%
University cooperation	8	6%
Speech recognition	6	4%

From Table 7, it is evident that the participants are most concerned about the practical improvement of technology for its future development, including the enhancement of language corpora, speech recognition technology, and convenience of use. The participants widely believe that interpreters should be involved in the development of technology and hope that relevant companies can strengthen cooperation with universities. In addition, the participants oppose the idea of "replacement" and are averse to excessive promotion.

5 Research Findings and Discussion

5.1 Use and Perception of "AI-Assisted Interpreting Technology" Among Student Interpreters

As future practitioners in the interpreting industry, student interpreters should establish an early awareness of assistive technology and consciously improve their technological literacy. But according to the survey results, student interpreters have a vague concept of "AI-assisted interpreting technology" and a fuzzy understanding of the use of technology. In the case of "speech transcription," the usage rates in "pre-interpreting/during interpreting" reached 44.81% and 14.15% respectively, but only 8.02% and 7.08% of the participants believed they had used assistive technology in "pre-interpreting/post-interpreting" or "pre-interpreting/during-interpreting/post-interpreting." Most participants defined "using assistive technology" as "using machine interpreting software during the interpreting process."

The survey results show that in all stages of interpreting (pre-interpreting, during interpreting, post-interpreting), only three electronic tools, namely language models, online dictionaries, and search engines, have usage rates exceeding 50%; the usage rate of traditional pen-and-paper tools still exceeds 60%. Efficiency-improving electronic tools such as vocabulary management software, machine interpreting/translation systems, and electronic databases all have usage rates of less than 30%. It is evident that assistive technology has not yet been widely used in the interpreting activities of student interpreters.

5.2 Inspiration for Interpreter Education

The research results show that the majority of student interpreters have an open-minded attitude towards technology. They not only have a strong willingness to use technology but also have a strong demand for learning about it. Over 70% of the participants believe that "it is necessary to introduce technology teaching in MTI (Master of Translation and Interpreting) education" and hope to receive training in this area. However, participants from the four universities in Shanghai were unable to reach a consensus on the question of whether "the university offers 'machine-assisted interpreting' related courses" and none of the four universities had relevant programs listed in their 2022 graduate program catalogs. The "2020 China Language Service Industry Development Report" released by the China Translation Association stated that "the proportion of schools offering translation technology courses is relatively low [10]," further confirming the finding of "insufficient development of technology teaching in universities" in this survey.

We require an integrated training system, and corresponding education and teaching methods need to adapt to the times and respond to the trends. Currently, technology teaching system has not been established, leaving universities with a broader space for exploration. Translation teaching in the new era should focus on cultivating students' awareness of complementary advantages in human-machine translation and enhancing students' competence in conducting human-machine collaborative translation. The author believes that a three-dimensional approach to interpreting teaching can be achieved by focusing on the following four aspects.

5.2.1 Using AI-Assisted Tools to Strengthen Pre-interpreting and Pre-class Preparation

Pre-interpreting preparation can not only help interpreters understand interpreting topics from a comprehensive and systematic perspective but also alleviate the pressure during interpreting, enabling interpreters to perform more effectively and confidently. Furthermore, AI-assisted tools can also help students deepen their understanding of the topic. Taking ChatGPT as an example, students can prepare for consecutive interpreting classes for document preprocessing, terminology concept learning and understanding of the topic area.

5.2.2 Applying AI-Assisted Technology in Interpreting Classrooms

The development of artificial intelligence provides a more diverse approach to the forms of interpreting teaching, and increasing the use of AI in interpreting classrooms is a top priority for the current development of interpreting teaching. Improvements in interpreting classrooms can be made in the following three aspects.

First, relying on technology to conduct real or virtual simulated human-computer interactive translation practice [9]. The author believes that VR (virtual reality) assisted teaching can construct situations in the pre-translation, during-translation, and post-translation stages, providing students with a comprehensive and systematic professional interpreting simulation experience.

Second, exploring the potential of subtitle translation development. Interlingual real-time subtitle translation is a new mode that has emerged in the field of audiovisual translation in recent years. The University of Leeds in the UK, the Autonomous University of Barcelona in Spain, and the University of Roehampton in the UK have begun to incorporate related content in audiovisual translation master's courses or online training, focusing mainly on intralingual real-time subtitles. In response to new market demands, there are currently a few institutions offering courses in interlingual real-time subtitle translation, such as the University of Antwerp in Belgium (English to Dutch) and the University of Vigo in Spain (English to Spanish and Galician) [11].

Interlingual real-time subtitle translation practice has not been prevalent in China for long. Currently, no universities in China offer related courses. However, in 2017, Graduate Institute of Interpretation and Translation (GIIT) in Shanghai International Studies University (SISU) established the "SISU-iFlytek Joint Laboratory for Intelligent Interpreting and Translation" in collaboration with iFlytek Research Institute, providing students with more opportunities and avenues to access and use relevant technologies. In addition, since 2020, GIIT of SISU has been experimenting with offering "patchwork classes" for interpreting majors, inviting technical developers from the interpreting industry to explain the relevant technological principles and applications to the students.

Third, actively utilizing AI interpreting teaching software to enrich classroom activities. With the development of modern technology, teachers can use test, discussion, live broadcast and other functions in the platforms such as Zoom, Dingding, Tencent Meeting, etc. Based on the multi-modal teaching perspective, flexibly use relevant corpus data platforms or computer-aided translation software such as Trados, CAT, Wordfast, OmegaT, etc. [9].

5.2.3 Use of AI Technology in Post-interpreting Self-training and Group Training

In interpreting teaching, effective practice is key to enhancing interpreting abilities. Transitioning from a novice interpreter to an expert requires thousands of hours of deliberate practice [12].

Firstly, utilizing AI-assisted interpreting software to recreate real interpreting scenarios and simulate live combat during practice. Professional tools such as IRIS, Marius, Interpretations, and Black Box have been developed and applied in interpreting teaching practice, continuously adjusted and improved in functionality, gradually integrating with interpreting courses [8].

Secondly, using interpreting teaching platforms to review classroom interpreting. For interpreters, post-interpreting debriefing and improvement are crucial for enhancing subsequent interpreting quality. Through interpreting teaching platforms such as the Cloud Classroom Learning Platform developed in China, teachers can upload all classroom materials, including speaker speeches and student interpreting recordings, to the cloud, monitoring students' post-class learning and providing complete materials for student post-training review. Students can review classroom interpreting materials, search for their interpreting recordings in the classroom corpus, and engage in post-class reflection on their own issues.

5.2.4 AI-Assisted Interpreting Performance Evaluation

Teachers' evaluation is of crucial importance to interpreting learning. It serves as a scaffolding or a steering wheel to the learning process. If every time the students' practice and excersise of interpreting can be assessed and reported by an AI algorism, scientifically calculating individual strong points and weaknesses, a long term analysis can be formed as a feedback. Thus, teachers should make full play to a multi-dimentional evaluation mechanism, including who to evaluate, what indicators to evaluate and in what way, in order to unleash the potential of AI assessment and it's supportive power in interpreter education.

6 Conclusion

The evolution trend of "human-machine collaboration" in the future language service industry is already clear. As future professionals in the industry, interpreting students need to remain sensitive to technological developments and proactively understand, recognize, and use technology during the learning stage of interpreting skills to prepare for their careers. Universities need to closely monitor the dynamic development of the industry and technology. Universities should consciously guide student interpreters to enhance their technological literacy and establish and improve the cultivation of students' interpreting technological abilities in the teaching process.

Student interpreters and universities need to clearly define the interpreter's position in interpreting activities, correctly understand the auxiliary role of technology, and insist on cultivating the core interpreting abilities in interpreting learning and teaching. Interpreter training should lead interpreting teachers to actively adapt to the current trend of informatization through various forms and approaches, enhancing their technological literacy from beliefs, cognition, skills, thinking, and actively applying the development achievements of information technology to various aspects of interpreting teaching. This includes exploring new teaching modes such as simulation training based on virtual scenarios, cross-language transmission based on intelligent pens, and adaptive learning based on big data [13]. By continuously innovating interpreting teaching ideas and methods, the effectiveness of interpreting teaching can be maximized.

References

1. Yue, F., Yu, J.: The development of language service industry and translation majors in colleges and universities语言服务行业的发展与高校翻译专业的应对策略. Shanghai J. Translators (03), 50–55 (2022)

2. National Accreditation Authority for Translators and Interpreters (NAATI). Annual Report (2019–2020). Canberra (2020)
3. Wang, H., Liu, S.: Smart Translation Education: Concept, Pathways and Prospects智慧翻译教育研究:理念、路径与趋势. Shanghai J. Translators (03), 47–51+95 (2023)
4. American Translators Association. ATA position paper machine translation: A clear approach to a complex topic. https://www.atanet.org/advocacy-outreach/ata-position-paper-machine-translation-a-clear-approach-to-a-complex-topic/,2018-08-14
5. Feng, Z.: Parallel development of machine translation and artificial intelligence机器翻译与人工智能的平行发展. J. Foreign Lang. **41**(06), 35–48 (2018)
6. Vieir, A.D.: Translating perceptions and managing expectations: an analysis of management and production perspectives on machine translation. Perspectives (2), 163–184 (2020)
7. Sun, H., Li, K., Lu, J.: Al-assisted simultaneous interpreting an experiment and its implications 人工智能赋能语音识别与翻译技术对同声传译的影响:实验与启示. Technol. Enhanced Foreign Lang. Educ. (06), 75–80+86+12 (2021)
8. Chen, J., Wu, Q.: IT-Assisted Interpreter Training in Retrospect and Prospect信息技术辅助下的中西口译教学:演变与展望. Chin. Translators J. **40**(02), 68–78+192 (2019)
9. Zhou, L.: Exploration on the Reform of Translation Undergraduate Teaching Driven by Intelligent Technology智能技术驱动下的翻译本科教学变革探索. English Square (20), 104–107 (2023)
10. Translators Association of China. Report on the development of China's Chinese language service industry 2020中国语言服务行业发展报告2020. Translators Association of China (2020)
11. Romero-Fresco, P.: Respeaking--subtitling through speech recognition. In: PÉREZ GONZÁLEZ L. The Routledge Handbook of Audiovisual Translation. London & New York: Routledge (2018)
12. Ericsson, K.A.: Expertise in interpreting: an expert-performance perspective. Interpreting **5**(2), 187–220 (2000)
13. Deng, J., Xu, M., Zhao, T.: Frontiers of interpreting technologies and informatization of interpreting education in the Al Era人工智能时代的口译技术前沿与口译教育信息化. Technol. Enhanced Foreign Lang. Educ. (04), 67–72+79+10 (2021)

Closed-Loop Automation with Python in Translation Technology Teaching – The Acquisition of a Meta-technology Competence Through Project-Based Learning

Zhengting Zhao[1](✉), Jing Wang[2], and Mingjiong Chai[1]

[1] Graduate Institute of Interpretation and Translation, Shanghai International Studies University, Shanghai, China
02512@shisu.edu.cn

[2] School of Foreign Languages and Cultures, North Minzu University, Yinchuan, China

Abstract. This paper proposes a project-based approach to teach and improve modern translator's skills in translation technology. Based on a three-level classification [2, 12, 14] of translation tools, it discusses the motivators and inhibitors of adopting current state-of-the-art translation technologies into a translator's workflow and the existing loopholes in workflow automation. Several translation scenarios in English-Chinese language pair are explored, such as Chinese term extracting, large-scale corpus building, mass process of structured language data, etc. It presents the initial finding that a high-level of workflow automation cannot be achieved with mere adoption of commercially available tools, and some ready-made tools have shortcomings like steep learning curve, high deployment cost, and hidden regulatory risks, etc.

Against this background, the paper turns away from the traditional tool-centered teaching and sets out to explore a meta-technology solution. Challenges and opportunities of introducing a digital "machine tool" technology, namely the programming languages, into the training of translators are discussed. The paper demonstrates how a translation-project-based Python course can be designed and carried out to help translation students working in English-Chinese language pair. The whole demonstration constructs a closed loop automation for a modern translator's workflow.

Keywords: Translation technology · Python programming · project-based learning · Chinese term extracting · big-data corpus

1 Introduction

To modernize the training of language service professionals, it is imperative to align with the developments of contemporary digital technologies, especially in the context of big data and artificial intelligence. In the era of exponential growth in international information exchange, translators and language professionals increasingly require advanced technological tools to support their daily operations. The new technological revolution

Z. Kubincová et al. (Eds.): SETE 2023, LNCS 14606, pp. 295–310, 2024.
https://doi.org/10.1007/978-981-97-4243-1_23

has elevated societal productivity, engendering social transformations and reforms, while simultaneously prompting the digital transformation of education [24].

For both translation practice and education, this presents both opportunities and challenges. Adapting to a rapidly evolving translation market, the ability of translation schools to produce qualified professionals is closely intertwined with the necessity to update and evolve traditional teaching methods. In recent years, undergraduate and postgraduate translation programs in China have witnessed robust development. The number of institutions offering translation programs has grown from a few experimental units to over 300, student enrollment has surged from a mere handful to tens of thousands, and faculties have expanded continuously. But in much of these teaching institutions, the training of the translator's technology competence still lacks an appropriate level of automation. This study proposes an innovative approach to teaching translation technology, seeking to integrate recent technological advancements in the field of artificial intelligence into the training of language professionals, and, in doing so, address issues inherent to traditional translation technology education models.

2 Closed-Loop Automation in Translation Technology Teaching

2.1 The Current State of Translation Technology Teaching in China

The process of a translation project typically involves several stages, such as translation service negotiations, review of the source text, terminology compilation, division of tasks, translation, consolidation of translated sections, review of translations, formatting, and final review [4]. Table 1 illustrates the various technological tools involved in a typical translation workflow.

Throughout this process, translators employ different technological tools to alleviate their workload and cognitive burden, thereby enhancing efficiency and work quality. Translation technology seeks to integrate information technology into the translation process to relieve the translator's workload and boost translation productivity [18]. Teaching translation technology involves simulating the integration of these tools in the classroom to help students become proficient in their use.

2.2 Automation Hurdles in Translation Technology Teaching

However, despite the significant progress made in translation technology, many educational institutions still face challenges in fully incorporating automation and advanced tools into their translation technology teaching. These challenges include:

(1) Overemphasis on Ready-to-Use Product Tutorials with Low Accessibility and Associated Risks

In some mainstream translation technology textbooks, the tools used for teaching are often mature software products, but they typically cover only a small portion of the translation process. These solutions come with steep learning curves [23], high deployment costs [22], and potential compliance and intellectual property risks.

Table 1. Technical Tools Used in a Typical Manual Translation Workflow, Based on Chai's Language Service Process [4].

Translation Stage	Activity	Tool
Pre-translation Process	Preparation of the translation document	Extractor
		Finereader
		Aligner
		TMX Editor
Translation	Term management	search engine
		Excel
		Multiterm
		Glossary Converter
	Task division	WORD
		XLIFFSplit
	Translating document	CAT
		WORD
	Compilation of divided tasks	XLIFFSplit
	Translation Review	Xbench
		CAT
		WORD
Post-translation Process	Typesetting	WORD
		Acrobat
		InDesign
	Final review	WORD
		CAT
	Document submission	Flash drive
		e-mail
		WeChat

(2) Low Level of Automation and Adaptability

Existing translation technology solutions often lack appropriate tools to cover the entire translation process [8, 19]. Even in the software technology solutions used in teaching, there are still steps that are challenging to automate, such as Chinese terminology extraction, document compilation, and corpus preparation. These uncovered translation processes remain labor-intensive tasks.

(3) Reinventing the Wheel and Neglecting Abundant NLP Resources

As one of the pivotal fields of artificial intelligence, the natural language processing (NLP) domain continuously produces new accomplishments and open-source resources.

The most prominent example is neural machine translation technology using deep learning technology. Additionally, there are technologies for text sentiment analysis, text classification, semantic extraction, and word segmentation, which hold substantial potential value for the professional translation domain. However, apart from machine translation, these emerging NLP technologies are rarely applied in the translation field. This is because most of these technologies are released in source code form on platforms like GitHub, lacking graphical user interfaces (GUIs) and comprehensive documentation. Translators with no programming background struggle to apply these technologies to their translation practice without external technical team assistance.

Faced with these challenges, if translation professionals try to tackle these automation hurdles solely by operating a pre-made software product, they become constrained by the tools, limiting their subjective initiative and preventing them from fully benefiting from the efficiency and convenience that digital tools can offer. If we can identify a "meta-technological approach" that integrates the needs of translation professionals into the design, programming, and development phases of these tools, then these tools can become more tailored and versatile. Once we can unlock this gate at the design phase, open-source resources in natural language processing and even other fields of artificial intelligence will have the opportunity to be directly applied to the translators' workflow, addressing existing challenges in translation technology.

3 Research Objectives

It is essential to acknowledge that whether it is student-centered, career-oriented [16], process-oriented [11], task-driven or project-based learning (PBL) [13], or causal models [6], they all empower student translators through real translation projects [13]. These approaches aim to enhance their acquisition of professional skills and cultivate their ability to tackle complex translation problems, laying a solid foundation for their future entry into the language service market. Therefore, our translation technology curriculum design in this study is guided by the relatively common PBL theory, as outlined in these principles. While introducing new technological tools into the classroom, teachers will base their approach on the translation management processes commonly seen in the language service industry, exploring the appropriate application of these new technologies. Specifically, the research objectives can be divided into three main levels:

(1) Identify the hurdles and bottlenecks in the translation process, leveraging advanced achievements in artificial intelligence and natural language processing to build a corresponding repository of solution cases.
(2) Explore patterns in students' acquisition of various technological solutions and design an ideal teaching gradient.
(3) Utilize state-of-the-art technological methods to develop a translation technology curriculum tailored for the language service market.

4 Research Process and Methods

4.1 Teaching Objectives

The primary objective of this research is to develop students' translation technology competence. For professional translators in the language service market, translation competence is fundamentally a "procedural knowledge" guiding "professional process behavior." Specifically, translation competence can be further subdivided into multiple sub-competence areas, including language (bilingual) competence, extralinguistic competence, domain-specific knowledge competence, technology tool competence, and translation project management competence [3, 5, 7, 17]. Based on the actual student context (first-year students majoring in Chinese-English translation), the focus of the teaching in this study is to enhance their "technology tool competence."

4.2 Teaching Content and Schedule

The course's teaching content is designed based on the aforementioned teaching principles and objectives, with each aspect centered around the teaching of technology competence (Table 2). In addition, to provide students with a continuous thread connecting all technological solutions, this course incorporates a module on project background introduction at the beginning of the semester. The teacher initially acquaints students with the work requirements of the current translation project based on project background information. The news corpus from the client's (in this case, a company called Veeva) website was used in this experiment. In the project background preparation phase, the teacher informs students, based on the corpus annotations, that this is a cloud technology company serving the global life sciences industry, encompassing computer science and biomedicine. The original project was commissioned in 2014, and the primary format for the translation is online web pages, targeted at potential clients and investors. All the technology solutions covered in the teaching are intended to facilitate the smooth execution of the translation work for this specific project.

4.3 Teaching Methods

The course's teaching activities are based on the eight essential components of translation courses as proposed by Colina [7]. These components include online discussion groups, classroom discussions, theory, translation tools, translation assignments (portfolio), translation activities, proofreading, and project operations. At the beginning of the first semester, with the assistance of the teaching staff, the class participating in the trial teaching established an online chat group. The 12 students were divided into four groups and engaged in both online and offline translation project practices and discussions.

Once the students understood the project background, they began their studies in the CAT module. In this module, students familiarized themselves with mainstream technological products in the language service industry. The teacher then introduced them to some challenging automation issues in the translation process, such as the division and compilation of large files, Chinese word segmentation, and handling big data corpora, thus prompting them to enter the next stage of learning with problem awareness.

(1) Basics and Translation Management

In the early stages of introducing the Python language, students are also exposed to the basic knowledge of XML language data. Following this, by becoming proficient in

Table 2. Teaching Content and Schedule

Semester	Competence Module	Course Content	Teaching Objectives
First semester	Project background and process introduction	Course Overview and Project Commission Overview	Understand the course schedule, understand the language service market structure and the needs of the technology company translation projects covered in the course
		Client translation outline and translation cases	Work in small teams to complete a client-assigned project case and grasp the fundamental points of the translation process
	CAT module	Language data asset management	Take several mainstream term databases and corpus management tools as examples to train students in language asset management skills
		CAT platform collaborative operation	Introduces the development of CAT translation and its impact on today's language service industry, helping students understand and practice various important translation technologies and practical tools
	XML language data	Introduction to XML and introduction to common text formats	Master the basic knowledge of XML language and understand the basic structures of common text formats such as HTML and DOCX

(*continued*)

Table 2. (*continued*)

Semester	Competence Module	Course Content	Teaching Objectives
Second semester	Regular expression	Regular expression basis for linguistic data	Introduce the characteristics of language data in translation tasks and learn to use computer language for intelligent data manipulation
	Python basics	basic grammar learning	Learn Python basic syntax application (Ad hoc)
		Natural language text processing automation	Train students to use automated scripts to solve text processing problems in translation projects
	Python advanced application	Online corpus data processing automation	Train students to use automated scripts to solve application problems of large-scale self-built corpora in translation projects
		Exploration on the application of SQL corpus and NLP technology	Comprehensive use of computer technology to build a SQL corpus and try to use the latest NLP toolkit to quantitatively analyze text readability and other indicators

basic Integrated Development Environment (IDE) operations and understanding fundamental data concepts like strings, lists, dictionaries, etc., students can break down the requirements of the translation process into if/else/for/while logic. This allows them to implement simple functionalities such as text division, compilation, and allocation for proofreading.

For instance, in the context of translation project division and compilation, without the assistance of a Translation Management System (TMS), the pre-translation task allocation for large projects can be quite labor-intensive. Even mainstream Computer-Aided Translation (CAT) tools may require tools like XLIFF Split for intervention, which, in turn, demands a certain amount of time to learn. However, in Python, with the help of the Python-docx module, it becomes relatively straightforward to achieve the division and compilation of Word documents.

As shown in Fig. 1 (left) and Fig. 1 (middle), after completing their respective tasks, the translated text was placed in the individual work files for each translator. At this point, a compilation was required. For large-scale projects, manually copying and pasting would be time-consuming and labor-intensive, and it could sometimes disrupt the original document's formatting.

Fig. 1. Translation Draft A for Compilation (Left), Translation Draft B for Compilation (Middle), Combined Draft after Compilation (Right)

Using the Python-docx module, the batch compilation of Word documents can be achieved. The core code for this process is as follows:

```
doc1 = Document('/track1.docx')
doc2 = Document('/track2.docx')
p1 = doc1.paragraphs
p2 = doc2.paragraphs
counter = 0
str=''
for n in p1:
    str += n.text
for pa1 in p1:
    for x in range(2,len(p2)):
        if p2[x].text.strip() not in str and p2[x-1].text.strip() ==
pa1.text.strip():
            counter += 1
            print(p2[x].text)
            pa1.text += '\n'
            pa1.text += p2[x].text
```

The variables p1 and p2 respectively contain the paragraph content of two documents. In the first for loop, we concatenate all the text within document 1 into a single string. In the second for loop, we insert the additional text from document 2 beneath the corresponding paragraphs in document 1. On the right side of Fig. 3, you can see the finalized bilingual combined draft after the compilation.

(2) English - Chinese Terminology Management

Chinese terminology extraction, also known as "terminology registration" or "keyword extraction," is a focal point in the field of artificial intelligence research. This process involves three primary steps: candidate keyword generation, feature engineering, and keyword extraction.

In the natural language processing domain, there are mature Chinese segmentation modules like Jieba (which utilizes the 1998 People's Daily Chinese corpus and BMES method for model design) and HanLP (which extracts text phrases based on mutual information and left-right entropy). With proper design, these modules can accomplish tasks such as word segmentation, N-grams, and part-of-speech tagging. After segmentation, features like term frequency, length, position, external knowledge bases, themes, word embedding vectors, and more can be used to extract the necessary terminology for translation work.

For example, in the case of the external translation project "Organizational Structure and Operational Procedures of the Chinese People's Political Consultative Conference" that the author participated in, a TF-IDF dictionary was trained using 18,707 news articles from the 1998 People's Daily that were closely related to the project's subject matter. Terms were then extracted based on this TF-IDF dictionary. TF-IDF is an unsupervised extraction method suitable for enhancing the level of automation in the translation process. This method is relatively simple to implement and yields good extraction results. When complemented with N-grams, part-of-speech tagging, thematic features, and other techniques, even better segmentation results can be achieved.

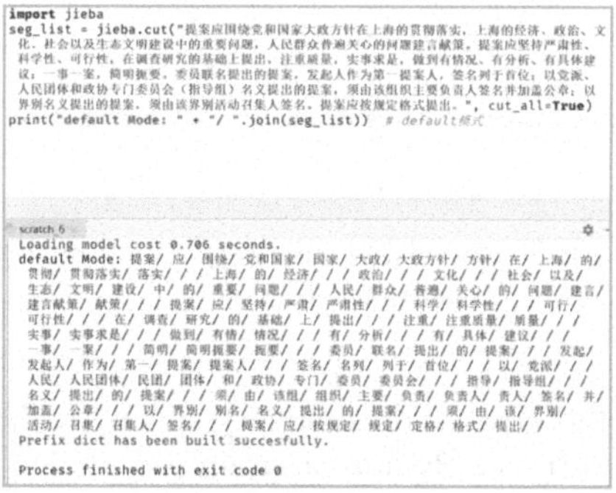

Fig. 2. Segmenting Text Using Jieba in PyCharm

From Fig. 2, we can see the segmentation results of the selected text using Jieba. In simple cases, calling this module only requires using the "import" command and the "jieba.cut" method. The entire code can be written as follows:

```
import jieba
from collections import Counter
def get_words(txt):
    seg_list = jieba.cut(txt)
    c = Counter()
    for x in seg_list:
        if len(x) > 2 and x != '\r\n' and u'\u4e00' <= x <= u'\u9fff':
            c[x] += 1
    for (k, v) in c.most_common(100):
        print(k, v))
```

In the code above, we use Counter to count the high-frequency terms after segmentation. Once the counting is completed, you can directly output the results to the command line. Alternatively, you can load the xlwt module to export the data to an Excel spreadsheet.

高频术语	计数	HanLP提取短语
市政协	655	提案办理
全体会议	174	优秀提案
秘书长	152	承办单位
社情民意	72	市政协党组
全国政协	50	重大问题
文史资料	48	界别委员
召集人	47	提案工作
民主党派	39	委员视察
监票人	38	主席会议
经济委员会	37	市政协全体会议
中共上海市委	34	运作程序
意见建议	34	组织实施
民主监督	34	地方委员会
市人大常委会	33	市政协委员
协商会	27	政协上海市委员会
通报会	26	市政协办公厅
人民团体	23	常委会议
港澳台侨委员会	23	政协工作
参政议政	22	界别活动
教科文卫体委员会	17	专门委员会

Fig. 3. High-Frequency Terms Extracted by Jieba Segmentation (Left), Phrases Extracted by HanLP (Right) Note: Only the top 20 items are listed here.

After processing an 80,000-word document, you can see the high-frequency terminology statistics generated by the Python program (on the left side of Fig. 3). On the right side of Fig. 3, HanLP module extracts phrases using a different algorithm, resulting in distinct extraction patterns and ordering compared to Jieba.

After completing terminology extraction, it's common to make some manual adjustments to these terms and then perform pre-translation. The results are typically stored in the form of a data table, as shown in Fig. 4.

Without using Computer-Aided Translation (CAT) tools, it's challenging to accurately present these pre-translated terms to the translators involved in the project within a regular Word interface. They would need to frequently switch between Word and the terminology table, which can significantly impact efficiency. To address this issue, you can also use the Pandas library to read the terminology table and import the source text and translations into a Python dictionary and give translation suggestions within the text.

高频术语	译文
市政协	CPPCC Shanghai Committee
全体会议	plenary sessions
秘书长	secretary-general
社情民意	social trends and popular opinions
全国政协	National Committee of the CPPCC
文史资料	cultural and historical data
召集人	convener
民主党派	democratic parties
监票人	scrutineer
经济委员会	Committee for Economic Affairs
中共上海市委	CPC Shanghai Municipal Committee
意见建议	views and suggestions
民主监督	democratic supervision
市人大常委会	Standing Committee of the SMPC
协商会	consultation meeting
通报会	briefing
人民团体	civil society organizations
港澳台侨委员会	Committee for Liaison with Hong Kong, Macao, Taiwan and Overseas Chinese
参政议政	political participation and discussion
教科文卫体委员会	Committee of Education, Science, Culture, Health and Sports

Fig. 4. High-Frequency Terms After Pre-Translation

(3) Corpus Management

The course project team possesses several gigabytes of Word documents, most of which are saved in the Chinese-English bilingual format shown on the left side of Fig. 5. To fully leverage the value of these language resources, these files need to be converted into a standard Translation Memory Exchange format (TMX file). By utilizing the Python-docx module mentioned earlier, the team successfully transformed these files into a translation memory.

Fig. 5. Bilingual Chinese-English Word Documents (Left) and Transformed TMX Documents (Right)

During the conversion process, to fully retain paragraph information, "paragraph alignment" was chosen as the unit, making the algorithm relatively simple. If you wish to align at the "sentence-paragraph" level, you can consider using PyWin32, which provides handles within the operation system, to call third-party software like ABBYY Aligner.

The applications in the first two stages were limited to writing code in an Integrated Development Environment (IDE), and these codes were not yet full-fledged programs.

To develop a complete program, it should include the design of a User Interface (UI). Creating a user interface in Python is convenient, as it offers Tkinter and PyQT, both of which are capable of effective UI design.

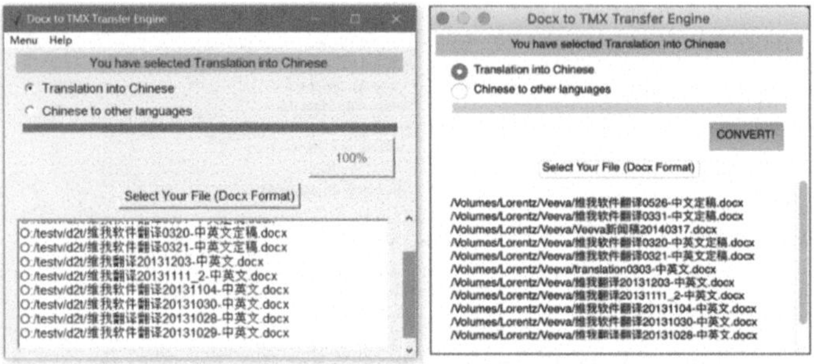

Fig. 6. UI Built for Python Programs Using Tkinter (Left: Windows Environment; Right: macOS Environment)

Figure 6 displays the UI created using Tkinter for the TMX conversion tool mentioned in the previous section. Thanks to Python's cross-platform capabilities and with the assistance of PyInstaller, we can distribute programs with UI to team members working on Windows, macOS, and Linux. Of course, for seamless collaboration with remote team members, we can utilize other Python networking modules and set up cloud platform services to enable the team to access this program from anywhere in the world.

(4) Big Data Application

The construction of parallel corpora is a crucial task for translation teams. For instance, organizing students to create a substantial shared corpus during the teaching process is common [7]. However, traditional manual methods for collecting parallel texts and corpora are inefficient, and individual efforts for building such corpora are not very feasible [20]. In practice, when our team worked on projects involving diplomatic content, we attempted manual collection of bilingual diplomatic documents and used alignment software to generate TMX files. However, due to the need to start and switch between different tools and the considerable time required for alignment operations, a team of five people could only create a corpus of about 20,000 words in an hour. Clearly, this scale of effort can limit the reference value of the corpus.

With the advancement of artificial intelligence and big data technologies, some researchers have started using automation tools to create large-scale corpora, encompassing languages beyond English, including Italian [21], and Arabic [1]. Many of these corpus-building solutions have relied on the BootCaT tool. As mentioned earlier, such software tools come with a learning curve and limited flexibility. Other scholars have begun to incorporate IT techniques into corpus construction. For instance, in the development of the renowned Corpus of Contemporary American English (COCA), the author, Davies [10], used VB.NET in conjunction with relational database technology to collect corpora on a scale of billions of words.

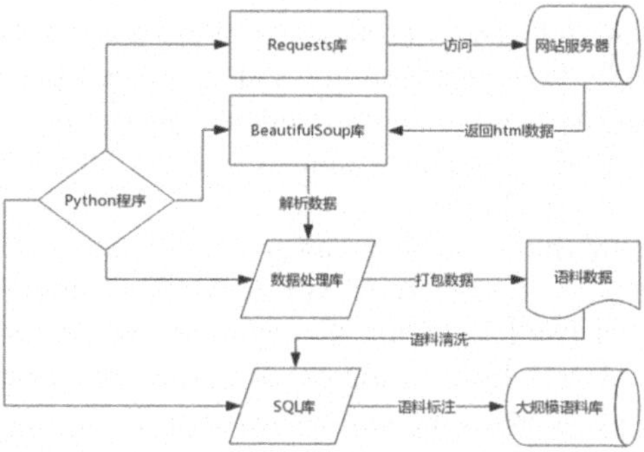

Fig. 7. Basic Program Architecture for Large-Scale Online Corpus Collection Using Python

By combining Python, Requests, and BeautifulSoup (or Xpath), we can design a similar tool for large-scale online corpus retrieval. The Requests library provides convenient HTTP access for users. Once we analyze the structure of web pages and locate the corpus, we can use this library to request data. BeautifulSoup offers users XML language filtering capabilities, allowing us to extract text from HTML web pages without the need for regular expressions [9]. Lastly, with a solid understanding of the structure of TMX files, we can directly use Python to write this content to TMX files. Furthermore, we can employ open-source relational databases like MySQL to build more secure and efficient SQL corpora. The specific workflow is illustrated in Fig. 7.

By employing the methods described above, the program collected 160,000 words of bilingual parallel corpus in just a few minutes, which is much more efficient than manual collection. Additionally, we can still leverage Python's powerful extensibility. The functional modules that have been developed can be combined like building blocks to meet various translation tasks. If we integrate the "Early Corpus Conversion into Translation Memory" module from the previous section at the end of the program, we can quickly convert this large-scale corpus data into the TMX format for use with CAT software. Furthermore, if we add the functionality to batch import online resources at the beginning of the program, the scale of corpus collection can expand to tens of millions or even billions of words.

4.4 Evaluation

The evaluation, also known as course assessment, primarily assesses the improvement in students' translation technology competence. During the design of the evaluation content, the author referred to automation-related issues in similar projects, assessing students' capabilities in analyzing and designing solutions. The evaluation criteria focus on the following aspects:

- Proficiency in the use of translation technology tools.
- The rationality and necessity of invoking translation technology tools.
- Awareness of translation automation.
- Completion of translation projects.

Firstly, in the evaluation phase of proficiency in using translation tools, the level of proficiency in tools like Python programming is included within the scope of the course evaluation as one of the criteria for assessing students' performance. Secondly, students' technical thinking is also assessed. For certain areas where simple methods can be used, over-reliance on large-scale technical tools may reduce efficiency and impact students' actual performance. Furthermore, students' awareness of automation when dealing with large-scale data operations is considered a key evaluation criterion. Lastly, the quality of the translation project itself is within the scope of assessment, as technical tools ultimately serve the goal of delivering high-quality translation projects. At the end of the semester, instructors can create a comprehensive performance distribution chart for students using a system to observe the overall performance of each individual and assign a final evaluation grade.

5 Research Findings and Conclusion

Teaching translation technology for the language service market involves numerous critical aspects, from establishing translation tools to overcoming automation bottlenecks, from handling large-scale data to ensuring customer data security. Python programming tools have proven to be a strong support for these aspects.

From the cases demonstrated in this study, we can see that introducing Python programming into translation technology teaching has several advantages for translation professionals:

(1) Addressing the challenges of existing translation technology, including steep learning curves, high deployment costs, and implicit compliance risks.
(2) Integrating artificial intelligence and big data technologies to achieve functions like Chinese term extraction and large-scale parallel corpus construction.
(3) Python's strong versatility and extensibility can cover the entire translation process, eliminating blind spots in workflow automation.
(4) Transforming the traditional dependence on specific software operations, helping translators shift to applications at the "meta-technical" level, significantly improving work quality and efficiency.

This integration is also highly beneficial for the training of translation talent. Some scholars have pointed out that as society rapidly develops, the demand for translation professionals has evolved from the previous single-language talent to the development of multi-skilled, compound professionals who combine language, technology, management, and market skills [5]. In the past, there may have been biases against students from a more humanities-oriented background, thinking that learning technical skills like programming languages might be challenging for them. However, Python's gentle learning curve and the abundance of learning materials in the age of big data greatly reduce this learning difficulty, making it suitable for students interested in translation technology. During the teaching process, the author also found that, after a single class, students with backgrounds in English and American literature were able to quickly write regular expressions and perfectly resolve tag issues that appeared in language corpora and translation files. After a few practice sessions, they also gradually learned to use dynamic programming to solve algorithm performance issues, such as the Fibonacci sequence summation. The fact is that the task of teaching translation major students a programming language seems daunting at first, with Python's ever decreasing learning curve among students and its rich resources, teaching this powerful meta-technology tool will gain momentum as today's CAT course. And some universities [15] are already working in this direction. Future research involving qualitative and quantitative evaluations of the courses will be carried out to determine how efficient this training approach is.

Acknowledgements. The work was substantially supported by The General Research Project Fund by Shanghai International Studies University.

References

1. Atwell, E.: Using the web to model modern and Qur'anic Arabic. In: McEnery , T. (ed.) Arabic Corpus Linguistics, pp. 100–119. Edinburgh University Press, Edinburgh (2019)
2. Austermühl, F.: Electronic tools for translators. St. Jerome Publishing, Manchester (2001)
3. Cao, D.: Translating law. Multilingual Matters, Clevedon, England (2007)
4. Chai, M.: Reflections on the construction of professional translation teaching: current status, issues, and strategies (对专业翻译教学建构的思考: 现状、问题和对策). East Transl. J. **01**, 15–18 (2010)
5. Chai, M.: Challenges in training translation talents(翻译人才培养所面临的挑战). East Transl. J. **03**, 4–7 (2019)
6. Chesterman, A.: Causality in translator training. Training for the new millennium: pedagogies for translation and interpreting (2005)
7. Colina, S.: Translation teaching: from research to the classroom. McGraw Hill, New York, San Francisco (2003)
8. Cui, Q., Liu, J.: Analysis and implications of language service needs in state-owned enterprises (国有企业语言服务需求调查分析及启示). Chin. Transl. J. **37**(04), 70–76 (2016)
9. Dale, K.: Data visualization with Python and JavaScript. O'Reilly, Beijing (2016)
10. Davies, M.: Multiple voices in the translation classroom: activities, tasks and projects. John Benjamins Publishing (2004)
11. Gile, D.: Basic concepts and models for interpreter and translator training. John Benjamins, Amsterdam/Philadelphia (2009)
12. Hutchins, J., Somers, H.: An introduction to machine translation. Academic Press, Ltd., London (1992)
13. Kiraly, D.: Project-based learning: a case for situated translation. Meta (2005)
14. Melby, A.: Multi-level translation aids in a distributed system. In: Horecký, J. (ed.), Proceedings of COLING 82, pp. 215–220. North Holland Publishing Company (1982)
15. Nitzke, J., Anke, T., Silvia, H.: Training the modern translator–the acquisition of digital competencies through blended learning. Interpret. Transl. Train. **13**(3), 292–306 (2019)
16. Nord, C.: Text type and translation method: an objective approach to translation criticism. Translator **2**(1) (1996)
17. PACTE. First results of a translation competence experiment: 'knowledge of translation' and 'efficacy of the translation process' In: John, K. (ed.) Translator and Interpreter Training. Issues, Methods and Debates, London: Continuum (2008)
18. Wang, H.: Translation technology tutorial. Shanghai Foreign Language Education Press, Shanghai (翻译技术教程) (2017)

19. Wang, H.: Research on terminology management in chinese language service enterprises: problems and measures (中国语言服务企业术语管理调研: 问题与对策). Chin. Transl. **39**(04), 67–72 (2018)
20. Yang, Q.: New trends in translation technology industry: commercialization of terminology databases (翻译技术产业新动向: 术语库商品化). Shanghai Transl. (06), 26–29+93 (2018)
21. Zanettin, F.: Translation-driven corpora: corpus resources for descriptive and applied translation studies. Routledge (2014)
22. Zhou, X.: Research on computer-aided translation collaborative model (计算机辅助翻译协作模式探究). Chin. Transl. **36**(02), 77–80 (2015)
23. Zhu, Y., Chen, J.: Theoretical concept and practical engineering of computer-aided translation teaching platform based on corpora (基于语料库的计算机辅助翻译教学平台的理论构想与工程实践). Comput.-Ass. Foreign Lang. Teach. **04**, 52–57 (2015)
24. Zhu, Z., Luo, H., Wang, C., et al.: Digital transformation and integrated innovation in foreign language education (外语教育数字化转型与融合创新). Comput.-Assist. Foreign Lang. Teaching, **206**(04), 7–17+110 (2022)

A Digitalized Approach to Discourse Production and Reception from the Perspective of Proximization Theory

Chengcheng Pan(✉)

Institute of Corpus Studies and Applications, Shanghai International Studies University, Shanghai, China
0224101596@shisu.edu.cn

Abstract. Previous research on Proximization Theory has mainly focused on the perspective of discourse production. This study attempts to compare the differences between discourse spaces of production and reception, specifically examining the differences in theme distribution in the two spaces, as well as discourse production and reception strategies from the perspective of Proximization Theory. Through thematic analysis and close reading, this study analyzes reports and comments on the incident of "Nuclear Wastewater Discharge from Fukushima Nuclear Power Plant in Japan" on the news aggregation website *Reddit*. The findings are as follows: 1) The themes in the discourse space of reception show significant expansion and exhibit an attitude of resistant reading; 2) The original report text, in order to deconstruct the legitimacy of Japan's wastewater discharge, employs spatial, temporal, and axiological proximization strategies, with spatial proximization being predominant; 3) Readers in the discourse space of reception employ five discourse strategies.

Keywords: Proximization Theory · Discourse Production · Discourse Reception · Discourse Strategies

1 Introduction

Proximization Theory (PT) is a potentially influential theory in the field of Critical Cognitive Linguistics, recently developed by Cap [1–3]. Proximization Theory is a discourse strategy employed by discourse producers to present events, situations, and ideologies that are spatially and temporally distant as imminent and potentially significant threats, causing harm to themselves and their audience [2]. It ultimately aims to provide a legitimizing background for their remarks and actions through forced construal, compelling readers to accept their viewpoints and behaviors.

Proximization Theory is developed based on the concept of "proximize/proximizing" [4], using IDC (inside deictic center) and ODC (outside deictic center) as two basic reference points. It operates from three dimensions: spatial, temporal, and axiological, forming the STA model. This is achieved through noun phrases, verb phrases, tense indicators, and related sentence structures [5]. Specifically, spatial proximization refers to

Z. Kubincová et al. (Eds.): SETE 2023, LNCS 14606, pp. 311–325, 2024.
https://doi.org/10.1007/978-981-97-4243-1_24

the constant approach of entities at the discourse space periphery, eventually surrounding the central entity; temporal proximization involves anticipating conflicts that are not only approaching from past to now but also having a significant impact in the future, requiring immediate response; axiological proximization involves conflicts between the central entity's "self values" and the external entity's "hostile values".

As a relatively new theory in critical cognitive linguistics, Proximization Theory is built on embodied philosophy, centered around the "self", and distinguishes between internal and external items. At the center, the discourse producer's space is marked as "here, now, right, us/self/speaker". The discourse producer then anchors other things around the "self", placing them at the periphery with markers as "there, then/past/future, wrong, them". Finally, through noun phrases, verb phrases, tense indicators, and related sentence structures, entities at the discourse periphery approach the discourse center, creating a sense of oppression and imminent danger for the discourse producer, prompting them to take resistant measures.

2 Literature Review

Currently, research on Proximization Theory involves theoretical introduction [3, 6, 7], empirical applications [8–10], and explorations of empirical methods [11]. Discourse types analyzed using Proximization Theory include political discourse [12], economic and trade discourse [13], environmental discourse [14], medical discourse [11], poverty alleviation discourse [15], so on and so forth.

However, past research has mainly unfolded from the perspective of discourse production, assuming that discourse may impose forced construal on the "ideal reader". There has been less consideration of the actual impact of proximization on the "real reader" from the perspective of discourse reception. In recent years, some scholars have explored from the perspective of discourse reception. For example, Zhang Hui provided theoretical construction for critical cognitive linguistics from the perspective of language perception and reception analysis, pointing out that previous research overlooked the reactions of discourse consumers. He holds the belief that we need to identify psychological representations and complex cognitive processes in language perception and reception, achieve "three identifications", and interpret induced linguistic materials [15]. Wang Zheng, Zhang Hui investigated the differences in proximization discourse strategies in discourse of Chinese poverty alleviation between Western and Chinese media. Subsequently, they examined the perceptual differences of real readers when reading poverty alleviation discourse with or without proximization discourse strategies through a survey questionnaire [16]. Kowalski suggested the simultaneous application of Proximization Theory to both discourse production and reception, forming a comprehensive model for discourse analysis. He also highlighted the challenges faced when applying this theory to empirical investigation of discourse reception [17]. Later, Kowalski applied this comprehensive model to the analysis of news texts and comments, qualitatively examining how discourse receivers use discourse strategies to construct and expand discourse spaces, forming microspaces that approach from the spatial periphery to the spatial center [18].

3 Research Design

3.1 Research Question

This study poses two research questions:

a. In terms of thematic content, how does the discourse space constructed by receivers differ from the discourse space constructed by the producers?
b. Through which discourse strategies do discourse receivers expand the discourse space constructed by the original text in the dimensions of space, time, and axiology?

3.2 Research Data

The research data consists of two parts: the original news texts and their reception data, i.e. the comments below. Both parts of the data are selected from *Reddit*, a U.S. social news aggregation, discussion, and content sharing website. On *Reddit*, users can post and share news or news links, and readers can leave comments; the news content covers various topics, including technology, culture, politics, sports, entertainment, and more. For this study, we focus on environmental discourse, specifically news and comments related to the disposal of Japan's nuclear wastewater. In fact, as a result of the massive earthquake and tsunami in 2011, the core of reactors 1 to 3 at the Fukushima Daiichi Nuclear Power Plant melted down. Following the incident, Tokyo Electric Power Company (TEPCO) has been consistently injecting water into the containment vessels of reactors 1 to 3 to cool the cores and recover contaminated water. As of March 2021, 1.25 million tons of nuclear-contaminated water have been stored, with an additional 140 tons added daily. In order to manage the radioactive pollutants generated post-accident, the Japanese government has implemented various measures, including the utilization of diverse filtration and purification technologies. However, there remain trace amounts of pollutants that cannot be entirely removed. Due to the vast volume of nuclear wastewater generated by the Fukushima nuclear power plant incident, it has surpassed the Japanese government's capacity to handle nuclear wastewater. Consequently, the Japanese government has been contemplating a plan to discharge the nuclear wastewater into the Pacific Ocean in recent years, triggering a wave of international media scrutiny and public discourse.

In particular, the first section involved the collection of nine relevant online news articles from May to July 2023 (Table 1), totaling 5128 tokens. The second section comprises comments located beneath these nine news articles. A total of 1519 comments were initially crawled by applying Python. After manual removal of duplicates and irrelevant comments, 1403 comments remained, amounting to 41557 tokens. The data retrieval was conducted on July 13, 2023.

Table 1. Data on 9 Event-Related Media News Reports

No	News Title	Time of release	Tokens	News Source
1	Opposition leader says Japan should use Fukushima water for drinking if it's safe	2023.5.15	247	https://en.yna.co.kr/view/AEN20230515004300315
2	Plan to release Fukushima nuclear plant water into sea faces local opposition: "The sea is not a garbage dump"	2023.5.31	697	https://www.cbsnews.com/news/fukushima-nuclear-plant-water-plan-release-into-sea-fear-controversy/
3	South Korean shoppers buy up salt before Japan's Fukushima water dump	2023.7.1	452	https://japantoday.com/category/national/south-korea-shoppers-buy-up-salt-before-japan's-fukushima-water-dump
4	China urges Japan to stop ocean discharge of Fukushima treated water	2023.7.4	423	https://english.kyodonews.net/news/2023/07/53b9416ea339-china-urges-japan-to-stop-ocean-discharge-of-fukushima-treated-water.html
5	Fukushima: Anxiety and anger over Japan's nuclear waste water plan	2023.7.5	1359	https://www.bbc.com/news/world-asia-66106162.amp
6	South Koreans protest the planned release of Fukushima wastewater during a visit by the head of IAEA	2023.7.8	710	https://apnews.com/article/south-korea-japan-fukushima-wastewater-iaea-37b42b2d442d15115dae462b48494fd6
7	Japan "strongly" asks Hong Kong not to ban food imports on Fukushima water release	2023.7.12	413	https://www.reuters.com/world/asia-pacific/japan-strongly-asks-hong-kong-not-ban-food-imports-fukushima-water-release-2023-07-12/
8	South Korea's imports of Japanese seafood down over 30% amid Fukushima concerns	2023.7.19	217	https://www.orissapost.com/south-koreas-imports-of-japanese-seafood-down-over-30-amid-fukushima-concerns/
9	Korean experts decry IAEA Fukushima report as "unscientific"	2023.7.19	610	https://english.hani.co.kr/arti/english_edition/e_international/1099203.html

3.3 Research Procedures and Methods

1) Research procedures are outlined as follows:
   a. Collect, crawl, and clean the corpus using Python 3.9;

b. Utilize Python to perform LDA (Latent Dirichlet Allocation) topic modeling on nine news articles and their corresponding readers' comments. This step examines the differences in thematic content between the two discourse spaces, addressing the first research question;
c. Select one news article for in-depth textual analysis. Apply the Proximization Theory to delineate the discourse space constructed by the article from the dimensions of space, time, and axiology. Generate a figure of proximization strategies, preparing for a comparative analysis for the second research question;
d. Under the guidelines of Proximization Theory, closely read all the comments on the selected article, studying discourse strategies employed and categorizing them.

2) Research Methods: Thematic analysis and textual analysis.

4 Data Analysis and Discussion

4.1 Analysis of Thematic Differences in Discourse Spaces of Production and Reception

Notably, the second set of data introduced new topics that either did not appear or had very low weights in the first set. In general, these topics reflected new issues and perspectives in the second set. After summarizing the thematic analysis, the discourse space in the comments expanded to cover four major additional topics, which we will elaborate on shortly.

Additionally, we observed a large number of instances of resistant reading during the dialogue with the original report. Participants engaged in resistant reading simultaneously maintain two discourse worlds: one is the discourse world they have formed in their thoughts, and the other is the discourse world the writer intends to convey [16]. The knowledge expressed in the latter is the knowledge the writer seeks to instill in the reader, hoping for the reader's acceptance. However, readers engaging in resistant reading may reject this knowledge, leading to a resistant reading of the discourse [19]. Resistant reading is based on cognitive perception [20]. Langacker identifies four primary modes of construal: specificity, focusing, prominence, and perspective [20]. Specificity involves concentrating attention on specific details or facts, neglecting other relevant information; Focusing entails concentrating attention on a particular aspect or issue; Prominence emphasizes the importance or significance of certain information or viewpoints; Perspective involves interpreting and understanding information from a specific angle or viewpoint.

We will now provide a brief analysis of the expanded topics and understanding perspectives in the discourse space constructed by readers' comments:

1) Different Perspectives on Safety Issues: Evaluating the safety issue of nuclear energy and its impact on fish and other aquatic life from various viewpoints, as expressed in the following comments:

   C#4:…I wished the general population had a better understanding of what radiation is and the what the risk is and is not. From another article: Tokyo has said levels of tritium—the one isotope that can't be filtered out—will be diluted to below 1/40th of the allowable level for discharge in Japan, and 1/7th the WHO ceiling for drinking water.

C#89: If they do this, they will singlehandedly destroy their fishing population and inadvertently poison themselves since the fish will have traces of radiation.

2) Focusing on Different Forms of Energy: Discussing comparisons and competition between nuclear energy and other forms of energy. For example:

   C#1134: Pollution from coal plants kills more people every day than nuclear power has in its entire history.

   C#1155:... Chernobyl killed about half as many people who die from respiratory illnesses caused by coal plants every single day. Go campaign against coal power.

3) Giving Prominence to Similar Situations in Other Countries: Highlighting the reasons for other countries' attitudes toward the event or comparing wastewater and gas emissions in other nations, for instance:

   C#1214: Both China and South Korea have political reasons to take jabs at Japan, and both countries know that there is little to no actual risks from this release plan.

   C#1266: The amount of tritiated water being released at Fukushima is less than the amount released into the ocean by South Korea's nuclear power plants.

4) Questioning the Government: Expressing doubts about government decisions and transparency, reflecting public concerns about the government's handling of nuclear incidents, for example:

   C#273: I think it's more the dumping part. I don't trust any government ever who said it's safe to dump something. In America these people who say it's safe are bought and paid for, I just assume it's the same everywhere.

   C#396: I don't trust any government ever who said it's safe to dump something. You're in a real pickle then, because most of the experts who know when something is safe to dump or not, work for governments.

In resistant reading, readers may use these cognitive modes of interpretation to selectively accept or reject the knowledge expressed by the author. This resistant reading can be driven by personal beliefs, viewpoints, experiences, and other factors. It reflects individuals' subjective preferences and cognitive tendencies in the process of receiving and perceiving new information.

4.2 Discourse Production from the Proximization Perspective

As introduced in the introduction, the STA model comprises three axes: spatial, temporal, and axiological. In this section, we focus on the fifth news article in our research database. The selected article for this section is titled *"Fukushima: Anxiety and Anger over Japan's Nuclear Waste Water Plan"*, published on the BBC official website on July 5, 2023. The article explores the anxiety and anger triggered by Japan's plan to release treated wastewater from the Fukushima nuclear power plant, both domestically and internationally. See Table 1 for specific information on this article.

Spatial Proximization Framework

The main categories and key items in spatial proximization used in the article are outlined in Table 2. In this text, entities within the IDC camp include local communities and fisheries, China, South Korean citizens, neighboring island nations, international organizations, UN human rights experts, and marine biologists, positioned at the center of the discourse space, perceived as the victims of wastewater discharge and active protesters against it. ODC entities encompass the Japanese government, Fukushima nuclear power plant, Tokyo Electric Power Company, Japanese scientists, the International organization displayed as threats approaching IDC in the spatial dimension. VP is categorized into motion and action, with the former emphasizing on the direction and process and the latter consequences and impacts. In this article, there is a prevalence of VP items related to consequences and impacts, primarily conceptualizing the panic and anger caused by ODC and highlighting the serious consequences, leading to public protests and import bans. These lend legitimacy to the condemnation by the Chinese government and relevant regulatory authorities, suggesting that Japan, regardless of the interests of other countries, insists on discharging into the sea, posing a threat to the IDC. For example:

(1) Beijing has also accused Tokyo of **violating** "international moral and legal obligations", and warned that if it proceeded with the plan, "it must bear all consequences".
(2) Thousands have **attended protests** in Seoul calling for government action, as some shoppers **fearing** food supply disruptions have stockpiled salt and other necessities.

Table 2. Spatial proximization framework and its key items

Categories	Key items
1. Noun phrases (NPs) construed as elements of the IDC	local communities, fishing and seafood industry groups in Japan; China/Beijing; South Korean public; several island nations; consumers; Greenpeace; UN-appointed human rights experts; marine biologists
2. Noun phrases (NPs) construed as elements of the ODC	Japan's government, Tokyo; Fukushima nuclear power plant; TEPCO; Japanese scientists; IAEA; South Korean government; Other nuclear plants in the region
3. Verb phrases (VPs) of motion and directionality construed as markers of movement of ODCs toward the deictic center	affect, violate
4. Verb phrases (VPs) of action construed as markers of impact of ODCs upon IDCs	fear, anger, attend protest, ban, make consumers even more anxious
5. Noun phrases (NPs) denoting abstract concepts construed as anticipations of impact of ODCs upon IDCs	risk
6. Noun phrases (NPs) denoting abstract concepts construed as effects of impact of ODCs upon IDCs	anxiety and anger, concerns, doubt

Temporal Proximization Framework

The main categories and key items in temporal proximization used in the article are outlined in Table 3. The article primarily employs two categories of temporal proximization: the contrastive combination of past tense and present perfect tense and modal verbs. These items are used to indicate that the threat from ODC extends from the past to nowadays and even into the future. Both categories express the impact of harm over different time spans, with the former interpretable as the ongoing and future effects of ODC's past actions, and the latter interpretable as such harm persisting from the present into the future. For example:

(3) But since it **was announced** two years ago, the plan **has been deeply controversial** in Japan with local communities expressing concerns about contamination. Fishing and seafood industry groups in Japan and the wider region **have also voiced concerns** about their livelihoods, as they fear consumers **will avoid** buying seafood.
(4) Critics say Japan **should**, for the time being, keep the treated water in the tanks.
(5) Beijing has also accused Tokyo of violating "international moral and legal obligations", and warned that if it proceeded with the plan, "it **must** bear all consequences".

Verbs inherently possess temporal attributes [21]. In example (3), from "was announced" to "has been controversial", "have also voiced", and further to "will avoid", the understanding is that the controversy and condemnation of the plan began two years ago. This threat and the concerns of various parties have persisted from the past to the present and extend to the fear of future seafood purchases. Additionally, the modal verbs "should" and "must" convey a strong tone, sternly informing Japan of the correct course of action, warning Japan to bear the consequences of its actions, thus deconstructing the legitimacy of ODC behavior. Temporal proximization can be viewed as a symbolic "compression" on the timeline.

Table 3. Temporal proximization framework and its key items

Categories	Key items
1. A combination of past tense and present perfect tense, the threat extending from the past into the future	did+have done+will do
2. Modal verbs indicating the impact of ODC from the present into the future	should, would, must

Axiological Proximization Framework

Axiological proximization primarily focuses on the ideological conflict between IDC and ODC. The categories and key items are outlined in Table 4. Within the axiological proximization, positive value terms such as "safety" and "standard" indicate that the IDC group emphasizes emission standards and the safety of marine fisheries. Simultaneously, terms like "doubt" "nonsense" "contamination disaster" are interpreted as negative values associated with ODC, placing them within an antagonistic discourse space. Another discursive item is the linear construction, interpreted as ODC's ideology progressively entering IDC's territory in an earnest manner. Deconstructing the legitimacy of the actions and ideology of being "selfish and disregarding the safety of others", this enhances the legitimacy of punishing and defending against potential harm from ODC.

Table 4. Axiological proximization framework and its key items

Categories	Key items
Noun phrases (NPs) expressing abstract notions conceptualized as values of IDCs	safety, standard
Noun phrases (NPs) expressing abstract notions conceptualized as values of ODCs	doubt, nonsense, concerns, serious pollution, contamination disaster, food supply disruptions
Linear discourse sequences	Since the disaster, power plant company Tepco has been pumping in water to cool down the Fukushima nuclear reactors' fuel rods. This means every day the plant produces contaminated water…It wants to gradually release this water into the Pacific Ocean over the next 30 years…

Based on the proximization theory, we attempted to construct a discourse space model with the side opposing the sea discharge as the IDC (Fig. 1). In the figure, the central point is the "trinity": spatially, it represents "local communities, fishing and seafood industry groups, China, South Korea, consumers, etc."; temporally, it means "now"; axiologically, it emphasizes safety and standards. The discourse space model is constructed around the central point, representing the discourse space through three main axes—the left-right axis (temporal axis from the past to the present), the front axis (axiological axis), and the upper axis (spatial axis). The model centers on the central point, grounded in embodied experience, and constructs a proximization model from a distant-to-imminent perspective. The dashed spherical shape in the figure represents the IDC space, while the rectangular prism symbolizes the oppressive discourse space constructed by the ODC.

At the spatial proximization level, since ODC's threat began in the past, it starts at the position where the T1 axis intersects with the S axis in the upper left of the model. ODC builds distance spatially, progressively approaching and signifying ODC's intrusion and impact on IDC, provoking IDC. In terms of temporal proximization, since the Fukushima nuclear power plant leakage in 2011, over a million tons of processed nuclear waste has already accumulated. Currently, Japan plans for sea discharge (as of the completion of this study, Japan is planning sea discharge but has not officially done so), with the intention to continue this action for the next 30 years. The threat extends from the past to the present and into the future. The resulting destruction has a sustained impact on the present and future, as indicated by the usage of past tense, present perfect tense, and future tense. Regarding axiological proximization, the corresponding axiological expressions for ODC are "nonsense", "disaster", "disruption", etc. The discourse producer constructs the discourse space from three dimensions, providing legal justification for the representatives of IDC to resist, revolt, and combat ODC.

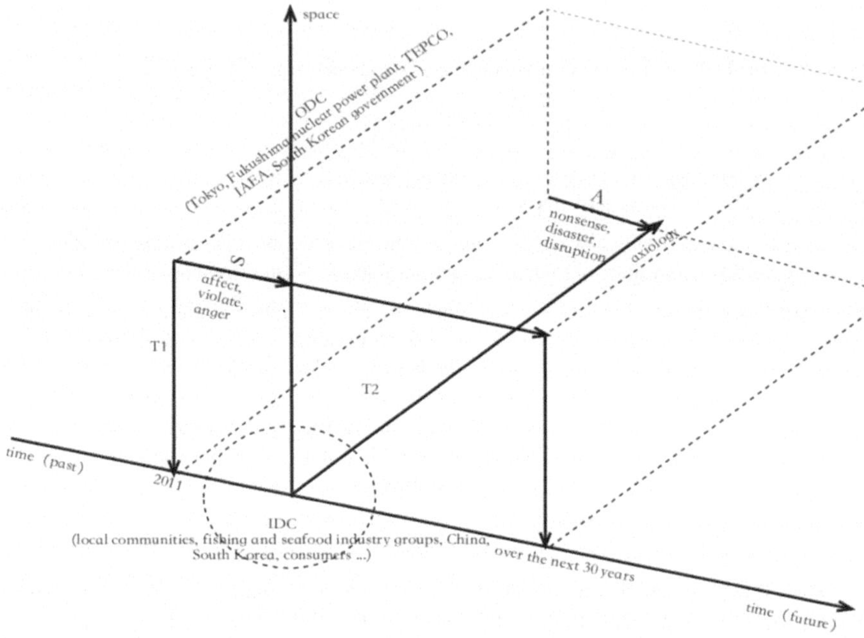

Fig. 1. Proximization model based on discourse production

4.3 Discourse Strategies in the Reception Space

Categorization

Categorization, where entities are classified into "us IDC" and "them ODC" based on attributes, characteristics, or viewpoints, operates within the spatial dimension. However, this process doesn't end once readers identify the positions of IDC and ODC constructed in the news text. Through the analysis of subsequent comments, this study find that once readers become familiar with the character roles presented in the news report, they may seek equivalent ODC or IDC roles in their self-perceived cognitive world—characters who have already established a certain image or status in the reader's discourse space. This process notably demonstrates reader preferences (and aversions). Let's examine the following comment:

C#26: On top of this, ***The USA*** already permission to dump the water. Japan has full authority to do this.

We can observe how the comment expands the categories of "us IDC" and "them ODC". The original news report did not mention the USA, but in comment C#26, the reader mentions that the USA has already allowed Japan to discharge nuclear wastewater and believes that Japan has the authority to do so. In this context, the USA is constructed as an expanded "them ODC" in the discourse space of the original text, specifically, a party supporting Japan's discharge of nuclear wastewater.

Readers, based on their constructed cognitive world, expand the scope of IDC and ODC by categorizing different countries or political entities. This expansion helps readers understand and evaluate events within their own cognitive framework, associating them with familiar countries or political entities. This comment falls into the category of the extended topic 3 in Sect. 4.1, also reflecting "resistant reading" mentioned above.

Historical Analogies

Historical analogies involve comparing and contrasting current situations, events, or issues with similar historical occurrences to support, explain, or evaluate specific viewpoints or arguments. It is a commonly used rhetorical device to enhance persuasiveness in understanding and assessing the current situation. Historical analogies can proximize viewpoints or perform persuasive, evaluative, historical contextualizing, predictive, resonant, and challenging functions, enriching the discourse space through temporal, spatial, and axiological dimensions. Let's examine a relevant example from a reader's comment:

C#64: And to those replying: don't forget that ***Chernobyl was "perfectly safe" until it melted down, water at Flint was "safe to drink" until folks started dying.***

The comment refers to the Chernobyl nuclear disaster in 1986, a severe nuclear accident that occurred at the Chernobyl Nuclear Power Plant in the Soviet Union (now Ukraine). The explosion of a reactor released a large amount of radioactive material, causing widespread environmental contamination and casualties. It is one of the most severe nuclear disasters to date. Another analogical event mentioned is the Flint water crisis, which occurred in Flint, Michigan, USA, from 2014 to 2015. The city's government, aiming to cut costs, switched its water supply from the nearby Flint River to Detroit's water supply system. Due to inadequate treatment of lead contamination in the water source, lead levels increased, posing a serious threat to residents' health. This crisis garnered public attention and protests, becoming a significant warning event regarding water resource management and government accountability.

This comment implicitly draws attention to past (temporal), distant (spatial), and catastrophic (axiological) events as warnings for the current Japanese water discharge. Events with established images in the reader's discourse space are incorporated, connecting them to the current event. This comment aligns with the expanded topic 4.

Emotional Reaction

Emotional reaction operates within the axiological dimension. It is a discourse strategy used to respond to others' viewpoints, comments, emotions, or feelings, aiming to establish an emotional connection and resonance. It involves expressing understanding, concern, and sharing of others' emotions to enhance the effectiveness of communication. Emotional reaction can manifest as positive responses, such as encouragement, support, and praise, or negative responses, such as empathy, consolation, and comfort. For instance:

C#6: And it's ***fine***. Stop ***scaremongering***.

C#28: I was going to say this. Stop the ***scare tactic***. Godzilla will only happen if we all focus our intentions on making him real. Manifesting Godzilla by 2030, that's the goal.

In C#6, the expressions "fine" and "stop scaremongering" suggest that the commenter holds a relatively relaxed and optimistic attitude. They believe that concerns about releasing nuclear wastewater from the Fukushima nuclear power plant into the ocean are exaggerated or sensationalized. In C#28, the commenter seems to respond in a sarcastic or exaggerated manner. They use the term "scare tactic" to imply skepticism and mention the goal of "Manifesting Godzilla by 2030" in a humorous and exaggerated way to lighten the atmosphere of concern.

Quoting Authorities

In employing the strategy of quoting authorities, discourse practice aligns with the spatial (third-party) and axiological (objective) dimensions, seeking proximity through referencing viewpoints and research findings from experts, authoritative figures, or reliable sources. By citing authorities, resonance is established within the framework of axiological judgments. When authoritative figures endorse a particular standpoint, it can be interconnected with one's own values, enhancing persuasive impact. This approach leverages the recognition of authority to convey to the readers that one's position is shared with credible figures, emphasizing the moral legitimacy and acceptability of one's arguments. Consider the following comment:

C#43:……TEPCO says that the resulting concentration of tritium is around 1,500 becquerels (a measure of the radioactivity of a substance) per litre—around one-seventh of the ***World Health Organization's guidelines*** for tritium in drinking water. The company suggests that the concentration of tritium will drop to background ocean levels within a few kilometres of the discharge site…. and this will reduce further with the seawater dilution that takes place before the water is discharged.

Comment #43, the mention of the tritium concentration in the discharged nuclear wastewater, approximately 1500 becquerels per liter, is highlighted. This concentration is about one-seventh of the threshold for tritium in drinking water set by the World Health Organization. By referencing standards from an international authoritative organization, the position supporting the discharge into the ocean is substantiated.

Relative Argumentation

The method of relative argumentation is a discourse strategy that approaches the IDC through the dimensions of space, time, and axiology. It involves contrasting and comparing one's own argument with the points raised by the opposing side to demonstrate the reasonability or superiority of one's own position. Through comparative analysis, this method highlights the rationality and advantages of one's own standpoint, showcasing a deep understanding of the issue and logical reasoning skills.

C#35: You do realize your tap water would be considered safe for drinking if ***it contained higher levels of radiation*** than what they plan to release? And it may just as well ***be more radioactive***. Each hour you spend in an airplane at 30,000 feet exposes you to ***as much radiation as spending 20 min in Fukushima exclusion zone***. Which is about the same you got for each ***30 bananas you ate*** over your lifetime. So, if apart from it being sea water.. its WELL below the safety limits for DRINKING WATER. Let alone to be dumped into the open and be even further diluted to safe levels.

C#35 engages in relative argumentation by contrasting the viewpoints presented in the news report. The comment highlights that the radiation present in tap water consumed daily is comparable. Additionally, it provides a comparison stating that the radiation absorbed during one hour at 30,000 feet in an airplane is equivalent to spending 20 min in the exclusion zone of the Fukushima nuclear disaster. The comment further notes that this radiation level is akin to the radiation absorbed by an individual consuming 30 bananas. The perspective emphasized in this comment is that the radiation level of Fukushima's nuclear wastewater is relatively low. Through relative argumentation, commentators attempt to support the stance of releasing Fukushima's nuclear wastewater into the ocean by comparing it to other sources of radiation in daily (temporal dimension) events (spacial dimension), such as drinking water at home, eating bananas, and flying on an airplane and discussing radiation levels and safety standards (axiological dimension). They underscore the relatively low radiation levels of Fukushima's nuclear wastewater, asserting that such discharge is safe.

5 Conclusion

Proximization Theory, analyzed from a cognitive-pragmatic perspective, dissects the representational strategies employed in the legitimacy of discourse. While previous studies have predominantly applied this theory to analyze discourse production, this research extends the application of the theory to discourse reception, contrasting the thematic and discursive strategy differences between discourse production and reception.

The study reveals that, thematically, discourse space of reception predominantly expand in four aspects: varying perspectives on safety issues, focusing on different forms of energy, giving prominence to similar situations in other countries, and questioning the government. In terms of content, the space exhibits a resistant reading attitude. In discourse production, spatial proximization is particularly evident, with rich categories and key items. In discourse reception, readers employ such discourse strategies as categorization, historical analogies, emotional responses, referencing authority, and relative argumentation.

The data for this study was collected from an American social news aggregation website, representative of emerging digital platforms that are reshaping discourse behavior and communication interaction. Future research could further explore the multimodal intertextuality of discourse production and reception on such platforms, providing a broader and more advanced perspective and methodology for discourse studies.

Acknowledgements. The work was substantially supported by Postgraduate Research & Innovation Program of Institute of Corpus Studies and Applications, Shanghai International Studies University.

Disclosure Statement. No potential conflict of interest was reported by the author.

References

1. Cap, P.: Towards the proximization model of the analysis of legitimization in political discourse. J. Pragmat. **40**(1), 17–41 (2008)
2. Cap, P.: Proximization: the pragmatics of symbolic distance crossing. John Benjamins, Amsterdam (2013)
3. Cap, P.: Discourse studies: between social constructionism and linguistics. A critical overview. Top. Linguist. **20**(2), 1–16 (2019)
4. Chilton, P.: Analyzing political discourse: theory and practice. Routledge, London (2004)
5. Zhang, H., Zhang, T.W.: Critical cognitive linguistics (批评认知语言学). Foreign Language Teaching and Research Press, Beijing (2022)
6. Wu, J.G., Lin, J.R., Li, Y.: A new method to critical discourse analysis - proximization (批评性话语分析的新方法——趋近化理论). J. Foreign Lang. **39**(05), 75–82 (2016)
7. Zhang, H., Yang, Y.Q.: Critical cognitive linguistics: theoretical foundations and its current research (批评认知语言学:理论基础与研究现状). Foreign Lang. Educ. **40**(03), 1–11 (2019)
8. Yan, B., Zhang, H.: A Critical Cognitive Analysis of China-US Trade War Discourses—from the Perspective of Proximization Theory (基于中美贸易战话语的批评认知语言学研究——趋近化理论的视角). Foreign Lang. Res. **35**(06), 16–22 (2018)
9. Wu, J.G., Niu, Z.J.: Analyzing legitimization in political discourse from the perspective of proximization theory: a case study of trump's immigration policy (趋近化理论视域下的政治话语合法化分析——以特朗普的移民政策为例). Foreign Lang. China **15**(06), 48–53 (2018)
10. Guo, R.T., Pan, Y.Y.: A study on the proximization of institutional anti-epidemic discourse: taking scripts of American CDC's telebriefings on COVID-19 as examples (抗疫机构话语的趋近化研究——以美国CDC的COVID-19电讯简报会文本为例). J. Zhejiang Int. Stud. Univ. **02**, 1–10 (2020)
11. Zhang, Y.M., Zhang, H.: Critical cognitive analysis of public health emergency discourse - a case study of chinese and foreign reports of 2018 vaccine scandal (突发公共卫生事件话语的批评认知语言学分析——2018"疫苗事件"中外媒体报道的个案研究). J. PLA Univ. Foreign Lang. **43**(06), 73–81+158 (2020)
12. Zhang, H., Yan, B.: A critical cognitive linguistic analysis of political conflict discourses: a case study based on discourses of syrian war (政治冲突话语的批评认知语言学研究——基于叙利亚战争话语的个案研究). Foreign Lang. Their Teach. (04), 14–27+146 (2019)
13. Yan, B., Zhang, H.: A critical cognitive analysis of china-us trade war discourse—from the perspective of proximization theory (基于中美贸易战话语的批评认知语言学研究——趋近化理论的视角). Foreign Lang. Res. **35**(06), 16–22 (2018)
14. Zhang, H., Lin, Z.J., Dong, X.M.: Study on ecological discourse in chinese and american climate change news reports from the perspective of proximization theory (中美气候变化新闻报道中生态话语的趋近化研究). J. Xi'an Int. Stud. Univ. **29**(01), 35–40+128 (2021)
15. Wang, Z., Zhang, H.: A critical cognitive linguistic study of chinese poverty alleviation discourses in chinese and western media from the perspective of triangulation (三角互证视域下中西媒体中国扶贫话语的批评认知语言学研究). Foreign Lang. Educ. **43**(06), 15–21 (2022)
16. Zhang, H.: Critical cognitive linguistics: an analytical perspectives from language comprehension and reception—revisiting the theoretical construction of critical cognitive linguistics (批评认知语言学: 语言理解与接受的分析视角———再论批评认知语言学的理论建构). Foreign Lang. Their Teach (03), 31–43+147–148 (2021)
17. Kowalski, G.: Proximization as reception. Bulletin of the Transilvania University of Braşov Series VII: Social Sciences. Law **11**(60), 1 (2018)

18. Kowalski, G.: Proximization and dialogue in internet news texts and comments. Lang. Dial.. **12**(2), 218–244 (2022)
19. Browse, S.: Cognitive rhetoric. John Benjamins, Amsterdam (2018)
20. Langacker, R.: Cognitive grammar: a basic introduction. Oxford University Press, Oxford (2008)
21. Wang, W.B., He, Q.Q.: An analysis of English "Be" and Chinese Shi/You/Zai (论英语"be"与汉语"是/有/在"). J. Foreign Lang. **37**(05), 2–10 (2014)

Research on the Teaching Model Design and Application of Corpus-Based Curriculum Group in Micro-translation Major

Caihong Han[1,2(✉)]

[1] School of Foreign Languages, Tongji University, Shanghai, China
hancaihong@163.com
[2] Zhengzhou University of Science and Technology, Zhengzhou, China

Abstract. Based on the practice of translation teaching in private colleges and universities, this research summarizes the research on corpus translation and translation research conducted by domestic and foreign scholars, and combines the application-oriented translation of private colleges and universities with the orientation of training goals, curriculum group design, teaching content selection, and implementation path planning so as to propose a new corpus-based micro-course teaching model. The results of teaching practice show that the new teaching mode is helpful to optimize the professional development teaching ecological environment of student translators, improve their English-Chinese bilingual expression level, diversify their learning methods, and significantly improve their sustainable and autonomous learning ability. In view of this, translation teaching in the construction of micro-translation major should further enrich corpus teaching resources and dynamically track students' use of corpus; translation teachers need to continuously improve corpus use technology, improve interdisciplinary ability, and adapt to the teaching reform of micro-translation major under the new situation needs.

Keywords: Corpus · translating curriculum group · micro-translation major

1 Introduction

With the rapid development of computer network technology, the use of corpora to empower foreign language education and teaching has become increasingly sophisticated. Corpus has the advantages of large corpus size, authentic examples, convenient retrieval, and accurate results. In recent years, corpus-based translation teaching has attracted the attention of frontline teachers due to its significant advantages such as electronic text, intuitive learning, diversified analysis, and scientific conclusions. From early monolingual corpora to bilingual corpora, from comparable corpora to parallel corpora, student translation archives, translation corpora, interpretation corpora, etc. (Kaibao 2011), and then to the "Translator Corpus" (Zhengting et al. 2021), the types of corpora and their teaching applications are becoming increasingly widespread.

Z. Kubincová et al. (Eds.): SETE 2023, LNCS 14606, pp. 326–335, 2024.
https://doi.org/10.1007/978-981-97-4243-1_25

Previous studies have mostly relied on a single type of corpus to teach a certain translation course, with less emphasis on the construction of micro translation majors. By combining multiple types of corpora and integrating different types of corpora into the micro translation course system, it can not only innovate educational models and teaching methods, but also to some extent make up for the limitations of traditional talent cultivation and teaching models, create an ecosystem of translation course teaching based on the professional literacy and abilities of student translators, empowering teachers and students with technical awareness and autonomy in the process of translation practice.

2 Teaching Model Design of Corpus-Based Curriculum Group in Micro-translation Major

2.1 Construction Plan for Course Group of Micro-translation Major

The corpus-based curriculum system for micro-translation major is mainly based on the development concept of "English + micro-major + humanistic literacy", promoting the transformation of educational content, leveraging the advantages of private universities, and collaborating with industries and enterprises to build a micro major with 4 credits of workplace general courses, 4 credits of multilingual courses, and 8 credits of business translation courses. With the National Talent Examination and Shanghai Interpretation Examination as vocational qualifications, it provides internship and employment opportunities for outstanding students, form a complete system of "teaching + assessment + practice + employment" and a translation course group based on the translator's business translation position: Translation Theory and Practice (4 credits) → Business Translation (2 credits) → Business Interpretation (2 credits), as shown in Table 1.

2.2 Compilation of Corpus Resources Based on Course Group Construction

Given that the micro business translation course group is composed of three interrelated courses, it is necessary to select suitable corpus resources based on the course objectives. At present, students participating in course practice can utilize three types of corpus resources, mainly including domestic and foreign free corpora, teacher-built corpora, and collected student translation corpora.

Free Monolingual and Parallel Corpora Both Domestically and Internationally. These corpora can provide authentic dynamic contexts for translation teaching and research. Monolingual corpora mainly include BNC corpus, COCA corpus, CQP web online corpus from Beijing International Studies University, BCC Chinese corpus from Beijing Language and Culture University, CCL corpus from Beijing University, Modern Chinese Universal Balanced Corpus from the National Language Commission, Ancient Chinese corpus, etc. Free parallel corpora available include the Chinese English Bilingual Online of Beijing International Studies University, the Shakespeare Drama English Chinese Parallel Corpus of Shanghai International Studies University, the Chinese English Parallel Corpus World of Shaoxing University of Arts and Sciences, and the Medical English Chinese Bilingual Parallel Corpus developed by Southern Medical University.

Table 1. Teaching model design of course group in micro translation major

Curriculum Group	Class Hours and Credits	Course Description
Corpus+ *Translation Theory and Practice Course*	64 h/4 credits	The corpus based "Translation Theory and Practice" course is an extension of data-driven teaching, aimed at strengthening students' technical awareness and self-learning ability in translation practice. Integrating descriptive methods into corpus translation teaching can not only provide students with the opportunity to observe language usage rules, but also help them understand the essence of translation activities
Corpus+ *Business Translation Course*	32 h/2 credits	The corpus based "Business Translation" course focuses on a practical platform for digital driven student translator professionalization. Based on an understanding of translation theory, students can master typical types of written communication tasks, writing points and methods, commonly used sentence structures, and classic cases in the workplace
Corpus+ *Business Interpretation Course*	32 h/2 credits	The corpus based "Business Translation" course focuses on a practical platform for digital driven student translator professionalization in interpreting. Based on an understanding of interpreting theory, students can master typical types of oral communication tasks, communication points and methods, commonly used expressions, and classic cases in the workplace
Totel	128 h/8 credits	

A Self-built Chinese English Parallel Corpus. The author has self-built a Chinese English parallel corpus of "Business Translation Classroom Teaching Record" and "Practical Interpretation Classroom Teaching Record". The annotation methods mainly involve professional terminology knowledge annotation, part of speech annotation, long and difficult sentence annotation, discourse theme annotation, and skill annotation. Skill annotation includes subject selection, correspondence, alliterative rhetoric, tense awareness, positive and negative awareness, stylistic awareness, semantic logic, discourse markers, anaphoric coherence, temporal coherence, etc., in order to enhance the applicability of parallel corpora in translation teaching. Students can improve their bilingual translation abilities based on a large amount of authentic language materials.

A Self-built Student Translation Corpus. Mainly by collecting electronic versions of students' after-school translation assignments, establishing a monolingual and parallel corpus of student translations, providing reference translations for students to compare and check, and cultivating their self-learning ability. Considering the actual demand of the translation market, these translation materials do not lean towards literary works, but rather focus on applied texts. In addition, relevant materials such as TEM-4 and TIME-8, CATTI, *Shanghai Interpretation Qualification Examination*, and postgraduate entrance examination were selected for training. On the one hand, a student translation corpus helps teachers use quantitative statistical methods to compare students' translation practices horizontally and vertically, identify common translation problems among students, and conduct a comprehensive, systematic, and objective evaluation of students' translations. On the other hand, students can refer to the translation on their own to discover their own shortcomings and improve their translation skills.

3 Teaching Model Implementation of Corpus -Based Translation Course Group

The corpus-based translation course group teaching can follow the following steps: corpus presentation → students browsing corpus → students summarizing, observing, and thinking → pretest and posttest → teachers and students discussing translation strategies together. Corpus can be used throughout the three stages of translation course group teaching: pre class preparation, in class learning, and post class practice.

3.1 Preparation Before Class

Students can use the free domestic foreign language corpus to learn about the application modules of the corpus, as well as the pragmatic features and common collocations of related content in advance. For example, students can learn the translator's handling of an important vocabulary or special sentence pattern through parallel corpora before class, use English corpora to understand the usage of English vocabulary in real contexts, or use Chinese corpora to verify their native language intuition and terminology accuracy.

3.2 Learning in Class

A teacher led, student-centered, and teacher-student interactive and cooperative classroom teaching model can be adopted. Firstly, teachers present representative teaching materials through monolingual or parallel corpora, guiding students to observe and establish a cognitive correlation between form meaning internalization; Then, through specific examples and annotations, organize students to discuss the language features, translation skills, etc. of relevant content in groups, and select one or two groups of students for classroom presentation; Next, the teacher demonstrates the use of various corpora, demonstrating how to use modules such as word frequency, collocation, and index lines to examine the collocation patterns, semantic tendencies, and semantic prosody of a certain word in a given text; Finally, arrange a small amount of classroom exercises to help students consolidate their knowledge points and familiarize themselves with corpus usage skills.

3.3 Practice After Class

Teachers use corpus resources to design after-school exercises. When students are translating, they can use translation memory software to improve translation quality and efficiency. After submitting the homework, students can see the reference answers and compare them with their own translations to analyze the gaps and shortcomings. Teachers can use tools such as Wordsmith and Para Conc to evaluate student translations, such as word meaning selection, idiomatic collocations, and grammatical structures, to identify common features in student translations and improve the efficiency of teacher homework correction.

4 Teaching Model Effective Evaluation of Corpus-Based Translation Curriculum Group

4.1 Test Subjects

The subjects of this study are third year undergraduate students majoring in translation from a certain university, with 30 students in each class. Class 1 is the experimental class, and Class 2 is the control class. From September to December 2021, pre testing, corpus assisted translation course group teaching, post testing, and questionnaire surveys were conducted for the experimental class. At the same time and under the same testing conditions, the control class also conducted pretest and posttest activities, aiming to form an objective comparison with the experimental class.

4.2 Homogeneity Testing of Experimental and Control Classes

In order to demonstrate the homogeneity of translation proficiency between the experimental class and the control class, both classes of students underwent a pretest. The research group conducted statistical analysis on the pretest results. The pretest for the experimental and control classes is scheduled for the first week of teaching, with the content of translating paragraphs into Chinese and translating them into English, as well as translating them into Chinese visually. The duration is 40 min, and the location is in the language laboratory. Students can use various resources such as the internet and dictionaries. The evaluation is based on the analytical scoring rules for learners' Chinese English translation proposed by Wang Jinquan & Wen Qiufang (2009), which combine semantic content scoring and language form scoring for evaluation. To ensure the objectivity and impartiality of the evaluation, two other translation teachers were invited to rate the translation content of the experimental class and the control class. The author analyzed the pretest data using SPSS 22.0 software, and the statistical results showed that the two teachers had good reliability in scoring the semantic and language form dimensions of the experimental and control classes. Moreover, both the experimental and control classes showed inconsistent semantic and language form scores in the pretest, indicating that students find it difficult to balance semantic accuracy and language form issues in the translation process. Overall, the translation proficiency of the subjects showed good homogeneity ($p > 0.05$).

4.3 Comparative Analysis of Pre-test and Post Test Scores Between Experimental and Control Classes

From weeks 2–16, students in the experimental class will receive systematic training on the use of various types of corpora. The teaching method will balance classroom teaching and practice, and focus on post class consolidation exercises. The posttest content for week 17 is to translate paragraphs of equal difficulty into Chinese and English. Before conducting the posttest activity, the teacher inspected the experimental class students' ability to use the corpus, ensuring that they have mastered the skills of using the corpus, and asked them to take time to practice and consolidate it specifically. In the post test, the reliability of the raters was 0.871 and 0.808, respectively, indicating that the two teachers had good scoring reliability. Paired sample t-tests were conducted on the pre and post test scores of the experimental class, and it was found (as shown in Table 2) that there were significant differences in the semantic and linguistic form scores of the experimental class ($p = 0.000 < 0.05$), indicating that the corpus-based translation course group teaching model helps to enhance teaching effectiveness.

Table 2. Paired sample T-test for pre and post test scores in the experimental class

		Mean value	Standard deviation	Standard error of the mean	95% confidence interval of difference		t	df	Sig
					Minimum	Maximum			
Group1	Semantic score	3.52	2.12	.42	2.64	4.39	8.29	28	.000
Group2	Language Form Score	2.00	1.87	.37	1.23	2.77	5.35	28	.000

The control class still adopts the traditional classroom teaching mode and does not use corpora for translation teaching. They also participated in the post test in week 17. In the post test, the reliability of the two raters was 0.863 and 0.917, respectively, indicating good consistency in their ratings. Paired sample t-test found see Table 3) that there was no significant difference in the semantic score and language form score of the control class (p-values greater than 0.05), indicating that the traditional classroom teaching mode did not significantly improve the semantic and language form teaching effect of translation.

Table 3. Paired sample T-test for pre and post test scores in the control class

		Mean value	Standard deviation	Standard error of the mean	95% confidence interval of difference		t	df	Sig
					Minimum	Maximum			
Group1	Semantic score	.40	6.29	1.26	−2.20	3.00	_	28	.0754
Group2	Language Form score	1.24	3.47	.69	−.19	2.67	1.78	28	.086

Statistical analysis was conducted on the semantic and language form scores of the experimental and control classes in the post test (see Table 4). It was found that the semantic and language form scores of the experimental class were higher than those of the control class in the post test, and the semantic and language form scores of the experimental class were closer to those of the control class. The average semantic score of the control class in the post test decreased slightly to 77.21, while the average language form score decreased to78.06. Relatively speaking, the semantic scores of the control class showed a greater degree of dispersion, indicating that there is a more significant differentiation in students' cognition, understanding, and transmission of semantic information under traditional classroom teaching models.

Table 4. Grouping statistics of semantic and language form scores in the experimental and control classes after post-test

		Mean Value	N	Standard deviation	Standard error of the mean
Semantic score	Group-E	80.76	30	3.36	.63
	Group-C	77.21	30	5.02	.63
Language Form Score	Group-E	81.04	30	3.33	.53
	Group-C	78.06	30	3.81	.64

To further compare the teaching effectiveness of the experimental class and the control class, an independent sample t-test was conducted on the scores of the two classes. The results showed (as shown in Table 5) that there was a significant difference in semantic and linguistic form scores between the experimental class and the control class in the post test (p-values were both less than 0.05). It can be seen that compared to traditional classroom teaching models, the corpus-based translation course group teaching model is not only conducive to helping students grasp semantic information, convey semantic content and main semantic points, improve the "faithfulness" of students' translation expression, but also helps to optimize the expression form of the translation, improve the accuracy and appropriateness of students' target language expression to a certain extent.

Table 5. Independent sample t-test before and after testing in experimental and control classes

		Levene test for variance equation		T-test for the mean equation						
		F	Sig	t	df	Sig (Bilateral)	Mean difference	Standard error of the mean	95% confidence interval of difference	
									Min	Max
Semantic score	Assuming equal variance	8.94	.004	3.01	48	.004	3.64	1.21	1.21	6.07
	Assuming variance is not related	–	–	3.01	41.94	.004	3.64	1.21	1.19	6.08
Language Form Score	Assuming equal variance	1.339	.253	2.60	48	.012	2.64	1.01	.60	4.69
	Assuming variance is not related	–	–	2.59	45.81	.013	2.64	1.02	.59	4.69

4.4 Questionnaire Survey Results

After the post test, students in the experimental class are required to fill out a paper questionnaire, which is required to be completed within 10 min. The types of questions include multiple-choice questions, multiple-choice questions, open-ended questions, etc. The questionnaire content includes the advantages and disadvantages of corpus assisted translation course group practice, difficulties in corpus usage, self-evaluation of translations assisted by corpus, whether the corpus is worth recommending, and overall evaluation of corpus usage.

From the survey results, it can be seen that the main advantages of the corpus assisted translation course group teaching model are as follows: ① more than 62% of students believe that using a corpus can make the translated language more pure, especially in terms of vocabulary matching, difficult word processing, word context determination, synonym discrimination, etc.; ② about 45% of students believe that corpora can help reduce translation errors, eliminate word creation issues, and improve translation quality; ③ about 19% of students believe that corpus assisted translation course groups help coordinate the gradual progress between courses within the course group, making it easier to motivate themselves; ④ about 10% of students believe that corpora can to some extent increase translators' confidence. Other advantages include helping translators understand the original text, understanding cultural differences between English and Chinese, improving translation speed, translators' English proficiency, and the accuracy of Chinese understanding. The main drawbacks of corpus assisted translation include: ① the complexity of corpus retrieval technology, the time required for translators to determine the optimal combination, and the longer time required for translators to obtain useful information; ② the main difficulties of corpus assisted translation include: unfamiliar vocabulary in index rose, incomplete sentences, too few sentences, too many sentences, etc., which can lead to difficulties in using the corpus, and difficulties in analyzing indexes or collocations; ③ the slow internet speed in schools affects the use of corpora, etc.

In summary, the teaching model of corpus-based translation courses has both advantages and disadvantages, but the advantages outweigh the disadvantages. After a semester of corpus-based translation course group teaching practice, most students in the experimental class can persist in using corpora to carry out translation practice after the course ends. In translation practice, participants prefer parallel corpora, followed by monolingual corpora, comparable corpora, etc. Some corpus beginners believe that corpus retrieval techniques are complex and time-consuming to obtain information. However, once proficient in using them, corpus can effectively improve translation quality and efficiency.

5 Conclusion and Enlightenment

This study integrates and utilizes various types of corpora to carry out translation course group teaching practice. By reviewing the design of talent cultivation plans for micro translation majors, the availability of corpus resources, the design of translation course group teaching content, and implementation paths, a new corpus-based teaching model for micro translation majors is proposed and teaching effectiveness is evaluated. The survey results show that the translation course group teaching model based on the integration of multiple corpora can effectively improve students' translation skills, and has characteristics such as richer teaching resources, reasonable content arrangement, and flexible assessment methods. It has a stronger sense of presence, experience, and practicality, which helps to optimize the expression form of students' translations, improve their corpus usage ability, and lay the foundation for them to enter the translation career in the future.

At the same time, as a translation teacher, one should enhance their translation skills and enhance their digital application abilities by participating in corpus training courses, visiting students outside, observing teaching and research, and communicating with peers. Given the limitations of this study, future research can select a portion of students for long-term and in-depth case studies to effectively grasp the changes in students' translation abilities.

Acknowledgments. This study was funded by The 2022 Henan Province Philosophy and Social Science Project "Application Research of Explainable Artificial Intelligence in the Construction of Interpretation Automatic Evaluation System" (2022BYY023), the 2022 Shanghai Social Science Planning Project "Emergency Language Service Research for Public Emergencies" (2022BYY009) General Project of the National Social Science Foundation of China "Research on the Intersubjective Evolution and Reconstruction of English Teaching Paradigm in Chinese Universities over the Forty Years of Reform and Opening up" (Project No. 19BYY216).

The authors have no competing interests to declare that are relevant to the content of this article

References

Jinquan, W., Qiufang, W.: Development of analytical scoring rules for chinese english translation of learners. J. Foreign Lang. Teach. **30**(4), 96–99+112 (2009)

Kaibao, H.: Introduction to corpus translation. Shanghai Jiao Tong University Press, Shanghai (2011)

Libo, H., Kefei, W.: Analysis of the development stage and frontier trends of corpus translation studies. J. Foreign Lang. Teach. Res. **55**(5), 18–25 (2023)

Ramos, S.M.D.M.: Documentation in specialized contexts: A quasi-experimental corpus-based study in public service interpreting and translation studies. J. Transl. Translang. Multilingual Cont. **8**(1), 313–331 (2022)

Xiaowan, Q., Keming, P.: Book review: extending the scope of corpus-based translation studies. Int. J. Transl. Interpret. Appl. Linguist. **5**(1) (2023)

Xu, J.: Translation studies from the perspective of corpus translation studies and digital humanities. J. Educ. Teach. Soc. Stud. **5**(3) (2023)

Zhengting, Z., Mingjie, C.: A study on the corpus translation teaching model for the language service market in the technology era: a case study based on the "translator" corpus translation teaching platform. J. Foreign Lang. Electron. Teach. (05), 88–95+13 (2021)

Zheng, M.: Cross disciplinary research path of translation: taking the topic selection of national social science foundation major projects as an example. J. Shanghai Transl. 03 (2023)

Author Index

Z. Kubincová et al. (Eds.): SETE 2023, LNCS 14606, pp. 337–338, 2024.
https://doi.org/10.1007/978-981-97-4243-1

GPSR Compliance

The European Union's (EU) General Product Safety Regulation (GPSR) is a set of rules that requires consumer products to be safe and our obligations to ensure this.

If you have any concerns about our products, you can contact us on ProductSafety@springernature.com

In case Publisher is established outside the EU, the EU authorized representative is:

Springer Nature Customer Service Center GmbH
Europaplatz 3
69115 Heidelberg, Germany

The manufacturer's authorised representative in the EU is Springer Nature Customer Service Centre GmbH, Europaplatz 3, 69115 Heidelberg, Germany. If you have any concerns regarding our products, please contact ProductSafety@springernature.com

Printed and bound by CPI Group (UK) Ltd, Croydon, CR0 4YY
01/10/2026
02225834-0010